ITEM	AMOUNT	SUGGESTED SERVING TEMP.	POWER LEVEL	APPROX. TIME MINS.
Sandwiches				
Moist Filling; such as sloppy joe, barbecue, ham salad, etc. in bun ⅓ cup / serving	1 serving	110°	M. High	1-1½
	2 servings	110°	M. High	1½-2½
	4 servings	110°	M. High	2½-4
Thick Meat-Cheese Filling; with firm bread	1 serving	110°	M. High	1½-2½
	2 servings	110°	M. High	2½-3½
	4 servings	110°	M. High	5-7
Soup				
Water Base 1 cup /serving	1 serving	150°-170°	High	2½-3½
	2 servings	150°-170°	High	4-5½
	4 servings	150°-170°	High	7-9
	1 can 10-oz. reconstituted	150°-170°	High	5-7
Milk Base 1 cup / serving	1 serving	140°	M. High	3-4
	2 servings	140°	M. High	5-7
	4 servings	140°	M. High	10-12
	1 can 10-oz. reconstituted	140°	M. High	8-10

Tip: Use paper towel or napkin to cover sandwiches. Cover soups with wax paper or plastic wrap.

ITEM	AMOUNT	SUGGESTED SERVING TEMP.	POWER LEVEL	APPROX. TIME MINS.
VEGETABLES				
Small Pieces such as peas, beans, corn, etc. ½ cup / serving	1 serving	150°-160°	High	1-2
	2 servings	150°-160°	High	2-3
	4 servings	150°-160°	High	3-4
	1 can 16-oz.	150°-160°	High or M. High	4-4½
Large pieces or whole such as asparagus spears, corn on the cob, etc.	1 serving		High	2-2½
	2 servings		High	3-3½
	4 servings		High	4-4½
	1 can 16-oz.		High	4-4½
Mashed ½ cup / serving	1 serving	150°-160°	High	1-2
	2 servings	150°-160°	High	2-3
	4 servings	150°-160°	High	6-7

Tip: Cover vegetables for most even heating.

ITEM	AMOUNT	SUGGESTED SERVING TEMP.	POWER LEVEL	APPROX. TIME MINS.
SAUCES				
Dessert such as chocolate, butterscotch				
Room Temp	½ cup	125°	High	¼-½
	1 cup	125°	High	½-1
Ref. Temp.	½ cup	125°	High	1-1½
	1 cup	125°	High	2-2½
Meat or Main Dish				
Chunky type such as giblet gravy, spaghetti sauce, etc.	½ cup	150°-160°	High	1½-2
	1 cup	150°-160°	High	2½-3½
	1 can 16-oz.	150°-160°	High	5-6
Creamy Type	½ cup	140°-150°	High	1-1½
	1 cup	140°-150°	High	2-2½

Tip: Cover food to prevent spatter.

ITEM	AMOUNT	SUGGESTED SERVING TEMP.	POWER LEVEL	APPROX. TIME MINS.
BAKERY FOODS				
Room Temperature				
Cake, Coffee Cake, Doughnuts, Sweet Rolls, Nut or Fruit Bread.	1 piece	90°	Low	½-1
	2 pieces		Low	1-1½
	4 pieces		Low	1½-2½
	9-in. cake or 12 rolls or doughnuts	90°	Low	2-4
Dinner Rolls, Muffins	1	90°	Medium	¼-½
	2		Medium	½-¾
	4		Medium	½-1
	6-8		Medium	1-1¾
Pie, Fruit or Nut ⅛ of 9-in. pie = 1 slice	1 slice	110°	High	½-1
	2 slices		High	1-1½
	4 slices		M. High	2½-3½
	9-in. pie	110°	M. High	5-7
Pie, Custard ⅛ of 9-in. pie = 1 slice	1 slice	110°	M. High	½-1
	2 slices		M. High	1½-2
	4 slices		M. High	2½-3½
	9-in. pie	110°	M. High	5-7

ITEM	AMOUNT	SUGGESTED SERVING TEMP.	POWER LEVEL	APPROX. TIME MINS.
GRIDDLE FOODS				
Room Temperature				
Pancakes				
Plain, no topping	Stack of 3	120°	High	½-1
Syrup & butter	Stack of 3	120°	High	1-1¼
With 2 sausage patties	Stack of 3	120°	High	1¼-1½
French Toast				
Plain, no topping	2 slices	120°	High	½-1
With syrup & butter	2 slices	120°	High	1-1¼
Waffles 3" x 4"				
Plain, no topping	2	120°	High	½-1
With syrup & butter	2	120°	High	1-1¼

ITEM	AMOUNT	SUGGESTED SERVING TEMP.	POWER LEVEL	APPROX. TIME MINS.
BEVERAGES				
Coffee, Tea, Cider, other water based	1 cup	160°-170°	High	1½-2½
	2 cups		High	3½-4½
	4 cups		High	6-7
Cocoa, other milk based	1 cup	140°	M. High	2-3
	2 cups		M. High	4-5
	4 cups		M. High	7-8

Tip: Do not cover bakery foods, griddle foods (pancakes, etc.) or beverages.

3rd printing 3/80

How to Use This Book

This unusual, new book is both a guide and a cookbook. It grew out of nationwide cooking schools and extensive consumer research, from which we learned what people need to know to become confident, successful and expert microwave cooks.

To make the most effective use of this book, first read the introductory guide, which teaches you the principles and techniques of microwaving. Many will be familiar, some, new. All are clearly illustrated with photographs.

Then go on to the recipe chapters where Microlessons demonstrate how to cook specific foods. We show you what to do, what to expect, how the food should look, and how to tell when it's done. You'll soon learn that successful microwaving is not only faster, but often easier than conventional cooking.

Diana Williams Hansen

Diana Williams Hansen
Manager-Home Economics
Range Marketing Department

Many thanks
to home economists,
Jean E. Kozar
Joyce Elliott Blair
Brigid Lally Bowles
Marita A. Duber
Paula Cooper Matthews

D.W.H.

The photographs in this book were designed to help you learn by seeing examples of foods and cooking techniques. All foods were microwaved according to recipes in the book, and photographed exactly as they came from the oven, using Kodak's new, no pollution E & G film and processing system.

Contents

Microwaving: A New Cooking Term

Water Boils in a paper cup. One of the remarkable characteristics of microwave energy is that it heats the food, not the utensil. Utensils become warm only when heat from food has transferred to them.

Television is radio waves converted to a picture on the screen. Microwave energy is very short radio waves converted to heat in food.

The microwave oven has added a new term to our cooking language. "Microwaving" means to cook, heat or defrost foods with microwave energy. Microwaving is a new type of cooking, which has its own special benefits, and produces its own food characteristics. Some microwaved foods may be different from what you expect when cooking in a conventional oven or on the range top. The difference may be in appearance, in improved flavor and juiciness, or in cooking technique.

The microwave oven is called an "oven" because it looks more like an oven than any other conventional appliance, but it can take over many of your top-of-range jobs with less time, attention and clean-up. Foods which you used to bake in a conventional oven will taste the same, but may look different. For example, a casserole will heat through quickly, but will not crust over, because the air in a microwave oven is room temperature, not hot and dry.

Like any new skill, microwaving takes a little practice. Until you are used to its speed, you may overcook. Some foods will be removed from the oven before they look done, because they finish cooking with internal heat. This book is designed to teach you what to expect, and how to achieve successful results with microwaving. You'll find learning to microwave easy and exciting.

HOW MICROWAVE WORKS

Microwaves are very short, high-frequency radio waves, and your microwave oven is similar to a miniature broadcasting system. Microwaves are the same type of energy as AM, FM or CB radio, but the wave length is much shorter.

Where other types of radio waves broadcast over a distance, the microwave broadcasting system is self-contained. When the door is closed and the oven is turned on, a transmitter, called a magnetron, sends a signal to a receiver within the oven. The moment you open the door, the microwave oven stops broadcasting, just as your radio will not play if the station has "signed off". No energy will be received from the oven while the door is open.

The receiver deflects the microwave energy into the metal-lined oven cavity, where it agitates food molecules. Since microwaves cannot penetrate metal, all the energy remains inside the oven, where it turns to heat in the food.

"HEAT" PHOTOS SHOW HOW MICROWAVES COOK

A new process, called thermography, which makes images of heat, demonstrates the different ways in which foods cook. At the General Electric Major Appliance Laboratory, potatoes were heated on a range top, in a conventional oven, and in a microwave oven, then cut in half and thermographed to show how heat is distributed in each cooking method.

On the thermograph scale, blue stands for cool areas, red represents warmth and yellow indicates the hottest area. The "halo" of blue around the potatoes is thermal reflection and occurs when the potatoes are removed from heat to room temperature for photography.

RANGE TOP

Cut Potato in a skillet is placed on a range surface unit set at medium heat. Potato was sliced so that a large flat surface could be exposed.

After 3 Minutes some heat from the surface unit has transferred through the pan to the cut side of the potato. On a range top, the bottom part of the food is always hottest.

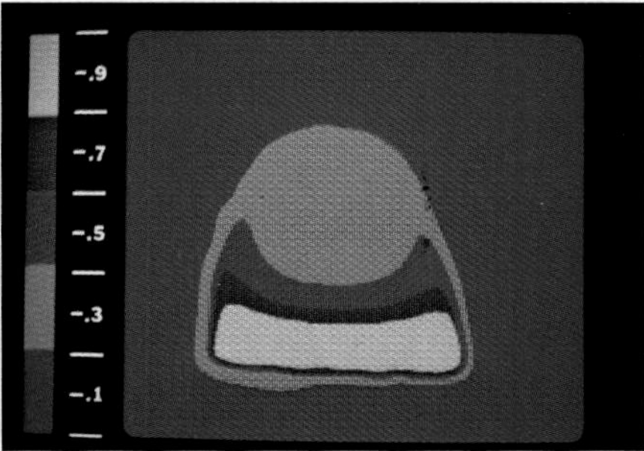

After 8 Minutes the hot yellow area has increased and heat is being conducted into the red, warm portions. The top of the potato is still cool.

CONVENTIONAL OVEN

Whole Potato is placed on the shelf of a conventional oven preheated to 400°. The air inside the oven is hot and dry.

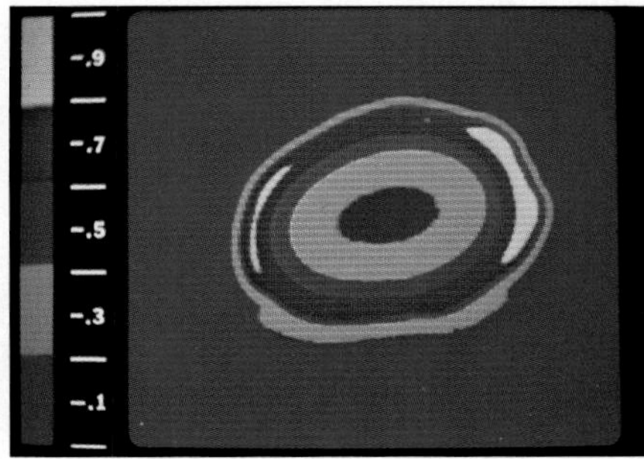

After 7 Minutes, thin yellow areas indicate that air in the oven has heated the surface of the potato. Prolonged exposure to hot, dry air will make the outside dry and crusty.

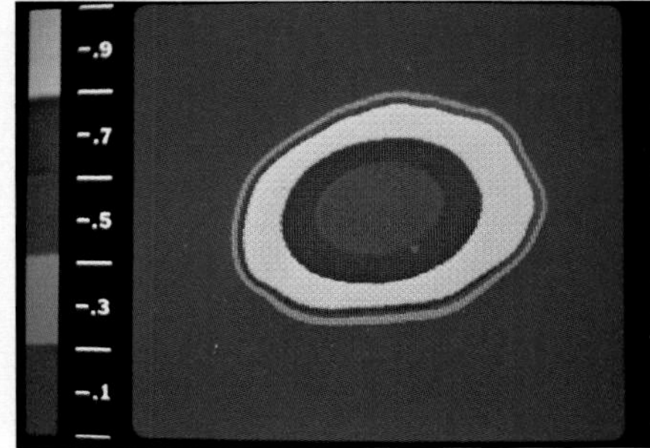

After 15 Minutes, heat is gradually spreading to the interior through conduction, although the center is still cool. It takes about 1 hour to bake a potato conventionally.

MICROWAVE

Potato is placed on the oven floor with a paper towel or napkin to absorb moisture, and is microwaved at High Power. Air in the oven is room temperature.

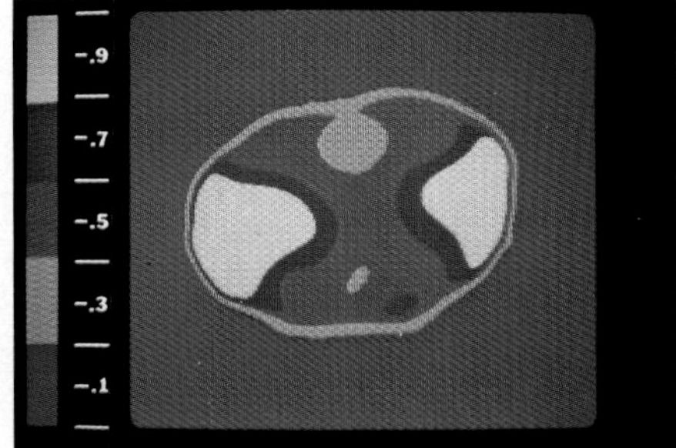

After 1 Minute, yellow areas of heat appear inside the potato, showing that microwave energy penetrates ¾ to 1¼-in. through food surfaces. Heat is then conducted inward and outward.

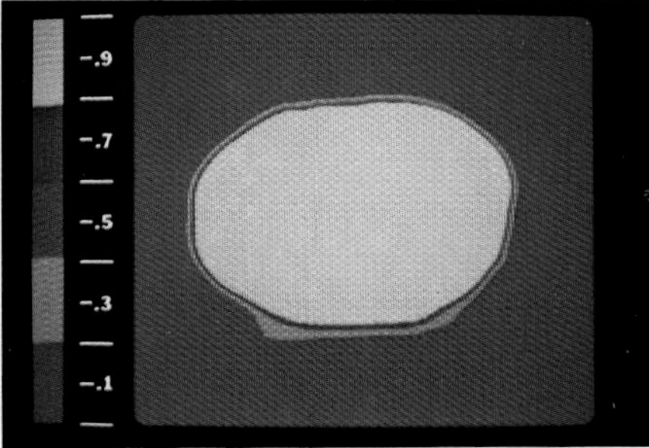

After 4 Minutes, potato is heated throughout, although it is not ready to serve. During a brief standing time, heat within the potato cooks it thoroughly.

COMPARISON OF MICROWAVE & CONVENTIONAL COOKING

Range Top. On the range top, heat from the surface unit transfers through the pan to the bottom of the food. Stirring the food while it cooks brings heated portions to the top and prevents scorching. Covering the pan holds in steam and speeds cooking. Rearranging or turning foods over helps them cook evenly. Because the bottom of the pan is hot, fried or griddled foods become crisp or crusty.

Conventional Oven. In a conventional oven, the heating units heat the air inside the oven. The oven may be preheated until the air reaches the proper cooking temperature. Heat from this hot dry air enters the food through its exterior surfaces, and gradually spreads to the interior through conduction. The process is usually slow, so by the time the center is done, the surfaces have become dry and crusty.

Microwave Oven. Microwaves penetrate ¾ to 1¼-in. through all food surfaces; top, bottom and sides. At this depth they are absorbed by moisture, sugar or fat molecules, which begin to cook. Heat is then conducted into the center and out to the surfaces. The food cooks by internal heat, not by contact with hot air or a hot pan. Because microwaves penetrate foods and cook them below the surface, cooking is faster for most foods, but the surface remains moist, not dry and crusty. Occasionally, the surface is the last place to cook.

COMPARISON OF MICROWAVE & CONVENTIONAL ENERGY CONSUMPTION

Microwaving can save energy and reduce electric bills, but savings depend on what, and how much, you cook. Some foods make efficient use of microwave energy. Others, such as popcorn, use less energy when cooked conventionally.

The amount of food cooked affects energy consumption, too. Four baked potatoes require 61% less energy when microwaved, but about 12 potatoes bake more efficiently in a conventional oven. Greatest savings result when heating medium or small quantities of dense foods.

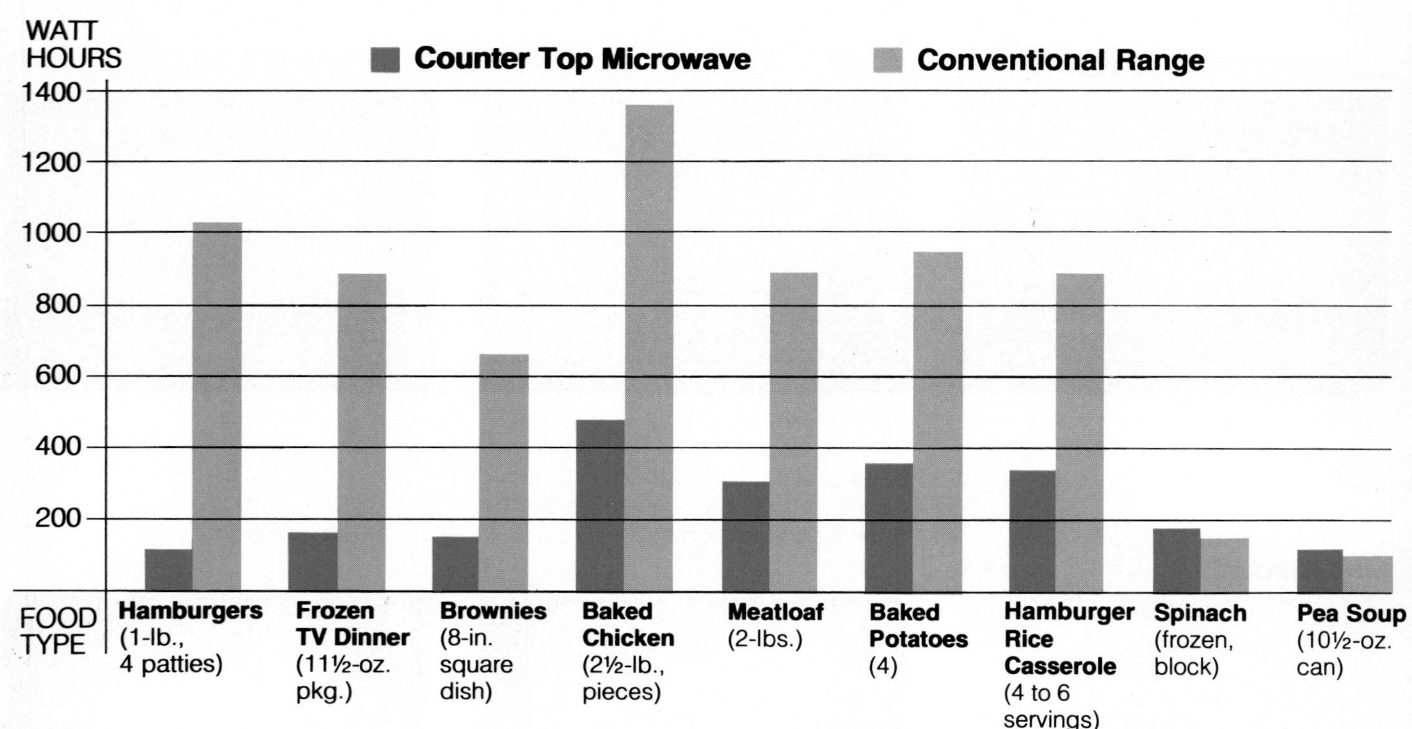

PRECAUTIONS TO AVOID POSSIBLE EXPOSURE TO EXCESSIVE MICROWAVE ENERGY

1. **Do Not Attempt** to operate the oven with the door open since open-door operation can result in harmful exposure to microwave energy. It is important not to defeat or tamper with the safety interlocks.
2. **Do Not Place** any object between the oven front face and the door or allow soil or cleaner residue to accumulate on sealing surfaces.
3. **Do Not Operate** the oven if it is damaged. It is particularly important that the oven door close properly and that there is no damage to the (1) door (bent), (2) hinges and latches (broken or loosened), (3) door seals and sealing surfaces.
4. **The Oven Should** not be adjusted or repaired by anyone except properly qualified service personnel.

SOME FOODS MICROWAVE WITH EXCEPTIONAL QUALITY

Some foods microwave so well that you may never want to cook them any other way. Foods which demand constant stirring on the range top, such as sauces, puddings, frostings and candies, need only an occasional stir in the microwave oven. Many can be measured, mixed and cooked in the same utensil for easy clean-up.

The excellent flavor and texture of microwaved fish, vegetables and fruits makes superior flavor the principle reason for cooking them by microwaves. Saving in time, while important, becomes a secondary advantage. In addition, there are some things unique to microwaving which cannot be done any other way.

Vegetables retain their fresh, crisp texture and bright color when microwaved according to chart, page 188.

Baked Potato microwaves fluffy, moist and tender. As an added benefit, you save time and energy. A potato microwaves in about 5 minutes.

Leftovers stay moist and taste freshly cooked. Roasted meats don't have a "leftover" flavor, rice reheats without overcooking.

Defrost foods rapidly. 1 pound of ground beef is ready to cook in 8 to 9 minutes. "I forgot to defrost", is never an emergency.

Melt Chocolate right in its paper wrapper. You have nothing to clean up and no danger of scorching or overcooking.

Eggs scramble fluffy, with greater volume. Compare 1 egg, cooked conventionally, left, with 1 microwave scrambled egg.

Reheat a meal right on the serving plate. If family members eat at different times, cook once and serve everyone a hot meal.

Fish steam tender and moist in their own natural juices, without additional water, for delicate flavor and pleasing texture.

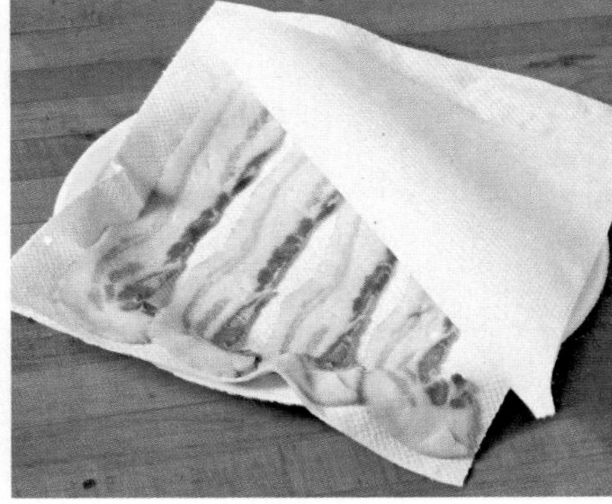

Bacon microwaves crisp, brown and flat on paper towels. You don't have to turn it over, drain it, or scour a crusty pan.

MORE FOODS THAT MICROWAVE WITH EXCEPTIONAL QUALITY

Rich, fudgy brownies can be microwaved in 6 minutes for a quick dessert or impromptu treat.

Casseroles can be microwaved, refrigerated and reheated in the same dish. They'll taste just as fresh the second day.

Hot Appetizers and snacks microwave in seconds on a paper napkin. They're so easy you can treat your family or guests to a variety.

Cakes rise higher and cook moist and tender when microwaved. Compare microwaved cake (right) with conventionally baked (left).

Puddings and custards cook smooth and creamy with no more than an occasional stirring. Cook and serve them from one dish.

Blanch vegetables for the freezer when they are at the peak of flavor. You and your kitchen will keep cool.

Candies that used to take constant stirring and attention are simplified by microwaving. The real, old-fashioned flavor is the same.

Hot Fruit desserts take less water to cook, so juices have true fruit flavor. Fruit keeps its fresh color and texture.

Heat frozen entrees rapidly whether you buy them ready-made or freeze leftovers in single servings for quick meals.

THESE MICROWAVED FOODS SAVE TIME AND RESULTS COMPARE TO CONVENTIONAL COOKING

A Hamburger microwaves in 1 to 2 minutes, right on a paper or microwave ovenproof plate. It won't stick to the dish, so you save clean-up time.

Chicken pieces are tender, juicy and ready to serve quickly. A cut up broiler-fryer microwaves in about 20 minutes. Skin will not be crispy.

Meatloaf takes about 15 to 20 minutes to microwave. Add another 8 to 9 minutes if you must defrost the meat first.

Upside-down Cake becomes a last-minute dessert or afternoon snack when it takes only about 10 minutes.

Sirloin Tip roast will be tender and medium-rare when microwaved at Medium Power for 11 to 16 minutes per pound.

Coffee Cake microwaves in 5 to 7 minutes when neighbors drop in for coffee. It also makes an easy surprise for family breakfast.

SOME FOODS DO NOT MICROWAVE WELL

No single appliance does everything well, and your microwave oven is no exception. Some things should not be done, either because results are not satisfactory, or because conventional cooking is more efficient.

Eggs in Shells and shelled boiled eggs can burst.

Pancakes do not crust, however, they reheat well.

Popcorn is too dry to attract microwave energy.

Canning requires prolonged high temperatures.

Deep Fat frying could cause burns.

Bottles with narrow necks may shatter if heated.

Large food loads, such as a 25-lb. turkey or a dozen potatoes cook more efficiently in a conventional oven.

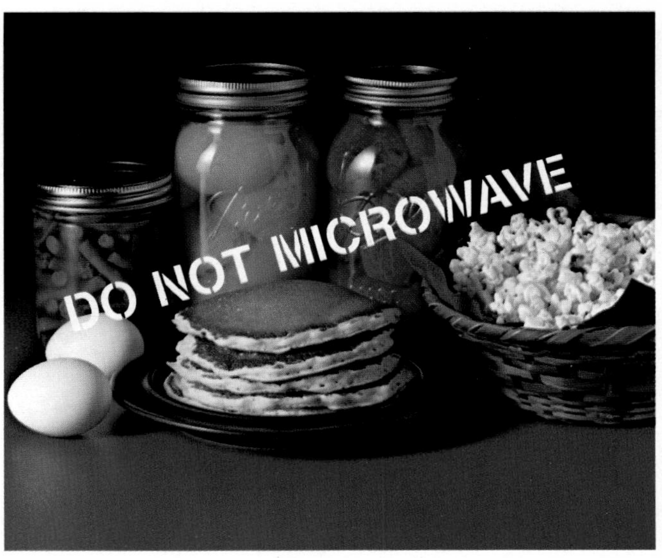

Microwaving Techniques

Many of the techniques used in microwaving are the same ones you use in conventional cooking. Most of them either speed cooking or promote even heating. While the techniques may be familiar, their application may be somewhat different because of the unique way in which microwave energy cooks.

Stirring. In range-top cooking, you stir foods up from the bottom to help them heat evenly. When microwaving, you stir cooked portions from the outside to the center. Foods which require constant stirring conventionally will need only occasional stirring.

Turning Over. In range top cooking you turn over foods such as hamburgers, so both sides can directly contact hot pan. When microwaving, turning is often needed during defrosting, or when cooking foods such as hamburgers without a cover, or from frozen state.

Arranging on Oven Shelf. In conventional baking, you position foods, such as tomatoes or potatoes, so that hot air can flow around them. When microwaving, you arrange foods in a ring, so that all sides are exposed to microwave energy.

Rearranging. In conventional cooking, you reposition foods in the pan, especially when there are several layers. When microwaving, you also rearrange foods part way through the cooking period.

Standing Time. In conventional cooking, foods such as roasts or cakes are allowed to stand to finish cooking or set. Standing time is especially important in microwave cooking. Note that the microwaved cake is not placed on a cooling rack.

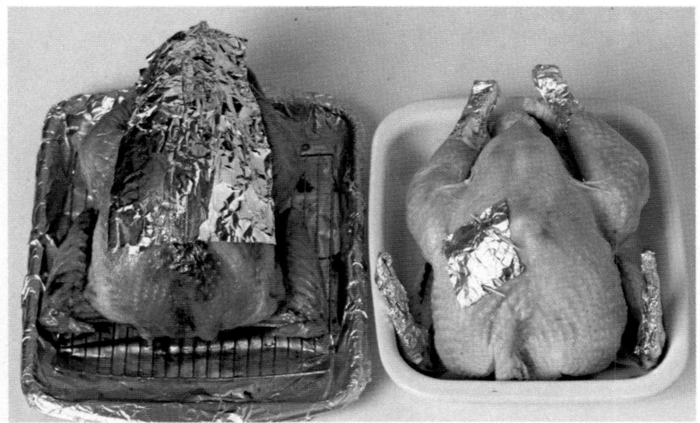

Shielding. In a conventional oven you shield turkey breasts or baked foods to prevent over-browning. When defrosting, you use small strips of foil to shield thin parts, such as the tips of wings and legs on poultry, which would cook before larger parts were defrosted.

Covering. In both conventional and microwave cooking, covers hold in moisture and speed heating. Conventionally, partial covering allows excess steam to escape. Venting plastic wrap or covering with wax paper serves the same purpose when microwaving.

SOME TECHNIQUES ARE UNIQUE TO MICROWAVING

Arranging in Dish. When microwaving, arrange foods with the thickest portions to the outside of the dish. This enables them to cook through without overcooking the thinner areas. Arrange foods of equal size in a ring, leaving the center empty.

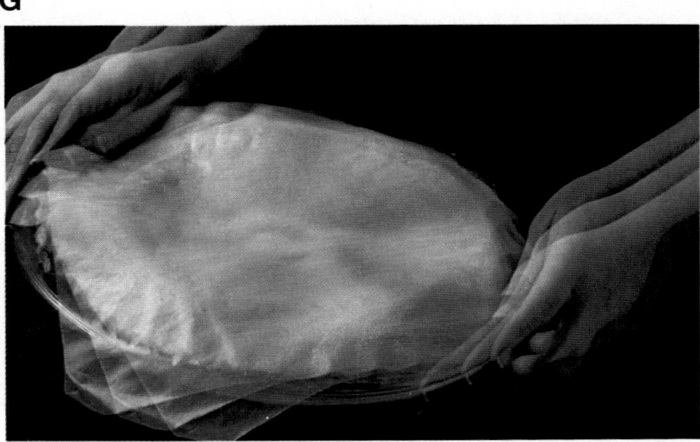

Rotating. Repositioning a dish in the oven helps food cook evenly. To rotate ½ turn, turn the dish until the side which was to the back of the oven is to the front. To rotate ¼ turn, turn the dish until the side which was to the back of the oven is to the side.

MICROWAVING BAKED POTATOES DEMONSTRATES SEVERAL TECHNIQUES

Prick potatoes in several places to allow steam to escape.

Arrange potatoes in a ring so that all sides can be exposed to equal amounts of microwave energy.

Turn Over and rearrange potatoes half way through cooking.

COVERING TECHNIQUES FOR RETAINING MOISTURE IN FOODS

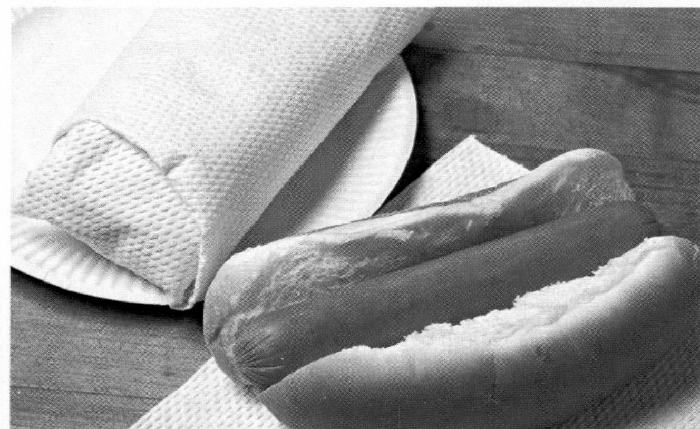

Porous Cover, such as paper towel or napkin, allows steam to escape while it promotes even heating and prevents spatters. Use to cover bacon, sandwiches and some vegetable custards.

Light Cover of wax paper holds in heat for faster cooking without steaming food. It is frequently used to cover some fruits and meats, such as chicken, hamburgers or roasts, which do not need steam to tenderize them.

Tight Cover of plastic wrap holds in steam as well as heat. Turning back one edge as a vent allows excess steam to escape, so wrap will not split during cooking. Vegetables and fish should be steamed.

Utensil Cover can be used instead of plastic wrap when you are microwaving vegetables, saucy casseroles and meats which require moisture and steam to tenderize them.

Cooking Bags also hold in steam. If the bag has a foil strip on the end, remove it. Cut a ½-in. wide strip from the open end of the bag to serve as a tie. Do not use metal twist ties. Make an X-shaped slash to vent.

Freezer Bags hold moisture in foods and serve as both cooking utensil and cover. Pierce the top of the bag with a knife to vent. Package leftovers in single portions for easy-to-heat homemade frozen entrees.

HOW TO ADD MOISTURE TO FOODS

Sprinkle a little fruit juice or water over dried fruits, cover with plastic wrap and microwave ½ to 1 minute at High to moisten and plump them.

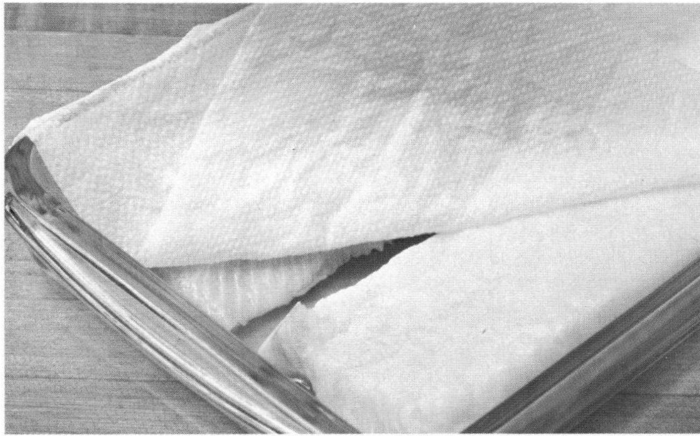

Wet Paper Towel, with excess water squeezed out, provides enough moisture to steam fish fillets and scallops. Wrap tortillas or crepes in damp towel and microwave at High ½ minute or more to soften them.

Add Water or sauce when reheating dry leftovers. A tablespoon of water or sauce is sufficient, and will not change the flavor of food or cause overcooking. Moisture creates steam for even reheating.

Soften lumpy brown sugar by placing in a microwave ovenproof container with a slice of apple. Cover or seal tightly and microwave ¼ minute or more, until moisture from the apple has softened the sugar.

HOW TO REMOVE MOISTURE FROM FOODS

Freshen Snacks, chips, pretzels, etc. by microwaving them, uncovered, for a few seconds. Let stand a minute or two to crisp. Dry a quart of bread crumbs or croutons at High 6 to 8 minutes, stirring every 2 minutes.

Paper Napkin or towel will absorb excess moisture. Dry herbs between 2 layers of towel or napkin until they can be crumbled. Line a cake dish with a paper towel to absorb moisture during cooking and make cake easy to turn out of the dish.

FACTORS WHICH AFFECT COOKING

Several factors which influence timing and results in conventional cooking are exaggerated by microwave speed. From conventional cooking you are familiar with the idea that more food takes more time. Two cups of water take longer to boil than one. Size of food is important, too. Cut up potatoes cook faster than whole ones. These differences are more apparent in microwaving, since energy penetrates and turns to heat directly in the food. Knowing what affects the speed and evenness of cooking will help you enjoy all the advantages of microwaving.

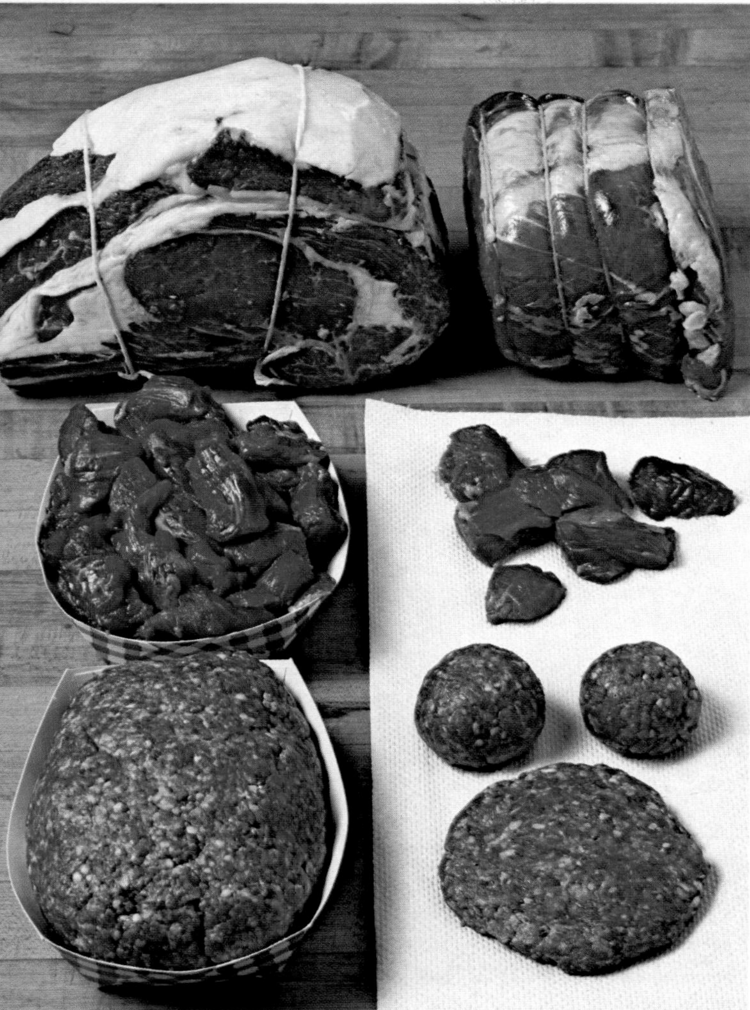

Piece Size. In both conventional and microwave cooking, small pieces cook faster than large ones. Pieces which are similar in size and shape cook more evenly.

Starting Temperature. Foods taken from the refrigerator take longer to cook than foods at room temperature. Timings in our recipes are based on the temperatures at which you normally store the foods.

Density of Food. In both conventional and microwave cooking, dense foods, such as a potato, take longer to cook or heat than light, porous foods, such as a piece of cake, bread or a roll.

Quantity of Food. In both types of cooking, small amounts usually take less time than large ones. This is most apparent in microwave cooking, where time is directly related to the number of servings.

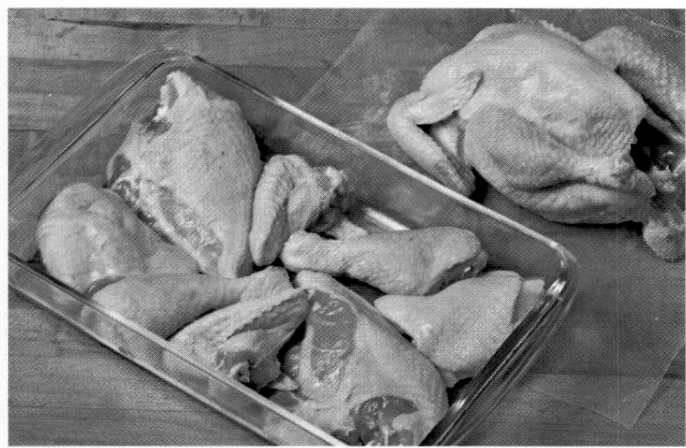

Shape of Food. In both types of cooking, thin areas cook faster than thick ones. This can be controlled in microwaving by placing thick pieces to the outside edge with thin pieces to the center.

Height in Oven. In both types of cooking, areas which are closest to the source of heat or energy cook faster. For even microwaving, turn over or shield vulnerable foods which are higher than 5 inches.

Boiling. Microwaves exaggerate boiling in milk-based foods. A temperature probe turns off the oven before foods boil over. Use a lower power setting and watch carefully when not using a probe.

Prick Foods to Release Pressure. Steam builds up pressure in foods which are tightly covered by a skin or membrane. Prick potatoes (as you do conventionally), egg yolks and chicken livers to prevent bursting.

Round Shapes. Since microwaves penetrate foods to about 1-in. from top, bottom and sides, round shapes and rings cook more evenly. Corners receive more energy and may overcook. This may also happen conventionally.

Bury Vulnerable Foods. Foods which attract microwave energy, such as cheese or meat, should, when possible, be buried in sauce or other ingredients. In conventional stewing or pot roasting, meat not covered with liquid dries out.

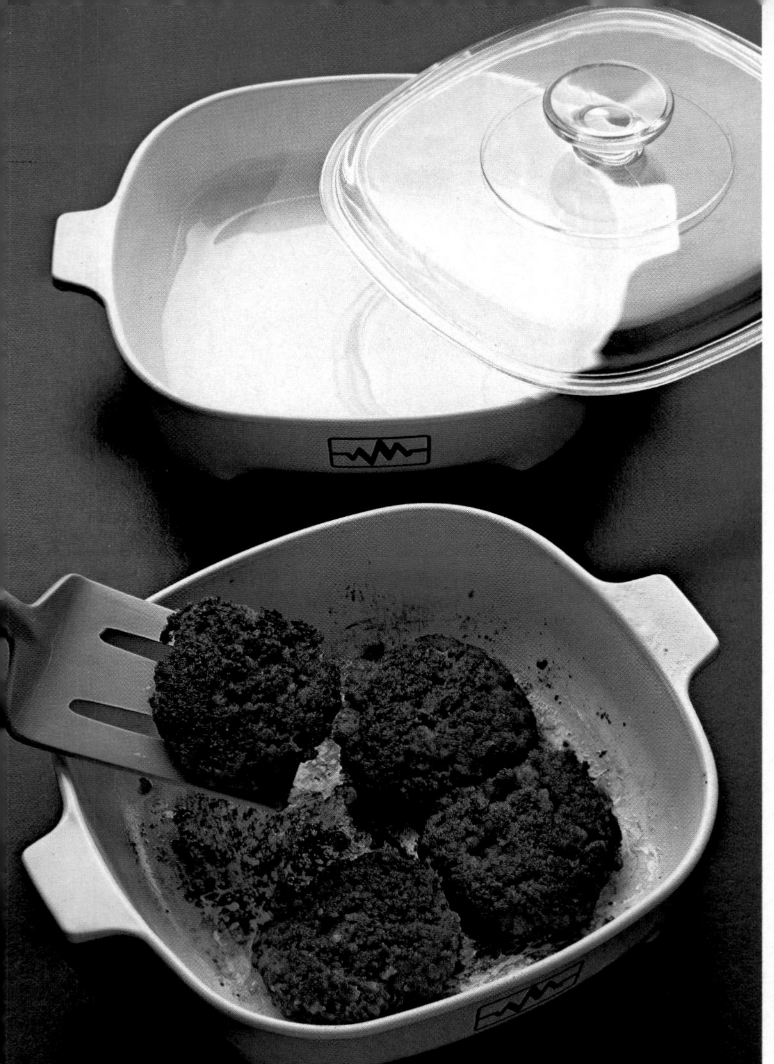

Microwave Utensils

Special Utensils for microwaving are now available because of the increasing popularity of microwave ovens. These utensils are made of microwave ovenproof materials and satisfy some of the special needs of microwave cooks.

Many manufacturers are designing utensils which can be used both in microwave and conventional ovens. Special utensils also include many everyday items of glass, pottery, plastic and paper which were never considered cooking utensils until microwaving made it possible to use them.

Brown 'N Sear Dish (9-in. square) has a special coating on the bottom which attracts microwave energy. When preheated, it fries eggs and browns hamburgers or chicken. A cover controls moisture and spatters.

BROWN 'N SEAR COOKING CHART POWER LEVEL: **High**

Preheat Brown 'N Sear Dish before each use. Use potholders and avoid touching bottom. If cooking many foods consecutively, preheat dish 1 to 1½ minutes between foods. Use the cover when cooking the foods listed on the chart below.

ITEM	AMOUNT	PREHEAT TIME/MINUTES	FIRST SIDE TIME/MINUTES	SECOND SIDE TIME/MINUTES
Steaks, Rib Eye or Delmonico (6-oz. each, ½-in. thick)	2	7 to 8	1	1½ to 2
Hamburgers, (¼-lb. each, ½-in. thick)	1 or 2	4 to 6	2 to 2½	1 to 1½
	3 or 4	6 to 8	2½ to 3	1½ to 2
Pork Chops (5-oz. each, ¾-in. thick)	1	3 to 4	2	4 to 6
	2	5 to 6	4	4 to 6
Pork Sausage Links (Uncooked, 8-oz.)	6 to 8	4 to 5½	1	2 to 2½
Ham Slice (¼ to ½-in. thick)	1	3½ to 4½	1 to 2	1 to 2
Chicken, Fried (pieces coated with seasoned flour and paprika)	3	6 to 7 (add 1 tablespoon oil after preheat)	3	3 to 4
	6	7 to 8 (add 1 tablespoon oil after preheat)	4	3 to 5
Fish Fillets (6-oz. each, ½-in. thick) (seasoned flour on outsides)	2	5 to 6 (add 1 tablespoon oil after preheat)	1½ to 2½	2 to 3
Lamb Chops (4-oz. each, ¾-in. thick)	2	5 to 6	3	3 to 4
	4	6 to 8	3 to 4	4 to 5

Browning Griddle (11½×14-in.) browns larger pieces or more items than the Brown 'N Sear Dish. A well around the outside of the griddle catches drippings. The griddle has no cover.

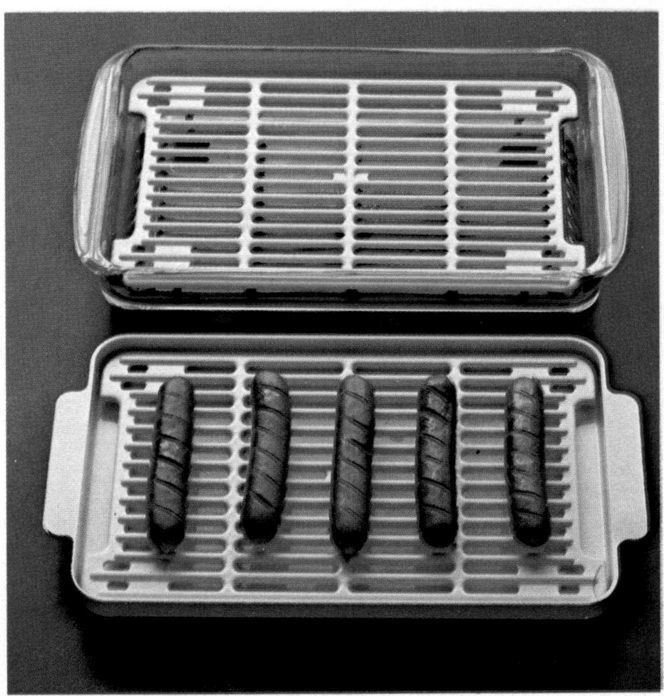

Microwave Trivet fits in its own plastic dish or may be placed in a 12×8×2-in. cooking dish. Like a conventional roasting rack, it holds meat out of its juices to prevent stewing.

Bacon Tree holds up to 6 slices. Set in a dish or 1-qt. measure to catch the fat as bacon microwaves.

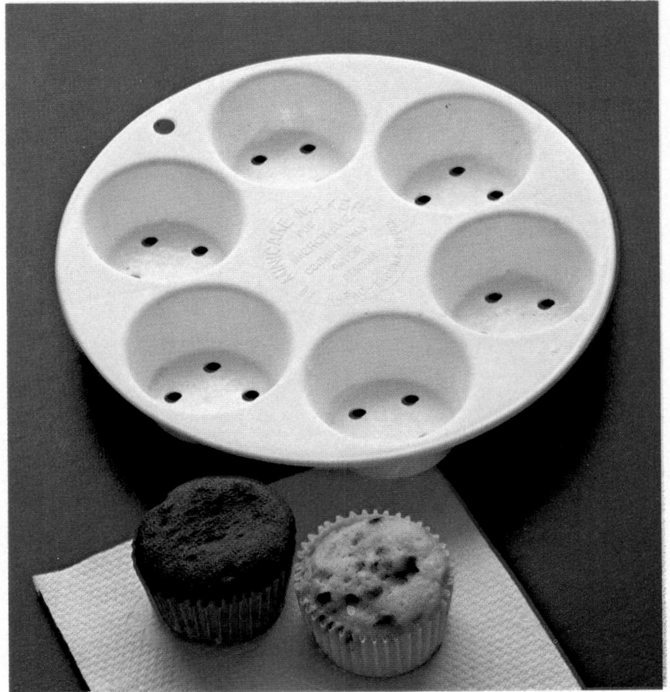

Cupcaker arranges and spaces muffins and cupcakes in the ring shape recommended for even microwaving.

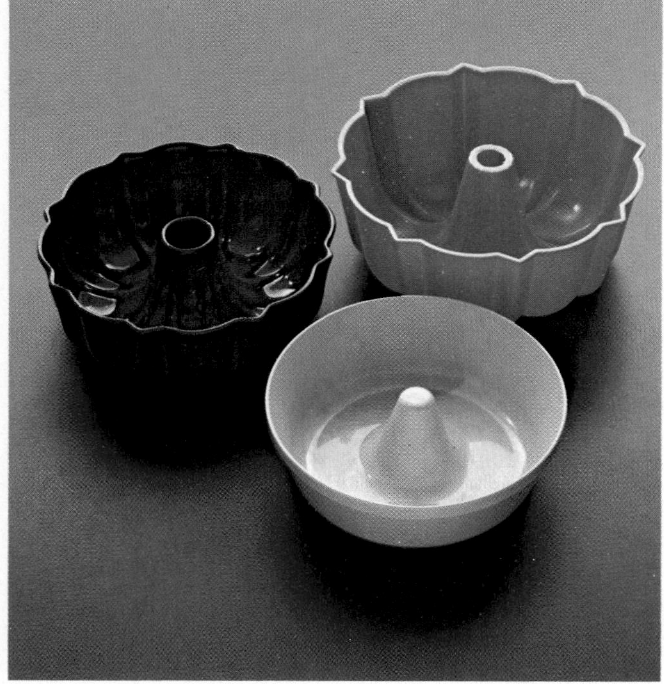

Ring Molds (fluted and straight sided) of plastic or ceramic are ideal for cakes, quick breads and meatloaves. They give them the ring shape preferred for microwaving, as well as an attractive appearance.

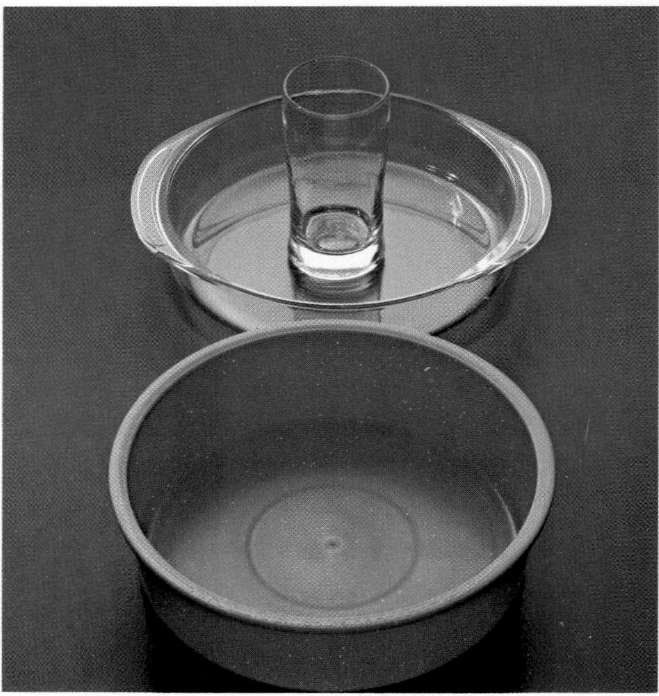

High Sided Cake Pans of plastic, glass or ceramic are especially designed for cake mixes, which rise higher in the microwave oven. Pans hold half of the cake mix batter. Make your own ring mold by placing a 3-in. diameter glass in an 8-in. round dish or casserole.

Utensils You Already Have may be suitable for microwaving. Oven glass casseroles, cooking dishes, measuring cups and custard cups are common household utensils. Pottery or china dinner ware which does not have gold or silver trim or glaze with a metallic sheen can be used. Most glass ceramic oven-to-table ware is labeled "suitable for microwave". If you are uncertain about a dish or container, use the dish test described below.

WHAT TO LOOK FOR WHEN BUYING UTENSILS FOR MICROWAVING

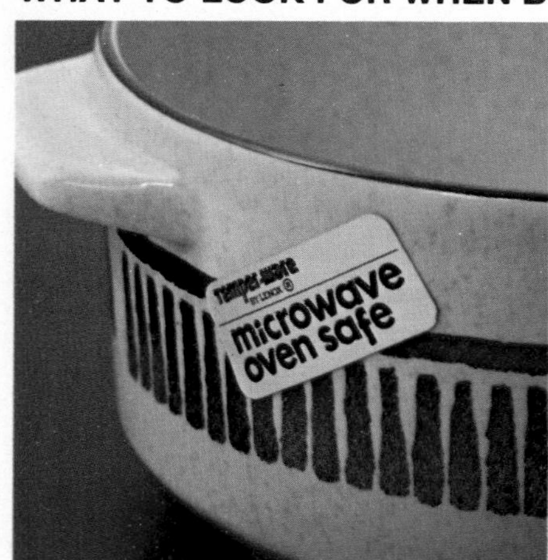

"Suitable for Microwave" or "Microwave Safe" may appear on the label or sticker, or may be stated in the warranty.

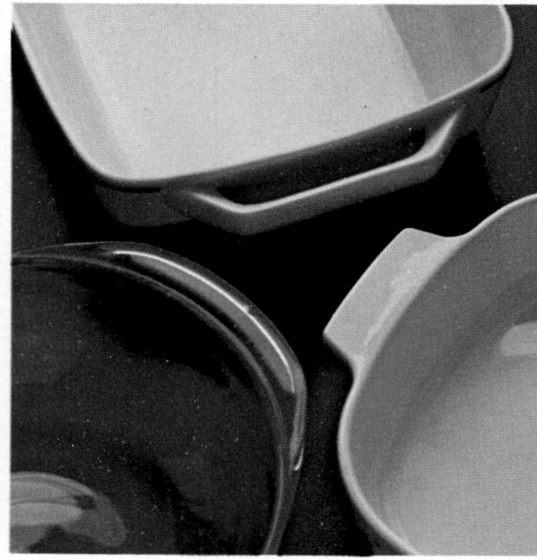

Lugs and Handles make dishes easier to use. While microwave energy does not heat the dish directly, heat from foods will transfer to the bottom and sides of it. Lugs and handles generally do not become hot.

Test Dishes. Measure 1 cup of water in a glass cup. Place in oven on or beside dish. Microwave 1 minute at High. If water becomes hot, dish is microwave safe. If dish heats, it should not be used for microwaving.

MICROWAVE UTENSIL GUIDE

Use this guide to help you evaluate and select utensils for microwaving. Some items can only be used for heating. Others are suitable for cooking. Many microwave utensils are designed both for cooking and attractive serving. Brands listed are among those recommended by their manufacturers for microwaving.

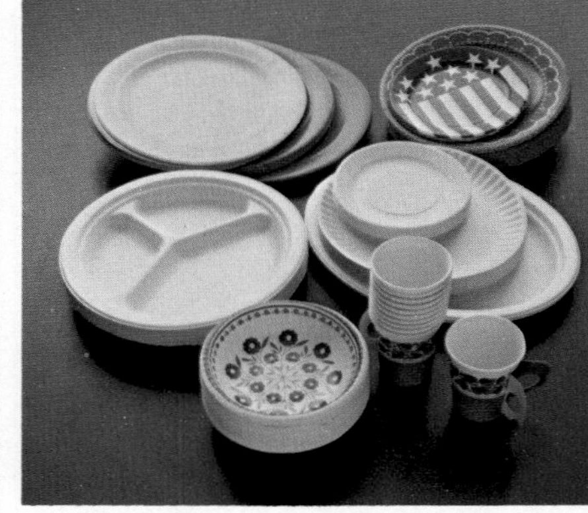

TYPE OF UTENSIL	**Paper Towels and Napkins, Wax Paper**	**Paper Plates and Cups (plain and plastic coated), such as:** Chinet, Diamond International, Dixie, St. Regis.
MICROWAVE USES	Cooking Bacon. Absorbing moisture and preventing spatters. Heating and serving sandwiches or appetizers. Light covering to hold in steam.	Heating and serving foods and beverages.
COMMENTS	Recycled paper products can contain metal flecks which may cause arcing or ignite. Paper products containing nylon or nylon filaments should be avoided, as they may also ignite. Dye from some colored paper products may bleed onto food.	Use plastic coated plates for moist or saucy foods. Use "hot drink" cups for soups and beverages. Also, see column to left.

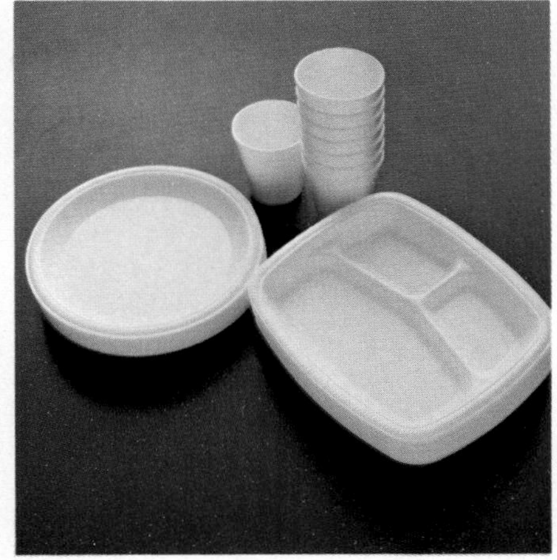

Plastic Foam Plates and Cups, such as: Sweetheart	**Plastic Wrap, Cooking Bags, Boil-in-bags, Storage Bags, such as:** Glad Wrap, Handi-Wrap, Saran Wrap, Cooking Magic, Reynolds, Baggies, Ziploc.	**Boilable Hard and Soft Plastics, such as:** Rubbermaid.
Short term heating to low temperatures and serving.	Covering to hold in steam (wrap). Cooking (cooking and boil-in-bags). Heating (storage bags).	Cooking ground beef (colander). Defrosting. Heating.
Distort when used with bacon and foods with high fat content.	Storage bags can melt at high temperatures.	May discolor from fat. May distort when used with foods with high fat content (except colander).

TYPE OF UTENSIL	**Microwave Plastics such as:** Anchor Hocking Microwave, Bangor Plastics, Mister Microwave, Nupac	**Oven Glass such as:** Anchor Hocking, Fire King, Glassbake, Heller, Jena, Pyrex	**Glass-Ceramic (Pyroceram), such as:** Corning Ware, Progression G. by Noritake
MICROWAVE USES	Specialized cooking (see pages 17 and 18 for details.)	Cooking and heating.	Cooking and heating.
COMMENTS	Some pieces may be available from appliance or housewares departments.	Inexpensive and readily available in supermarkets, hardware and department stores.	Attractive for serving. Plastic storage lids, available with individual casseroles, should not be used for microwaving.

		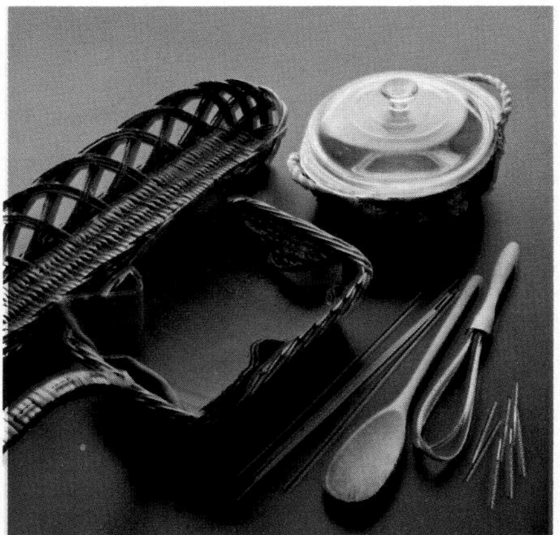	
TYPE OF UTENSIL	**Specialty Glass-Ceramic and Porcleain, such as:** El Camino, F. B. Rogers, Heller, Marsh Industries, Pfaltzgraff, Shafford	**Straw and Wood**	**Boxes lined with paper or plastic, Paper or plastic packages, Styrofoam base, Shallow frozen dinner tray.**
MICROWAVE USES	Recommended for microwave oven-to-table cooking of special foods.	Short term heating (baskets and boards). Cooking (spoons, whisks, picks and skewers).	Refresh foods, defrost meat and baked goods. Cook vegetables. Heat frozen foods.
COMMENTS	Microwave ovenproof ceramics may be sold with metal holders. Ceramic part, but not holders, may be used in microwave oven.	Spoons and whisks may be left in foods while microwaving.	Do not use foil trays higher than ¾-in.

Handmade Pottery, Porcelain, Stoneware

Cooking and heating.

Avoid glazes with metallic sheen. Use the dish test, page 18, to determine if hand-made pottery is microwavable.

Regular Dinnerware, such as: Corelle by Corning, Dansk Generation, Denby, El Camino, Franciscan, International Stoneware, Lenox Temperware, Marsh, Mikasa, Pfaltzgraff

Heating and some cooking.

Check for "Recommended for microwave" seal, or use dish test. Avoid metal trim.

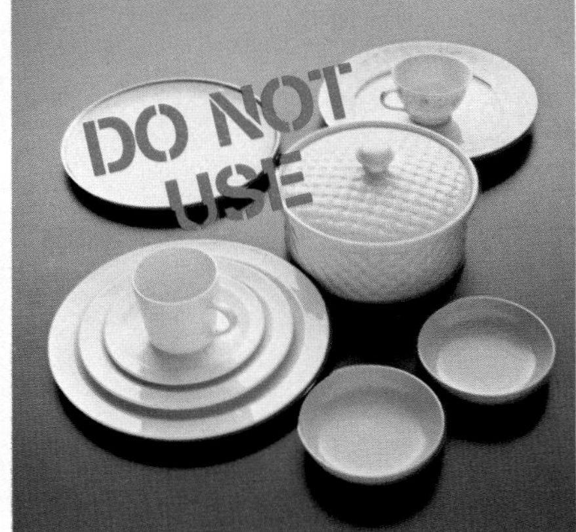

Unsuitable Dinnerware, such as: Corning Centura, Fitz and Floyd Oven-to-table Ware, Malamine, Dishes with metal trim

None

Warranty for Centura and Fitz and Floyd dishes states unsuitability for microwave.

Foil-lined Paper Bags, Boxes and Baking Trays

Avoid

Check for foil lining before attempting to microwave food in original packages.

Metal or part metal pots, Pans, Thermometers, Skewers and Foil Trays

Avoid

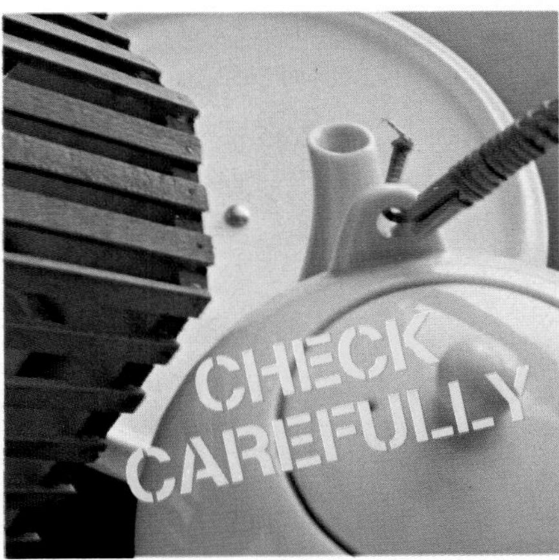

Glass, pottery, pyroceram, wood or straw with metal fittings (screws, handles, clamps, etc.)

Avoid or remove metal parts.

Block of Ice was defrosted for several minutes. Melted water has tunneled through ice, leaving some areas intact.

HOW TO DISTRIBUTE MICROWAVE ENERGY EVENLY DURING DEFROSTING

Stir vegetables, casseroles and saucy foods part way through defrosting time.

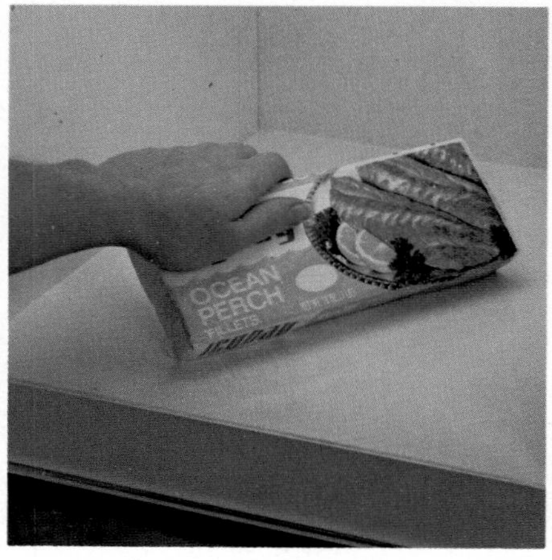

Turn Over or rotate foods which cannot be stirred, such as meats, layered casseroles or cakes.

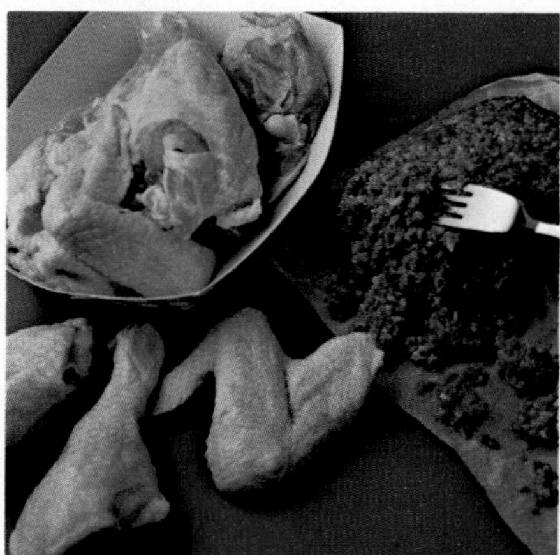

Separate Pieces, such as chicken parts or fish fillets, as soon as possible. Let large items stand to complete defrosting.

Defrosting

Ice absorbs microwave energy slowly, while water and moisture respond rapidly. Where microwaves penetrate frozen foods and moisture appears, melting is exaggerated. Defrosting techniques which redistribute microwave energy help foods defrost evenly and speed defrosting as well. If you try to defrost food without any attention, vulnerable spots, such as edges and thin areas, will start to cook before centers or thick areas are defrosted. Step-by-step instructions for defrosting specific foods are included throughout the recipe sections. Be sure to observe standing time where directed. Some microwave ovens allow you to program standing time.

TIPS FOR MICROWAVING FROZEN DINNERS

Remove food from trays over ¾-in. high and arrange on plate. Peel off foil lid from shallow trays. Return tray to box. (Check box for microwave directions.)

Place Box in oven 1-in. from sides. Microwave at Medium High 8 to 12 Minutes, or at High 5 to 8 Minutes. (Rotate ½ turn after ½ of time at High.) Plated foods take less time.

Avoid French fries, doughs and foods which do not microwave well, or remove them and cook conventionally.

HOW TO FREEZE FOODS FOR MICROWAVING

Package single portions for future heating in pouches. Make additional servings or use leftovers.

Freeze and defrost foods in plastic or cardboard cartons from deli foods, sour cream, etc. Pop out foods from foil pans.

Freeze and heat homemade dinners in shallow foil trays. Select foods which microwave well, and follow directions above.

Heating

Heating is one of the advantages of microwaving. Food can be prepared earlier in the day, when cooking may be more convenient, and reheated at serving time. Plates of food can be set aside and heated to give late comers a hot meal. Leftovers will taste freshly cooked when reheated.

Consult the chart on the inside front cover for times and power levels recommended for various types and quantities of food. When heating by time, stir, turn over or rotate foods as needed.

Starting Temperature. Foods taken from the refrigerator take longer than foods stored on your pantry shelf.

Quantity. One serving heats faster than several. Heat large amounts at Medium High and rotate or stir after ½ of time for even heating.

Automatic Temperature Probe. Heat foods by temperature for accuracy. Moist casseroles heat well. Serve at 150° to 160°.

Soften Ice Cream for easy scooping. Remove any foil and microwave at Defrost ½ minute per pint, or 1½ to 2 minutes for ½ gallon.

Soften Butter to spreadable stage. Unwrap ¼ lb. and place on plate. Microwave at Defrost ½ minute (refrigerated) or 1 minute (frozen).

Melt Butter in small bowl or glass measure, using High Power. To clarify, heat until bubbly and pour off clear liquid.

HEATING SINGLE PLATES OF FOOD

Arrange plates with hardest to heat foods on the outside of dish. Make a depression in dense foods like mashed potatoes, to give them a ring shape. Where possible, spread foods out to keep a low, even profile.

When assembling plates from leftovers, start with foods of the same temperature; all refrigerated or all room temperature. Fast heating items can be added at the end.

Cover most foods with wax paper to hold in heat and prevent spatters without steaming. When more moisture is desired, cover with plastic wrap. Be careful of steam when removing wrap.

For accurate heating, use the temperature probe inserted into the largest piece of food and set to 150° to 160°, which is serving temperature.

When heating by time at High, you may want to rotate the plate after ½ the time. Heat for 2 to 3 minutes and test by feeling the bottom of the plate. If plate is warm, it indicates that food is hot enough to transfer heat to the plate. If plate is cool, food may be warm, but will lose heat to the plate and taste cool when served.

Arrange thick areas and dense foods to the outside of dish, with easy-to-heat foods on the inside.

Speed heating of uniform foods like beef stew by stirring from edges to center while heating.

Spread saucy, moist foods, such as chow mein or creamed tuna with noodles flat for absorption of energy. Rotate layered foods.

Add Sauce to sliced meat and a pat of butter to dry pasta or rice, to speed heating. Add frozen roll last ½ to 1 minute.

Delicate foods which can overheat, such as macaroni and cheese or seafood, may be microwaved at Medium to keep them tender.

Use temperature probe for accurate, carefree reheating of moist, saucy foods. Cover plate with plastic wrap.

The Automatic Temperature Probe

The automatic temperature probe takes the guesswork out of timing. Factors which influence time cooking, such as the amount, type and starting temperature of food are automatically adjusted in temperature cooking. Foods cook to a pre-set internal temperature, then the oven signals you and turns off. With Automatic Simmering the probe regulates temperature so that foods cook slowly.

With temperature cooking, roasting most meats and poultry becomes carefree. If you follow directions for covering, probe placement and power level, the roast will need no attention during cooking.

Probe placement is important for accurate results. Throughout this book you will find pictures and instructions for positioning the probe in different types of food. Here are a few general rules:

Insert probe into foods as directed in recipes, making sure the disc does not touch food. Probe is easiest to use when inserted from the front. Use the clip to keep probe in place while heating. Cover foods as directed for moisture control and speedy, even heating. When simmering automatically, submerge the tip of the probe in liquid.

Where choice of power levels is given, lower setting will heat more evenly, but requires a little more time.

If food has been frozen, make sure it is completely defrosted before inserting the probe. Do not use the probe with TV dinner trays or with the Brown 'N Sear Dish.

ACCURATE COOKING

Roast Beef to rare, medium or well done at Medium or Low Power. Insert probe into center of meaty areas, without touching fat or bone.

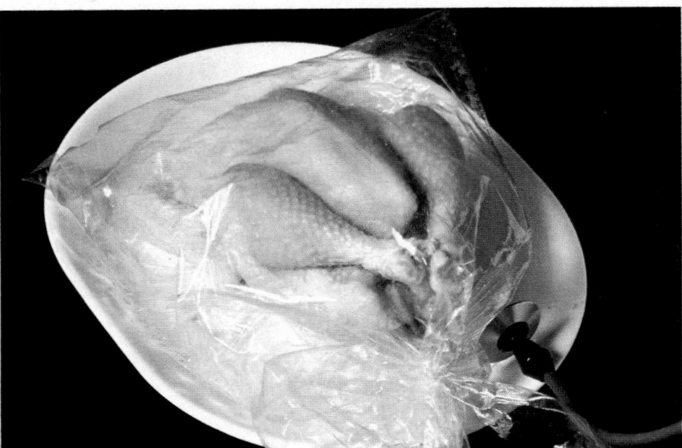

Roast Poultry at Medium or Medium High to an internal temperature of 190°. Insert probe into meatiest area of inner thigh, from below the end of, and parallel to the leg.

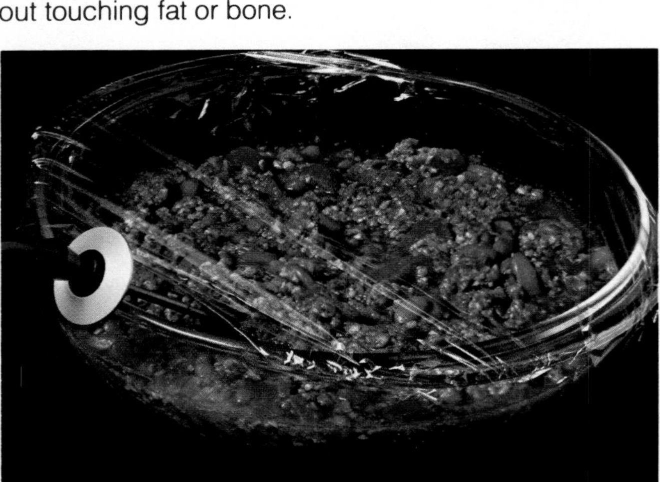

Cook Casseroles at High to Medium, to accurate internal temperature as directed in recipes. Insert probe so tip is in center of casserole.

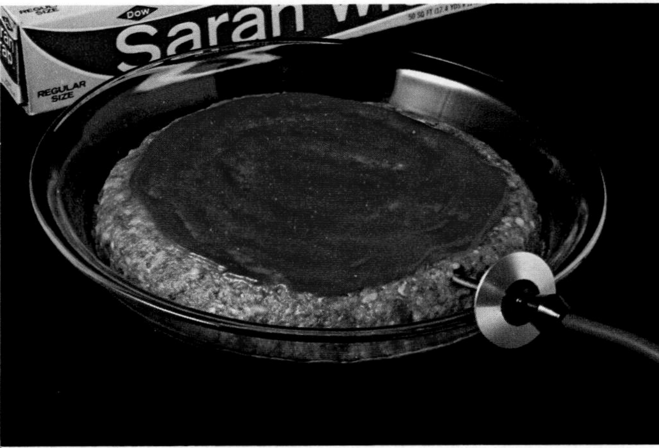

Cook Meatloaves without special attention, following recipes for power levels and internal temperatures. Insert probe into center of loaf or ring.

ACCURATE HEATING

Dips may be served hot (130°), or softened to proper scooping temperature (90°), at Low or Medium. Insert probe so tip is in center of dip.

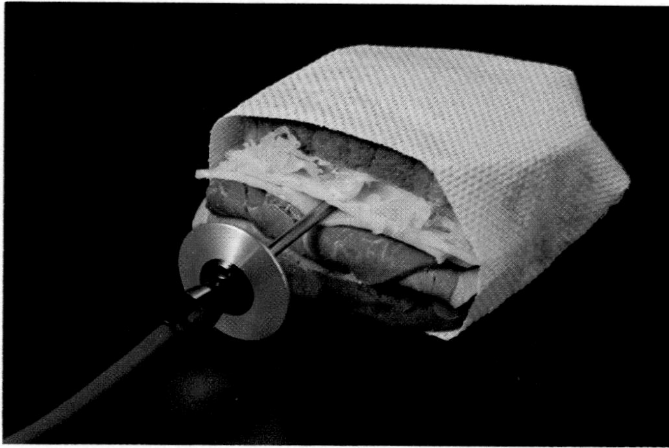

Heat Sandwich at Medium High to 110° or 120°. Wrap sandwich in paper towel or napkin and insert probe so tip is in center of filling.

Milk-Based soups and beverages won't boil over when heated at Medium High to 140°. Place probe in center of liquid. Use clip to hold it in place.

Warm Syrup for pancakes or waffles in glass measure or microwave ovenproof pitcher. Insert probe in center using clip. Heat at Medium High to 120° to 140°.

Warm Baked Goods, such as nut bread, coffee cake or pound cake at Low to 90° or 110°. Insert probe so tip is in center. *(Do not use with frozen foods.)*

Heat Casseroles containing precooked foods at Medium or High to 150° to 160°. Bubbling will probably appear at edges before center reaches 150°. If foods are not precooked, temperatures above 160° may be needed.

Menu Planning

As with any meal, microwave menus begin with balanced nutrition and contrast of color, texture and taste for eye and appetite appeal. As with conventional cooking, plan your meals so that all the foods will not need last-minute cooking or attention at the same time.

Some special features of microwaving make it easy to serve meals with every food piping hot. Cooking of some foods may be interrupted while you start others, without harm to the food.

A recipe which requires standing time can be microwaved first, and another food cooked while it stands. Dishes prepared in advance can be reheated briefly before serving.

Use these sample menus as a guide to planning microwave meals. They are well-balanced, good tasting dinners made with every-day, popular foods. Follow the step-by-step microwaving order to have everything hot and ready to eat at the same time.

Chicken Dinner

CHICKEN DINNER

Crumb Coated Chicken
page 122

Frozen Beans
page 188

Tossed Salad

Warm Rolls
page 213

Fruit-Topped Cake
page 242

45 minutes before serving time:

Prepare Fruit-Topped Cake

While cake is cooking, skin chicken (if desired). and coat with crumbs.

When cake is ready, microwave chicken. While chicken cooks, prepare and refrigerate salad greens and get beans ready to microwave.

When chicken is done, set it aside to keep warm and microwave beans.

Toss salad and warm rolls just before serving.

MENU PLANNING TIPS

Appetizers. Early in the day, get appetizers ready to microwave and refrigerate them if necessary. At serving time, microwave them and serve them hot. If you must remove another food from the oven while you heat appetizers, it will not harm the food.

Meats and Main Dish Casseroles. As a general rule, start cooking the meat or main dish casserole first. Meats cooked with a sauce or other ingredients improve in flavor if allowed to stand a few minutes before serving. Many meats and main dishes require standing time to finish cooking.

Vegetables. We recommend a short standing time of 4 to 6 minutes for frozen vegetables and most fresh vegetables. During this time, heat rolls or microwave a beverage.

Desserts. Many desserts such as cakes, brownies or refrigerated pies may be microwaved several hours ahead of serving time. Others, such as baked apples or defrosted frozen cakes and pastries, may be prepared while dishes from the main course are being cleared from the table.

Baked Breads and Rolls. Warm breads and rolls for only a few seconds just before serving dinner.

MEATLOAF DINNER

Lemon Lovers Meatloaf
page 78

Baked Potatoes
with Bacon Crumbles and Sour Cream
page 190

Frozen Carrots and Peas
page 189

Apple Graham Pie
page 237

Early in the day:

Make Apple Graham Pie. Refrigerate if made more than 4 hours in advance.

About 50 minutes before serving time:

Microwave Bacon.

Prepare and microwave meatloaf.

While meatloaf cooks, scrub potatoes and prick them in several places with fork. Crumble bacon.

When meatloaf is done, set it aside in a warm place to stand while microwaving potatoes. When potatoes are done (still slightly firm to the touch), set them aside. Microwave carrots and peas.

Reheat pie while clearing the table.

Meatloaf Dinner

Power Levels

Microwave ovens vary in the number of power levels available, depending upon the model selected. Each power level serves a definite purpose, and should be used when recommended, if possible.

Where a choice of power levels is given, the lower setting will cook and heat more evenly, although it will take a little more time.

If your oven does not have the recommended setting, you will not get the same results. Some foods may be cooked at a higher power level with additional attention, such as frequent stirring, turning over or rotating. Other foods, especially those which are delicate or require slow simmering, should not be attempted at higher settings.

High Power is full (100%) power and used for fast cooking, and for foods which tolerate heat and speed. Many recipes in this book call for High Power.

Medium High Power is about ⅔ (70%) the oven's full power and used for ease in heating and cooking amounts or types of food which require extra attention at High Power.

Medium Power is about ½ (50%) the oven's full power and used for slower cooking and most meat cookery.

Low Power is about ⅓ (30%) the oven's full power and recommended for delicate foods which are not tolerant of fast cooking, or for foods which require slow simmering to tenderize them.

Warm is about ¹/₁₀ (10%) the oven's full power and used for extremely gentle cooking or for holding foods at serving temperature.

Additional Settings of up to 10 levels offer greater flexibility. You can match the power to the food by lowering or increasing the setting.

HOW TO ADAPT OUR RECIPE TIMES

These recipes were developed for microwave ovens of 625 watts. However, house power varies from one part of the country to another, or during periods of peak consumption, such as early evening or extremely hot or cold weather. To prevent overcooking, recipes which are cooked by time direct you to check for doneness after the minimum cooking time, then add more time if needed. Fluctuations in power do not affect cooking with the temperature probe.

If you are uncertain about your house power, or have purchased this book for use with a different microwave oven, you can determine wattage with the following test. You will need a 1-qt. measure, a 1 cup measure and a watch or clock with a second hand.

Bring tap water from cold to boil as shown in pictures below. Time how long it takes. If your oven has 625 watts, timing will be approximately 3½ minutes, and recipe times in this cookbook should be correct for you. If your timing is significantly longer, expect recipe times to be about maximum or more. If your timing is shorter, use minimum or less time.

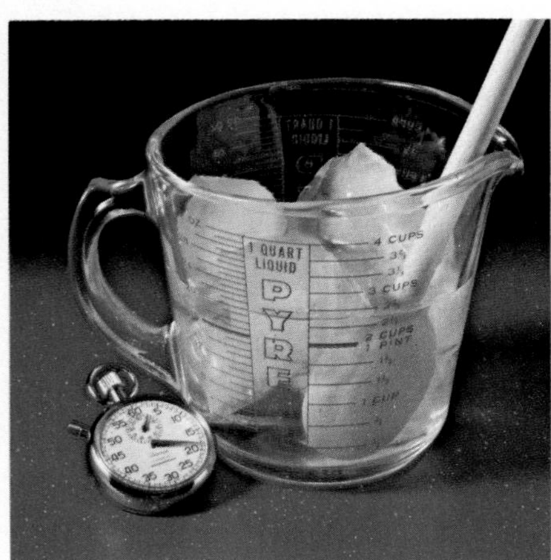

Combine 1 cup cold tap water with 8 ice cubes. Stir together for 1 minute.

Pour Off 1 cup of water without ice cubes. Temperature of water will be about 38°.

Timing Carefully, microwave water at High until many bubbles break on the surface (212°).

HOW TO CONVERT CONVENTIONAL RECIPES FOR MICROWAVING

Before converting your recipe, study it in terms of microwaving. Is it one of the many foods which microwave well? Look for cooking techniques which are similar to microwaving techniques, such as covering, steaming or cooking in sauce or liquid. If the food requires a crisp, fried crust or very dry surface, you will prefer to cook it conventionally. Some recipes may not be exactly the same when microwaved, but you will be pleased with the results.

If the food is suitable for microwaving, refer to a Microlesson or similar recipe for cooking techniques, power level, timing and possible changes in ingredients.

Many recipes will not need changing. Moist, rich cakes, candies and moist meatloaves are examples.

Since liquids do not evaporate when microwaved, reduce the amount or add more thickening to sauces and gravies. Reduce seasonings; lack of evaporation intensifies flavors. Salt meats and vegetables after cooking. If an ingredient takes longer to microwave than the others, substitute one which is precooked or quick-cooking, as we have done in the following example.

CONVENTIONAL SPANISH RICE

COOKING TIME: 45 to 50 min., total

Use Chuck — **1 lb. ground beef** ...... In 10-in. skillet crumble ground beef. Cook over medium high heat 10 minutes, uncovered. — Use 3qt. casserole — Skip

Omit — **1½ cups water** .... Add water, rice, chili powder, onion, salt pepper and tomatoes. Stir very well. Cover and cook over medium heat 35 to 40 minutes. — Microwave at High 12 to 14 minutes, stirring after 6 minutes

Substitute 1 cup precooked rice — **¾ cup long grain rice**
2 tablespoons chili powder
Reduce — **2 tablespoons instant minced onion**
2 teaspoons salt
⅛ teaspoon pepper
1 can (1-lb. 12-oz.) tomatoes

Makes 4 to 6 servings

MICROWAVE SPANISH RICE

POWER LEVEL: High
MICROWAVE TIME: 12 to 14 min., total

1 lb. ground chuck beef .. Into 3-qt. casserole crumble beef. Add remaining ingredients and mix well, cutting tomatoes to distribute evenly. Cover. **Microwave at High 12 to 14 Minutes,** stirring after 6 minutes. If top of food appears dry during cooking, stir again, then return to oven to finish cooking.

1 cup packaged precooked rice (minute)
1 can (1-lb. 12-oz.) tomatoes
1 tablespoon instant minced onion
2 tablespoons chili powder
2 teaspoons salt
⅛ teaspoon pepper

Makes 4 to 6 servings

Beef Stew simmers 6 to 8 hours, controlled automatically by the temperature probe.

In the Morning, prepare vegetables and combine with beef, liquid and seasonings in the casserole. Place the probe with its tip submerged in liquid.

In the Evening, serve savory, tender beef stew. Microwave a dish of brownies in 6 to 7 minutes for a popular family dessert.

Automatic Simmering & Slow Cooking

If your microwave oven is equipped with a simmer or slow cook setting, use it to prepare delicious, old-fashioned in-a-pot dishes. Most of these hearty foods are a meal in themselves, made from popular yet inexpensive meats and vegetables.

In-a-pot meals are versatile enough to serve as a sustaining family dinner or easy-on-the-hostess party fare. Just add a crisp green salad, crusty French bread and microwave a quick dessert.

Slow cooked dishes need no attention during microwaving. The temperature probe controls cooking automatically, keeping foods at a slow simmer to develop rich homemade flavor and fork tender texture. If desired, however, you may check or stir the food at any time while it's cooking.

Our recipes call for refrigerated meat, but you may also start with frozen meat. Adjust the cooking time according to the chart below. Fresh vegetables in large chunks may be started with frozen meat and will not overcook in the minimum time.

Recipes for crocks and slow cookers may be used for microwave simmering. Check food at the minimum time recommended for slow cookers.

AUTOMATIC SIMMERING AND SLOW COOKING CHART

Always add at least ½ cup liquid when simmering foods. Place the temperature probe IN THE LIQUID with the tip submerged. It should rest on the bottom of the utensil, about halfway between the center and side of dish.

Use the minimum time for meat which is very tender but firm enough to hold its shape when lifted from the pot. Maximum time will produce "fall off the bone" tenderness.

The special stoneware casserole available with some models is suitable for microwaving beans, stews and pieces of meat in recipes calling for casserole of under 3 to 3½-qt. capacity. For larger recipes and solidly frozen or unevenly shaped meats, other microwave ovenproof utensils of glass, pyroceram or pottery are available. Even the glass bowl of your electric mixer makes a good simmering pot. The microwave stoneware casserole has a special slotted cover which allows the probe to be placed in the covered dish, yet prevents escape of steam needed for tenderizing. If you do not have this accessory, cover the dish tightly with plastic wrap, rather than a conventional casserole lid.

ITEM	APPROXIMATE AUTOMATIC SIMMER TIME/HOURS
Beef Chuck Roast (5-lb.)	
Fresh	6 to 8
Frozen	9 to 11
Beef Stew	6 to 8
Larger Quantity	9 to 11
Chicken, Stewing (4 to 6-lb.)	
Fresh	11 to 12
Frozen	12 to 14
Chicken, Broiler-Fryer (2½ to 3½-lb.)	
Fresh	4 to 6
Frozen	6 to 8
Chili and other Saucy Hamburger Mixtures	11 to 13

ITEM	APPROXIMATE AUTOMATIC SIMMER TIME/HOURS
Corned Beef and Brisket (3 to 4-lb.)	5 to 7
Ham or Pork Roast (5-lb.)	4 to 6
Pork and Beans	9 to 11
Punch, Mulled Cider	4 to 6
Rice Pudding	½
Soup Stock	4 to 6
Split Pea Soup	13 to 15
Swiss Steak	6 to 8
Tongue, boiled	10 to 12
Vegetable Soup	3 to 4

Chili

Beef

Savory stews, tender pot roasts and hearty casseroles microwave carefree with automatic simmering. To keep these meats tender and juicy, bury them beneath vegetables or cover them with liquid or sauce.

TIP: Pour water over the back of a spoon when adding it to saucy hamburger mixtures. The water will form a layer over surface to keep the top from drying out. Stir water into mixture before serving.

GERMAN MEATBALLS

POWER LEVEL: Automatic Simmer
MICROWAVE TIME: 6 hr. to 8 hr.

2 lb. ground veal, pork and beef mixture
1 medium onion, finely chopped
2 eggs
2 tablespoons flour
2 tablespoons dry onion soup mix
1 teaspoon salt
¼ teaspoon pepper
Boiling water
2 bay leaves
2 tablespoons dry onion soup mix
1 teaspoon salt
1 teaspoon brown bouquet sauce (optional)

In mixing bowl mix together ground meat, onion, eggs, flour, soup mix, salt and pepper. Form into medium sized balls (up to ¼ cup per ball). Set aside. Pour 1-qt. boiling water into stoneware accessory or 3-qt. casserole. Add bay leaves, soup mix, salt and brown bouquet sauce. Carefully add meatballs. Add more boiling water if needed to cover. Insert temperature probe so tip rests in liquid on bottom of dish, halfway between center and side.

Use accessory cover; or cover tightly with plastic wrap, arranging loosely around probe to vent. Attach cable end at receptacle. **Microwave at Automatic Simmer 6 to 8 Hours.** Thicken broth (below), if desired.

To Thicken Broth: Remove meatballs from broth and keep warm. Into hot broth in dish, stir mixture of ¼ cup cornstarch and ¼ cup water. Add additional dry onion soup mix for onion gravy. **Microwave at High 4 to 6 Minutes,** stirring every 2 minutes.

Makes 16 to 18 meatballs

CHILI

POWER LEVEL: High and Automatic Simmer
MICROWAVE TIME: 11 to 13 hr.

To Prepare Beans: In 3-qt. casserole place **½ lb. dry pinto beans** and **2 qt. water.** Soak overnight. Before finishing chili, drain beans and add **6 cups fresh water. Microwave uncovered at High 60 Minutes.** Drain.

2 lb. ground chuck beef

In 4-qt. casserole crumble beef. **Microwave at High 8 to 10 Minutes,** stirring after 4 minutes. Drain off fat.

2 cans (1-lb. each) tomatoes
1 can (6-oz.) tomato paste
2 medium onions, coarsely chopped
1 green pepper, coarsely chopped
2 cloves garlic, crushed
2 to 3 tablespoons chili powder
½ teaspoon pepper
½ teaspoon cumin
2 teaspoons salt
1 cup water

Add drained beans, tomatoes, tomato paste, onions, peppers, garlic, chili powder, pepper, cumin and salt. Stir well. Over back of spoon, gently pour water onto top surface; do not stir in. Insert temperature probe so tip rests on bottom of dish, halfway between center and side.

Cover tightly with plastic wrap, arranging loosely around probe to vent. Attach cable end at receptacle. **Microwave at Automatic Simmer 10 to 12 Hours.** Stir before serving.

Makes 8 to 10 servings

NOTE: 2 cans (1-lb. each) pinto or kidney beans, drained, may be substituted for the dry beans. No overnight soaking or cooking of beans is needed.

HOW TO MICROWAVE BEEF STEW WITH AUTOMATIC SIMMERING

Combine 1 can undiluted beef broth, 1½ cups liquid, ⅓ cup minute tapioca and 2 tablespoons brown bouquet sauce in casserole.

Bury stew meat and vegetables under liquid. Place probe halfway between center and side of dish with tip submerged in liquid.

Vary the recipe with different meats and vegetables. Special seasonings give stews international flavors.

BASIC BEEF STEW

To lengthen cooking of all beef stews by 1 or 2 hours, add one more can of beef broth and increase tapioca to ½ cup.

POWER LEVEL: Automatic Simmer
MICROWAVE TIME: 6 to 8 hr.

- **2 lb. beef stew meat, cut in 1-in. cubes**
- **2 large potatoes, peeled, cut into chunks**
- **5 medium carrots, peeled, sliced**
- **2 medium onions, sliced**
- **2 stalks celery, sliced**
- **1 can (10½-oz.) beef broth**
- **1½ cups water**
- **⅓ cup minute tapioca**
- **2 tablespoons brown bouquet sauce**
- **2 teaspoons salt**
- **¼ teaspoon pepper**
- **¼ teaspoon garlic powder**

In stoneware accessory or 4-qt. casserole place beef, potatoes, carrots, onions, celery, broth, water, tapioca, brown bouquet sauce, salt, pepper and garlic powder. Mix together very thoroughly. With the back of a spoon, press chunks of meat to submerge under liquid. Insert temperature probe so tip rests on bottom of dish, halfway between center and side. Use accessory cover; or cover tightly with plastic wrap, arranging loosely around probe to vent. Attach cable end at receptacle. **Microwave at Automatic Simmer 6 to 8 Hours.** Stir before serving.

Makes about 6 servings

For Larger Amount of Beef Stew: Use a 5-qt. casserole. Increase the above recipe by ½ the amount, except reserve 1 cup water. Invert a microwave oven proof saucer over stew to hold meat and vegetables under liquid. Gently pour reserved water around edge of dish. **Automatic Simmer 9 to 11 Hours.**

VARIATIONS:

Beef Curry: Prepare Beef Stew, omitting potatoes and carrots. Blend ½ cup raisins and 3 tablespoons curry powder into mixture and microwave as in recipe, left. Serve over rice.

Beef Goulash: Prepare Beef Stew, omitting potatoes and carrots. Stir 2 tablespoons paprika into mixture and microwave as in recipe, left. Just before serving, stir in 1 cup (8-oz.) sour cream. Serve over noodles.

Irish Stew: Substitute lamb for beef. Just before serving, stir in 1 pkg. (10-oz.) frozen peas. **Microwave at High 5 to 10 Minutes,** until peas are tender.

BEEF STEW WITH WINE

This French beef stew is also called Boeuf Bourguignon. Serve with buttered wide noodles.

POWER LEVEL: Automatic Simmer
MICROWAVE TIME: 6 to 8 hr.

Make Basic Beef Stew (left), except omit potatoes and celery. Add 1 can (6-oz.) tomato paste, 1 can (8-oz.) mushrooms, drained and substitute 1 cup red burgundy for 1 cup of the water.

Insert temperature probe so tip rests on bottom of dish, halfway between center and side. Use cover; or cover tightly with plastic wrap, arranging loosely around probe to vent. Attach cable end at receptacle. **Microwave at Automatic Simmer 6 to 8 Hours.** Stir before serving. If desired, garnish each serving with crumbled bacon, (Microwave 4 to 6 strips bacon at High 4 to 6 minutes.), and chopped parsley.

Makes 8 to 10 servings

HOW TO MICROWAVE POT ROAST WITH AUTOMATIC SIMMER

Frozen roast may be substituted for fresh. Use large chunks of fresh vegetables or frozen stew vegetables. See page 33 for time.

Shield high roasts, such as rump, as suggested in recipe, right. Flat roasts, such as chuck or round, need no shielding.

Place probe, with tip submerged in liquid, next to meat in microwave ovenproof cooking dish.

CORNED BEEF OR BEEF BRISKET

Horseradish Sauce, page 173, is a good accompaniment.

POWER LEVEL: Automatic Simmer
MICROWAVE TIME: 5 to 7 hrs.

1 corned beef* or beef brisket, 3 to 4 lb. **½ cup chopped onion** **2 garlic cloves, crushed** **2 bay leaves** **2 cups water***	In 13×9×2-in. dish place meat. Cover with onion add garlic and bay leaves. Add water. Insert temperature probe so tip rests in water on bottom of dish.

Cover tightly with plastic wrap, arranging loosely around probe to vent. Attach cable end at receptacle. **Microwave at Automatic Simmer 5 to 7 Hours.** To serve, remove from broth and slice thinly and diagonally across the grain. If desired, serve slices with some of the broth.

*Corned beef must be covered with water and cooked in stoneware accessories or 3-qt. casserole.

Makes 8 to 10 servings

VARIATIONS:

Corned Beef and Cabbage: Cook corned beef as in recipe above. Remove from broth and keep warm. To broth, add 1 head cabbage, cut into 6 wedges. **Microwave at High 20 to 25 Minutes,** rearranging wedges after 10 minutes, until tender. Serve cabbage with sliced corned beef.

Barbecued Brisket: Cook brisket as in recipe above. After simmering, drain off liquid. Coat top surface with bottled barbecue sauce. **Microwave at High 5 to 8 Minutes,** until sauce begins to form glaze. Slice and serve with more sauce, if desired.

SAVORY BEEF TONGUE

Serve with mustard and sweet pickles. Most people think of tongue as a favorite sandwich filling. Marinate in Italian dressing, if desired, before slicing.

POWER LEVEL: Automatic Simmer
MICROWAVE TIME: 10 to 12 hr.

2 qt. water **8 whole cloves** **4 whole peppercorns** **1½ teaspoons salt** **4 to 5 bay leaves** **⅓ cup vinegar** **1 beef tongue, 3 to 4-lb.**	In 5-qt. casserole place water, cloves, peppercorns, salt, bay leaves and vinegar. Stir to blend. Add tongue. Insert temperature probe so tip rests in water on bottom of dish.

Cover tightly with plastic wrap, arranging loosely around probe to vent. Attach cable end at receptacle. **Microwave at Automatic Simmer 10 to 12 Hours.** Drain and cool tongue slightly. Remove skin over tongue with sharp knife. Slice thinly. Serve hot or cold.

Makes about 8 to 10 servings

AUTOMATIC SIMMERING POT ROASTS

Depending on your time schedule, select a flat roast, like beef chuck or blade roast, or a chunky roast, such as rolled rump or sirloin tip. Flat roasts may be simmered for 6 or more hours while chunky roasts must be checked after 3 to 4 hours.

CHUCK ROAST

Arrange vegetables as flat as possible in dish. If vegetables cover roast, microwave for minimum time.

POWER LEVEL: Automatic Simmer
MICROWAVE TIME: Fresh 6 to 8 hr. - Frozen 9 to 11 hr.

1 fresh or frozen beef chuck or arm roast, about 5-lb.
2 to 3 potatoes, peeled and cut in large chunks
4 to 6 carrots, scraped and cut in chunks
2 large onions, cleaned and quartered
1 can (10½-oz.) beef consomme or beef broth

In 13×9×2-in. dish place roast. Arrange vegetables around edges of dish. Pour consomme over top. Insert temperature probe so tip is in liquid on bottom of dish. Cover tightly with plastic wrap, arranging loosely around probe to vent. Attach cable end at receptacle. **Microwave at Automatic Simmer 6 to 8 Hours,** for fresh meat, or **9 to 11 Hours,** for frozen.

Makes 6 to 8 servings

VARIATIONS:

Pot Roast with Wine: Use above recipe except omit vegetables and consomme. Sprinkle 1 cup chopped onions over top of roast; top with mixture of 1 can (10-oz.) beef gravy and ½ cup red cooking wine.

With Other Vegetables: Fresh rutabagas, turnips, and parsnips, peeled and cut in large chunks, or 1 pkg. (32-oz.) frozen stew vegetables may be substituted for carrots and potatoes in basic recipe.

To Automatic Simmer Chuck Roast 1 to 2 Hours Longer: Use larger dish, such as pyroceram 12x10 roasting dish and add 1 cup water.

RUMP ROAST AND SIRLOIN TIP

Use this method for rolled and tied roasts, including veal, less tender lamb and pork cuts, which are pot roasted.

The high chunky shape of these roasts can cause them to become dry on top if simmered more than 4 hours. Check roast after 3 to 4 hours. To prevent dryness, protect top of roast by spreading over top surface one of the following:

1. 1 can (10-oz.) undiluted condensed tomato soup.
2. A double-thick layer of bacon. (This gives a delicious flavor to roast.)

Cover with plastic wrap and microwave as for chuck roast. Be sure to include the beef broth, or about 1 to 1½ cups water or wine. Thick soup or gravy toppings may be stirred into broth to flavor and thicken it.

Chuck Roast

SWISS STEAK

POWER LEVEL: Automatic Simmer
MICROWAVE TIME: 6 to 8 hr.

3 lb. round steak, ½-in. thick
1 cup flour
1 teaspoon salt
¼ teaspoon pepper

Cut round steak into serving pieces. Tenderize with meat mallet or foil-covered brick. Dredge all pieces in flour seasoned with salt and pepper. In 12×8×2-in. dish arrange meat.

2 cans (10½-oz. each) condensed chicken gumbo soup

Spoon undiluted soup over meat. Insert temperature probe so tip rests in liquid on bottom of dish, halfway between center and side.

Cover tightly with plastic wrap, arranging loosely around probe to vent. Attach cable end at receptacle. **Microwave at Automatic Simmer 6 to 8 Hours.**

Makes 6 to 8 servings

VARIATION: Substitute any of the following for the chicken gumbo soup: cream of mushroom, onion, tomato or vegetable soup.

Smothered Swiss Steak: Prepare as above, using cream of mushroom soup, except stir in 1 cup (8-oz.) dairy sour cream just before serving.

SHORT RIBS IN SPICY SAUCE

POWER LEVEL: High and Automatic Simmer
MICROWAVE TIME: 6 hr. to 8 hr.

3 to 4 lb. lean beef short ribs
1 onion, sliced
Spicy Sauce (below)

Line 13×9×2-in. dish with 2 layers paper towel. Add trimmed ribs. **Microwave at High 10 Minutes,** turning meat over after 5 minutes. Remove paper towels, which have absorbed grease. Add onion and sauce, stirring to coat each piece.

Insert temperature probe so tip rests in sauce on bottom of dish, halfway between center and side. Cover tightly with plastic wrap, arranging loosely around probe to vent. Attach cable end at receptacle. **Microwave at Automatic Simmer 6 to 8 Hours.** If desired, serve with noodles.

Spicy Sauce: In small bowl, stir together 2 cups bouillon, 1 tablespoon mustard, 2 tablespoons ketchup, 1 teaspoon salt, ¼ teaspoon black pepper and 1 teaspoon caraway.

Makes 3 to 4 servings

BEEF ROLLS IN TOMATO SAUCE

POWER LEVEL: Automatic Simmer
MICROWAVE TIME: 4 to 5 hr.

1½ lb. round steak, ¾-in. thick
3 tablespoons butter, softened
4 tablespoons fresh parsley, chopped
1 clove garlic, crushed
1 teaspoon rosemary
6 thin dill pickle slices
6 thin onion slices

Cut steak into 6 serving pieces. Pound ½-in. thick with meat mallet or foil covered brick. Spread each piece with butter; sprinkle with parsley, garlic and rosemary. Top each piece with a pickle and onion slice. Roll up each piece, securing roll with toothpick or string. In 10×6×2-in. dish, arrange rolls.

1 can (8-oz.) tomato sauce
¼ cup Worcestershire sauce
½ teaspoon pepper
Dash cayenne pepper

In small bowl blend together tomato sauce, Worcestershire sauce, black pepper and cayenne. Spoon over beef rolls.

Insert temperature probe so tip rests in sauce on bottom of dish. Cover tightly with plastic wrap, arranging loosely around probe to vent. Attach cable end at receptacle. **Microwave at Automatic Simmer 4 to 5 Hours.** Just before serving, remove toothpicks or string.

Makes 6 servings

GINGER BEEF

POWER LEVEL: Automatic Simmer
MICROWAVE TIME: 4 to 5 hr.

2½ lb. flank steak

Trim and cut steak diagonally into strips ¾-in. thick.

1 can (16-oz.) stewed tomatoes
1 pkg. (½ of 2¾-oz. box) dry onion soup mix
2 medium onions, chopped
3 cloves garlic, minced
1½ teaspoons salt
1 tablespoon ground ginger
1 teaspoon turmeric
¼ teaspoon dry chili peppers, optional

In stoneware accessory or 3-qt. casserole combine steak strips, tomatoes, soup mix, onions, garlic, salt, ginger, turmeric and chili peppers. Insert temperature probe so tip rests in liquid on bottom of dish, halfway between center and side. Use accessory cover; or cover tightly with plastic wrap, arranging loosely around probe to vent. Attach cable end at receptacle. **Microwave at Automatic Simmer 4 to 5 Hours.** Serve hot over rice.

Makes 6 to 8 servings

Pork & Ham

Pork and ham products are delicious when simmered slowly, but they can become dry on top and care must be taken to prepare them properly for automatic simmering. Small pieces, such as ribs, chops or sausages can be buried beneath vegetables or in liquid. Arrange a pork roast in the cooking dish with the bone side up to form a natural shield.

HOW TO AUTOMATIC SIMMER PORK ROAST

POWER LEVEL: Automatic Simmer
MICROWAVE TIME: 4 to 6 hr.

Place 4 to 6 lb. fresh pork roast in 13×9×2-in. dish, bone side up and fat side down. Add 1½ cups water.

Insert temperature probe so tip rests in water on bottom of dish. Cover tightly with plastic wrap, arranging loosely around probe to vent. Attach cable end at receptacle.

Microwave at Automatic Simmer 4 to 6 Hours. Meat will be very tender and juicy, but top fat will not be brown. If desired, turn roast over and conventionally broil, or brush brown bouquet sauce over fat, until brown color is achieved.

TIP: Traditional barbecued pork starts with pork roasts tender enough to be shredded before combining with barbecue sauce and simmered to mellow flavors. This technique gives you the type of meat which you can use for such barbecue.

HOW TO AUTOMATIC SIMMER HAM

A thick rind is an asset on hams to be automatically simmered because it acts as a covering to keep the top areas moist and juicy. Look for rind on both hams and smoked picnics when you buy them for automatic simmering. If rind is thick, omit paper towel covering.

POWER LEVEL: Automatic Simmer
MICROWAVE TIME: 4 to 5 hr.

Place about 5 lb. ham cut side down in 13×9×2-in. dish. Add 3 cups water.

Cover top of ham with several (about 5) thicknesses of paper towels which have been saturated with water until dripping wet.

Insert temperature probe so tip rests in water on bottom of dish. Cover tightly with plastic wrap, arranging loosely around probe to vent. Attach cable end at receptacle.

Microwave at Automatic Simmer 4 to 5 Hours. Note that when finished, paper towel will have brown spots, similar to brown spots found on paper towels used to cook bacon. These are caused by sugar curing in these pork products.

Sausage and Tomato Stew

Ham: Saturate five layers of paper towels with water until dripping wet. Place them over a ham arranged with the cut side down. Add three more cups of water to the dish. This prevents overcooking the large meaty area. Brown spots which appear on the towels during cooking are due to the process used in curing ham, and are similar to brown spots seen on paper towels on which you cook bacon.

Fresh Pork Roast: Invert pork roast, bone side up when using Automatic Simmer. Add 1½ cups water.

OLD FASHIONED BAKED BEANS

POWER LEVEL: Automatic Simmer
MICROWAVE TIME: 18 to 22 hr., total

To Simmer Beans: In stoneware accessory or 3½ qt. casserole, place **1½ lb. (3½ cups) navy (pea) beans, 1 teaspoon soda and 9 cups water.** Use accessory cover; or cover tightly with plastic wrap arranging loosely around probe to vent. Attach cable end at receptacle. **Microwave at Automatic Simmer 10 to 12 hours or overnight.** Drain and return to same casserole.

1 cup brown sugar, packed
1 cup ketchup
2 cups water
½ cup chopped onion
¼ cup prepared mustard
¼ cup molasses
¼ cup vinegar
1 tablespoon salt
6 slices bacon, microwaved and crumbled.

In small bowl stir together well the brown sugar, ketchup, water, onion, mustard, molasses, vinegar, salt and bacon. Add and blend well into drained beans. Use accessory cover or cover tightly with plastic wrap, arranging loosely around probe to vent. Attach cable end at receptacle. **Microwave at Automatic Simmer 8 to 10 hours.** Stir before serving.

Makes 8 to 10 servings.

SAUSAGE AND TOMATO STEW

Of Polish origin, sometimes called Hunters Stew. Very hearty. Sauerkraut becomes mild over the long cooking period.

POWER LEVEL: Automatic Simmer
MICROWAVE TIME: 9 to 10 hr.

2 lb. polish sausage (kielbasa) sliced diagonally in 1-in. pieces
2 cans (4-oz. each) mushroom pieces, undrained
2 large apples, peeled, cored and sliced
3 cans (1-lb. each) sauerkraut, drained
2 medium onions, chopped
2 bay leaves
10 peppercorns
1 clove garlic, minced
2 cans (1-lb. each) tomatoes
5 strips microwaved bacon, crumbled

In 5-qt. casserole layer ½ of each of the following, in the order listed: sausage, mushrooms, apple, sauerkraut, onion, bay leaves, peppercorns, garlic and tomatoes. Sprinkle with all of bacon. Repeat layers. Insert temperature probe so tip rests in liquid in bottom of dish. Cover tightly with plastic wrap, arranging loosely around probe to vent. **Microwave at Automatic Simmer 9 to 10 Hours.**

Makes about 10 servings

SPARERIBS APPLES AND SAUERKRAUT

POWER LEVEL: High and Automatic Simmer
MICROWAVE TIME: 8 to 10 hr.

3 to 4 lb. lean pork spareribs, cut in serving pieces

In stoneware accessory or 3-qt. casserole place ribs. Cover. **Microwave at High 15 Minutes,** rearranging meat after 7 minutes. Drain off liquid.

1 teaspoon salt
¼ teaspoon pepper
1 teaspoon dill weed
2 apples, quartered, cored and sliced
2 large onions, thinly sliced
1 can (16-oz.) sauerkraut
1 cup water

Sprinkle salt, pepper and dill weed over ribs. Cover with apple slices, onion slices, undrained sauerkraut, then water. Insert temperature probe so tip rests in water on bottom of dish.

Use accessory cover; or cover tightly with plastic wrap, arranging loosely around probe to vent. Attach cable end at receptacle. **Microwave at Automatic Simmer 8 to 10 Hours.**

Makes 3 to 4 servings

HAM HOCKS WITH FRESH GREEN BEANS

POWER LEVEL: Automatic Simmer
MICROWAVE TIME: 10 to 11 hr.

4 ham hocks
1 lb. fresh green beans, washed and cut
2 onions, sliced
2 cups water
1 bay leaf
1 clove garlic, minced
1 teaspoon salt
¼ teaspoon pepper

In stoneware accessory or 3-qt. casserole place ham hocks, spacing evenly in dish. Add beans around and between hocks. Cover with onions. In 1-qt. measure stir together water, bay leaf, garlic, salt and pepper. Add to casserole.

Insert temperature probe so tip rests in water on bottom of dish, halfway between center and side. Use accessory cover; or cover tightly with plastic wrap, arranging loosely around probe to vent. Attach cable end at receptacle. **Microwave at Automatic Simmer 10 to 11 Hours.** Remove skin, bone and fat from ham hocks; dice meat and return to beans.

Makes about 4 servings

Poultry

Slowly simmered chicken is an international favorite. It's tender, tasty and economical, too. With automatic simmering you can microwave stewing chickens or broiler-fryers, either fresh or frozen, without attention. Just put them in the pot and forget about them until dinner time. See chart, page 33, or recipes for times.

Simmered Chicken

ROASTING CHICKEN EN CASSEROLE

POWER LEVEL: Automatic Simmer
MICROWAVE TIME: 6 to 7 hr.

4 medium potatoes, peeled, sliced ½-in. thick
4 small onions, peeled, sliced ⅛-in. thick
3 carrots, peeled, sliced ½-in. thick.
6 strips microwaved crisp bacon

In stoneware accessory or 3-qt. casserole layer potatoes, onion and carrots. Sprinkle with 2 slices of bacon, crumbled.

1 roasting chicken, 3-lb.
2 teaspoons dried parsley flakes
1 teaspoon salt
⅛ teaspoon pepper
¼ cup water

Sprinkle ½ of parsley, salt and pepper inside cavity of chicken and other ½ over top. Place chicken over vegetables and add water.

Crumble remaining bacon over chicken. Insert temperature probe so tip rests in water on bottom of dish. Use accessory cover; or cover tightly with plastic wrap, arranging loosely around probe to vent. Attach cable end at receptacle. **Microwave at Automatic Simmer 6 to 7 Hours.**

Makes 4 to 5 servings

SIMMERED CHICKEN

One of the simplest of ways to cook chicken, and one of the best. The stoneware casserole accessory is an excellent utensil for small, whole chickens.

POWER LEVEL: Automatic Simmer
MICROWAVE TIME: Fresh 4 to 6 hr. - Frozen 6 to 8 hr.

1 whole chicken (2½ to 3½-lb.)
Paprika
1 cup chicken broth

In stoneware accessory or 3-qt. casserole place chicken. Rub top of chicken with paprika. Add chicken broth. Insert temperature probe so tip is in liquid on bottom of dish. Use accessory cover; or cover tightly with plastic wrap, arranging loosely around probe to vent. Attach cable end at receptacle. **Microwave at Automatic Simmer 4 to 6 Hours** for fresh chicken; or **6 to 8 Hours** for frozen meat.

Makes 4 servings

HOW TO STEW CHICKEN WITH AUTOMATIC SIMMERING

Submerge chicken pieces in liquid and add seasoning. Place the probe with the tip in liquid halfway between the center and side of the dish.

Strip Meat from bones after microwaving. Use meat in cooked chicken recipes or return it to the casserole.

Vary chicken in broth by dropping dumplings on top or adding rice or noodles. Microwave as directed in the recipes below.

STEWING CHICKEN

POWER LEVEL: Automatic Simmer
MICROWAVE TIME: 11 to 12 hr.

1 stewing chicken (4 to 6-lb.) cut up
1 large onion, chopped
3½ cups water
2 tablespoons chicken bouillon granules
1 teaspoon salt

In 5-qt. casserole arrange chicken and onion. In small bowl mix water, bouillon granules and salt. Pour over chicken. Insert temperature probe so tip rests in liquid on bottom of dish, halfway between center and side. Cover tightly with plastic wrap, arranging loosely around probe to vent. Attach cable end at receptacle. **Microwave at Automatic Simmer 11 to 12 Hours.** Let pieces stand in broth until cool. Strip off skin and remove bones. Skim fat from broth.

Makes about 1 quart meat

CHICKEN 'N' NOODLES

While chicken stews, prepare homemade noodles, page 81, (recipe with Short Ribs), except do not dry them by microwaving; or use 1 to 1½ cups packaged egg noodles. After meat has been removed, **Microwave** broth **at High 5 to 8 Minutes,** until boiling. Add noodles. **Microwave at High 10 to 12 Minutes,** until noodles are tender. Add chunks of chicken. **Microwave at High 10 Minutes** more, until thickened, well blended and bubbly

Makes 6 to 8 servings

CHICKEN 'N' DUMPLINGS

Return stripped meat to broth in casserole. Stir in mixture of ¼ cup each cornstarch and cold water. **Microwave at High 5 to 8 Minutes,** until hot and bubbly. Meanwhile, prepare Fluffy Dumplings, page 83. Stir well. Drop dumplings around edges of dish. **Microwave at Medium 7 to 9 Minutes,** until dry in appearance and no longer doughy.

CHICKEN 'N' RICE

Before returning stripped meat to broth, bring broth to boil: **Microwave at High 10 to 15 Minutes,** until boiling. Stir in ¾ cup long grain rice. Cover. **Microwave at High 15 to 20 Minutes** more, stirring after about 9 minutes. To cooked rice, add chicken; **Microwave 5 to 8 Minutes** more, until hot.

SPANISH STYLE CHICKEN

This is a version of the famous Arroz Con Pollo.

POWER LEVEL: Automatic Simmer and High
MICROWAVE TIME: 4 hr. to 6 hr.

1 chicken (2½ to 3½-lb.) cut up
1 teaspoon salt
¼ teaspoon pepper
¼ teaspoon chili powder
1 clove garlic, minced
⅛ teaspoon saffron powder
3 cups chicken broth or bouillon
2 tablespoons sherry

In stoneware accessory or 3-qt. casserole combine chicken, salt,pepper, chili powder, garlic and saffron. Pour broth and sherry over chicken. Insert temperature probe so tip rests in liquid on bottom of dish, halfway between center and side. Use accessory cover; or cover tightly with plastic wrap, arranging loosely around probe to vent. Attach cable end at receptacle. **Microwave at Automatic Simmer 4 to 6 Hours.**

2 cups cooked rice
1 pkg. (10-oz.) frozen peas, defrosted
½ cup stuffed green olives, sliced

Add to chicken, broth, peas, olives and rice. Recover. **Microwave at High 5 Minutes,** until vegetables are hot.

Makes 4 to 6 servings

CHICKEN FRICASSEE

POWER LEVEL: Automatic Simmer and High
MICROWAVE TIME: 11 to 12 hr.

1 stewing chicken (4 to 6-lb.), cut up
2 teaspoons salt
1 teaspoon paprika
1 bay leaf
2 medium onions, sliced
3 stalks celery, sliced
2 carrots, pared and sliced
1 cup chicken broth

In 5-qt. casserole arrange chicken pieces. Sprinkle with salt, paprika and top with bay leaf. Add onions, celery and carrots. Pour chicken broth over top. Insert temperature probe so tip rests in broth on bottom of dish, halfway between center and side.

Cover tightly with plastic wrap, arranging loosely around probe to vent. Attach cable end at receptacle. **Microwave at Automatic Simmer 11 to 12 Hours.** Cool. Strip off skin and remove bones from chicken. Skim fat from broth and thicken (see below) just before serving.

To Thicken Broth: Stir together ½ cup flour and ½ cup water well. Add chicken pieces to broth and stir in flour-water mixture. **Microwave at High 10 to 13 Minutes,** until hot and bubbly. Serve over mashed potatoes or noodles.

CHICKEN IN SPAGHETTI WINE SAUCE

Sometimes known as Chicken Marengo.

POWER LEVEL: Automatic Simmer and High
MICROWAVE TIME: 4 to 6 hr.

1 chicken (2½ to 3½-lb.) cut up
1 pkg. (1½-oz.) spaghetti sauce mix
½ cup water or dry white wine

In stoneware accessory or 2-qt. casserole place chicken parts. Combine sauce mix with water or wine, pour over chicken.

Insert temperature probe so tip rests in liquid on bottom of dish, halfway between center and side. Use accessory cover; or cover tightly with plastic wrap, arranging loosely around probe to vent. Attach cable end at receptacle. **Microwave at Automatic Simmer 4 to 6 Hours.** Garnish as described below.

To Garnish: Stir **2 peeled fresh tomatoes,** cut in quarters and **¼ lb. fresh mushrooms,** cut in ½-in. slices, into chicken. **Microwave at High 5 Minutes** to heat. If desired, serve with ½ cup sliced black olives and ¼ cup snipped fresh parsley. Serve over rice.

CHICKEN IN WINE

Coq au Vin is its French name. This makes a delicious supper when served with rice and a salad.

POWER LEVEL: Automatic Simmer
MICROWAVE TIME: 4 to 6 hr.

1 chicken (2½ to 3½-lb.) cut up
3 tablespoons minute tapioca
1 qt. large mushrooms, cut in quarters
1 medium onion, chopped (¾ cup)
1 large carrot, sliced
Sauce (below)

In stoneware accessory or 3-qt. casserole place chicken. Sprinkle with tapioca, then layer mushrooms, onion and carrot over top. Pour sauce (below) over all. Insert temperature probe so tip rests in sauce on bottom of dish. Use accessory cover; or cover tightly with plastic wrap, arranging loosely around probe to vent. Attach cable end at receptacle. **Microwave at Automatic Simmer 4 to 6 Hours.**

Makes about 4 servings

Sauce: In small bowl stir together 1 cup white wine, 2 tablespoons dried parsley flakes, ½ bay leaf, ½ teaspoon thyme, 1 teaspoon salt and ⅛ teaspoon freshly ground pepper.

Soups & Sauces

Vegetable Soup

Make Soup or Basic Stock ahead and freeze in one cup containers. Defrost rapidly by microwaving when ready to use. Any main dishes which call for water will taste richer if you substitute stock.

With automatic simmering you can microwave good, old-fashioned soups, mellowed sauces and the full-bodied broth essential to many Italian, French and Chinese recipes. Freeze poultry carcasses, or roast bones with some meat on them, until you have enough for stock. If you bone meat before cooking, save these scraps, too. When making stock for soup, add extra chicken backs or beef soup bones for flavor.

VEGETABLE BEEF SOUP

POWER LEVEL: Automatic Simmer
MICROWAVE TIME: Stock 4 to 6 hr. - Soup 3 to 4 hr.

For stock:
2 lb. soup bones or 1 lb. beef shortribs
1 teaspoon salt
1 teaspoon celery salt
1 small onion, chopped
1 cup diced carrots
½ cup diced celery
Water

In 4-qt. casserole place meaty bones, salt, celery salt, onion, carrots, celery and water to cover. Insert temperature probe so tip rests on bottom of dish, halfway between center and side. Cover tightly with plastic wrap, arranging loosely around probe to vent. Attach cable end at receptacle. **Microwave at Automatic Simmer 4 to 6 Hours.** Remove fat from surface. Remove meat from bones; chop and return to broth.

For soup:
2 cups diced, peeled potatoes
1 can (1-lb.) whole kernel corn, undrained
1 can (1-lb.) tomatoes, cut up
2 diced, peeled turnips
1 can (6-oz.) tomato paste
4 beef bouillon cubes
½ teaspoon marjoram
½ teaspoon salt
¼ teaspoon pepper

To stock, add potatoes, corn, tomatoes, turnips, tomato paste, bouillon, marjoram, salt and pepper. Stir. With back of spoon press meat and vegetable chunks to submerge under water. Insert temperature probe so tip rests in liquid on bottom of dish, halfway between center and side. Cover tightly with plastic wrap, arranging loosely around probe to vent. Attach cable end at receptacle. **Microwave at Automatic Simmer 3 to 4 Hours.**

Makes 8 to 10 servings

HOW TO MAKE BASIC STOCK

Save meat and bones until you have enough. (See Vegetable Beef Soup.) Add water, seasonings and carrots, onions and celery tops for flavor.

Strip meat from bones after microwaving and return it to stock when making soup. Or, strain stock and freeze for broth.

Skim fat if using immediately, or refrigerate stock until fat solidifies and can be lifted off.

MINESTRONE

The popular Italian vegetable soup.

POWER LEVEL: Automatic Simmer
MICROWAVE TIME: Stock 8 to 12 hr. - Soup 6 to 8 hr.

To Prepare Stock: In 4-qt. casserole place **2 to 3 lb. beef shank bone** and **1 to 2 lb. beef marrow bone.** Add water to cover. Insert temperature probe so tip rests in liquid on bottom of dish, halfway between center and side. Cover tightly with plastic wrap, arranging loosely around probe to vent. Attach cable end at receptacle. **Microwave at Automatic Simmer 8 to 12 Hours.** Cool. Remove meat and marrow from bones, return to stock.

For soup: **1 medium onion, chopped** **2 carrots, diced** **2 stalks celery with tops sliced** **1 cup diced leeks, optional** **1 can (1-lb.) tomatoes** **1 pkg. (10-oz.) frozen mixed vegetables** **½ cup uncooked vermicelli, broken into 2-in. pieces** **1 zucchini, sliced** **1 cup shredded cabbage** **1 tablespoon dried basil** **1 clove garlic, minced** **2 teaspoons salt** **1 teaspoon oregano** **1 can (6-oz.) tomato paste**	To stock, add onion, carrots, celery, leeks, tomatoes, mixed vegetables, vermicelli, zucchini, cabbage, basil, garlic, salt and oregano. Add tomato paste for heartier flavor. Submerge the chunks beneath broth surface. Insert temperature probe so tip rests on bottom of dish, halfway between center and side. Recover. Attach cable end at receptacle. **Microwave at Automatic Simmer 6 to 8 Hours.** To serve, ladle into bowls and sprinkle with Parmesan cheese. Serve with crusty bread.

Makes 8 to 10 servings

BEAN SOUP

POWER LEVEL: High and Automatic Simmer
MICROWAVE TIME: 13 to 15 hr.

1 lb. navy beans **Water**	Wash and sort beans. Place in 4-qt. casserole with water to cover and soak overnight. In the morning, drain beans and add 6 cups fresh water. **Microwave uncovered at High 60 Minutes.**
1 meaty ham bone or 2 cups diced cooked ham **1 cup celery, finely chopped** **1 onion, finely chopped** **2 tablespoons parsley, finely chopped** **1 teaspoon salt** **¼ teaspoon pepper** **1 bay leaf**	To beans, add ham, celery, onion, parsley, salt, pepper and bay leaf. Insert temperature probe so tip rests in liquid on bottom of dish, halfway between center and side. Cover tightly with plastic wrap, arranging loosely around probe to vent. Attach cable end at receptacle.

Microwave at Automatic Simmer 12 to 14 Hours, until beans are very tender. Remove ham bone and bay leaf. Cut meat off bone, return meat to bean soup. Add water to thin, if desired. Serve hot.

Makes 8 to 10 servings

CHICKEN NOODLE SOUP

A very nice chicken soup may be made by adding about 1-qt. chicken broth to Chicken 'N' Noodles, page 42.

Split Pea Soup

SPLIT PEA SOUP

For a creamy version of this chunky soup, puree in blender before adding ham.

POWER LEVEL: High and Automatic Simmer
MICROWAVE TIME: 13 to 15 hr.

1 lb. dried split peas.... In 4-qt. casserole place peas with water to cover. Soak overnight. Drain. Add 6 cups fresh water. **Microwave uncovered at High 60 minutes.**

1 can (1-lb.) tomatoes, cut up
1½ cups sliced carrots
1 cup chopped celery
¾ cup chopped onion
1 clove garlic, minced
1 teaspoon salt
1 meaty ham bone

Add tomatoes, carrots, celery, onion, garlic and salt. Stir well and add ham bone. Insert temperature probe so tip is in liquid touching bottom of dish. Cover tightly with plastic wrap, arranging loosely around probe to vent.

Attach cable end at receptacle. **Microwave at Automatic Simmer 12 to 14 Hours.** Cut meat off bone and return to soup. Thin with water, if desired.

Makes about 12 servings.

SPAGHETTI SAUCE

POWER LEVEL: Automatic Simmer
MICROWAVE TIME: 3 to 4 hr.

2 cans (1-lb. 14-oz.) tomatoes, cut up
2 cans (6-oz.) tomato paste
2 cups chopped onion
½ cup snipped parsley
2 tablespoons brown sugar
2 teaspoons salt
1 tablespoon dried oregano, crushed
½ teaspoon dried thyme, crushed
2 bay leaves

In stoneware accessory or 3-qt. casserole place tomatoes, tomato paste, onion, parsley, brown sugar, salt, oregano, thyme and bay leaf. Mix together well. Insert temperature probe so tip is in liquid on bottom of dish. Use accessory cover; or cover tightly with plastic wrap, arranging loosely around probe to vent. Attach cable end at receptacle. **Microwave at Automatic Simmer 3 to 4 Hours.**

Makes 2 to 3 quarts

TIP: Freeze in ice cube trays. When frozen hard, remove to plastic bags. Only amounts needed can be easily thawed and/or heated.

MARINARA SAUCE

This sauce starts with convenience ingredients and results 3 to 4 hours later, in a rich homemade taste. Serve over meatballs and spaghetti, if desired, or use as a sauce over other meats.

POWER LEVEL: Automatic Simmer
MICROWAVE TIME: 3 to 4 hr.

1 jar (2-lb.) spaghetti sauce
1 can (28-oz.) tomatoes, cut up
1 can (16-oz.) stewed tomatoes, cut up
1 can (10½-oz.) tomato puree
1 cup onion, chopped
½ cup red cooking wine
1 tablespoon sugar
2 teaspoons garlic powder
1 teaspoon thyme

In stoneware accessory or 4-qt. casserole mix together spaghetti sauce, tomatoes, stewed tomatoes, tomato puree, onion, wine, sugar, garlic powder and thyme. Insert temperature probe so tip rests on bottom of dish, halfway between center and side. Use accessory cover; or cover tightly with plastic wrap, arranging loosely around probe to vent. Attach cable end at receptacle. **Microwave at Automatic Simmer 3 to 4 Hours.**

Makes 2 to 3 quarts

Desserts & Beverages

Old-fashioned desserts and beverages can be started early in the day and simmered automatically without further attention. Slow cooking brings out their full flavor.

HOMEMADE APPLESAUCE

This recipe is tangy and very fresh tasting. The lemon helps keep the apples from turning brown, and imparts a good flavor, too.

POWER LEVEL: Automatic Simmer
MICROWAVE TIME: 5 to 7 hr.

10 medium large apples, peeled, quartered and cored
2 tablespoons lemon juice
½ cup sugar
1 teaspoon cinnamon

In stoneware accessory or 3-qt. casserole place apples. Sprinkle with lemon juice, sugar and cinnamon. Insert temperature probe so tip rests in juice in bottom of dish, halfway between center and side. Use accessory cover; or cover with plastic wrap, arranging loosely around probe to vent. Attach cable end at receptacle. **Microwave at Automatic Simmer 5 to 7 Hours.** When tender, break up applesauce with table fork, potato masher or electric mixer.

Makes 6 to 8 servings

RICE PUDDING

POWER LEVEL: Automatic Simmer
MICROWAVE TIME: ½ hr.

4 eggs
2 cans (13-oz. each) evaporated milk
⅔ cup water
1 cup raisins
1 cup sugar
1 teaspoon salt
2 teaspoons vanilla
3 cups cooked long grain rice

In stoneware accessory or 3-qt. casserole beat eggs. Stir in evaporated milk and water. Add raisins, sugar, salt, vanilla and rice. Stir well. Insert temperature probe so tip rests in liquid on bottom of casserole, halfway between center and sides. Use accessory cover; or cover tightly with plastic wrap, arranging loosely around probe to vent. Attach cable end at receptacle. **Microwave at Automatic Simmer ½ Hour.** Serve warm or cool.

Makes about 6 servings

Mulled Spicy Cider

MULLED SPICY CIDER

This punch has a piquant, spicy flavor. For more mellow flavor, substitute 2 cups orange juice for equal amount cider in recipe below.

POWER LEVEL: Automatic Simmer
MICROWAVE TIME: 4 to 6 hr.

½ cup brown sugar (packed)
1 teaspoon whole allspice
1 teaspoon whole cloves
¼ teaspoon salt
Dash nutmeg
1 stick cinnamon
2 qt. apple cider

In stoneware accessory or 3-qt. casserole place sugar, allspice, cloves, salt, nutmeg, cinnamon and cider. Insert temperature probe so tip rests on bottom of dish, halfway between center and side. Use accessory cover; or cover tightly with plastic wrap, arranging loosely around probe to vent. Attach cable end at receptacle. **Microwave at Automatic Simmer 4 to 6 Hours.** If desired, garnish each serving with orange or thin lemon wedge, stuck with few cloves, or cinnamon sticks.

Makes 8 servings

Appetizers & Hot Snacks

Microwaving makes exciting hot appetizers and snacks as easy to serve as the more ordinary cold ones. A minute or two after your guests arrive, you can offer them hot and tempting nibbles to stimulate appetites and conversation. Since all the preparation is done ahead, you can serve an unusual variety without last minute fuss.

1. Bacon Poles, page 55
2. Seaside Cheese Dip, page 53
3. Curried Pineapple and Piggies, page 57
4. Cheese Crock, page 54

MICROLESSON:

Appetizers and snacks are among the easiest foods to microwave. On these pages you'll find the basic principles of microwaving which assure success, some possibilities unique to microwave, and helpful ideas for using your microwave oven to make entertaining easier and more varied.

Arrange pieces, such as meatballs, mushrooms or canapes in a circle for even heating. To serve, place a bowl of sauce or another snack, such as pretzels, in center.

The Temperature Probe heats dips, such as Chili Con Queso, page 53, to correct serving temperature. Stir dip well before serving.

Dry Mixtures, such as Party Mix, page 53, must be stirred, as in conventional cooking, but they cook much faster.

Wooden or Plastic Picks, even those with frills, may be used in the microwave oven. Use bamboo skewers instead of metal, when making kabobs.

Cover foods according to the amount of moisture needed. Paper towels absorb it, waxed paper holds in a little, plastic wrap and lids seal it in.

Soften Cream Cheese for spreads or dips. Remove foil wrap and microwave at Medium 1 to 1½ Minutes.

Dry Croutons, page 53, for snacks, using leftover bread, herbs and butter. Also great for salads and soups.

Sloppy Joe Filling, canned or deli, spooned on buttered bun, makes an easy snack in ½ Minute at High.

Warm Cheese from refrigerator ½ to 1 Minute at Medium High to make it easy to slice.

Use Paper Plates for heating and serving. Let guests microwave their own hors d'oeuvres.

Shell Nuts easily. Microwave 2 cups pecan or Brazil nuts in 1 cup water 4 to 5 Minutes at High.

Soften Tortillas and crepes in the package or damp towel by microwaving at High ½ to 1 Minute.

Refresh Salty Snacks, by microwaving a few seconds at High. Let stand to crisp.

For Fast Canapes, spread ham salad or cheese spread on crackers. Microwave at High a few seconds.

SOUR CREAM DIPS WITH VARIATIONS

POWER LEVEL: Low TEMP:* 90°
APPROX. MICROWAVE TIME: 4 to 5 min.

1. Use **1 cup (8-oz.) dairy sour cream** as a basis for the following variations. In 1-qt. casserole or microwave ovenproof bowl, stir sour cream together with ingredients of one of the variations. Insert temperature probe so tip is in center of dip. Cover with plastic wrap, arranging loosely around probe to vent.
2. Attach cable end at receptacle. **Microwave at Low. Set Temp, Set 90°.** Stir before serving.

NOTE: Due to the delicate nature of sour cream, it is best microwaved at **Low.**

* On models not equipped with probe use minimum microwave time and check for doneness.

VARIATIONS:

ONION DIP

1 packet (½ of 2⅞-oz. box) onion soup mix
1 teaspoon lemon juice
1 tablespoon sherry wine (optional)

Makes about 1 cup

ZIPPY DIP

2 tablespoons chili sauce
1 tablespoon minced green pepper

Makes about 1 cup

DEVILED HAM DIP

1 can (4½-oz.) deviled ham
2 tablespoons chopped green olives
2 teaspoons instant minced onion
⅛ teaspoon pepper

Makes about 1½ cups

PUB DIP

POWER LEVEL: Medium TEMP:* 130°
APPROX. MICROWAVE TIME: 6 to 8 min.

2 jars (5-oz. each) sharp Old English cheese spread, softened
1 pkg. (8-oz.) cream cheese, softened
⅓ cup beer
1 teaspoon Worcestershire sauce
5 to 6 drops hot pepper sauce (optional)

In 1½-qt. casserole stir together cheeses, beer, Worcestershire sauce and pepper sauce. Insert temperature probe so tip is in center of dip. Attach cable end at receptacle. **Microwave at Medium. Set Temp, Set 130°.**

4 strips bacon, microwaved crisp and crumbled

When oven signals, stir in crumbled bacon. Serve with pretzels, crackers or other crisp dippers.

Makes about 1½ cups

* On models not equipped with probe use minimum microwave time and check for doneness.

CREAM CHEESE DIPS WITH VARIATIONS

POWER LEVEL: Medium TEMP:* 130°
APPROX. MICROWAVE TIME: 4 to 7 min.

1. Use **1 pkg. (8-oz.) cream cheese** as a basis for the following variations. In 1-qt. casserole place cream cheese. **Microwave at Medium 1 to 1½ Minutes,** to soften. Stir in ingredients of one of the variations. Insert temperature probe so tip is in center of dip. Cover with plastic wrap, arranging loosely around probe to vent.
2. Attach cable end at receptacle. **Microwave at Medium. Set Temp, Set 130°.** Stir before serving.

* On models not equipped with probe use minimum microwave time and check for doneness.

VARIATIONS:

SHRIMP DIP

1 can (7-oz.) broken shrimp, drained
2 teaspoons ketchup
1 teaspoon instant minced onion
1 teaspoon prepared mustard
1 teaspoon Worcestershire sauce
¼ teaspoon garlic salt

Makes about 2 cups

HOT CRAB DIP

1 can (6 - 8-oz.) crab meat, drained and flaked
2 tablespoons milk
1 tablespoon instant minced onion
1 tablespoon lemon juice
1 tablespoon sherry wine (optional)
1½ teaspoons grated lemon rind
1 teaspoon cream-style horseradish

Makes about 2 cups

APPETIZER CONVENIENCE FOODS

Many pastry-style frozen appetizers can be microwaved rapidly at High Power. However, pastry will not be as crisp as when baked conventionally for longer time.

Frozen Egg or Pizza Rolls: For 1-pkg. of 6 rolls (12-oz.) place on plate suitable for microwave oven. **Microwave at High 3 to 4 Minutes,** turning rolls over after 2 minutes. Let stand to crisp about 5 minutes before serving.

Frozen Prepared Sandwiches: Remove from foil package and wrap in paper towel. For each sandwich, **Microwave at High 1 to 1½ Minutes.** Let stand about 5 minutes to continue heating through.

Canned Sausages: (About 5-oz.) Drain and cut into pieces of desired size. Place on plate suitable for microwave oven. Add ½ cup chili sauce or cocktail sauce as desired. Cover with wax paper. **Microwave at High 1 to 1½ Minutes.**

CHILI CON QUESO DIP

Served fondue style, and accompanied by a salad, Chili Con Queso makes a nice informal luncheon. Dip is very thick and should be served with sturdy dippers such as large tortilla chips.

POWER LEVEL: Medium High TEMP:* 140°
APPROX. MICROWAVE TIME: 12 to 14 min.,

1 lb. block pasteurized processed cheese, diced in 1½-in. pieces
1 can (1-lb.) chili with beans
. . .In 1½-qt. casserole stir together diced cheese and chili.

Insert temperature probe so tip is in center of dip. Attach cable end at receptacle. **Microwave at Medium High. Set Temp, Set 140°.**

When oven signals, stir well. Let stand a few minutes before serving. Serve with tortilla chips.

Makes about 3 cups

VARIATION: A smaller amount can be made by using a 1-qt. casserole, an 8-oz. block of cheese and 1 can (7½-oz.) of chili with beans. Approximate microwave time is 5 to 7 minutes.

* On models not equipped with probe use minimum microwave time and check for doneness.

SEASIDE CHEESE DIP

POWER LEVEL: Medium TEMP:* 130°
APPROX. MICROWAVE TIME: 11 to 14 min.

1 can (6½-oz.) minced or chopped clams
2 jars (5-oz. each) sharp Old English cheese spread, softened
1 pkg. (8-oz.) cream cheese, softened
1 tablespoon Worcestershire sauce
½ medium green pepper, chopped (about ⅓ cup)
2 green onions, chopped (about 2 tablespoons)
. . .Drain clams, saving ¼ cup juice. In 1½-qt. casserole place drained clams, with reserved juice, along with sharp cheese spread, cream cheese, Worcestershire sauce, pepper and onion. Stir together well.

Attach cable end at receptacle. **Microwave at Medium. Set Temp, Set 130°.**

When oven signals, stir before serving. Excellent with fresh raw vegetables such as celery, cucumbers, radishes and cauliflowerets.

Makes about 2 cups

* On models not equipped with probe use minimum microwave time and check for doneness.

PARTY MIX

POWER LEVEL: High
MICROWAVE TIME: 6 to 7 min., total

6 tablespoons butter
4 teaspoons Worcestershire sauce
1 teaspoon seasoned salt
. . .In 13×9×2-in. dish place butter, Worcestershire sauce and salt. **Microwave at High 1 Minute,** or until butter is melted. Stir well.

2 cups corn chex
2 cups wheat chex
2 cups rice chex
2 cups thin stick pretzels
1½ cups (12-oz.) mixed nuts
. . . . . .Add cereals, pretzels and nuts, mixing thoroughly to coat. **Microwave at High 5 to 6 Minutes,** stirring after 3 minutes, until evenly toasted.

Makes about 2½ quarts

CROUTONS ITALIANO

This is a delicious snack food as well as a great way to use up dry bread. Croutons may also be used as soup accompaniment or topping for tossed salad.

POWER LEVEL: High
MICROWAVE TIME: 10 to 12 min., total

1½ qts. bread cubes (6 cups)
. . . . . .In 12×8×2-in. dish place cubes. **Microwave at High 6 Minutes,** stirring after 2 minutes, until cubes begin to dry.

2 tablespoons Italian herb seasoning
½ teaspoon garlic salt
½ cup (¼-lb.) melted butter
. . .Sprinkle herb seasoning and garlic salt evenly over bread cubes. Drizzle with butter, tossing to coat cubes.

Microwave at High 4 to 6 Minutes, stirring every minute, until crisp and dry.

Makes 1½quarts

SPREADS ON CRACKERS

POWER LEVEL: High
MICROWAVE TIME: ¼ to ½ min., per plate

12 crackers
¼ cup canned meat spread or deli filling
. . . . Spread about 1 teaspoon spread on each cracker. Arrange in circle on a paper plate. **Microwave at High ¼ to ½ Minute,** rotating dish ½ turn after ¼ minute, if necessary.

NOTE: If spread has a delicate mayonnaise base, Microwave at Low, increasing time by ¼ minute. Refrigerated spreads as well as larger amounts may take slightly longer to heat.

Soft Smokey Cheese Ball

MEXICAN CORN CHIP SNACKS

A version of the popular Nachos.

POWER LEVEL: High
MICROWAVE TIME: ¼ to ½ min., per plate

Large corn chips (plain or taco flavored)
Jalapeno bean dip or refried beans
Hot pepper cheese

Mound about 1 teaspoon bean dip or refried bean mixture on each tortilla corn chip. Top with ⅛-in. thick slice of cheese to cover bean dip. Place 8 to 12 pieces in circle on paper plate or small pottery plate. **Microwave at High ¼ to ½ Minute,** until cheese is melted.

CRAB-SWISS CRISPS

POWER LEVEL: High
MICROWAVE TIME: ¾ to 1 min., per plate

1 can (7½-oz.) crab, drained and flaked
1½ tablespoons sliced green onion
1¼ cup shredded Swiss cheese
½ cup mayonnaise
1 teaspoon lemon juice
¼ teaspoon curry powder
36 crisp round crackers

Combine crab, onion, cheese, mayonnaise, lemon juice and curry powder. Shortly before serving, place level teaspoonful on each cracker round. Place appetizers in circle on paper plates or other plates suitable for microwave oven. Cook about 12 at a time. **Microwave at High ¾ to 1 Minute,** rotating dish ¼ turn after ½ minute,

Makes 36 appetizers

SOFT SMOKEY CHEESE BALL

This cheese ball is soft and easily spreadable on crackers. For a more smokey flavor, add a few drops liquid smoke or smoke-flavored salt to taste.

POWER LEVEL: High
MICROWAVE TIME: 2 to 2¼ min., total

1 roll-shaped pkg. (6-oz.) smokey cheese spread
2 pkgs. (3-oz. each) cream cheese
1 teaspoon Worcestershire sauce
1 cup (4-oz.) shredded sharp cheddar cheese

Unwrap cheeses. In 1½-qt. casserole place smokey cheese. **Microwave at High 1 Minute.** Add cream cheese. **Microwave at High 1 to 1¼ Minutes** more, until cheeses can be mixed together. Add Worcestershire sauce and blend mixture well. Stir in shredded cheese. Mixture should remain gold-flecked.

½ cup chopped fresh parsley
½ cup chopped pecans

Chill cheese mixture about 15 to 30 minutes in freezer or about 1 hour in refrigerator, until it can be formed into a ball with the hands. Roll cheese ball in parsley, then pecans. Chill to set. Serve with crackers.

Makes 1 (14-oz.) cheese ball

CHEESE CROCK

Cheese Crock may be used immediately; however, aging truly improves the flavor. This makes an excellent gift.

POWER LEVEL: Medium
MICROWAVE TIME: 4 to 6 min., total

4 cups (1-lb.) shredded sharp cheddar cheese
1 pkg. (3-oz.) cream cheese
2 to 3 tablespoons brandy
1 to 2 tablespoons olive oil
1 teaspoon garlic salt
1 teaspoon dry mustard

In large glass mixing bowl place cheeses. **Microwave at Medium 4 to 6 Minutes,** until soft, stirring after 2 minutes. Stir in brandy, oil, salt and mustard. Beat well until thoroughly blended. Mixture will be soft and creamy. Pack into a container with a tight-fitting lid or cover well. Refrigerate 1 week to age before using. Spread on crackers or cocktail rye rounds.

Makes about 3 cups

BACON POLES

POWER LEVEL: High
MICROWAVE TIME: See Recipe

10 strips bacon . . . . With scissors, cut bacon strips in half lengthwise, making 2 long, thin strips from each slice. Wrap one strip in a spiral "barber pole fashion" around each bread stick.

20 long, thin garlic bread sticks or sesame bread sticks

TO MICROWAVE ENTIRE RECIPE: Place 2 paper towels in bottom of 13×9×2-in. dish. Distribute wrapped bread sticks so they don't touch each other. Cover with paper towel. **Microwave at High 10 to 13 Minutes,** rotating dish ½ turn after 5 minutes, until bacon is cooked.

TO MICROWAVE 7 ON A PAPER PLATE: Makes 3 plates. Place 2 paper towels on a paper plate. Arrange wrapped bread sticks on top. Cover with paper towel. **Microwave at High 2½ to 4 Minutes,** until bacon is cooked.

Total recipe makes 20

BACON-WRAPPED CHICKEN LIVERS

This is often known by its Polynesian name of Rumaki.

POWER LEVEL: High
MICROWAVE TIME: 6½ to 7½ min., per plate

1 lb. thinly sliced bacon . . **Microwave at High 1 Minute,** in the package, until slices easily separate. Divide bacon slices between 4 paper towel lined paper plates. Cover with paper towel. Microwave one plate at a time. **Microwave at High 2½ Minutes.** Cut each partially cooked slice in half.

1 can (8-oz.) water chestnuts . . . . Drain and cut each chestnut in half.

½ lb. chicken livers (about 20) . . . . . . Rinse and drain livers. Cut in half.

To assemble, sprinkle bacon strips lightly with ground cloves and brown sugar. Place one piece of chicken liver and one piece of water chestnut at the end of each bacon strip. Roll up, securing with a toothpick. Arrange 10 in a circle on each of 4 paper towel lined (1 sheet) paper plates. Cover with paper towel. Recipe may be refrigerated at this point if desired. Microwave one plate at a time. **Microwave at High 3 to 4 Minutes,** rotating dish ½ turn after 1½ minutes. When microwaving from refrigerator temperature, increase time for each plate ½ to 1 minute.

Makes 40 hors d'oeuvres

Tacos

TACOS

POWER LEVEL: High
MICROWAVE TIME: 11 to 13 min., total

1 lb. ground chuck beef
½ cup chopped onion
½ cup chopped green pepper
1 clove garlic, minced . . . . . . In 2-qt. casserole break up ground beef in very small chunks. Add onion, green pepper and garlic. Cover. **Microwave at High 6 to 7 Minutes,** stirring every 2 minutes. Drain well.

1 can (8-oz.) tomato sauce
1 teaspoon Worcestershire sauce
⅛ to ¼ teaspoon cayenne pepper
½ teaspoon chili powder
½ teaspoon salt . . . . . Add tomato sauce, Worcestershire sauce, pepper, chili powder and salt. Cover. **Microwave at High 5 to 6 Minutes,** stirring after 3 minutes.

Use meat to fill prebaked, packaged taco shells, filling about half full. Finish tacos by topping with 2 or more of the following: shredded lettuce, shredded cheese, chopped tomatoes and chopped onions. Add hot sauce if desired.

Makes 12 tacos

EASY TACOS

POWER LEVEL: High
MICROWAVE TIME: 9 to 11 min., total

1 lb. ground chuck beef
1 can (8-oz.) tomato sauce
1 pkg. (1⅛ - 1¼-oz.) taco seasoning mix . . . . In 2-qt. casserole crumble beef. **Microwave at High 6 Minutes,** stirring after 3 minutes. Drain well. Mix in tomato sauce and taco seasoning mix. **Microwave 3 to 5 Minutes.** Stir well and serve as above.

CURRIED BEEF BALLS

For convenience, make meatballs ahead of time and refrigerate on cooking dish or paper plate. Microwaving time may be slightly longer.

POWER LEVEL: High
MICROWAVE TIME: See Recipe

½ cup buttery flavored cracker crumbs or slightly crushed herb seasoned stuffing mix **⅓ cup evaporated milk** **¼ teaspoon salt** **1½ to 2 teaspoons curry powder** **1 lb. ground chuck beef**	In large mixing bowl thoroughly combine crumbs, milk, salt and curry powder. Add beef and blend well. Shape meat mixture into 48 (1-in.) balls.

TO MICROWAVE ENTIRE RECIPE: In 12×8×2-in. dish place about 24 balls. Cover with wax paper. **Microwave at High 4 to 5 Minutes,** rotating dish ½ turn after 2 minutes. Repeat with other half of beef balls.

TO MICROWAVE A DOZEN BEEF BALLS IN CIRCLE ON PAPER PLATE: Cover plate with wax paper. **Microwave at High 2 to 3 Minutes,** rotating dish ½ turn after 1 minute.

Makes 4 dozen hors d'oeuvres

EASY MEXICAN MEATBALLS

1 lb. ground chuck beef **1 egg** **½ pkg. (1⅛ - 1¼-oz., about 2 tablespoons) taco seasoning mix**	In large mixing bowl, thoroughly combine beef, egg and seasoning mix. Shape into 48 (1-in.) balls. Cook as directed above.

Makes 4 dozen hors d'oeuvres

APPETIZER FRANKS

If desired, 2 cans (4-oz. each) Vienna sausages, drained and halved, may be substituted for frankfurters.

POWER LEVEL: High
MICROWAVE TIME: 2 to 3 min., per plate

3 frankfurters **¼ cup apricot preserves or apple jelly** **1 tablespoon prepared mustard**	Cut frankfurters into eighths and arrange in circle on plastic coated paper plate. Mix together preserves and mustard. Spread over pieces. Stick each piece with wooden pick. **Microwave at High 2 to 3 Minutes,** until hot.

Chili Franks: Substitute chili sauce for preserves and mustard.

Makes 24 hors d'oeuvres

BEEF TERIYAKI BITES

POWER LEVEL: High
MICROWAVE TIME: 1½ to 2 min., each plate

1 lb. beef tenderloin or sirloin	Cut tenderloin into ¼-in. slices, then into 1-in. squares to make about 90 pieces.
¼ cup cocktail sherry **¼ cup honey** **¼ cup soy sauce** **30 thin bamboo skewers, 5-in. long**	In a deep bowl stir together sherry, honey and soy sauce. Add meat and stir to coat all pieces with teriyaki mixture. Cover with plastic wrap and marinate at least 1 hour or overnight, stirring once or twice so all meat is marinated.

On each skewer thread 3 pieces of meat, skewering each piece twice, in opposite corners, so it looks as though there are 3 diamond shapes on each skewer. Place 6 skewers on a plate suitable for microwave oven. **Microwave at High 1½ to 2 Minutes,** rotating dish ½ turn after ¾ minute until beef is just cooked. Repeat with rest of skewers.

Makes about 30 skewers

SWEET-TART FRANKS FOR A CROWD

POWER LEVEL: High
MICROWAVE TIME: 5 to 8 min., total

1 jar (10-oz.) currant jelly **1 jar (6-oz.) prepared mustard**	In 3-qt. casserole stir together jelly and mustard. **Microwave at High 1 to 2 Minutes** until mixture can be stirred smooth.
2 lbs. frankfurters cut into 1-in. pieces	Stir in franks stirring to coat each piece. Cover. **Microwave at High 4 to 6 Minutes,** stirring after 2 minutes, until franks are hot. Serve immediately, or transfer to chafing dish, if desired.

Makes about 80 hors d'oeuvres

TIP: Other recipes which make excellent appetizers are:

Meatballs Hawaiian, page 71
Swedish Meatballs, page 70
Tavern Franks (cut in 6ths or 8ths), page 113
Barbecued Franks (cut in 6ths or 8ths), page 113
Sweet-Sour Spareribs (cut into small riblets), page 98

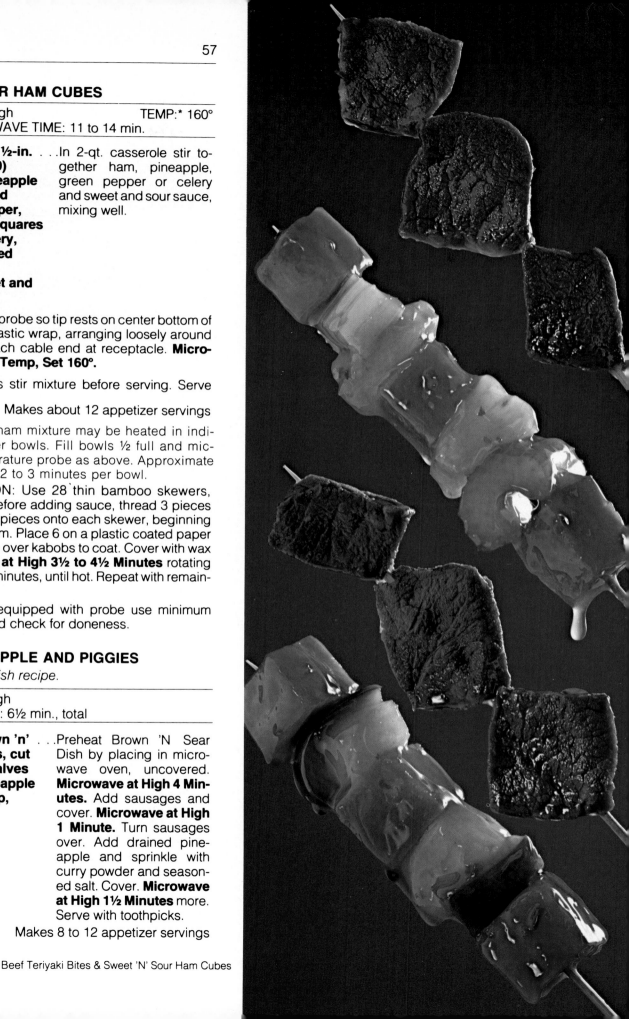

SWEET 'N' SOUR HAM CUBES

POWER LEVEL: High TEMP:* 160°
APPROX. MICROWAVE TIME: 11 to 14 min.

1 lb. ham cut into ½-in. cubes (60 to 70)
1 can (20-oz.) pineapple chunks, drained
1 large green pepper, cut into ½-in. squares or 2 stalks celery, diagonally sliced ½-in. thick
1 jar (10-oz.) sweet and sour sauce

. . . In 2-qt. casserole stir together ham, pineapple, green pepper or celery and sweet and sour sauce, mixing well.

Insert temperature probe so tip rests on center bottom of dish. Cover with plastic wrap, arranging loosely around probe to vent. Attach cable end at receptacle. **Microwave at High. Set Temp, Set 160°.**

When oven signals stir mixture before serving. Serve with cocktail picks.

Makes about 12 appetizer servings

NOTE: If desired, ham mixture may be heated in individual 10-oz. paper bowls. Fill bowls ½ full and microwave with temperature probe as above. Approximate microwave time is 2 to 3 minutes per bowl.

KABOB VARIATION: Use 28 thin bamboo skewers, about 5-in. long. Before adding sauce, thread 3 pieces of ham and 4 other pieces onto each skewer, beginning and ending with ham. Place 6 on a plastic coated paper plate. Spoon sauce over kabobs to coat. Cover with wax paper. **Microwave at High 3½ to 4½ Minutes** rotating dish ½ turn after 2 minutes, until hot. Repeat with remaining kabobs.

* On models not equipped with probe use minimum microwave time and check for doneness.

CURRIED PINEAPPLE AND PIGGIES

A Brown 'N Sear dish recipe.

POWER LEVEL: High
MICROWAVE TIME: 6½ min., total

1 pkg. (8-oz.) brown 'n' serve sausages, cut crosswise in halves
1 can (13-oz.) pineapple chunks in syrup, drained
Curry powder
Seasoned salt

. . . Preheat Brown 'N Sear Dish by placing in microwave oven, uncovered. **Microwave at High 4 Minutes.** Add sausages and cover. **Microwave at High 1 Minute.** Turn sausages over. Add drained pineapple and sprinkle with curry powder and seasoned salt. Cover. **Microwave at High 1½ Minutes** more. Serve with toothpicks.

Makes 8 to 12 appetizer servings

Beef Teriyaki Bites & Sweet 'N' Sour Ham Cubes

ESCARGOTS MICROWAVE

POWER LEVEL: High
MICROWAVE TIME: 2 to 2½ min., per plate

½ cup (¼-lb.) butter
1 teaspoon garlic powder
½ teaspoon minced parsley flakes

In 1-pt. glass measure, place butter, garlic and parsley. **Microwave at High 1 Minute,** or until melted. Stir well.

1 can (4-oz.) medium size escargot (about 24 snails) with shells

Drain and rinse snails. Pour small amount of butter sauce into each shell, add snail, then a little more sauce. Snail should be placed into shell loosely, not plugging hole, because steam will cause it to pop out in heating. Place 6 snails on each of 4 plates. Microwave one plate at a time. **Microwave at High 1 to 1½ Minutes.**

Makes about 24

NOTE: If snails come without shells place 6 snails each in 4 small sauce dishes with ¼ of sauce. Or, use the special glass or pottery snail dishes which have 6 small compartments. Half fill each compartment with sauce, then add snails.

SHRIMP IN SPECIAL GARLIC BUTTER

POWER LEVEL: High TEMP:* 180°
APPROX. MICROWAVE TIME: 5 to 7 min.

1 lb. raw, shelled, deveined shrimp

In 2-qt. casserole place shrimp.

½ cup (¼-lb.) butter
2 tablespoons sauterne wine
2 teaspoons freeze dried or frozen chives
⅛ teaspoon instant minced garlic or 1 clove fresh garlic, crushed
1 to 2 drops liquid pepper seasoning (tabasco)

Stir together butter, wine, chives, garlic and pepper seasoning. Pour over shrimp and stir to coat. (Butter mixture will solidify because of temperature of shrimp.) Insert temperature probe so tip rests on center bottom of dish. Cov- with plastic wrap, arranged loosely around probe. Attach cable end at receptacle **Microwave at High. Set Temp, Set 180°.**

When oven signals, stir shrimp before serving with cocktail picks.

Makes about 1 pound

NOTE: If desired, shrimp can be cooked in individual 10-oz. paper bowls. Fill bowls ½ full and microwave with probe. Approximate time is 1 to 2 minutes per bowl.

* On models not equipped with probe use minimum microwave time and check for doneness.

STUFFED MUSHROOMS

Choose large or medium-sized firm, fresh mushrooms. When fresh, mushrooms are pale grey or white and the gills (the accordian-like vents on the underside of the cap) should be tightly closed and firmly attached.

POWER LEVEL: See Recipe
MICROWAVE TIME: 3 to 4 min., per plate

1. For each of the following stuffings, use **12 large, fresh mushrooms,** 2-in. in diameter.
2. Wash mushrooms well, removing stems. Dry.
3. Prepare one of the following stuffing recipes. Divide evenly among caps and mound slightly. Arrange caps in a circle on plate suitable for microwave oven.
4. **Microwave at High 3 to 4 Minutes,** rotating plate ½ turn after 2 minutes. If mushroom size is not uniform, smaller caps may cook in a shorter time.

NOTE: Mushroom stems may be finely chopped (about ⅔ cup) and added to stuffing, except Spinach Stuffing, if desired.

MUSHROOM STUFFINGS:
HAM OR BACON-ONION STUFFING

Stems from mushrooms, finely chopped
½ cup finely chopped onion

In 1½-qt. casserole place chopped stems and onion. Cover. **Microwave at High 4 Minutes,** stirring after 2 minutes.

1 pkg. (3-oz.) cream cheese
¼ cup fine dry bread crumbs
½ cup chopped, cooked ham or bacon (8 slices)

To hot mixture above, add cream cheese, mashing and mixing well. Stir in crumbs and ham or bacon.

Stuffs 12 large mushrooms

Stuffed Mushrooms

CLAM STUFFING

1 pkg. (3-oz.) creamed cheese, softened
1 can (7-oz.) minced clams, drained
1 tablespoon minced parsley
½ teaspoon garlic powder

. . .In small bowl mix together cream cheese, clams, parsley and garlic powder.

¼ cup crushed French fried onions

. . .Sprinkle onion pieces over top.

NOTE: If mushroom stems are used, in 1-qt. casserole place chopped stems, ⅓ cup finely chopped onion and 2 tablespoons butter. **Microwave at High 2 Minutes,** stirring after 1 minute. Add remaining ingredients.

Stuffs 12 large mushrooms

CRUNCHY STUFFING

2 tablespoons butter
⅓ cup finely chopped or grated onion
½ cup finely chopped walnuts
1 tablespoon chili sauce
1 teaspoon lemon juice
⅛ teaspoon salt

. . . .In 1-qt. casserole place butter and onions. **Microwave at High 3 Minutes,** until onion is limp. Add walnuts, chili sauce, lemon juice and salt.

NOTE: If mushroom stems are used, add chopped stems to butter and onions. Microwave following recipe directions.

Stuffs 12 large mushrooms

SAVORY BREAD CRUMB STUFFING

¼ cup finely chopped onion
¼ cup finely chopped green pepper
¼ cup finely chopped celery
3 tablespoons butter

. . . .In 1-qt. casserole place onions, green pepper, celery and butter. **Microwave at High 3 Minutes,** until slightly cooked.

1 pkg. (3-oz.) cream cheese, softened
1 cup fine, soft bread crumbs (3 slices)
1 teaspoon lemon juice
½ teaspoon salt
⅛ teaspoon pepper

. . . . . .Add cream cheese, crumbs, lemon juice, salt and pepper. Mix together well.

NOTE: If mushroom stems are used, add chopped stems to butter and onions. Microwave following recipe directions.

Stuffs 12 large mushrooms

SPINACH STUFFING

1 pkg. (12-oz.) frozen spinach souffle

. . . .Remove from foil container. With sharp knife cut in half. Return half to freezer, place other half in 1-qt. casserole. **Microwave at Medium 1 to 1½ Minutes,** until partially defrosted. Mash with fork.

½ cup softened bread crumbs (about 1 slice)
1 teaspoon lemon juice
½ teaspoon instant minced onions
¼ teaspoon salt

. . . .Mix in crumbs, lemon juice, onion and salt.

Stuffs 12 large mushrooms

Since it starts with triangles of dough, Pizza-On-A-Plate may be slightly irregular, but quick and good.

PIZZA-ON-A-PLATE

POWER LEVEL: Medium High
MICROWAVE TIME: 11 to 15 min., per plate

1 can (8-oz.) refrigerated crescent roll dough
2 teaspoons cooking oil

On each of two 12-in. pieces of wax paper, press ½ of dough to form a 9-in. circle. Press perforations together to seal. Brush each lightly with cooking oil. Place wax paper on microwave ovenproof plates. Microwave one pizza at a time. **Microwave at Medium High 4 Minutes.** Holding wax paper. Flip dough over onto plate and carefully peel off wax paper. **Microwave at Medium High 3 to 4 Minutes** more, until set and crisp. There will be some brown spots.

1 can (8-oz.) tomato sauce
1 pkg. (4-oz.) pepperoni
1 cup (4-oz.) shredded mozzarella cheese

Divide tomato sauce evenly between crusts, spreading to edges. Top each with half of pepperoni and sprinkle with half of cheese. **Microwave at Medium High 4 to 6 Minutes,** rotating plate ½ turn after 2 minutes. Remove immediately to cooling rack for crisper crust.

Makes 2 (9-in.) pizzas

REHEATING PIZZA

POWER LEVEL: High
MICROWAVE TIME: See Recipe

Pizza, with the exception of Pizza-On-A-Plate, is best *reheated,* in the microwave oven *after* it has been cooked conventionally. A frozen, uncooked pizza, if microwaved, will not have a crisp crust and the center tends to be soggy as there is no hot air to dry out the crust or topping.

1. To reheat a 10" pizza, cut into 8 wedges. Place each wedge on a paper towel or paper plate. Microwave one wedge at a time. **Microwave at High** according to chart below.

	MINUTES PER WEDGE
Room Temperature	¼ to ½
Refrigerated	½ to ¾
Frozen	¾ to 1

2. Time may vary due to the size of pizza and amount of topping. Pizza topped with pepperoni and cheese was used to determine times above.

TIPS: If more than 1 pizza wedge is heated at one time, use amount of time given for *each* wedge, rotating dish ½ turn after half of total time. Place points to center of plate, as they are usually the first to melt.

For more even heating, use a lower power and increase time slightly.

For crisper bottom crust, place on cooling rack immediately after heating so crust can dry out.

CHEESE PASTRY SNACKS

POWER LEVEL: High
MICROWAVE TIME: 2¾ to 3¼ min., per plate

1 cup shredded cheddar cheese **¾ cup unsifted all-purpose flour** **¾ cup coarsely crushed crisp rice cereal** **½ cup chopped walnuts** **½ teaspoon garlic salt** **⅓ cup butter, softened** **6 strips crisp cooked bacon, crumbled** **2 tablespoons cold water**	In large mixing bowl mix together cheese, flour, cereal, walnuts, garlic salt, butter, bacon and water with a fork until a dough forms. Drop 7 level tablespoonfuls in a circle onto each of 3 lightly buttered plates suitable for microwave. (Butter plates only around edges, where dough will be placed.)
Paprika	Sprinkle with paprika. Microwave one plate at a time. **Microwave at High 2¾ to 3¼ Minutes.** Dough will be slightly puffed when done and will crisp on drying. Remove immediately from plate. Serve hot or cold. Repeat with remaining mixture.

Makes 21 Snacks

TIP: Another pastry appetizer is Quiche. See page 164 for several variations.

ALMOND FILLED CHEESE BALLS

POWER LEVEL: High
MICROWAVE TIME: 1¾ to 2¼ min., per plate

2 tablespoons soft butter **1 cup (4-oz.) shredded sharp cheese** **½ cup unsifted all-purpose flour** **Dash cayenne pepper** **½ teaspoon celery seed**	In small mixing bowl, mix together butter and cheese until smooth. Add flour, pepper and celery seed, blending well, kneading dough with hands if necessary to form a ball.
1 pkg. (3-oz.) hickory smoked, barbecue or cheese flavored almonds	Measure dough by level teaspoonfuls and shape smoothly around each almond to form a ball.

Place 9 balls in a circle on each of 4 paper plates. **Microwave at High 1¾ to 2¼ Minutes,** rotating dish ¼ turn after 1 minute. Dough will be slightly puffy and dry when cooked. Remove from dish and cool a few minutes before serving. Repeat, cooking all cheese balls.

Makes about 3 dozen cheese balls

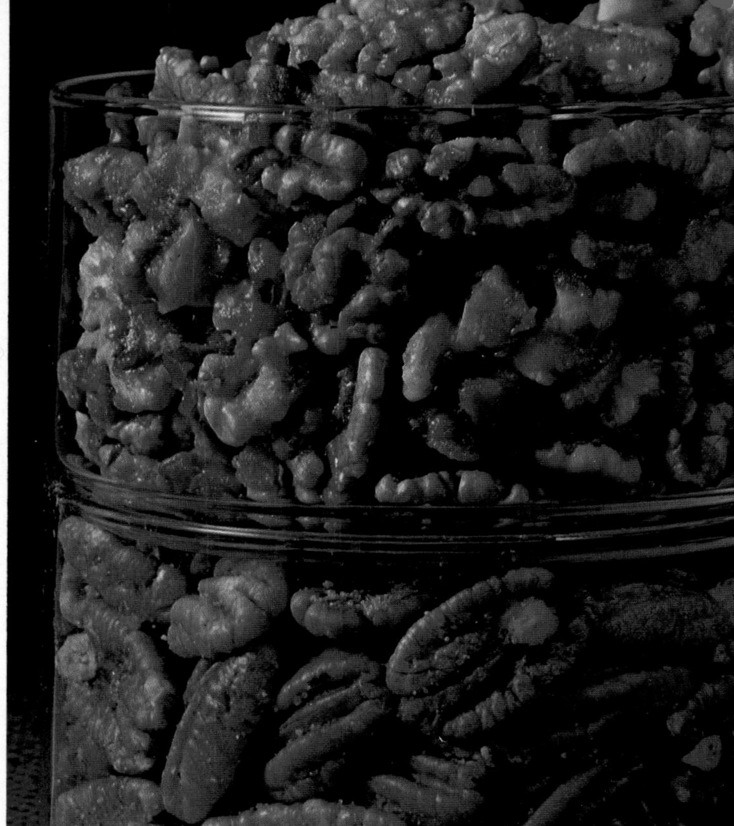

Sugar Glazed Walnuts & Toasted Butter Pecans

SUGAR GLAZED WALNUTS

POWER LEVEL: High
MICROWAVE TIME: 6 to 8 min., total

½ cup (¼-lb.) butter	In 1½-qt. casserole place butter. **Microwave at High 1 Minute,** or until melted.
1 cup brown sugar (packed) **1 teaspoon cinnamon**	Stir in brown sugar and cinnamon. **Microwave at High 2 Minutes.** Mix well to combine butter and sugar.
1 lb. walnut halves or large pieces (about 4 cups)	Add nuts and mix to coat. **Microwave at High 3 to 5 Minutes.** Spread out onto wax paper and cool slightly. Serve warm or cold.

Makes 1 pound

TOASTED BUTTER PECANS

POWER LEVEL: High
MICROWAVE TIME: 5 to 6 min., total

1 lb. pecan halves (about 4 cups) **1 tablespoon seasoned salt** **¼ cup butter**	In 1½-qt. casserole place pecan halves. Sprinkle with seasoned salt. Cut butter into 4 pieces and arrange evenly over top

Microwave at High 5 to 6 Minutes. Mix to evenly distribute butter. Serve warm or cold.

Makes 1 pound

Soup & Sandwiches

Hot soups or sandwiches are popular choices for a between meal break, lunch, or, together, as a hearty supper. Microwaving makes both fast and easy-to-clean-up. Soups can be heated right in the serving dish or cup. Most sandwiches are heated in a paper napkin or towel, so if you serve them casually, there's no clean up at all!

Some sandwiches are such meal-time staples that we have featured them in other sections. See:

Frankfurters, page 112; Melted Cheese, page 178; Hamburgers, page 72; Sloppy Joes, page 51 and 67; Bacon-Lettuce-Tomato, using your microwave oven to cook the bacon, page 109.

TIPS FOR HEATING SOUPS BY MICROWAVE

When you're serving soup and sandwich together, don't heat them together. Do the soup first; it will stay hot during the short time it takes to warm the sandwich.

Water-Based Soups can be heated at High. A can of condensed soup, diluted with water in a 1½-qt. casserole takes 5 to 7 minutes. One cup (⅔ to ¾ full) takes 2½ to 3½ minutes; or use temperature probe. **Set Temp, Set 150° to 170°.**

Cream Soups should be heated at Medium because milk boils over rapidly so times will be slightly longer. For care-free heating, use the temperature probe. **Set Temp, Set 140°.**

CORN CHOWDER SOUP

POWER LEVEL: High
MICROWAVE TIME: 17 to 19 min., total

1 can (10¾-oz.) cream of potato soup
2 cans (1-lb. 1-oz. each) cream-style corn
1 can (13-oz.) evaporated milk
1½ cups milk
¼ cup finely chopped green pepper (optional)
1 tablespoon instant minced onion
1 teaspoon salt
¼ teaspoon pepper

In 3-qt. casserole combine soup, corn, milks, green pepper, onion, salt and pepper. Cover. **Microwave at High 17 to 19 Minutes,** stirring after 10 minutes, until hot.

Fresh frozen or freeze dried chives . . . Add chives and serve.

Makes 8 one-cup servings

INTERNATIONAL SANDWICH

POWER LEVEL: High
MICROWAVE TIME: 2 to 3 min., total

1 thick (1-in.) slice French bread
Butter
1 slice bologna
1 slice salami
½ cup sauerkraut*
½ cup grated mozzarella cheese

Spread the bread with butter. Cut bologna and salami in halves. Alternate the half-slices over bread, then top with sauerkraut. Sprinkle cheese over top.

Place sandwich on paper or china plate. **Microwave at High 2 to 3 Minutes,** giving sandwich ½ turn after 1 minute.

Makes 1 sandwich

*8-oz. can sauerkraut, drained, makes 2 sandwiches, 1-lb. to 1-lb. 4-oz. can makes 5 to 6 sandwiches.

NOTE: To heat 4 sandwiches, place on plate or platter and heat 6 to 7 minutes, giving plate ½ turn after 3 minutes.

HOT HOAGIE SANDWICH

POWER LEVEL: Medium High — TEMP:* 110°
APPROX. MICROWAVE TIME: 5 to 7 min.

½ loaf unsliced Italian or French bread (10 to 12-in. in length)
Mayonnaise
Mustard
½ lb. meat**
3 to 4 oz. cheese**

Cut bread lengthwise to make two long, thin layers. Spread both cut sides evenly with mayonnaise and mustard, spreading completely to edges. Cover both sides with meat slices, then cover bottom of loaf with cheese.

Place meat covered top half of bread over bottom half. This arrangement results in cheese in center of sandwich with meat on either side. Place on board or platter with piece of paper towel over sandwich and tucked under edges. Insert temperature probe about ⅓ the length of bread loaf so tip is "sandwiched" into center of filling. Attach cable end at receptacle. **Microwave at Medium. Set Temp, Set 110 °.** Let stand a few minutes before slicing.

Makes 3 to 4 servings

* On models not equipped with probe use minimum microwave time and check for doneness.

****Meat Fillings:** Choose thin sliced hard salami, pastrami, pepperoni, corned beef, boiled ham, or a combination of these.

****Cheese Fillings:** Choose sharp or mild cheddar, brick, Monterey Jack, Swiss, or a combination of these.

Hot Hoagie Sandwich

TIPS FOR MICROWAVING HOT SANDWICHES

Layer filling with cheese in the center. Cheese attracts microwaves and by hiding it in the middle of the sandwich you promote rapid heating and avoid overcooking the cheese.

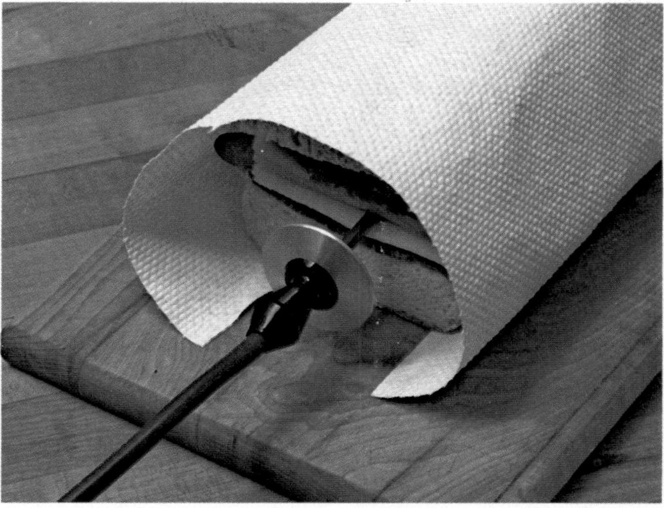

Wrap the sandwich in a paper towel or napkin, to absorb moisture from the bread. For an attractive presentation, microwave the sandwich on a wooden board. (Wood is not affected by short heating times.)

Meats

Microwaved meats cook tender and juicy in ⅓ to ½ the time it takes to cook them conventionally. Some meats are microwaved at High Power, but for most meats, the lower power settings allow you to cook with less care and attention. The automatic temperature probe gives you truly carefree microwaving. You simply set the dial for the finished temperature, and the oven signals you when the meat is ready.

Since meat continues to cook on standing, we recommend that you carve rare meats immediately. For well done meats, especially poultry, roast pork and meatloaf, the standing time is especially important, since it is actually part of the cooking process. The meat finishes cooking while it stands.

In this chapter, we've included all your favorite types and cuts of meat, beginning with beef. Each section starts with small pieces and progresses to large, from simple recipes to the more complex, from hearty everyday food to party fare.

Each cut of meat has its own instructions for defrosting and microwaving, located where they will be most available and useful to you while cooking, plus special tips which will help you microwave all of them.

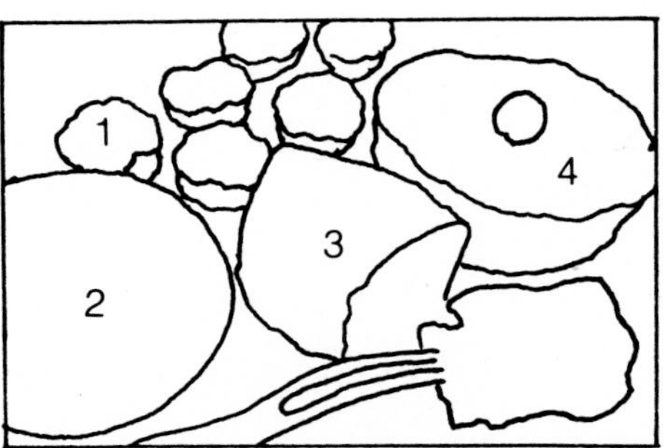

1. Favorite Stuffed Peppers, page 69
2. Barbecued Franks, page 113
3. Sirloin Tip, page 88
4. Ham Slice, page 103

GROUND BEEF DEFROSTING CHART

POWER LEVEL: **Defrost**

AMOUNT	FIRST SIDE	SECOND SIDE	SCRAPE OFF BREAK UP AND FINISH
1 pound	3 minutes	3 minutes	2 to 3 minutes
2 pounds	6 minutes	6 minutes	5 to 6 minutes
5 pounds	12 minutes	12 minutes	11 to 12 minutes*

*Second scraping may be needed after minimum time.

HOW TO DEFROST GROUND BEEF

Ground Beef is packaged in a variety of shapes. Defrosting procedure is the same, but some shapes take more time and attention. Flat, circular packages, 1 to 1½-inches thick, are easiest to defrost. Tubes should be rotated frequently and broken up as soon as possible. The ends defrost rapidly and may cook before center is defrosted.

Place Package wrapped in plastic or paper in oven set at **Defrost.** Microwave first side. Turn package over. Microwave second side. With a fork, scrape softened meat onto wax paper and set aside. Scraping off defrosted meat is a very important step. Break remaining block into small pieces and return to oven. Continue defrosting, turning pieces over often.

When Properly Defrosted, crumbled beef should be cool, soft and glossy. Meat is red and fat still white. (Fat which turns transparent is beginning to cook.) It looks much like fresh ground beef, but feels colder. Some moisture may be apparent. It will make patties that hold together during cooking.

Ground Beef Crumbled

Crumbled ground beef is the basic ingredient for a variety of popular main dishes, which take a minimum of time and attention when microwaved. Many can be mixed, cooked and served in the same casserole.

Our recipes were written for 1-step ease, but if you wish to lower calories, you may cook ground beef until it loses its pink color, then drain off fat. Add a little more water to the recipe if it seems dry.

To cook and drain fat from ground beef in one easy step, try our simple colander method. (Plastic colanders are widely available in the housewares section of department or hardware stores and supermarkets.)

Place crumbled ground beef in plastic colander, set over a casserole or bowl. For one pound of meat **Microwave at High 5 to 6 Minutes,** until meat loses its pink color, stirring after ½ the time. Discard fat and place meat in cooking dish.

HOW TO DEFROST & COOK FROZEN GROUND BEEF IN 1-STEP

Unwrap 1 pound of frozen ground beef and place it in the same cooking utensil called for in the recipe you plan to follow. **Microwave at High 10 to 12 Minutes,** breaking up and stirring meat with a fork every 5 minutes. Some areas will still be pink. Let meat stand 1 to 2 minutes until the pink color disappears.

Sloppy Joes

SLOPPY JOES

POWER LEVEL: High
MICROWAVE TIME: 11 to 12 min., total

1½ lb. ground beef **⅔ cup finely chopped onion** **½ cup diced celery** **¼ cup diced green pepper**	In 1½-qt. casserole crumble beef. Add onion, celery and green pepper. Cover. **Microwave at High 6 Minutes,** stirring after 3 minutes. Drain meat well.
½ cup ketchup **1 tablespoon Worcestershire sauce** **½ teaspoon salt** **⅛ teaspoon pepper**	To cooked meat mixture, add ketchup, Worcestershire sauce, salt and pepper. Cover. **Microwave at High 5 to 6 Minutes,** stirring after 3 minutes, until hot. To serve, spoon onto buns or crusty French rolls.

Makes 6 to 8 sandwiches

Sloppy Joes With Cheese: Add 1 cup (4-oz.) shredded cheddar cheese to meat mixture along with ketchup.

Sloppy Joes With Beans: Add 1 can (16-oz.) pork and beans to meat mixture along with ketchup.

BEEF AND CORN CASSEROLE

POWER LEVEL: High
MICROWAVE TIME: 14 to 16 min., total

1 lb. ground chuck beef
¼ cup chopped onion
¼ cup chopped green pepper

Into 2-qt. casserole crumble beef. Add onion and green pepper. **Microwave at High 6 Minutes,** stirring after 3 minutes.

1 can (16-oz.) tomatoes
1 can (12-oz.) whole kernel corn, drained
1 can (8-oz.) tomato sauce
½ cup sliced stuffed olives
1 to 2 teaspoons chili powder

Drain tomatoes, reserving ¼ cup juice. Dice tomatoes and add to meat mixture with reserved tomato juice, corn, tomato sauce, olives and chili powder. Cover. **Microwave at High 6 to 8 Minutes,** until hot.

1 cup coarsely crushed corn chips
½ cup shredded cheddar cheese

Remove cover, sprinkle corn chips and cheese over top. **Microwave at High 2 Minutes,** uncovered, until cheese melts.

Makes 4 to 6 servings

CHILI

Microwaved with the temperature probe, this chili requires no stirring during cooking. Ground beef is softer with this 1-step method. For more texture, precook ground beef before combining with other ingredients.

POWER LEVEL: High TEMP:* 190°
APPROX. MICROWAVE TIME: 40 to 45 min.,

1½ lb. ground chuck beef

Into 2½ to 3-qt. casserole crumble beef.

1 can (28-oz.) tomatoes, undrained
1 can (6-oz.) tomato paste
2 cans (1-lb.) kidney beans, undrained
1 medium green pepper, finely chopped
3 teaspoons instant minced onion
1 to 2 tablespoons chili powder
2 teaspoons salt

Mix in tomatoes, tomato paste, beans, green pepper, onion, chili powder and salt. Insert temperature probe so tip rests on center bottom of dish. Cover tightly with plastic wrap, arranging loosely around probe to vent. Attach cable end at receptacle. **Microwave at High. Set Temp, Set 190°.** When oven signals, stir and let chili stand about 10 minutes to blend flavors before serving.

Makes 6 to 8 servings

* On models not equipped with probe use minimum microwave time and check for doneness.

BEEFBURGER STROGANOFF

POWER LEVEL: High
MICROWAVE TIME: 15 to 18 min., total

1 lb. ground chuck beef
½ cup finely chopped onion
1 garlic clove, minced
1 can (8-oz.) mushrooms, undrained
1 can (10½-oz.) condensed cream of mushroom soup
3 tablespoons all-purpose flour
1 teaspoon salt
¼ teaspoon pepper

Into 2-qt. casserole crumble beef. Add onion, garlic, mushrooms, soup, flour, salt and pepper. Mix thoroughly. Cover. **Microwave at High 15 to 18 Minutes,** stirring after 8 minutes.

1 cup (8-oz.) dairy sour cream
½ teaspoon bottled brown bouquet sauce

Stir casserole thoroughly, then stir in sour cream and bouquet sauce. Serve over cooked rice or chow mein noodles.

Makes 6 servings

CABBAGE ROLLS ITALIAN STYLE

POWER LEVEL: High
MICROWAVE TIME: 22 to 26 min., total

8 large cabbage leaves (from outer layers of cabbage)
½ cup water

In 3-qt. casserole place cabbage and water. Cover. **Microwave at High 7 to 9 Minutes,** until leaves are pliable.

1 lb. ground chuck beef
1 egg
1 cup packaged precooked (minute) rice
3 tablespoons chopped onion
1 teaspoon salt

While cabbage is cooking, mix together ground beef, egg, rice, onion and salt. Divide meat mixture into 8 equal portions. Place one portion on each partially-cooked cabbage leaf and roll meat into leaf, securing with toothpick if necessary. Return to 3-qt. casserole, placing rolls seam-side-down.

2 cans (8-oz. each) tomato sauce
1 tablespoon sugar
1 teaspoon oregano

Blend tomato sauce, sugar and oregano. Pour over cabbage rolls. Cover casserole.

Microwave at High 15 to 17 Minutes, rotating dish ½ turn and basting with sauce after 9 minutes.

Makes 8 cabbage rolls

FAVORITE STUFFED PEPPERS

For crisper pepper and brighter color, remove cooked peppers from dish immediately. Separate them and let stand uncovered. Sprinkle top with grated, rather than sliced, cheese to assure melting.

POWER LEVEL: High TEMP:* 175°
APPROX. MICROWAVE TIME: 28 to 32 min.

6 medium green peppers .... Cut off tops of green peppers; remove seeds and membrane.

1½ lb. ground chuck beef
1 cup cooked long grain rice
1 small onion, chopped (about ½ cup)
1½ teaspoons salt
¼ teaspoon pepper
1 clove garlic, minced ..... Mix beef with rice, onion, salt, pepper and garlic. Fill peppers with meat mixture. Arrange snugly in 3-qt. casserole so one pepper is in center of dish.

1 can (10¾-oz.) condensed tomato soup
½ cup water .... Mix together soup and water; pour over and around peppers. Insert temperature probe so tip is in middle of center pepper. Cover tightly with plastic wrap, arranging loosely around probe to vent. Attach cable end at receptacle. **Microwave at High. Set Temp, Set 175°.**

6 slices (1-oz. each) sharp cheese (optional) .... When oven signals, remove peppers and let stand, covered, 5 to 10 minutes before serving. If desired, cheese slices may be placed over tops of peppers to melt before casserole stands. Recover loosely with plastic wrap.

Makes 6 servings

NOTE: Peppers should fit snugly in dish so steam and heat conduction help cook them evenly.

* On models not equipped with probe use minimum microwave time and check for doneness.

HOW TO FORM CABBAGE ROLLS

Shape meat mixture into 8 rolls, each about 3-inches long. Place meat roll on the base of the cabbage leaf over heavy vein. Fold sides of leaf over meat and roll up. Secure roll with wooden pick if necessary and place in the casserole, seam side down.

LAYERED TACO CASSEROLE

With the exception of lettuce, this casserole has the texture and flavor of Mexican tacos.

POWER LEVEL: High
MICROWAVE TIME: 25½ to 29½ min., total

1 lb. ground chuck beef .. In 2-qt. casserole place beef. **Microwave at High 5 to 6 Minutes,** stirring after 3 minutes. Drain beef and remove from casserole.

2 tablespoons butter
1 medium onion, chopped (about ½ cup)
2 tablespoons diced green chilies
1 can (8-oz.) tomato sauce
1 pkg. (1¼-oz.) taco seasoning mix
½ cup water ..... In 1-qt. glass measure place butter, onions and chilies. **Microwave at High 2 to 2½ Minutes,** stirring after 1 minute. Add tomato sauce, taco seasoning mix and water. **Microwave at High 1½ to 2 Minutes** more.

2 eggs
1 cup dairy half & half .... Beat eggs; blend in half & half. Add this mixture slowly to tomato sauce, stirring constantly.

1 pkg. (6-oz.) corn chips
8 oz. Monterey Jack cheese, shredded or sliced .... Place half of corn chips in same 2-qt. casserole. Top with half of ground beef, half of cheese and half of sauce. Repeat layers. **Microwave at High 15 Minutes,** rotating dish ½ turn after 8 minutes.

1 cup (8-oz.) dairy sour cream
½ cup grated cheddar cheese .. Top with sour cream and grated cheese. **Microwave at High 2 to 4 Minutes,** until cheese is melted.

Makes about 6 servings

Basic Meatballs

Ground Beef Meatballs

Meatballs microwave exceptionally well, and turn brown after a short standing time, so they need no special browning.

For loose meatballs, place about ¾" apart in dish. Rearrange them after half the cooking time. To cook meatballs with a minimum of attention, arrange them in a ring around the edge of a 9 or 10-in. pie plate, depending on size. After half the cooking time, rotate the dish ½ turn. These recipes are all well-tested favorites. Using them as models, you'll find it easy to adapt your own special recipes for microwaving.

BASIC MEATBALLS

POWER LEVEL: High
MICROWAVE TIME: 9 to 12 min., total

1 lb. ground chuck beef
1 egg
½ cup fine bread crumbs
1 teaspoon salt
¼ teaspoon paprika
⅛ teaspoon pepper

Mix together beef, egg, crumbs, salt, paprika and pepper. Shape into 12 balls and arrange in a circle in 9 or 10-in. pie plate. Cover with wax paper. **Microwave at High 9 to 12 Minutes,** rotating dish ½ turn after 5 minutes, until done. If desired, serve with Italian Sauce, page 176.

Makes 12 meatballs

VARIATIONS:
Add one of the following flavor combinations:

1 tablespoon Worcestershire sauce and ¼ cup chopped onion
1 tablespoon steak sauce and 1 clove crushed garlic (or ½ teaspoon garlic powder)
1 tablespoon chili sauce and ¼ cup finely chopped green pepper
1 tablespoon ketchup and 1 teaspoon prepared mustard
2 tablespoons red wine and 1 teaspoon oregano

SWEDISH MEATBALLS

POWER LEVEL: High
MICROWAVE TIME: 16 to 22 min., total

2 lbs. ground chuck beef
2 cups soft bread crumbs
½ cup milk
1 egg
1 pkg. (½ of 2¾-oz. box) onion soup mix
½ teaspoon salt
½ teaspoon nutmeg

Mix together beef, crumbs, milk, egg, soup mix, salt and nutmeg. Shape meat mixture into 40 balls. Cook 20 at a time in 13×9×2-in. dish. Cover with wax paper. **Microwave at High 6 to 8 Minutes,** rearranging meatballs after 3 minutes. Remove meatballs from dish and keep warm, reserving meat drippings. Repeat.

2 tablespoons unsifted all-purpose flour
1 cup milk
2 tablespoons brown bouquet sauce
1 cup dairy sour cream (8-oz.)

To ¼ cup drippings in dish, add flour, stirring until smooth. Gradually stir in milk and brown bouquet sauce. **Microwave at High 3 to 4 Minutes,** stirring every minute, until thickened. Add sour cream. Stir well. Return meatballs to dish, mixing to coat evenly. **Microwave at High 1 to 2 Minutes,** until hot. Serve over noodles or rice.

Makes 40 meatballs (1-in.)

PORCUPINE MEATBALLS

Fast cooking rice is used in this recipe because the short cooking time does not allow regular rice to soften.

POWER LEVEL: High
MICROWAVE TIME: 9 to 13 min., total

1 lb. ground chuck beef
1 cup packaged precooked (minute) rice
1 can (10-oz.) condensed tomato soup (divided)
1 egg
½ cup water
1 teaspoon onion salt

Mix together beef, rice, ½ can of soup (about ½ cup), egg, water and onion salt. Shape into 12 balls and arrange in a circle in 9 or 10-in. pie plate. Cover with wax paper. **Microwave at High 7 to 9 Minutes,** rotating dish ½ turn after 4 minutes.

Spoon Topping over meatballs. **Microwave at High 2 to 4 Minutes** to heat. If desired, mound center of meatball ring with rice before serving.

TOPPING: Into remaining ½ can undiluted tomato soup, stir 2 tablespoons ketchup and 1 teaspoon prepared mustard.

Makes 4 to 6 servings

COLORFUL RING OF MEATBALLS

POWER LEVEL: High
MICROWAVE TIME: 15 to 17 min., total

1 lb. ground chuck beef
1 egg
½ cup fine bread crumbs
1 teaspoon salt
¼ teaspoon paprika
⅛ teaspoon pepper

Mix together beef, egg, crumbs, paprika, salt and pepper. Shape into 12 balls and arrange in a circle in 9 or 10-in. pie plate. Cover with wax paper. **Microwave at High 8 Minutes.**

1 medium onion
1 medium lemon
1 medium green pepper
1 cup dairy sour cream (8-oz.)
½ cup chili sauce
2 tablespoons brown sugar (packed)

While meatballs are cooking, peel onion and lemon. Slice onion, lemon and pepper ¼-in. thick. Mix together sour cream, chili sauce and brown sugar. Rotate dish ½ turn. Distribute onion rings and lemon and pepper slices over meatballs. Pour sour cream mixture evenly over slices.

Microwave at High 7 to 9 Minutes, uncovered. Serve with buttered noodles, if desired.

Makes 4 to 5 servings

Porcupine Meatballs

MEATBALLS HAWAIIAN

These meatballs microwave very quickly because of the moist pineapple filling.

POWER LEVEL: High
MICROWAVE TIME: 7 to 9 min., total

1 can (1-lb. 4-oz.) pineapple chunks

Drain pineapple well, reserving syrup.

1 lb. ground chuck beef
1 egg
2 slices fresh bread, crumbled
1 tablespoon instant minced onion
1 teaspoon salt
⅛ teaspoon cloves
⅛ teaspoon allspice
2 tablespoons reserved pineapple syrup

Mix together beef, egg, bread crumbs, onion, salt, cloves, allspice and syrup. Mold small amount of mixture around each pineapple chunk. Place meatballs in 12×8×2-in. dish. Cover with wax paper. **Microwave at High 4 Minutes.** Pour off meat juices.

⅓ cup reserved pineapple syrup
½ cup ketchup
⅓ cup brown sugar (packed)

Stir together syrup, ketchup and brown sugar. Pour over drained meatballs. **Microwave at High 3 to 5 Minutes** longer, until done. Serve with rice or noodles, or serve with toothpicks as an appetizer.

Makes about 24 to 30 meatballs

Ground Beef Hamburger Patties

Hamburgers are America's all-time favorite for lunch or supper. (Some people even like them for breakfast.) With microwaving, hamburgers defrost and cook so quickly and successfully that, if you keep a supply in the freezer, you can serve hamburgers at a moment's notice. You may microwave hamburgers in the Brown 'N Sear Dish or browning griddle, but they will be equally delicious when cooked on a paper or pottery plate suitable for microwaving; and you'll save even more cooking and clean up time.

Cover patties with wax paper for a juicy hamburger. Microwave at **High.** After half the cooking time, rotate dish ½ turn. For a drier surface, microwave uncovered and turn patties over after ½ the cooking time.

MICROLESSON:

Illustrated below are several ways additional browning can be achieved. Browning agents should be added before cooking.

Plain hamburger immediately after microwaving Barbecue Sauce Teriyaki Sauce

Let Pattie Stand a few minutes, covered with wax paper. On removal from the oven, hamburgers will look grey, but they will turn brown after standing.

Serve on buttered buns with your favorite condiments. Notice the change in appearance after standing time. This hamburger was cooked without a browning agent.

Onion Soup Mix

Brown Bouquet Sauce With Butter

Brown 'N Sear Dish

TIPS FOR MICROWAVING GROUND BEEF PATTIES

Thickness and type of ground beef determine cooking time. The time chart is for medium-lean ground chuck. Fattier hamburgers might take less time, very lean ones, more.

A Paper Plate lined with a double thickness of paper towel gives you no-clean-up convenience. Cover patties with a single paper towel.

For Lower Calorie hamburgers, place patties on a trivet set over a plate or dish. Cover with wax paper and rotate dish ½ turn after half the cooking time. Fat drains into dish.

GROUND BEEF PATTY COOKING CHART

Timings are based on medium-lean ground chuck shaped into 6, 4 or 2 patties per pound and microwaved to well done. Use paper, pottery or glass plate.

Preheat Brown 'N Sear dish or browning griddle when using this cooking method. Follow the timings given on the chart below, but turn fresh hamburgers over after ⅔ cooking time. For frozen hamburgers, turn as directed on the chart. Use the Brown 'N Sear dish cover to prevent spatters, but preheat dish uncovered.

Extended Hamburgers. Hamburgers may be extended with soy protein, following directions on the package. You may also use oatmeal, crushed corn flakes or crackers, according to your favorite recipe. Extended hamburgers microwave in ½ to 1 minute less time per patty, and give greater volume per pound of meat. The following recipe uses bread as an extender.

Meatloaf Burgers. Mix together 1 pound ground chuck, 1½ cups cubed bread (2 slices), 1 egg and ½ teaspoon salt. Shape into size and thickness of patties preferred. Microwave ½ to 1 minute less time per pattie than for regular hamburgers.

POWER LEVEL: **High**

PATTY SIZE	NO. OF PATTIES	FRESH TIME/MINUTES	FROZEN TIME/MINUTES		PREHEAT BROWNING DISH OR GRIDDLE TIME/MINUTES	
6 per pound	1	1 to 1¼	2	Turn over after ½ of time	4	
(about ½" thick)	2	1½ to 2	4 to 4½		4	
	3	2 to 2½	5 to 5½		6	
	4	2½ to 3	6 to 6½		6	
	5	3 to 4	7½ to 8	Turn over every ⅓ of time	8	Griddle only
	6	4 to 5	9 to 10		8	
4 per pound	1	2 to 3	3 to 3½	Turn over after ½ of time	4	
(about ¾" thick)	2	3 to 4	4½ to 5½		6	
	3	4 to 5	7 to 8	Turn over every ⅓ of time	6	
	4	5 to 6	10 to 11		8	
2 per pound	1	2½ to 3½	5 to 7	Turn over every ⅓ of time	6	
(about ¾" thick)	2	6 to 7	12 to 14		8	– Griddle only

SALISBURY STEAKS

If you prefer creamy gravy, substitute milk for water.

POWER LEVEL: High
MICROWAVE TIME: 10 to 13 min., total

1 lb. ground chuck beef
½ small onion, chopped
1 teaspoon seasoned salt
⅛ teaspoon pepper

Combine beef, onion, salt and pepper. Shape into 2 large oval patties in 8-in. square dish. Cover with wax paper. **Microwave at High 7 to 9 Minutes,** rotating dish ½ turn after 3 minutes. Remove patties from dish and keep warm.

3 tablespoons flour
½ cup water
½ teaspoon brown bouquet sauce
1 can (2-oz.) mushroom stems and pieces, undrained

Mix flour and water to make a smooth paste. Add quickly to hot drippings, stirring until smooth. Add brown bouquet sauce and mushrooms, stirring well. **Microwave at High 2 Minutes,** stirring after 1 minute, until gravy thickens. Place patties in gravy, spooning some over the top. **Microwave at High 1 to 2 Minutes,** until hot.

Makes 2 generous servings

HAMBURGER PATTY STEW

When arranging this casserole, be sure that the top layer of beef patties is well covered with vegetables or it will overcook.

POWER LEVEL: Medium High
MICROWAVE TIME: 45 to 50 min., total

3 medium potatoes
3 medium carrots
3 medium onions

Peel vegetables and slice into ¼-in. slices.

2 lbs. ground chuck beef
1 tablespoon salt
¼ teaspoon pepper
⅓ cup water
Paprika

Form beef into 24 small flat patties. In 3-qt. casserole make 3 layers of beef with vegetables, sprinkling layers with salt and pepper, ending with vegetables. Add water. Press down into casserole. Sprinkle with paprika. Cover. **Microwave at Medium High 45 to 50 Minutes,** rotating dish ½ turn after 20 minutes.

Makes 8 to 10 servings

Stuffed Hamburgers

STUFFED HAMBURGERS

POWER LEVEL: High
MICROWAVE TIME: 7 to 9 min., total

1 lb. ground chuck beef
Salt
Pepper
Filling (below)

Shape beef into 8 thin patties. Sprinkle with salt and pepper. Place selected filling over 4 patties and top with other 4 patties. Seal fillings inside by pinching firmly around edges. Arrange 4 stuffed patties in 8-in. square dish. Cover with wax paper. **Microwave at High 7 to 9 Minutes,** rotating dish ½ turn after 4 minutes. Serve on buttered buns.

Makes 4 patties

FILLINGS:

Ham 'N' Cheese: Use a thin ham slice and 1 thin cheese slice per patty.

Cordon Bleu: Use ¼-in. thick slices Canadian bacon and 1 tablespoon crumbled bleu cheese per patty.

Hot Dog Burgers: Use ½ of a hot dog sliced lengthwise, 1 tablespoon ketchup and scant teaspoon mustard per patty.

Maxi Burgers: Use thin slice onion and thin slice tomato per patty. Before cooking raw, but filled patties, microwave 4 long bacon strips until barely done, but still limp. Quickly wrap strips around patties to encircle edges and secure with toothpicks. Place each patty on a slice of drained pineapple. Microwave as above, adding 1 additional minute for pineapple. Top Maxi Burgers with pimiento cheese slice after cooking. Allow to melt by returning to microwave oven few seconds.

Ground Beef Meatloaf

In the microwave oven, meatloaf cooks in 15 to 20 minutes, instead of the hour, or hour and a half you expect conventionally. Microwaved meatloaves are round and flat. We do not recommend square or loaf shapes, because the corners absorb too much energy and will be overcooked by the time the center is done.

A conventionally baked meatloaf occasionally has areas on the top which are overbrown. When microwaved, these areas may appear on the bottom edges of the loaf. Because microwave energy is attracted to sweet mixtures, toppings which contain sugar, syrup or preserves can increase overbrowning if they come in contact with the bottom edges. When applied before microwaving, they should be brushed only on the top.

Plain meatloaf looks grey. It needs a topping, sauce or browning agent for attractive color. For this picture, we brushed the left side of the meatloaf with a browning sauce, leaving the right side plain. Ketchup, chili or barbecue sauces make easy toppings. For delicious flavor variety, try one of our homemade toppings.

Basic Meatloaf

HOW TO MICROWAVE PIE-SHAPED MEATLOAF

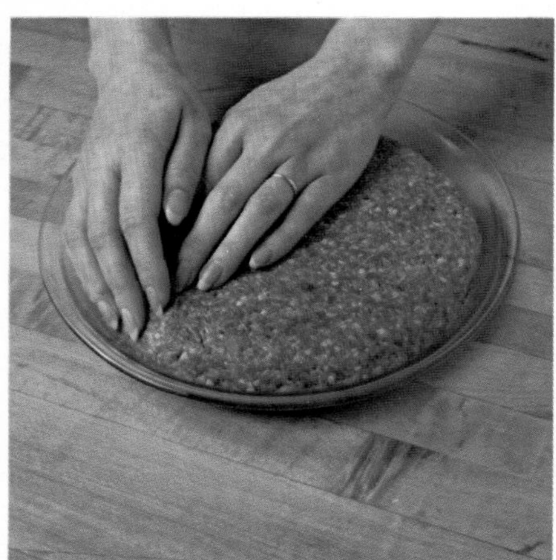

Use 1 to 2 pounds ground beef. If you are adapting a recipe, choose a moist mixture. Spread the mixture directly in a pie plate, not on a trivet. The top should be very flat and about even with the top of the dish.

Brush the top with a browning agent or sauce. If you are not using a probe, cover dish tightly with plastic wrap, turning back about 2-in. at edge to vent. After cooking, let loaf stand 5 to 10 minutes to complete cooking and make it easier to slice.

Insert temperature probe as horizontally as possible, so that tip is in the center of the loaf. Make sure disc does not touch the food. Cover tightly with plastic wrap, arranging loosely around probe to vent.

BASIC MEATLOAF

Add 1/4 teaspoon herbs or dry mustard to vary flavor.

POWER LEVEL: High TEMP:* 170°
APPROX. MICROWAVE TIME: 15 to 20 min.

1½ lbs. ground chuck beef
¾ cup chopped onion
½ cup fine dry bread crumbs
1 egg
2 tablespoons ketchup
1 cup milk
1 teaspoon salt
¼ teaspoon pepper
⅛ teaspoon paprika

Mix together beef, onion, crumbs, egg, ketchup, milk and seasonings. Mold into a rounded, flat loaf in 9-in. pie plate.

2 tablespoons ketchup . . Spread ketchup evenly over top of loaf.

Insert temperature probe and cover as shown in picture on preceding page. Attach cable end at receptacle. **Microwave at High. Set Temp, Set 170°.**

When oven signals, remove meatloaf and let stand about 10 minutes to firm before serving. Serve in wedges.

Makes 6 servings

* On models not equipped with probe use minimum microwave time and check for doneness.

SOUPER MEATLOAF

POWER LEVEL: Medium High TEMP:* 170°
APPROX. MICROWAVE TIME: 22 to 25 min.

2 lbs. ground chuck beef
½ cup fine dry bread crumbs
⅓ cup chopped onion
1 egg, slightly beaten
1 can (10½-oz.) condensed cream of mushroom soup, (divided)
2 tablespoons beef bouillon granules

Mix together beef, crumbs, onion, egg, ½ of soup and bouillon. Shape into flat loaf in 10-in. pie plate. Insert temperature probe as shown in picture at left. Attach cable end at receptacle. **Microwave at Medium High. Set Temp, Set 170°.** When oven signals, let loaf stand 10 minutes. Serve with Topping.

Topping: Mix remaining soup with 1 teaspoon beef bouillon granules and ⅓ cup water. **Microwave at High 2 to 3 Minutes,** stirring every minute, until hot.

For best results, this loaf must be cooked in the 10-in. pie plate at Medium High Power.

* On models not equipped with probe use minimum microwave time and check for doneness.

1½-pound Loaf Shaped Meatloaf can be microwaved at Medium High to 170°, about 25 to 30 minutes.

CHEESE STUFFED MEATLOAF

This meatloaf tastes like a cheeseburger and will be popular with your family.

POWER LEVEL: High TEMP:* 170°
APPROX. MICROWAVE TIME: 25 to 30 min.

1½ lbs. ground chuck beef
3 slices fresh bread, cubed
1 cup milk
2 teaspoons salt
½ teaspoon pepper

Make meatloaf mixture: In large mixing bowl, mix together beef, bread, milk, salt and pepper.

½ cup chopped onion
¼ cup chopped green pepper
¼ cup chopped celery
2 tablespoons lemon juice
1 egg, slightly beaten
1 cup (4-oz.) shredded cheddar cheese
3 slices fresh bread, finely crumbled

Make cheese stuffing: In 1½-qt. casserole place onion, pepper, celery and lemon juice. **Microwave at High 3 Minutes,** until lightly sauteed. Add egg to hot vegetables and stir to blend well. Stir in cheese and fine bread crumbs.

To assemble meatloaf: Pat half of meat mixture in bottom of 9-in. pie plate. Mound filling over meat leaving about 1-in. uncovered at edges. Spread remaining meat mixture over filling. (Meat mixture is soft and spreads easily.) Seal around edges. Brush assembled meatloaf with 1 tablespoon Worcestershire sauce.

Insert temperature probe so tip is in center of stuffing. Cover tightly with plastic wrap, arranging loosely around probe to vent. Attach cable end at receptacle. **Microwave at High. Set Temp, Set 170°.**

When oven signals, remove meatloaf and let stand about 10 minutes to firm before serving. Serve in wedges.

Makes 4 to 6 servings

LEMON LOVERS' MEATLOAF

Lemon juice and a garnish of lemon slices add tang to this meatloaf.

POWER LEVEL: High TEMP:* 170°
APPROX. MICROWAVE TIME: 15 to 20 min.

¾ cup ketchup
¼ cup brown sugar (packed)
¾ teaspoon dry mustard
¼ teaspoon allspice
Dash ground cloves

In small bowl mix together ketchup, brown sugar, dry mustard, allspice and cloves. Set aside.

1½ lb. ground chuck beef
3 slices day-old bread, cubed
1 egg, slightly beaten
⅓ cup lemon juice
¼ cup chopped onion
2 teaspoons seasoned salt

Mix together beef, bread cubes, egg, lemon juice, onion and salt. Mold into rounded flat loaf in 9-in. pie plate.

6 very thin lemon slices

Spread half the reserved sauce over loaf and arrange lemon slices on top.

Insert temperature probe so tip is in center of loaf. Cover tightly with plastic wrap, arranging loosely around probe to vent. Attach cable end at receptacle. **Microwave at High. Set Temp, Set 170°.**

When oven signals, remove loaf and let stand 5 minutes to firm before serving. Remove plastic wrap and spread remaining sauce over loaf before serving.

Makes 6 servings

* On models not equipped with probe use minimum microwave time and check for doneness.

Mini Meatloaves: Shape meat mixture into 6 individual loaves and arrange in 12×8×2-in. dish. Cover with wax paper. **Microwave at High 4 Minutes.** Evenly divide half of sauce over loaves. Top each loaf with a lemon slice. Recover with wax paper. Rotate dish ½ turn. **Microwave at High 7 to 9 Minutes,** until done. Heat and spoon remaining sauce over loaves before serving.

SAUERBRATEN BEEF RING

POWER LEVEL: High TEMP:* 180°
APPROX. MICROWAVE TIME: 17 to 22 min.

1¼ cups finely crushed gingersnap cookies
2 cups beef broth
½ cup brown sugar (packed)
¼ cup raisins
¼ cup lemon juice

Reserve ½ cup gingersnap crumbs for meatloaf. In 1-qt. glass measure, mix together remaining ¾ cup crumbs, broth, brown sugar, raisins and lemon juice. **Microwave at High 8 to 10 Minutes,** stirring every 3 minutes, until thickened. Set aside.

2 lbs. ground chuck beef
1 cup soft bread crumbs (1½ slices)
½ cup chopped onion
¼ cup lemon juice
¼ cup water
1 teaspoon salt
¼ teaspoon pepper

In 2-qt. casserole mix together reserved crumbs, beef, bread crumbs, onion, lemon juice, water, salt and pepper. Invert 6-oz. custard cup in center of same 2-qt. casserole. Divide meat into 12 equal parts. Shape into ovals and arrange as shown below around custard cup. Pour 1 cup sauce over meat.

Insert temperature probe so tip is in center of one meatball. Cover dish tightly with plastic wrap, arranging loosely around probe to vent. Attach cable end at receptacle. **Microwave at High. Set Temp, Set 180°.**

When oven signals, remove loaf from oven and let stand 10 minutes. Invert serving plate over casserole. Carefully but quickly invert beef ring onto serving plate. (*Caution:* custard cup in center of ring will be filled with hot meat liquid. Keep casserole over serving plate until meat and custard cup slip onto plate.) Remove custard cup full of liquid. Serve beef ring with remaining sauce, heated before serving, if necessary.

Makes 6 to 9 servings

HOW TO MAKE A MEATLOAF RING

Place inverted 6-oz. custard cup in center of casserole. Pack oval-shaped meatballs around it.

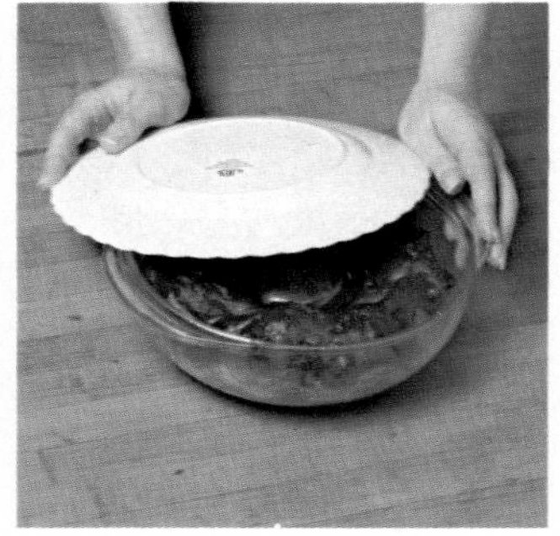

Cover casserole with serving plate after microwaving and standing for 10 minutes.

Invert casserole over plate. When meat and cup slip onto plate, remove casserole.

Lift out custard cup with tongs. Cup will be filled with hot meat liquid.

Beef Convenience Foods

Canned convenience foods, or foods frozen in metal trays, should be removed from their containers to suitable microwave plates or casseroles. Small boil-in-bag pouches (about 5 to 10-oz.) can be placed directly in the oven. Slit or pierce the top of the pouch before microwaving and open carefully after heating to avoid burns from steam. Large boil-in-bags may be placed in a serving dish. When contents are partially defrosted, open the bag, slide food into the dish and stir before continuing to microwave.

TIPS FOR MICROWAVING BEEF CONVENIENCE FOODS

Stirring. Part way through the heating period, stir food from the outside to the center of the dish. Foods which cannot be stirred, such as meatloaf, lasagna or salisbury steak, should be rotated, rearranged or turned over.

Covering. To shorten cooking time and prevent spatters, use a covered casserole. When heating foods on a serving plate, or in a dish without a cover, use wax paper or plastic wrap to cover the food. Prick or slash plastic wrap and remove carefully when stirring.

Probe. Before inserting temperature probe, make certain that frozen foods are completely defrosted. Heat fully cooked foods to 150° to 160°. For probe placement, and temperature of uncooked foods, follow instructions given with similar home-cooked recipes.

CONVENIENCE GROUND BEEF COOKING CHART

Main Dishes such as canned or frozen barbecue beef, chili, hash, meatballs, patties or pieces with gravy, stew, meatloaf, salisbury steak, stuffed cabbage rolls and stuffed peppers can be microwaved following directions below.

Dry Casserole Mixes. Always use hottest tap water and 3-qt. casserole for dishes containing pasta or rice. Stir once or twice during cooking. Let them stand, covered, 5 minutes after cooking.

POWER LEVEL: **High**

CANNED AMOUNT	TIME MINUTES	COMMENTS
Up to 16-oz.	3 to 5	Stir after ½ of time or use temperature probe set for 150°.
Over 16-oz.	5 to 8	

FROZEN AMOUNT	TIME MINUTES	COMMENTS
8 to 16-oz.	5 to 11	Stir, redistribute or rotate after ½ of time. Use temperature probe only if completely defrosted.
16 to 32-oz.	11 to 22	

CASSEROLE MIXES	TIME MINUTES	COMMENTS
Add Hamburger	18 to 22	Microwave crumbled ground beef 5 minutes, stirring after 3 minutes. Drain before adding remaining ingredients.
Add Cooked Beef	18 to 22	If milk is used for part of liquid add 2 to 3 minutes cooking time.
One-pot Main Dish (freeze-dried beef)	11 to 13	Add crumb topping just before serving.

Beef Strips & Chunks

Round Steak Stew

Less tender beef, such as round or chuck, microwaves best when cut in small pieces and simmered gently at Low or sometimes Medium power setting. The temperature probe is not appropriate for small pieces of less tender meat. Recipes which call for Low power setting will not be as tender if cooked at Medium. Slower cooking allows the meat to simmer in its sauce until it is fork tender. When defrosting strips or chunks, place them in the cooking dish, separate and spread them out as soon as possible. Any juices which appear during defrosting can be added to the liquid in the recipe.

HOW TO DEFROST STRIPS & CHUNKS

1. Place plastic or paper wrapped package in oven. **Microwave at Defrost** ½ the minimum total time.
2. Turn package over and defrost second ½ of time.
3. Separate pieces with a table knife and let stand to complete defrosting, or microwave 1 to 2 minutes more.

DEFROSTING TIME: 4 to 8 minutes per pound

TIPS FOR MICROWAVING BEEF STRIPS & CHUNKS

Browning Agents eliminate the pre-browning step associated with conventional cooking. These may be soy or teriyaki sauce, brown bouquet or steak sauce. Brown gravy mix, dry onion soup mix or bouillon may also be used.

A Tight Cover not only speeds cooking but holds in steam which helps tenderize meat. If your casserole does not have a tight cover, seal the top with plastic wrap, turning back about 2-in. at one edge to vent. Be careful when removing the cover to avoid scalding hot steam.

Low Power Setting cooks meat gently in liquid and steam until it becomes fork tender. Microwave time will be slightly shorter than conventional cooking. Some recipes may call for Medium power.

SHORT RIBS AND HOMEMADE NOODLES

POWER LEVEL: High and Low
MICROWAVE TIME: 1½ hr. to 1 hr. 42 min., total

2 lb. short ribs, cut into 2 or 3 rib pieces **1 small onion, sliced** **1 stalk celery with leaves, cut in half** **2 teaspoons salt** **3 cups water**	In 3-qt. casserole place short ribs, onion, celery, salt and water. Cover. **Microwave at High 20 Minutes.** Stir. Cover. **Microwave at Low 60 to 70 Minutes,** stirring after 30 minutes, until tender.
Homemade Noodles or 1½ cups (½ of 6-oz. pkg.) narrow egg noodles	Remove ribs and keep warm. Add dry noodles to broth. Cover. **Microwave at High 10 to 12 Minutes,** until tender.

Makes 2 to 3 servings

HOMEMADE NOODLES

Beat together 1 egg, 2 tablespoons milk and ½ teaspoon salt. Add 1 cup unsifted all-purpose flour and mix to make a stiff dough. Roll out very thin on floured surface; let stand 20 minutes. Roll up loosely; slice ¼-in. wide. Spread loosely in 13×9×2-in. dish. **Microwave at Low 10 to 12 Minutes,** stirring after 5 minutes, until noodles are dry.

Makes 3 cups cooked noodles.

ROUND STEAK STEW

POWER LEVEL: High and Low
MICROWAVE TIME: 2 hr. 3 min. to 2 hr. 9 min., total

2 beef bouillon cubes **2 cups water**	In 3-qt. casserole place bouillon cubes and water. Cover. **Microwave at High 3 to 4 Minutes.** Stir.
2 lbs. round steak, cubed	Add round steak to bouillon. Cover. **Microwave at Low 1 Hour 45 Minutes,** stirring every 30 minutes.
¼ cup cold water **3 tablespoons cornstarch** **2 large potatoes, cut up** **1 cup sliced carrots** **½ cup sliced celery** **1 tablespoon diced onion** **1½ teaspoon salt** **¼ teaspoon pepper** **1 pkg. (10-oz.) frozen peas**	In small bowl stir together water and cornstarch. Slowly add to hot mixture, stirring well. Add potatoes, carrots, celery, onion, salt and pepper. Stir to distribute evenly. Cover. **Microwave at High 10 Minutes.** Add peas and stir well. Cover. **Microwave at High 5 to 10 Minutes,** until vegetables are tender.

Makes 6 to 8 servings

CUBE STEAK STEW

POWER LEVEL: Medium and High
MICROWAVE TIME: 49 to 58 min., total

4 cube steaks, cut in ½-in. strips **1 large onion, thinly sliced** **1 teaspoon bottled brown bouquet sauce** **1½ teaspoons salt** **¼ teaspoon pepper** **1 can (16-oz.) tomatoes** **1 can (8-oz.) tomato sauce**	In 3-qt. casserole combine meat, onion, brown bouquet sauce, salt, pepper, tomatoes and tomato sauce. Stir well. Cover. **Microwave at Medium 35 to 38 Minutes.** Stir well.
4 medium potatoes, peeled and cut in eighths	Add potatoes to stew, stirring well. Cover. **Microwave at High 10 to 15 Minutes,** until potatoes are tender.
1 pkg. (10-oz.) frozen peas, defrosted **½ medium green pepper, cut in strips**	Add peas and pepper to stew. Cover. **Microwave at High 4 to 5 Minutes,** until peas are tender but pepper still crisp. Stir well before serving.

Makes about 6 servings

STEWED BEEF WITH VEGETABLES

POWER LEVEL: Medium and Medium High
MICROWAVE TIME: 1 hr. 50 min. to 2 hr. 10 min., total

2 lb. beef stew meat, cut into 1-in. cubes **2 cups water** **2 cans (6-oz. each) tomato paste** **1 pkg. (½ of 2¾-oz. box) dry onion soup mix** **¼ teaspoon garlic powder** **¼ teaspoon pepper**	In 3-qt. casserole combine meat, water, tomato paste, onion soup mix, garlic powder and pepper. Stir well. If desired, marinate 3 to 4 hours or overnight. Cover. **Microwave at Medium 85 to 95 Minutes,** stirring every 30 minutes.
2 medium potatoes, cut into 1-in. cubes **2 medium carrots, sliced** **1 can (12-oz.) yellow kernel corn**	Add potatoes, carrots and corn to stew, stirring well. Cover. **Microwave at Medium High 25 to 35 Minutes** more, stirring after 15 minutes, until vegetables are tender. Stir well before serving.

Makes 8 to 10 servings

Beef Steaks Less Tender Cuts

Less tender steaks, such as round, flank or cubed should be microwaved in liquid at Low or Medium. Steam produced by the liquid softens the meat during its longer, slower cooking at the lower power settings. If power levels higher than medium are used, meat will not be as tender.

In some of our recipes, we recommend the traditional technique of pounding the meat, or having it processed through the butcher's tenderizing machine, before cooking.

Frequently, less tender steaks are cooked with a slightly acid liquid, such as tomato juice or wine, which helps tenderize them. Marinating both tenderizes and imparts a delicious flavor to steaks. Try one of the marinades on page 84, and use some of the marinade as the cooking liquid.

HOW TO DEFROST STEAKS

POWER LEVEL: **Defrost**

4 to 8 Minutes Per Pound

1. Place plastic or paper wrapped package in oven. Microwave at Defrost ½ the minimum total time.
2. Turn package over and defrost second ½ of time.
3. Separate pieces with a table knife and let stand to complete defrosting, or microwave 1 to 2 minutes more.

Separate steaks as soon as possible and let stand until ice is no longer apparent. If meat is to be cut into strips, do this while it is still partially frozen. It will slice neatly and easily. Any juices which appear during defrosting can be added to the liquid in the recipe.

Swiss Steak

SWISS STEAK

POWER LEVEL: Medium
MICROWAVE TIME: 70 to 80 min., total

1½ lb. round steak, ½-in. thick, tenderized or pounded with meat mallet
¼ cup flour
1½ teaspoons salt
⅛ teaspoon pepper
1 medium onion, sliced thin
1 can (1-lb.) tomatoes

Cut meat in 6 pieces, then coat with mixture of flour, salt and pepper. Place in 3-qt. casserole. Cover with onion. Break up tomatoes with fork and pour over top. Cover. **Microwave at Medium 70 to 80 Minutes,** rearranging meat after 40 minutes, until tender.

Makes 6 servings

Swiss Style Cube Steak: Substitute 1½ lb. cube steaks, ½-in. thick (about 6), for round steak. Cut in half, if desired.

NOTE: If thicker gravy is desired, stir in 2 tablespoons of flour per cup of juices. Microwave 2 to 3 minutes.

POLYNESIAN SWISS STEAK

Be sure meat is covered with sauce throughout cooking time to prevent overbrowning.

POWER LEVEL: Medium
MICROWAVE TIME: 70 to 80 min., total

2 lb. round steak, ½-in. thick, tenderized or pounded with meat mallet . . . Trim fat from meat and cut into serving pieces.

1 can (8-oz.) crushed pineapple, undrained
1 can (8-oz.) tomato sauce
1 pkg. (½ of 2¾-oz. box) dry onion soup mix
1 tablespoon prepared mustard . . . In small bowl or 1-qt. measure, mix together undrained pineapple, tomato sauce, soup mix and mustard. In 3-qt. casserole, alternately layer meat and sauce. Cover. **Microwave at Medium 70 to 80 Minutes,** rearranging meat after 40 minutes, until tender.

Makes 4 to 6 servings

PEPPER STEAK

POWER LEVEL: Medium High, Medium and High
MICROWAVE TIME: 36 to 39 min., total

4 cube steaks (6-oz. each)
⅓ cup steak sauce . . . In 12×8×2-in. dish place cube steaks, overlapping if necessary. Brush with steak sauce. Cover with wax paper. **Microwave at Medium High 10 Minutes.**

1 can (10-oz.) beef consomme
1 teaspoon seasoned salt . . . Transfer steaks to 2-qt. casserole. Add consomme and seasoned salt. Cover. **Microwave at Medium 20 Minutes.**

¼ cup cold water
2 tablespoons cornstarch
1 medium green pepper, cut into strips
2 medium firm tomatoes, cut into chunks . . . Mix together water and cornstarch. Add to sauce. Cover. **Microwave at High 2 to 3 Minutes,** until thickened. Stir well. Return meat to sauce and add green pepper and tomatoes. **Microwave at Medium 4 to 6 Minutes,** until hot. Let stand a few minutes before serving. Vegetables will be crisp-tender.

Makes 4 servings

BOHEMIAN STEAK

POWER LEVEL: Medium and Medium High
MICROWAVE TIME: 87 to 99 min., total

2 lb. round steak, tenderized or pounded with meat mallet
2 cups thinly sliced onion . . . Cut round steak into 8 to 10 serving size pieces. In 3-qt. casserole layer meat and onion.

½ cup water
1 can (12-oz.) beer
1 can (10-oz.) beef gravy
1 tablespoon sugar
2 teaspoons salt
½ teaspoon minced garlic
¼ teaspoon pepper . . . Measure water into 1-qt. measure. Add beer, gravy, sugar, salt, garlic and pepper and mix well. Pour over meat and onions. Cover. **Microwave at Medium 80 to 90 Minutes,** rearranging meat after 50 minutes.

¼ cup cold water
2 tablespoons unsifted all-purpose flour . . . Stir together water and flour. Gradually add to stew, mixing well. **Microwave at Medium 3 to 4 Minutes,** uncovered, until thickened. Stir well. Top with Fluffy Dumplings (below).

Makes 4 to 6 servings

Fluffy Dumplings: In small bowl mix together 2 cups buttermilk biscuit mix, ⅔ cup milk and 1 tablespoon parsley flakes just until moistened. Drop by tablespoonfuls around edges of hot stew. Cover. **Microwave at Medium High 4 to 5 Minutes,** until done.

ROUND STEAK SAVORY

A favorite recipe often made by our customers. A good variation is to use tomato soup in place of mushroom.

POWER LEVEL: Low
MICROWAVE TIME: 1 hr. 40 min. to 1 hr. 50 min., total

2 lb. round steak, ½-in. thick
1 teaspoon seasoned instant meat tenderizer . . . Cut steak in serving size pieces (about 2 to 3-in. strips). Sprinkle pieces evenly with meat tenderizer.

1 can (10½-oz.) condensed cream of mushroom soup
1 teaspoon beef bouillon granules . . . In small bowl mix together soup and bouillon. In 3-qt. casserole layer meat and sauce, ending with sauce. Cover. **Microwave at Low 1 Hour 40 Minutes to 1 Hour 50 Minutes,** rearranging meat after 50 minutes. Let stand 10 minutes before serving so flavor can blend.

Makes about 8 servings

TOMATO MARINADE

1 cup tomato juice
1 cup chopped onion
1 teaspoon basil
1 teaspoon sugar
1 teaspoon garlic powder

In cooking container or 1-qt. glass measure mix together tomato juice, onion, basil, sugar and garlic powder. Use as suggested.

Makes 1½ cups

TERIYAKI MARINADE

½ cup soy sauce
½ cup brown sugar (packed)
1 clove garlic, minced
2 teaspoons ground ginger
1 teaspoon monosodium glutamate (accent)
½ teaspoon pepper

In cooking container or 1-qt. glass measure mix together soy sauce, brown sugar, garlic, ginger, monosodium glutamate and pepper. Use as suggested.

Makes ¾ cup

LEMON OR VINEGAR MARINADE

½ cup lemon juice or white vinegar
½ cup oil
1 sprig parsley or 1 tablespoon chopped parsley
2 bay leaves
1 garlic clove, crushed
2 slices onion
1 tablespoon sugar
Pinch of nutmeg
2 drops liquid pepper seasoning (tabasco)

In cooking container or 1-qt. glass measure mix together lemon juice, oil, parsley, bay leaves, garlic, onion, sugar, nutmeg, liquid pepper. Use as suggested.

Makes 1 cup

WINE MARINADE

⅔ cup dry burgundy wine
⅓ cup cooking oil
1 medium onion, finely chopped
1 clove garlic, minced
½ teaspoon pepper
¼ teaspoon dried thyme

In cooking container or 1-qt. glass measure mix together wine, oil, onion, garlic, pepper and thyme. Use as suggested.

Makes 1 cup

HOW TO MARINATE LESS TENDER STEAKS

POWER LEVEL: **Medium**

25 to 30 Minutes Per Pound

Flank steak, chuck steak, round steak and cube steak are good choices for marinating. Select desired marinade, left.

For convenience, mix marinade in glass cooking dish and cover during marinating with plastic wrap. Dish and plastic can be reused for microwaving. Refrigerate while marinating.

The smaller the cut of meat, the more marinade flavor it will absorb because more surface is exposed. If you prefer mild marinade flavor, use large meat pieces.

1. Stir together marinade in 13×9×2-in. dish or 2-qt. casserole.
2. Cut steak into serving size pieces, or as desired. Arrange in marinade, turning over once. Refrigerate overnight in marinade, turning meat over after several hours.
3. Just before microwaving, turn meat over and, if desired, drain off some of marinade. Microwave at Medium 25 to 30 minutes per pound, turning over after ½ of time.

SPICY STEAK STRIPS

This is a variation of Greek Beef Stew, called Stifado. A good dinner dish to serve with rice, salad and hard rolls.

POWER LEVEL: High and Low
MICROWAVE TIME: 75½ to 85½ min., total

3 tablespoons butter
2 lb. round steak, cut in strips
½ teaspoon salt
⅛ teaspoon pepper
1 cup chopped onion

In 3-qt. casserole place butter. **Microwave at High ½ Minute,** until melted. Sprinkle meat with salt and pepper. Stir into melted butter until each piece is coated. Sprinkle onions over meat.

1 can (6-oz.) tomato paste
½ cup red wine
2 tablespoons vinegar
1 tablespoon brown sugar
1 clove garlic, minced
1 bay leaf
1 small stick cinnamon
½ teaspoon whole cloves
¼ teaspoon cumin
2 tablespoons raisins

In small bowl mix together tomato paste, wine, vinegar, brown sugar, garlic, bay leaf, cinnamon, cloves, cumin and raisins. Pour over meat and onions. Cover. **Microwave at Low 75 to 85 Minutes,** stirring after 40 minutes, until tender. Let stand 10 to 15 minutes before serving.

Makes about 6 servings

Beef Steaks Tender Cuts

Steaks microwaved on the browning griddle are juicy and tender. Your microwave oven can also be useful when cooking steaks conventionally. See tips below.

HOW TO DEFROST STEAKS

POWER LEVEL: **Defrost**

4 to 8 Minutes Per Pound

1. Place plastic or paper wrapped package in oven. Microwave at Defrost ½ the minimum total time.
2. Turn package over and defrost second ½ of time.
3. Separate pieces with a table knife and let stand to complete defrosting, or microwave 1 to 2 minutes more.

MICROWAVING STEAKS IN BROWN 'N SEAR DISH OR BROWNING GRIDDLE

Times are given for ¾ to 1-in. thick steaks cooked to medium (pink center). To test for doneness, cut with knife tip from edge toward center of steak. Area closest to bone is last to cook. **Preheat empty and uncovered browning utensil 8 minutes.**

POWER LEVEL: **High**

TYPE	NO. OF STEAKS	1st SIDE MINUTES	2nd SIDE MINUTES
Cube Steak or Minute Steak (4-oz. each)	1 or 2 4	1 2	1 to 1½ 2 to 2½
Rib Eye or Strip	1 or 2 3	2 5	2 to 2½ 3 to 3½
T-Bone	1	3	2
Filet Mignon	1, 2 or 4	2	2 to 2½

TIP: For browner color, butter both sides of steak before cooking, using 1 tablespoon of butter per steak. When using the Brown 'N Sear Dish, drain juices after cooking the first side of steak.

HOW TO REHEAT FROZEN PRE-COOKED STEAKS

Always undercook steaks slightly. This two-step process produces steak which is not dry or overdone.

1. Unwrap steak and place on microwave ovenproof serving plate. Cover with wax paper. **Microwave at Defrost,** allowing 4 to 8 minutes for each 1-lb. steak. Turn steak over after ½ the defrosting time. Let stand a few minutes before reheating.
2. While steak is still covered with wax paper, reheat it by **Microwaving at Medium,** using the following times for each 1-lb. steak:

DONENESS	TIME MINUTES	COMMENTS
Rare Medium Well	5 to 7 6 to 8 7 to 9	Turn steak over after ½ the time. Let stand a few minutes before serving.

Brown 'N Sear Steak

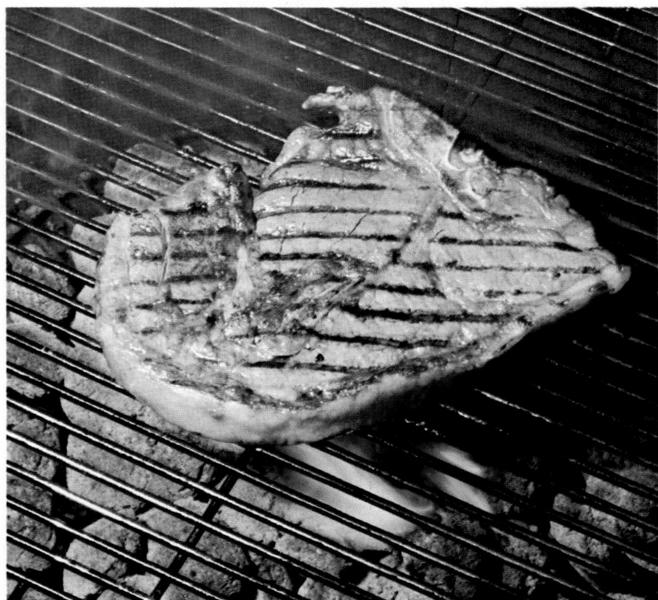

Sear extra 1-in. steaks while your charcoal grill is hot, but undercook them slightly. Cool, wrap in paper or plastic and freeze for future defrosting and microwaving. You'll have charcoal flavor without re-lighting the grill. This is also a good idea when you are grilling hamburgers.

Roast Defrosting

MICROLESSON

Defrosting is one of the major benefits of the microwave oven, but it is not miraculous. Roasts need attention dur-

HOW TO DEFROST ROASTS

POWER LEVEL: **Defrost**

10 to 12 Minutes Per Pound

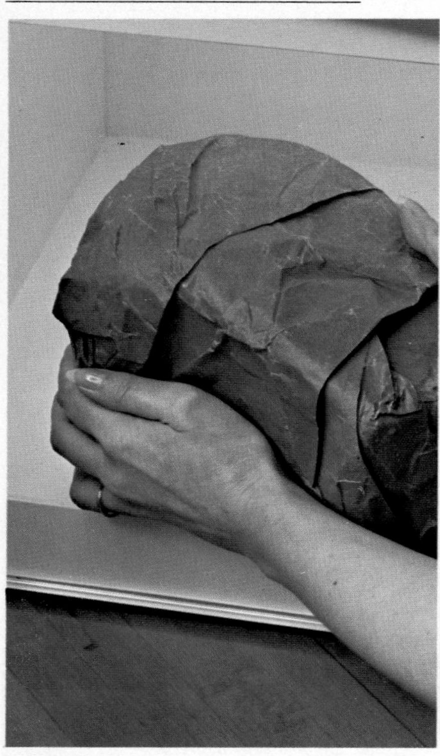

Place unopened paper or plastic wrapped package in oven. Microwave at Defrost for ½ the time.

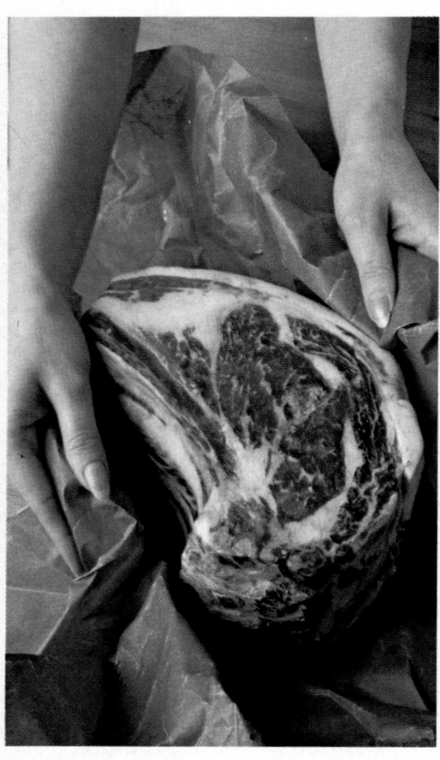

Remove wrappings, which will come off easily.

Turn roast over onto a trivet set over a cooking dish.

DEFROSTING ROASTS OVER 6 POUNDS

1. Place wrapped roast in oven and defrost for first ½ of time. Unwrap roast and shield any warm areas.
2. Turn roast over into baking dish. If roast is over 5-in. high, do not use trivet.
3. Defrost for second ½ of time. Let stand 30 minutes.

ing defrosting or they will start to cook. Follow directions carefully for successful defrosting of these expensive cuts of meat.

The procedure demonstrated here applies to pork, lamb and veal roasts as well as beef. Warm areas after defrosting indicate that the meat has started to cook and should be roasted immediately. If you are defrosting a roast for later cooking, be especially careful. We recommend that you defrost for ¾ the time and allow the roast to finish defrosting in the refrigerator.

Feel roast for warm spots, especially on edges and thinner areas. Shield warm areas with small pieces of foil. Defrost for final ½ of time.

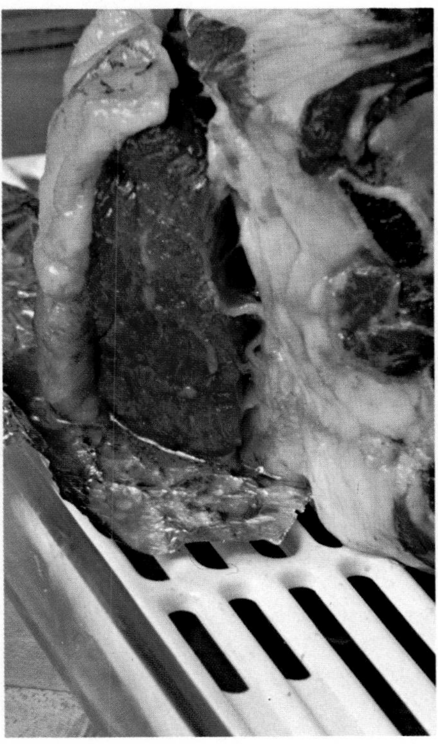

Juices begin to appear. Meat should look moist with glistening fat and should feel cool.

Test meat by inserting a skewer into the center. Do not insert the temperature probe until meat is completely defrosted.

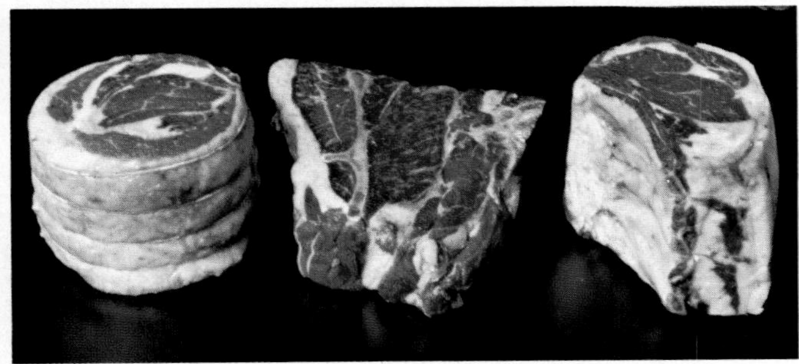

Shape of Meat as well as size influences defrosting time.

Thick roasts defrost evenly and turning over is very important. Allow some standing time to be sure interior is completely defrosted.

Flat roasts defrost quickly. Defrost for ½ of time and turn roast over.

Irregular roasts need more shielding on thinner areas. Check carefully for warm spots.

Beef Roasts Less Tender Cuts

In microwaving, as in conventional cooking, less tender cuts of beef call for some liquid, tight covering and Low or Medium Power setting to make them juicy and tender. Use sirloin tip, rump, arm or blade chuck for pot roasts, and brisket or corned beef for simmered beef.

If you want vegetables with your meat, you may use either of two methods. One is to cook vegetables separately, either before the roast or during standing time. Add them to the meat and heat briefly. Or you may add vegetables to the meat half way through the cooking period and microwave until meat is fork tender.

MICROLESSON

HOW TO MICROWAVE A POT ROAST

Arrange sirloin tip, rump or chuck roast weighing 3 to 5 pounds, in a roasting dish of appropriate size and shape. Brush all sides with a mixture of equal parts of brown bouquet sauce and water.

Pour in ½ cup water. If roast has been marinated (recipes page 84), substitute marinade for water. Cover tightly with plastic wrap, turning back corner to vent. **Microwave at Medium** for ½ the cooking time.

HOW TO MICROWAVE SIMMERED BEEF

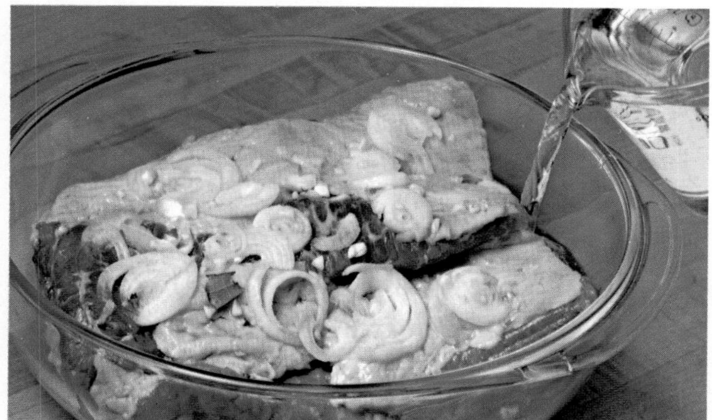

Combine brisket or corned beef, weighing 3 to 3½ pounds, with 3 cups water, onion, garlic, bay leaf and peppercorns in a casserole.

Cover and **Microwave at High 15 to 25 Minutes.**

Chuck Roast With Vegetables

Turn roast over. If meat is more than 3-in. higher than liquid, shield top with foil.

Arrange vegetables around roast, if desired. Cover and microwave until meat is fork tender. Thinner roasts cook faster than thick ones. Microwave time: **20 to 25 Minutes Per Pound.**

Turn meat over and recover. **Microwave at Medium 1 to 1½ Hours,** turning meat again after ½ of time, until fork tender.

Carve roast diagonally across the grain in thin slices for attractive, tender meat.

SIRLOIN TIP ROAST

POWER LEVEL **Medium**

11 to 16 Minutes Per Pound

High quality sirloin tip may be cooked to medium- rare or medium at Medium. It will be juicy, tender and pink. On removal from oven, the roast will appear moist, but the surface will dry and darken attractively after standing.

Brush roast with diluted brown bouquet sauce. Place meat in cooking dish, add ½ cup water or wine and cover tightly with plastic wrap. If you are using a temperature probe, arrange plastic wrap loosely around probe to vent and set for 90°. When oven signals, turn meat over and roast to 130° or 135°. If you are cooking by time, estimate 11 to 16 minutes per pound.

To cook by time, microwave for ⅔ total cooking time. Turn meat over and microwave for remaining time. Remove meat from oven and test for doneness with a meat thermometer. *Do not use meat thermometer inside the microwave oven.*

PEPPERED SIRLOIN TIP ROAST

POWER LEVEL: Medium TEMP:* See Recipe
APPROX. MICROWAVE TIME: 11 to 16 min. per pound

3 to 5 lb. rolled sirloin tip
Liquid smoke seasoning
Garlic powder
Cracked black pepper
. . . . Brush liquid smoke on roast to cover. Rub evenly with garlic powder. Press cracked pepper evenly over roast.

Insert temperature probe from cut side so tip rests in center of roast. Place roast in 12×8×2-in. dish. Add ½ cup red wine or water to roasting dish. Cover tightly with plastic wrap, arranging loosely around probe to vent. **Microwave at Medium. Set Temp, Set 90°.**

When oven signals, turn roast over. Recover with plastic wrap and return to microwave oven. **Reset Temp, Set 130°** for medium doneness.

VARIATION: For well done roast, cook on first side to 125°, then turn over and cook to 200°. Let stand 10 to 15 minutes before carving. Approximate microwave time is 21 to 24 minutes per pound.

Makes 6 servings

* On models not equipped with probe use minimum microwave time and check for doneness.

CHUCK ROAST

To microwave milk gravy as an accompaniment, see recipe page 173.

POWER LEVEL: Medium
MICROWAVE TIME: 21 to 24 min., per pound

3 to 5 lb. chuck roast
1 teaspoon seasoned salt
1 tablespoon Worcestershire sauce
1 teaspoon bottled brown bouquet sauce
½ cup water
. . . . Rub both sides of roast with salt. Mix together Worcestershire sauce and bottled brown bouquet sauce. Brush on roast. In 13×9×2-in. dish place roast and ½ cup water. Cover tightly with plastic wrap, turning back one corner to vent. **Microwave at Medium 21 to 24 Minutes** per lb. Turn roast over after ½ of total time. Let stand about 10 minutes before serving.

Makes 5 to 8 servings

Chuck Roast with Vegetables: After ½ of cooking time add 2 large onions, cut in 8ths; 4 medium potatoes, cut in 6ths or 8ths; and 6 carrots, cut in large chunks. Recover and continue microwaving.

ROLLED RUMP ROAST

Bacon cover over roast bastes it while cooking, keeps top surface moist and gives delicious flavor to roast.

POWER LEVEL: Medium
MICROWAVE TIME: 24 to 27 min., per pound

3 to 5 lb. rolled rump roast
1 teaspoon onion salt
1 tablespoon brown bouquet sauce
1 tablespoon water
. . . . . Rub both sides of roast with salt. Brush with brown bouquet sauce mixed with water.

Bacon strips, uncooked . . . . Cover roast, except cut sides, with bacon strips laying side by side and securing with toothpicks if necessary.

In 3-qt. casserole place roast and ½ cup water. Cover tightly with plastic wrap, turning back 2-in. at edge to vent. **Microwave at Medium 24 to 27 Minutes,** per pound, turning over after ½ of time. Let stand about 10 minutes before serving.

Makes 6 to 10 servings

Rump Roast with Vegetables: Add vegetables suggested under Chuck Roast after ½ of cooking time, if desired. Or, substitute peeled and cut up rutabagas for potatoes.

SIMMERED CORNED BEEF

POWER LEVEL: High and Medium
MICROWAVE TIME: 1 hr. 25 min. to 1 hr. 35 min., total

3 to 3½ lb. corned beef brisket
3 cups water
1 medium onion, thinly sliced
2 cloves garlic, minced
2 bay leaves

In 3-qt. casserole place brisket with water. Slice onion over brisket and add garlic and bay leaves. Cover. **Microwave at High 25 Minutes.** Turn brisket over. Recover. **Microwave at Medium 60 to 70 Minutes,** turning brisket over after 30 minutes. To serve: diagonally slice corned beef very thin for sandwiches or for serving with boiled vegetables.

Makes 6 to 8 servings

NEW ENGLAND BOILED DINNER

POWER LEVEL: High
MICROWAVE TIME: 1 hr. 50 min. to 2 hrs. 5 min., total

1 recipe Simmered Corned Beef (above)

Microwave corned beef as described above. Remove meat from broth and keep warm.

2 large potatoes, cut up
4 medium carrots, cut lengthwise
1 medium head cabbage cut in 6 wedges

Add potatoes and carrots to broth. Arrange cabbage in a pinwheel on top.

Cover. **Microwave at High 25 to 30 Minutes,** rearranging after 15 minutes, until vegetables are tender. Discard bay leaves. To serve: diagonally slice corned beef very thin and serve with vegetables.

Makes 6 servings

BEEF BRISKET

POWER LEVEL: High and Medium
MICROWAVE TIME: 1 hr. 35 min. to 1 hr. 45 min., total

3 lb. beef brisket
3 cups water
1 tablespoon salt
¼ teaspoon peppercorns
1 medium onion

In 3-qt. casserole place brisket, water, salt and peppercorns. Place onion slices on top of brisket. Cover. **Microwave at High 15 Minutes.**

Microwave at Medium 80 to 90 Minutes, until tender, turning brisket over after 45 minutes. For maximum juiciness, let brisket stand in juices 10 minutes before serving.

Makes 6 to 8 servings

New England Boiled Dinner

SPICY BEEF BRISKET

POWER LEVEL: High and Medium
MICROWAVE TIME: 1 hr. 45 min. to 2 hr., total

½ cup ketchup
1 medium onion, chopped
3 tablespoons brown sugar
2 tablespoons vinegar
1 teaspoon basil or bouquet garnish
½ teaspoon garlic salt
¼ teaspoon thyme
¼ teaspoon salt
⅛ teaspoon pepper
3 lb. beef brisket

In small bowl mix together ketchup, onion, brown sugar, vinegar, garlic salt, basil, thyme, salt and pepper. Pour half of sauce over brisket in 12×8×2-in. dish. Cover with plastic wrap turning back one corner to vent. **Microwave at High 15 Minutes.**

Microwave at Medium 45 Minutes. Turn brisket over and pour other half of sauce over meat. **Microwave at Medium 45 to 60 Minutes,** until meat is tender. Let stand 10 minutes, then carve into very thin slices and serve with sauce.

Makes 6 to 8 servings

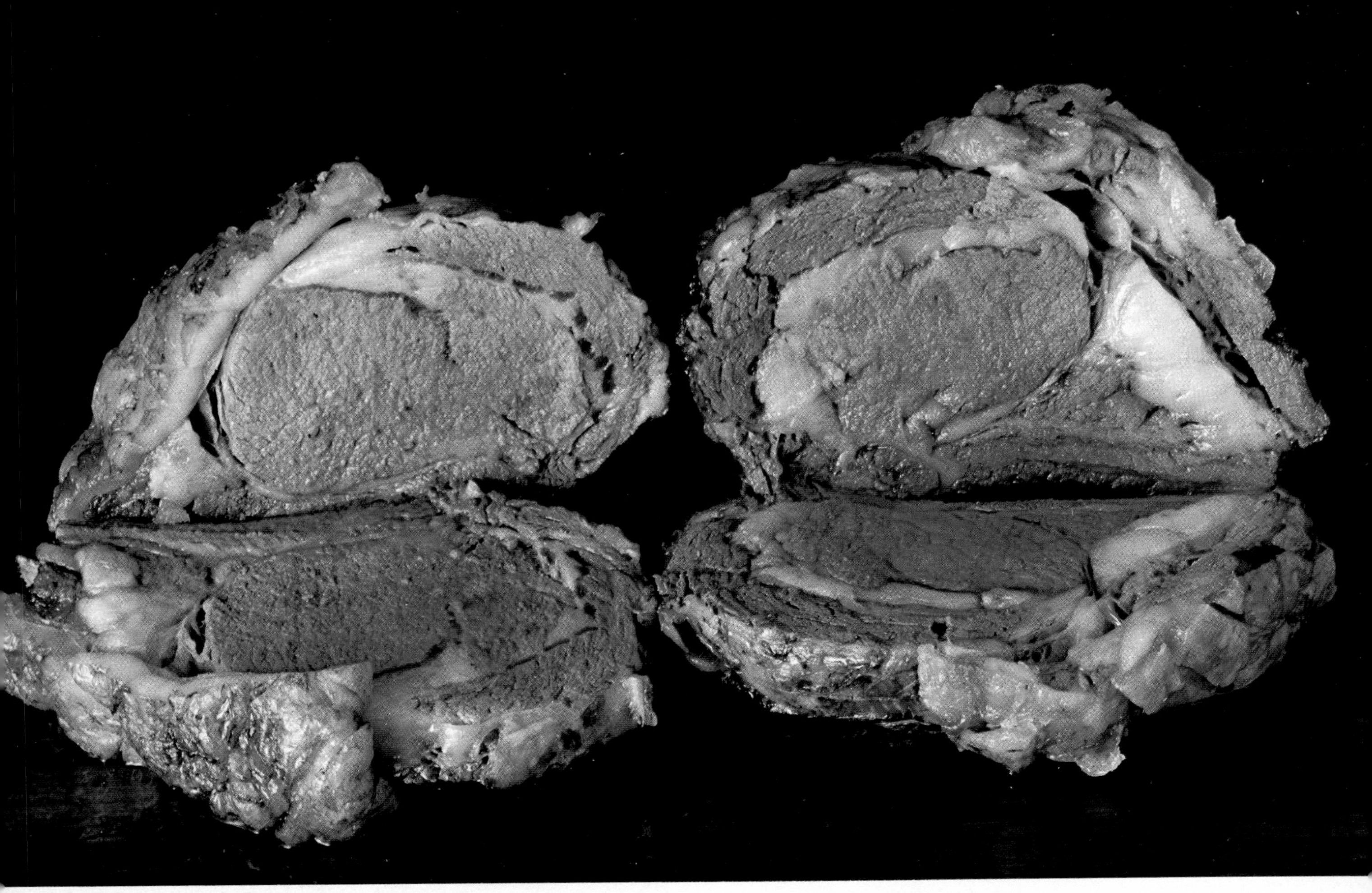

Microwave Roasted Beef. This rolled rib was microwave roasted to an internal temperature of 130°. It has the same medium color internally as conventionally roasted beef, although the temperature is lower. Roast was brushed with browning agent before microwaving.

Conventionally Roasted Beef. This rolled rib was roasted conventionally to an internal temperature of 140°. Both roasts stood about 15 minutes before carving.

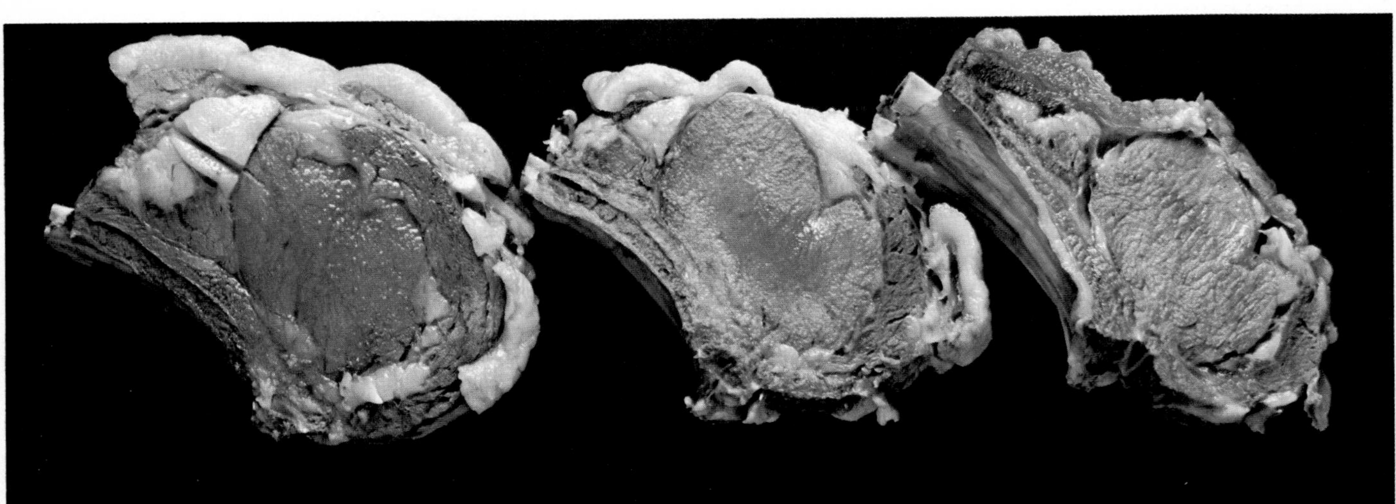

Rare. Meat microwaved to an internal temperature of 120° is red in the center, with running juices. Since microwaving is so fast, the exterior will not be browned. If you desire a brown color, brush the meat with a browning agent before roasting.

Medium. Meat microwaved to an internal temperature of 130° is rosy in the center, with pink juices. Some browning occurs on the outside. If you prefer a browner exterior, brush the meat with a browning agent before roasting.

Well Done. Meat microwaved to an internal temperature of 155° is brown in the center, with clear juices. The time needed to cook beef well done is enough to brown the exterior, so no browning agent is needed.

Beef Roasts Tender Cuts

Tender cuts of beef, such as rolled or standing rib, tenderloin, or eye of round, are ideal for microwave roasting. Lower power settings allow carefree, no attention roasting at faster than conventional speed.

Since these roasts are expensive, and generally reserved for special occasions, you'll want to follow directions carefully. Before you purchase roasts, select meat carefully; standards for grading beef have changed recently, which may affect grain and resulting tenderness. Pay special attention to internal temperatures so you don't overcook! Since meat continues to cook while standing, rare to medium roasts are microwaved to lower internal temperatures than conventional roasts. After 10 minutes standing they reach about the same final temperature as conventionally cooked.

Small, compact and evenly shaped roasts cook best. Just as in conventional cooking, a roast which is thinner on one end will be done first in that area. Long, thin roasts cook faster than short, thick ones.

Roasts of 5 to 6 pounds may be more done in the first two slices from the top than in the center, because these slices are closer to the source of energy. This can be useful if some guests prefer more doneness than others.

If you want a large roast done uniformly, it can be turned over halfway through the estimated roasting time.

If family or guests differ in preference between rare and well-done, roast the meat to the minimum doneness. Carve it, and return some slices to the microwave oven. It takes just a short time to bring a slice from rare to well-done.

Due to the slotted design of the microwave trivet accessory shown below, bottom areas of rare or medium done roasts may not be brown when meat is done. This allows greater area of rare or medium meat for serving. Flat glass or pottery trivets such as top of refrigerator dish, flat top of casserole, or china plate hold heat to bottom of roast and bottom browning will occur; or, turn roast over and continue microwaving for a few minutes.

HOW TO MICROWAVE TENDER BEEF ROASTS

Tie standing rib roasts across the meat to secure fat. Fold the thin end of a half tenderloin under and tie the roast to maintain an even, compact shape.

Brush half tenderloin or eye of round with equal parts of brown bouquet sauce and melted butter.

Place roast on a trivet in a 12×8×2 or 13×9×2-in. cooking dish. DO NOT SALT. Cover with wax paper.

MICROWAVING BEEF BY TEMPERATURE

If your oven is equipped with a temperature probe, be sure to use it when roasting tenderloin beef. See chart below for power level and internal temperature. Note that the internal temperature is lower for microwaved beef roast than it is for conventionally roasted beef.

When microwaving tenderloin and eye of round with the temperature probe, set for 90°, turn over and reset to finished temperature.

HOW TO INSERT THE TEMPERATURE PROBE

Measure the distance to the center of the roast by laying the temperature probe on top of the meat. If the roast is uneven in shape or contains fat or bone, select an angle which will bring the tip of the probe to the center of the thickest meaty area without touching fat or bone. Mark with your thumb and forefinger where the edge of the meat comes on the probe. Insert the probe up to the point marked off with your finger.

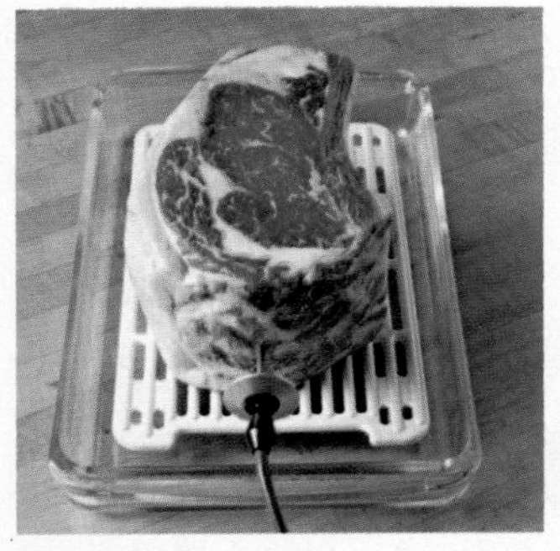

Standing Rib. Insert probe from the front of roast so that tip is in the center of roast.

Rolled Rib. Insert probe into the rolled side so that tip is in the center of roast.

Half Tenderloin. Insert probe into the cut end so that tip is in the center of roast.

Eye Of Round. Insert probe through side of roast so that tip is in the center of meat.

MICROWAVING BEEF BY TIME

Estimate the cooking time for the type, size and desired doneness of your roast. See chart below. Cook for the minimum time suggested on the chart. You may need to reset the timer to complete the minimum cycle for larger or well done roasts.

After the minimum time, remove the roast from the oven and test the temperature with a meat thermometer, following the directions for probe placement given with your type of roast. Remember that microwave roasted meats are cooked to a lower temperature than conventionally roasted meats. If the roast has not reached the desired doneness, remove the thermometer and return the meat to the oven for a few more minutes of cooking time. *Do not use meat thermometer in the microwave oven.*

TENDER BEEF ROAST COOKING CHART

The estimated microwaving times are based on meat at refrigerated temperature. Rib roasts up to 6 pounds microwave well. If meat has been frozen, be sure to thoroughly defrost before roasting, especially if you are using the temperature probe. Let roast stand about 10 to 15 minutes before carving.

ITEM	POWER LEVEL	INTERNAL TEMP.	MINUTES PER LB.
Standing Rib			
Rare	Medium	120° to 125°	11 to 13
Medium	Medium	130° to 140°	13 to 15
Well Done	Medium	155° to 165°	15 to 17
Rolled Rib			
Rare	Medium	120° to 125°	11 to 13
Medium	Medium	130° to 140°	13 to 15
Well Done	Medium	155° to 165°	15 to 17

ITEM	POWER LEVEL	INTERNAL TEMP.	MINUTES PER LB.
Half Tenderloin			
Rare	Low	120° to 125°	8 to 9
Medium	Low	130° to 140°	9 to 10
Well Done	Low	155° to 165°	10 to 12
Eye of Round			
Rare	Low	120° to 125°	9 to 10
Medium	Low	130° to 140°	10 to 11
Well Done	Low	155° to 165°	11 to 13

Ham & Pork Ground

Lower power settings are ideal for ground ham, which tends to become dry and crusty at high settings due to the curing process. The addition of some ground pork or beef not only makes ham go farther, but adds enough moisture so that it remains tender and juicy.

Patties containing ground ham do not require use of the Brown 'N Sear Dish or a browning agent because ham has a naturally attractive pink color; however, a light brushing of brown bouquet sauce may be used.

Defrosting Ground Pork. Ground pork should be defrosted in the same way as ground beef. See page 66. Ham does not freeze well, but small quantities of leftover ground ham may be frozen for use in appetizers, casseroles or Oriental and Italian dishes which call for small amounts of ham to heighten color and flavor.

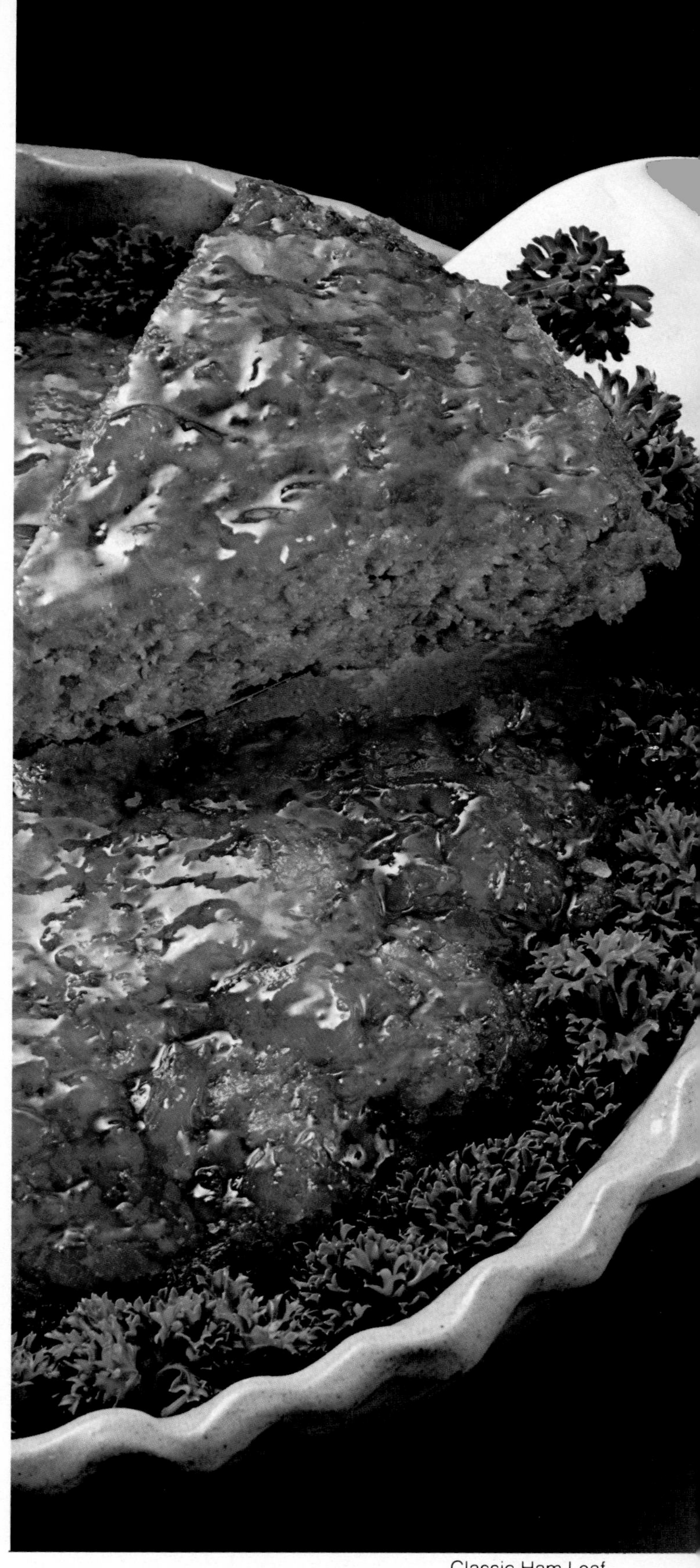

Classic Ham Loaf

Shape ham loaf in an oval or circle. Insert the temperature probe so the tip is in the center of the loaf. Cover tightly with plastic wrap, arranging loosely around probe to vent. Microwave to an internal temperature of 170°.

CLASSIC HAM LOAF

POWER LEVEL: Medium TEMP:* 170°
APPROX. MICROWAVE TIME: 25 to 30 min.

1 lb. ground ham
½ lb. ground fresh pork
½ cup soft bread crumbs
½ cup water
2 tablespoons instant minced onion
¼ teaspoon pepper

Mix ground ham and pork thoroughly with crumbs, water, onion, and pepper. Mold into flat oval loaf in 10×6×2-in. dish, or flat loaf in 9-in. pie plate.

Insert temperature probe so tip is in center of food. Cover tightly with plastic wrap, arranging loosely around probe to vent. Attach cable end at receptacle. **Microwave at Medium. Set Temp, Set 170°.**

When oven signals, remove loaf from oven and let stand 5 minutes before serving.

Makes 6 servings

* On models not equipped with probe use minimum microwave time and check for doneness.

NOTES:

1. If a fast simple glaze is desired, spoon pineapple or apricot preserves over cooked ham loaf a few minutes before serving.
2. For best cooking results, do not exceed recommended weight of meat.

Sweet 'N' Sour Porkies

TRIPLE MEATLOAF

POWER LEVEL: Medium and High TEMP:* 170°
APPROX. MICROWAVE TIME: 45 to 50 min.

1½ lb. ground cooked ham
1 lb. ground chuck beef
½ lb. ground fresh pork
3 eggs beaten
1¼ cup graham cracker crumbs, 16 squares
½ cup diced red or green pepper
1 teaspoon ground cloves

In large bowl place ham, beef, pork, eggs, crumbs, pepper and cloves. Mix together very well. In 12×8×2-in. dish form mixture into flat oval loaf. Insert temperature probe so tip is in center of loaf. Cover tightly with plastic wrap, arranging loosely around probe to vent.

Attach cable end at receptacle. **Microwave at Medium. Set Temp, Set 170°.** When oven signals, remove loaf and microwave Topping (below), spread over loaf. Let stand 10 minutes before slicing.

Makes 10 to 12 servings

* On models not equipped with probe use minimum microwave time and check for doneness.

Raisin Topping: In small bowl stir together ½ cup brown sugar, ½ teaspoon dry mustard, 1 tablespoon vinegar and ¼ cup raisins. **Microwave at High 3 to 5 Minutes.**

SWEET 'N' SOUR PORKIES

POWER LEVEL: High
MICROWAVE TIME: 15 to 18 min., total

1 lb. ground cooked ham
½ lb. ground fresh pork
½ cup soft bread crumbs
½ cup water
1 egg
¼ cup minced celery
2 tablespoons minced green pepper
2 tablespoons instant minced onion
½ teaspoon dry mustard
¼ teaspoon pepper

In large mixing bowl mix together ham, pork, crumbs, water, egg, celery, green pepper, onion, mustard and pepper. Shape mixture into 4 individual patties and place in 8-in. square dish.

8 to 12 whole cloves

Score tops of patties and place 2 or 3 whole cloves in top of each.

⅓ cup brown sugar (packed)
1 tablespoon prepared mustard
1 tablespoon vinegar

Stir together sugar, mustard and vinegar. Pour evenly over patties.

Cover dish with wax paper. **Microwave at High 15 to 18 Minutes,** rotating dish ½ turn after 10 minutes.

Makes 4 generous servings

HOLIDAY HAM LOAF

POWER LEVEL: Medium and High TEMP:* 170°
APPROX. MICROWAVE TIME: 40 to 50 min.

1½ lb. ground cooked ham
1½ lb. ground fresh pork
1½ cups fine bread crumbs
2 eggs beaten
½ cup chopped onion
½ cup milk

In large bowl mix together ham, pork, crumbs, eggs, onions and milk. In 12×8×2-in. dish form mixture into flat oval loaf. Insert temperature probe so tip is in center of loaf. Cover tightly with plastic wrap, arranging loosely around probe to vent.

Attach cable end at receptacle. **Microwave at Medium. Set Temp, Set 170°.** When oven signals, remove loaf and microwave Topping (below); spread over loaf. Let stand 10 minutes for topping to set and to allow loaf to firm before slicing.

Makes 10 to 12 servings

* On models not equipped with probe use minimum microwave time and check for doneness.

Spicy Topping: In small bowl stir together 2 tablespoons butter, 1 cup brown sugar (packed) and 1 teaspoon allspice. **Microwave at High 3 to 5 Minutes,** until dissolved.

Pork Spareribs

Everyone agrees that the barbecued sparerib is one of America's greatest inventions. No one agrees on how it should be cooked. One side advocates the moist, fork tender rib which falls off the bone and melts in the mouth. Another side is devoted to the dry, chewy rib, and considers eating ribs with anything but the fingers a sacrilege. Ever since our first Microwave Cookbook, in 1962, we've provided recipes for both types, because the staff couldn't agree on which rib was the real rib.

Whichever rib you fancy, the microwave oven cooks it fast and flavorful. The fork tender rib takes a little longer, because you add moisture which absorbs some power, and you cook part of the time at a lower power setting. Either way, turn or rearrange ribs half way through the cooking time. Both styles may be served as a main dish or as an appetizer.

HOW TO DEFROST SPARERIBS

POWER LEVEL: **Defrost**

4 to 8 Minutes Per Pound

1. Place plastic or paper wrapped package in oven. Microwave at Defrost ½ the minimum total time.
2. Turn package over and defrost second ½ of time.
3. Separate pieces with a table knife and let stand to complete defrosting, or microwave 1 to 2 minutes more.

NOTE: For a rack of ribs, let stand 15 minutes to completely defrost largest end.

CHEWY STYLE SPARERIBS

POWER LEVEL: High
MICROWAVE TIME: 30 to 35 min., total

3 lb. rack of spareribs . . . . In 13×9×2-in. dish place spareribs, bone side up. Cover with wax paper. **Microwave at High 15 Minutes,** turning over after 10 minutes. Drain off liquid.

1 medium onion, very thinly sliced
1 lemon, very thinly sliced
1 cup barbecue sauce, bottled, or page 176 . . . . Distribute onion and lemon slices over ribs, pour sauce over top. Cover. **Microwave at High 15 to 20 Minutes,** until no pink remains in meat. Spoon sauce over ribs before serving.

Makes about 4 servings

TO COOK RIBS IN PIECES: Cut into 2 or 3-rib pieces and microwave in 3-qt. covered casserole.

Chewy Style Spareribs — Fork Tender Spareribs

FORK TENDER SPARERIBS

POWER LEVEL: Medium
MICROWAVE TIME: 1 hr. 30 min. to 1 hr. 45 min., total

3 lb. rack of spareribs
2 cups hot tap water
1 medium onion, very thinly sliced
1 lemon, very thinly sliced . . . . In 13×9×2-in. dish place spareribs, bone side up. Add water. Cover tightly with plastic wrap, turning back one corner to vent. **Microwave at Medium 80 to 90 Minutes,** turning over and arranging onion and lemon over top after 40 minutes, until fork tender.

1 cup barbecue sauce bottled, or page 176 . . . . Drain liquid from ribs and pour sauce over top. **Microwave at Medium 10 to 15 Minutes,** loosely covered with plastic wrap, until sauce has dried on top. Spoon sauce over ribs before serving.

Makes about 4 servings

TO COOK RIBS IN PIECES: Cut into 2 or 3-rib pieces and microwave in 3-qt. covered casserole.

Sweet-Sour Spareribs

SWEET-SOUR SPARERIBS

POWER LEVEL: Medium and High
MICROWAVE TIME: 1 hr. 33 min. to 1 hr. 47 min., total

3 lb. spareribs, cut in serving pieces
1 large onion, chopped
2 cups hot tap water

In 3-qt. casserole place ribs. Add onion and water. Cover. **Microwave at Medium 80 to 90 Minutes,** rearranging after 40 minutes. Drain meat.

¾ cup cider vinegar
¾ cup sugar
½ cup sherry wine
1 tablespoon soy sauce
2 teaspoons ground ginger

In small bowl stir together vinegar, sugar, wine, soy sauce and ginger. Add to drained cooked ribs. **Microwave at High 5 to 7 Minutes,** until hot.

3 tablespoons cornstarch
2 tablespoons cold water

In small bowl stir cornstarch into cold water. Add to hot saucy ribs, mixing well. **Microwave at High 8 to 10 Minutes,** stirring after 5 minutes, until sauce is thickened.

Makes about 4 entree servings, or 8 appetizer servings

SMOKEY PINEAPPLE SPARERIBS

POWER LEVEL: Medium
MICROWAVE TIME: 80 to 90 min., total

3 lb. spareribs, cut in serving pieces
2 cups hot tap water

In 3-qt. casserole place ribs and water. Cover. **Microwave at Medium 40 Minutes.** Drain ribs.

1 can (8½-oz.) crushed pineapple
1 can (8-oz.) tomato sauce
⅓ cup vinegar
1 teaspoon garlic salt
1 teaspoon chili powder
2 tablespoons light molasses
1 tablespoon prepared mustard
1 tablespoon liquid smoke

In 1-qt. glass measure mix together pineapple, tomato sauce, vinegar, garlic salt, chili powder, molasses, mustard and liquid smoke. Pour over drained ribs, stirring to coat each piece. Cover. **Microwave at Medium 40 to 50 Minutes,** until ribs are tender.

Makes about 4 servings

TERIYAKI RIBLETS

Ribs may be marinated in sauce several hours or overnight before cooking, if desired.

POWER LEVEL: Medium and High
MICROWAVE TIME: 73 to 84 min., total

3 lb. spareribs

Have butcher cut rack of spareribs in half crosswise. Cut ribs into 3-in. pieces and place in 3-qt. casserole.

¼ cup soy sauce
½ cup sliced onion
2 tablespoons brown sugar
1 clove garlic, minced
1 teaspoon ground ginger
1 teaspoon salt
2 tablespoons sherry wine
3 cups apricot nectar or orange juice

In mixing bowl stir together soy sauce, onion, brown sugar, garlic, ginger, salt, sherry and nectar. Pour over ribs. Cover. **Microwave at Medium 70 to 80 Minutes,** rearranging after 40 minutes. Remove ribs to platter and keep warm. Skim fat from top of liquid remaining in dish.

1½ tablespoons cornstarch
2 tablespoons water

In small bowl, stir together cornstarch and water. Blend into liquid in dish. **Microwave at High 3 to 4 Minutes,** stirring every minute until sauce is clear and thickened. Serve sauce over ribs.

Makes about 8 appetizer servings, or 4 entree servings

Pork Chops & Steaks

Just as in conventional cooking, texture of pork chops depends upon the cooking method used. Fried chops are chewy; steamed chops are more soft. Some people prefer to brown chops in a skillet on the range top, then finish them by microwaving.

HOW TO DEFROST CHOPS & STEAKS

POWER LEVEL: **Defrost**

4 to 8 Minutes Per Pound

1. Place plastic or paper wrapped package in oven. Microwave at Defrost ½ the minimum total time.
2. Turn package over and defrost second ½ of time.
3. Separate pieces with a table knife and let stand to complete defrosting, or microwave 1 to 2 minutes more.

MICROWAVING CHOPS OR STEAKS

1. Select steaks or chops about ¾-in. thick. Cut steaks into pieces about 3×4-in. Arrange in suitable dish.
2. On each chop or steak, spread 2 tablespoons of Topping. (See suggestions below.)
3. Cover tightly with plastic wrap, venting 2-in. at one side. Microwave at Medium, rotating dish ½ turn after ½ of time.
4. Add salt and pepper after microwaving, as desired.

POWER LEVEL: **Medium**

AMOUNT	UTENSIL	TIME MINUTES	COMMENTS
2	Microwave-type dinner plate or 9-in. pie plate	14 to 18	Let stand covered 5 to 10 minutes before serving.
3	8-in. square	19 to 24	
4	8-in. square	26 to 32	
6	12×8×2-in.	33 to 37	

TOPPINGS

1. Equal parts Worcestershire or steak sauce and water.
2. Barbecue sauce (bottled or see recipe, page 176).
3. Teriyaki sauce, bottled.
4. Any marinade from page 84. Marinate chops several hours, if desired, then cook in marinade.
5. Brush meat with diluted brown bouquet sauce or soy sauce. Add 2 tablespoons water or red wine per chop.

Microwaved pork chops or steaks need to be browned or cooked in a colorful sauce. From the top: Conventional, Plain Microwaved, Steak Sauce and Water Topping, Brown 'N Sear Dish.

Golden Breaded Pork Cutlets

CHILI PORK CHOPS

POWER LEVEL: Medium
MICROWAVE TIME: 35 to 45 min., total

4 pork chops, 1-in. thick
4 onion slices, ¼ to ½-in. thick
4 green pepper rings, ¼ to ½-in. thick
1 bottle (12-oz.) chili sauce

Score fat on chops and arrange in 3-qt. casserole so "tails" are in center. Place onion and green pepper slices on top of chops. Pour chili sauce over top. Cover. **Microwave at Medium 35 to 45 Minutes,** rotating dish ½ turn after 20 minutes.

Makes 4 servings

PORK CHOPS WITH SAUERKRAUT AND BEER

When possible, assemble this dish ahead of time and allow to marinate several hours to blend flavor and tenderize meat.

POWER LEVEL: Medium
MICROWAVE TIME: 35 to 40 min., total

4 pork chops, 1-in. thick
½ cup chopped onion
1 can (16-oz.) sauerkraut, drained
1 teaspoon caraway seed (optional)
1 can (12-oz.) beer

In 8-in. square dish arrange chops with thickest meaty areas to edge and "tails" to center. Sprinkle evenly with onion. Spread sauerkraut over top. Sprinkle with caraway. Pour beer around chops.

Cover dish tightly with plastic wrap, turning back one corner to vent. **Microwave at Medium 35 to 40 Minutes,** rotating dish ½ turn after 17 minutes.

Makes 4 servings

GOLDEN BREADED PORK CUTLETS

Pounding the cutlets thin tenderizes them and allows for fast cooking at High.

POWER LEVEL: High
MICROWAVE TIME: 12 to 14 Minutes

6 lean pork rib chops (8-oz. each)

Remove bone from each chop leaving a single solid piece of meat. Pound each chop with wooden mallet or foil-covered brick until meat is ½-in. thick.

1¼ cups buttery cracker crumbs (about 45 crackers)
¾ teaspoon salt
2 eggs, beaten
¼ cup butter, melted

Combine crumbs and salt. Dip flattened cutlets into crumbs to coat, then in mixture of eggs and melted butter. Coat again with crumbs.

Place coated cutlets in 12×8×2-in. dish. Cover with wax paper. **Microwave at High 12 to 14 Minutes,** rotating dish ½ turn after 6 minutes. Let stand 5 to 10 minutes before serving. If desired, garnish with chutney.

Makes 6 servings

VARIATION: To crumb mixture add 1 tablespoon curry powder. Or, use a flavored snack cracker, such as onion or cheese cracker, to make crumbs for breading.

GOLDEN BREADED PORK CHOPS

Prepare above recipe, except use 1-in. pork chops with bone in and 13×9×2-in. dish, if necessary. **Microwave at Low 55 to 65 Minutes,** rotating dish ½ turn after 30 minutes.

MICROWAVING PORK CHOPS IN BROWN 'N SEAR DISH OR BROWNING GRIDDLE

Preheat empty dish or griddle at High. Add chops; cover (if Brown 'N Sear Dish is used), and cook first side. Turn chops and recover dish. Cook second side.

POWER LEVEL: **High**

NO. OF CHOPS	PREHEAT MINUTES	1st SIDE MINUTES	2nd SIDE MINUTES
1	3	2	4 to 6
2	4	4	4 to 6
3	4	4, then pour off juice	5 to 6
4 (griddle)	6	6	5 to 7
6 (griddle)	8	9	7 to 10

STUFFED 'N' TENDER PORK CHOPS

POWER LEVEL: Medium
MICROWAVE TIME: 35 to 40 min., total

1. Select **4 (1-in. thick) pork chops** with pocket cut in each.
2. Fill pocket with Apple Stuffing or Cornbread Stuffing (below), dividing all of stuffing among chops. Arrange chops in 12×8×2-in. dish, with thickest meaty areas to edge and "tails" in center. Brush half of glaze (below) over top of chops. Cover with wax paper.
3. **Microwave at Medium 35 to 40 Minutes,** rotating dish ½ turn after 15 minutes, until tender. Let stand 5 minutes. Brush with remaining glaze before serving.

Makes 4 servings

APPLE STUFFING WITH SWEET GLAZE

2 cups chopped apples
¼ cup raisins
1 egg, beaten
2 tablespoons butter, melted
½ teaspoon cinnamon
½ teaspoon salt
⅛ teaspoon pepper

In mixing bowl combine apples, raisins, egg, butter, cinnamon, salt and pepper. Divide evenly between chops.

Sweet Glaze: Mix together ⅓ cup currant jelly and 2 tablespoons orange juice.

Makes about 1½ cups

CORNBREAD STUFFING WITH SAVORY GLAZE

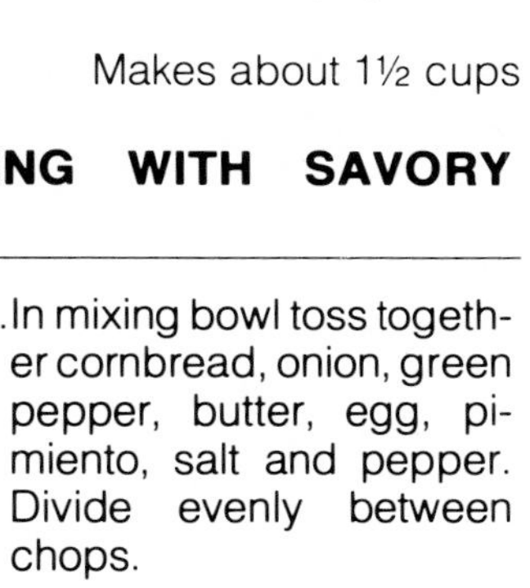

2 cups crumbled cornbread
¼ cup chopped onion
¼ cup chopped green pepper
¼ cup butter, melted
1 egg, beaten
1 tablespoon chopped pimiento
½ teaspoon salt
⅛ teaspoon pepper

In mixing bowl toss together cornbread, onion, green pepper, butter, egg, pimiento, salt and pepper. Divide evenly between chops.

Savory Glaze: Mix together ½ cup ketchup, 2 tablespoons brown sugar, 2 teaspoons prepared mustard and ¼ teaspoon chili powder.

Makes about 1½ cups

Cornbread Stuffed 'N' Tender Pork Chops

PORK CHOPS ROSADO

This dish is very saucy, so plan rice or noodles to serve under chops and sauce.

POWER LEVEL: Medium
MICROWAVE TIME: 35 to 45 min., total

4 center cut loin pork chops, 1-in. thick
1 large onion, cut in ¼-in. slices
1 medium lemon or lime, cut in ⅛-in. slices

In 12×8×2-in. dish arrange pork chops with thickest meaty areas to edge and "tails" in center. Place onion and lemon slices over top of chops.

1 cup ketchup
1 cup (8-oz.) dairy sour cream

Combine ketchup and sour cream. Pour over top. Cover dish with plastic wrap, turning back one corner to vent.

Microwave at Medium 35 to 45 Minutes, rotating dish ½ turn after 18 minutes.

Makes 4 servings

Sweet and Sour Pork

SWEET AND SOUR PORK

POWER LEVEL: Medium and Medium High
MICROWAVE TIME: 45 to 50 min., total

1½ lbs. fresh pork, cut into 1-in. cubes
1 tablespoon instant minced onion
1 tablespoon soy sauce
1 teaspoon brown bouquet sauce
1 can (8¾-oz.) pineapple chunks

In 2-qt. casserole place pork, onion, soy sauce and bouquet sauce. Reserving juice, drain pineapple. Set aside. Add reserved juice to meat, stirring well. Cover. **Microwave at Medium 30 Minutes,** stirring after 15 minutes.

1 cup water
¼ cup cider vinegar
¼ cup brown sugar (packed)
3 tablespoons cornstarch
1 can (5-oz.) water chestnuts, drained and sliced
1 medium green pepper, sliced in ½-in. strips

In small bowl stir together water, vinegar, brown sugar and cornstarch. Add to meat along with pineapple and water chestnuts. Cover. **Microwave at Medium High 15 to 20 Minutes,** stirring and adding green pepper after 8 minutes, until thickened and clear.

1 medium firm tomato cut into chunks

Fold in tomato chunks and let stand, covered, 10 minutes before serving. Serve over rice or crisp noodles.

Makes 6 servings

CHOW MEIN

POWER LEVEL: High
MICROWAVE TIME: 20 to 22 min., total

⅓ cup soy sauce
3 tablespoons cornstarch
2 cans (5-oz. each) water chestnuts, sliced and undrained
1 can (1-lb.) bean sprouts, undrained
1 can (7-oz.) mushroom stems and pieces, undrained
2 cups diced cooked pork or other meat
2 cups ½-in. diagonal slices celery
1 cup thinly sliced onion

In 3-qt. casserole stir together soy sauce and cornstarch. Stir in water chestnuts, bean sprouts and mushrooms, then meat, celery and onion. **Microwave at High 20 to 22 Minutes,** stirring well after 10 minutes. Stir thoroughly and serve over cooked rice or chow mein noodles.

Makes 4 to 6 servings

GOLDEN PORK CASSEROLE

POWER LEVEL: High
MICROWAVE TIME: 9 to 12 min., total

4 to 6 slices (½-in. thick) cooked pork roast (¾ to 1-lb.)
1 can (17-oz.) yams, drained and cut in 1-in. slices
1 cup coarsely shredded, unpeeled apple
½ cup grated sharp cheddar cheese
3 tablespoons brown sugar
1 tablespoon lemon juice
2 tablespoons butter

In 2-qt. casserole layer pork, yams, apple and cheese. Sprinkle on brown sugar and lemon juice. Dot with butter. Cover. **Microwave at High 9 to 12 Minutes,** until hot throughout.

Makes 4 to 6 servings

Ham Slices & Steaks

Slices and steaks of ready-to-eat ham are precooked, so they need only be reheated. Cooking times are short because the high sugar content attracts microwaves, but browning is not necessary, since ham has a naturally attractive color. When baking a ham slice, 1 to 2-in. thick, add some liquid to keep it juicy and cover the dish tightly with plastic wrap. Due to the salt, ham can become dry if moisture is not sealed in.

Baked Ham Slice. Use a slice of fully cooked ham, 1 to 2-in. thick. Slash the edges to prevent curling. Place ham in a baking dish large enough to hold it easily. Add a small amount of liquid. Cover the dish tightly.

Fried Ham. Thin slices and steaks of fully-cooked ham may be fried with a Brown 'N Sear Dish or griddle. Preheat the dish 3½ to 4 minutes. Cook ¼ to ½-in. thick slices 1 minute per side.

FRUITED HAM SLICE

POWER LEVEL: High
MICROWAVE TIME: 18 to 27 min., total

1 slice fully cooked ham, 1 to 2-in. thick
1 can (11-oz.) mandarin orange segments
1 can (8¼-oz.) crushed pineapple

Score or remove fat from ham. Depending on size of slice, place in 8-in. square dish or 12×8×2-in. dish. Drain fruit, reserving juice. Arrange fruit attractively over ham slice. Cover with wax paper. **Microwave at High 10 to 15 Minutes.**

Juice from fruits
2 tablespoons brown sugar
1 tablespoon cornstarch
¼ teaspoon ground cloves

Combine juice, sugar, cornstarch and cloves. Pour carefully over ham slice to avoid disturbing the arranged fruit. Rotate dish ½ turn. Cover. **Microwave at High 8 to 12 Minutes,** until hot. Spoon juice over fruit and serve.

Makes 4 to 6 servings

Brown 'N Sear Dish Ham and Eggs

Pork Roasts

Microwaved Pork Roast

Pork is leaner than it used to be, giving you more meat and less fat. Roasted conventionally or microwaved, this leaner meat has a firm texture. We recommend using a cooking bag and a small amount of water to keep roast pork tender and juicy. If you prefer, you may cover the roast with wax paper. Start the roast bone side up and turn it over after ½ the time. When using the temperature probe, set it for 120°. When oven signals, turn roast over and reset for 170°.

Microwaved pork roasts develop browning, especially when the fat coating is thin. If the roast has a heavy coating of fat, you may want to add brown bouquet sauce.

Microwave pork roast to 170° to cook it thoroughly and maintain juiciness. Be sure to allow the entire standing time, which allows meat to complete cooking and makes it more tender.

HOW TO INSERT THE TEMPERATURE PROBE

Rib end or center cut roasts. Identified by arch shaped bones on the edge of the roast and clearly-defined large muscle. Insert the temperature probe through the bag* slightly below center of the largest muscle, so tip is in the center of the roast.

*Roast is pictured without cooking bag for a clear view of probe placement.

Loin end roast. Identified by circular bone at one end of the roast and rack of bones at the bottom. Insert the temperature probe through the bag* into the end where the round bone is located, placing it ¾ to 1-in. above the bottom of the roast on the meatiest side of the round bone. Follow the bone structure, angling if necessary, so that tip of probe is in the center of the roast. Do not allow tip of probe to touch bone.

*Roast is pictured without cooking bag for a clear view of probe placement.

HOW TO DEFROST PORK ROAST

POWER LEVEL: **Defrost**

10 to 12 Minutes Per Pound

1. If roast is wrapped in paper or plastic, place the unopened package in the oven and defrost for half the time. (Foil wrapping must be removed before defrosting.)
2. Unwrap roast and feel it for warm areas. Shield any warm spots with small pieces of foil. Turn roast over, place it in a roasting dish and return it to the oven.
3. Defrost for second half of time and let the roast stand for 15 to 30 minutes. For step-by-step pictures of roast defrosting, see page 86.

MICROWAVING PORK ROAST

POWER LEVEL: **Medium**

13 to 15 Minutes Per Pound

Do not salt roast. Cut a ½-in. strip from the open end of a cooking bag. Place roast in the bag in a 13×9×2-in. dish. Add ½ cup water to the bag.

Tie end securely with the strip of plastic. Do not use metal twist ties in the microwave oven. Make an X-shaped slash in the bag near the closure.

Microwaving By Temperature. Insert temperature probe through the bag, following directions for probe placement on the previous page. Correct position of the probe is extremely important. Attach cable end at receptacle. **Microwave at Medium. Set Temp, Set 170°.** When oven signals, remove roast and let stand 20 minutes.

Microwaving By Time. Estimate the minimum total roasting time. If your oven has a 35 minute timer you will have to reset it to complete the cooking cycle. **Microwave at Medium.** After the minimum cooking time, test the internal temperature of the roast with a meat thermometer, following instructions given for probe placement. Allow 2 minutes for thermometer to register. If roast has not reached 170°, remove the thermometer and return roast to the oven for a few more minutes. When cooking is completed remove and let stand 20 minutes.

Do not place conventional metal meat thermometer in microwave oven; remove from roast if meat needs additional microwaving.

GLAZES FOR PORK ROASTS

The following glazes may be spooned or poured over pork roasts just before serving.

WINEBERRY GLAZE

POWER LEVEL: High
MICROWAVE TIME: 5 to 7 min., total

1 can (8-oz.) whole cranberry sauce
½ cup vermouth
1 tablespoon cornstarch
1 tablespoon steak sauce

In 1-qt. casserole mix together cranberry sauce, vermouth, cornstarch and steak sauce. **Microwave at High 5 to 7 Minutes,** stirring after 3 minutes, until thickened and clear.

Makes about 1½ cups

APRICOT PRESERVES GLAZE

POWER LEVEL: High
MICROWAVE TIME: 3 to 4 min., total

1 jar (12-oz.) apricot preserves
½ teaspoon ground ginger
1 tablespoon lemon juice

In 1-qt. casserole stir together preserves, ginger and lemon juice. **Microwave at High 3 to 4 Minutes,** until warm and well blended.

Makes about 1¼ cups

CHERRY ALMOND GLAZE

POWER LEVEL: High
MICROWAVE TIME: 8 to 12 min., total

1 teaspoon butter
¼ cup slivered almonds

In 8 or 9-in pie plate place butter and almonds. **Microwave at High 3 to 5 Minutes,** stirring every 2 minutes, until toasted. Set aside.

1 jar (12-oz.) cherry preserves
2 tablespoons white corn syrup
¼ cup red wine vinegar
¼ teaspoon salt
¼ teaspoon cinnamon
¼ teaspoon nutmeg
¼ teaspoon cloves

In 1½-qt. casserole stir together preserves, corn syrup, vinegar, salt, cinnamon, nutmeg and cloves. Cover. **Microwave at High 5 to 7 Minutes,** stirring very well after 4 minutes. Mixture should be well blended. Stir in toasted almonds just before glazing.

Makes about 1¾ cups

Ham Roasts

Most hams are now precooked and can be microwaved quickly and easily on Medium Power. The meat will be juicy and tender if you take care not to overcook. If your oven is equipped with a temperature probe, use it for carefree cooking. Hams which are already cooked need only be heated to internal temperature of 115°.

HOW TO MICROWAVE PRECOOKED OR CANNED HAMS

POWER LEVEL: **Medium**

10 to 13 Minutes Per Pound

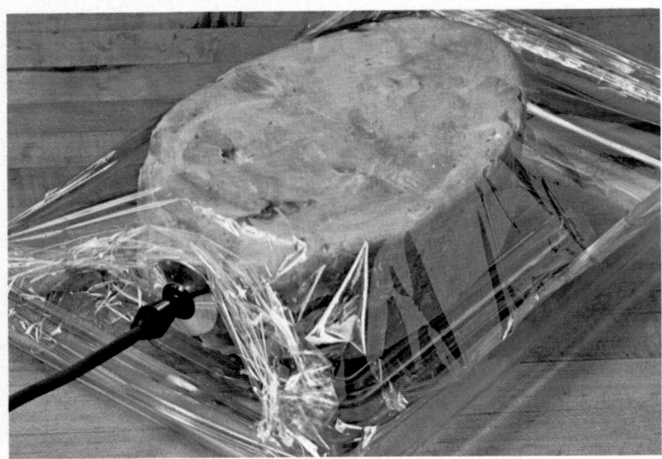

Place ham in a 12×8×2 or 13×9×2-in. roasting dish. Canned ham may be placed on a trivet, if desired, but precooked ham halves or pieces should be microwaved without a trivet to prevent overcooking top. Precooked ham should be arranged with fat side up and shielded on the top cut edge with a strip of foil. When roasting a ham over 5 pounds, tie butcher's string around and across it in several places to keep it from pulling apart. Cover tightly with plastic wrap, turning back corner to vent, or insert temperature probe, cover tightly and arrange plastic wrap loosely around probe to vent.

Microwaving By Temperature. Insert probe as close to the center as possible. **Microwave at Medium. Set Temp, Set 115°.** When oven signals, remove ham and let stand 5 to 10 minutes.

Microwaving By Time. Estimate the minimum roasting time. If your oven has a 35 minute timer you may need to reset the timer to complete the cooking cycle. **Microwave at Medium** for minimum time and test for an internal temperature of 115° with a meat thermometer following directions at right.

HOW TO MICROWAVE A RAW HAM

POWER LEVEL: **Medium**

12 to 15 Minutes Per Pound

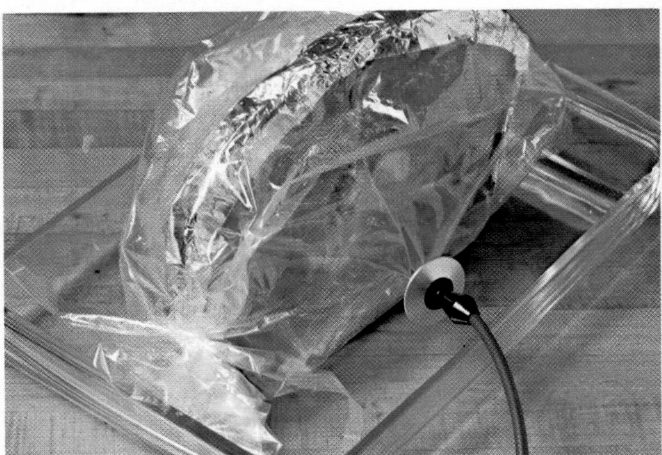

Shield top cut edge of ham with 1½-in. strip of foil. Place ham in cooking bag and arrange in baking dish so cut side will be to front of oven. Tie end of bag with string or strip of plastic cut from open end of bag. Make an X-shaped slash near closure.

Microwaving By Temperature. Insert probe through bag into the center of the lowest large muscle. **Microwave at Medium. Set Temp, Set 160°.** When oven signals, remove ham and let stand 10 minutes before carving.

Microwaving By Time. Estimate the minimum roasting time. **Microwave at Medium** to an internal temperature of 160°, resetting timer as needed.

Do not use meat thermometer in the microwave oven.

To Test Time-Cooked Hams With Meat Thermometer. Insert thermometer into ham, following directions for probe placement. Allow 2 minutes for thermometer to register. If specified temperature has not been reached, remove the thermometer and return to the oven for a few more minutes. After cooking remove ham and let stand 5 to 10 minutes before carving.

Microwaved Precooked Ham with Currant Jelly Glaze

Glazes. For an attractive finish, brush cooked ham with ½ cup jelly or preserves, such as pineapple, apricot or cherry; or, use bottled ham glaze. Use one of the following glazes, or the superb Kentucky Bourbon Sauce (right). Also try Raisin Sauce, page 175, or Horseradish Sauce, page 173.

Traditional Pineapple Glaze: Drain 1 can (8-oz.) pineapple slices, saving juice. Arrange pineapple over ham. In small bowl stir together ½ cup brown sugar, 2 tablespoons reserved pineapple syrup and 2 tablespoons prepared mustard. Pour over microwaved (finished) ham. **Microwave at High 5 Minutes,** to set.

Currant Jelly Glaze: In small bowl stir together 1 jar (10-oz.) currant jelly, 1 tablespoon prepared mustard and 1 tablespoon brown sugar. Brush over microwaved ham. Let stand few minutes to set.

Honey Glaze: In small bowl stir together ¼ cup honey, ¼ cup soy sauce and 1 teaspoon dry mustard. Brush over microwaved ham. Let stand few minutes to set.

KENTUCKY BOURBON SAUCE FOR HAM

POWER LEVEL: High
MICROWAVE TIME: 4 to 5 min., total

1 jar (10-oz.) currant jelly
¼ cup butter
½ teaspoon dry mustard
2 teaspoons prepared mustard
¼ cup Kentucky bourbon

In 1-qt. casserole place jelly. **Microwave at High 4 to 5 Minutes,** stirring after 2 minutes, until hot and melted. Add butter, mustards, and bourbon, stirring well.

Makes 6 to 8 servings

HAM-AGETTI CASSEROLE

POWER LEVEL: High
MICROWAVE TIME: 23 to 27 min., total

4 strips bacon .... With scissors, snip bacon into 1-in. pieces into 2-qt. casserole. **Microwave at High 4 to 5 Minutes.** Remove approximately half the fat.

2 cups cooked ham, cut into strips
1 can (1-lb. 14-oz.) tomatoes
1 cup spaghetti, broken into 1-in. pieces
½ cup chopped onion
¼ cup chopped green pepper
½ teaspoon salt
⅛ teaspoon pepper
.. Add ham, tomatoes, spaghetti, onion, green pepper, salt and pepper. Stir well. Cover. **Microwave at High 18 to 20 Minutes,** until spaghetti is tender, stirring after 8 minutes.

½ cup shredded cheddar cheese .... Sprinkle with cheese. **Microwave at High 1 to 2 Minutes,** uncovered, until cheese is melted.

Makes 6 servings

SWEET AND SOUR HAM

POWER LEVEL: High
MICROWAVE TIME: 14 to 17 min., total

⅓ cup pineapple juice
1 can (10½-oz.) condensed beef broth
3 tablespoons cornstarch
.... In 3-qt. casserole combine juice, broth and cornstarch.

2 cups cooked ham, cut into 1-in. cubes
1 can (1-lb. 4-oz.) pineapple chunks, drained
1 green pepper, cut into strips
1 small onion, thinly sliced
¾ teaspoon dry mustard
2 tablespoons brown sugar
3 tablespoons vinegar
.. Add ham, pineapple, green pepper, onion, mustard, brown sugar and vinegar. Cover. **Microwave at High 14 to 17 Minutes,** stirring every 5 minutes. Serve over rice or crisp noodles.

Makes 4 servings

PINEAPPLE HAM AND YAMS

POWER LEVEL: High
MICROWAVE TIME: 5¼ to 7½ min., total

1 tablespoon butter
1 can (8-oz.) yams or sweet potatoes, drained
2 tablespoons brown sugar
4 slices (about 4-oz.) packaged, thinly sliced cooked ham *
...... In 1-qt. casserole place butter. **Microwave at High ¼ to ½ Minute,** to melt. Add drained yams and mash well. Stir in brown sugar. Divide mixture equally over one end of each ham slice. Roll up into firm rolls.

1 can (8-oz.) sliced pineapple (4 slices) ...... Drain pineapple, reserving juice. Place pineapple slices in 8-in. square dish. Cover each with ham roll, seam side down.

¼ cup coarsely chopped pecans
¼ cup light brown sugar (packed)
¼ cup syrup reserved from pineapple
.... Combine pecans, sugar and pineapple syrup. Spoon over ham rolls. Cover with wax paper.

Microwave at High 5 to 7 Minutes, rotating dish ½ turn after 4 minutes.

Makes 4 servings

*Or use thinly sliced leftover ham, about 6-in. long by 3-in. wide.

CREAMED HAM

If ham is salty, omit salt when preparing White Sauce.

POWER LEVEL: High and Medium
MICROWAVE TIME: 16 to 19 min., total

2 cups (double recipe) White Sauce, page 173
2 cups diced cooked ham
2 hard-poached eggs, diced (below)
1 can (2-oz.) sliced mushrooms, drained
1 tablespoon chopped green pepper
1 tablespoon chopped pimiento
¼ teaspoon dry mustard
... In 2-qt. casserole, mix together white sauce, ham, eggs, mushrooms, green pepper, pimiento and mustard. Cover. **Microwave at High 8 to 10 Minutes,** stirring after 4 minutes, until hot. Serve as desired, over cornbread, rice or noodles.

Makes 4 to 6 servings

Hard-poached Eggs: In 1-qt. casserole, place 2 cups water. **Microwave at High 5 to 6 Minutes,** until boiling. Break eggs onto plate, puncture membrane. Gently slip eggs into water. Cover. **Microwave at Medium 3 Minutes.** Let eggs stand in water 5 minutes before removing to dice.

Bacon

Microwaving is a superior way to cook bacon. It is spatter-free. There is less curling and shrinkage than with conventional frying, and if you cook it on paper towels, there is no messy pan to wash.

When cooked until crisp, bacon will be evenly cooked and flat. Just as in conventional cooking, under-crisp bacon may be randomly cooked, with some spots fatty while others are crisp. Bacon varies in quality, depending upon the amount of sugar and salt used in curing and thickness of slices. The following chart is for average cure, commercially sliced, thin bacon. Cook less time for extra-sweet bacon, more for thick slices.

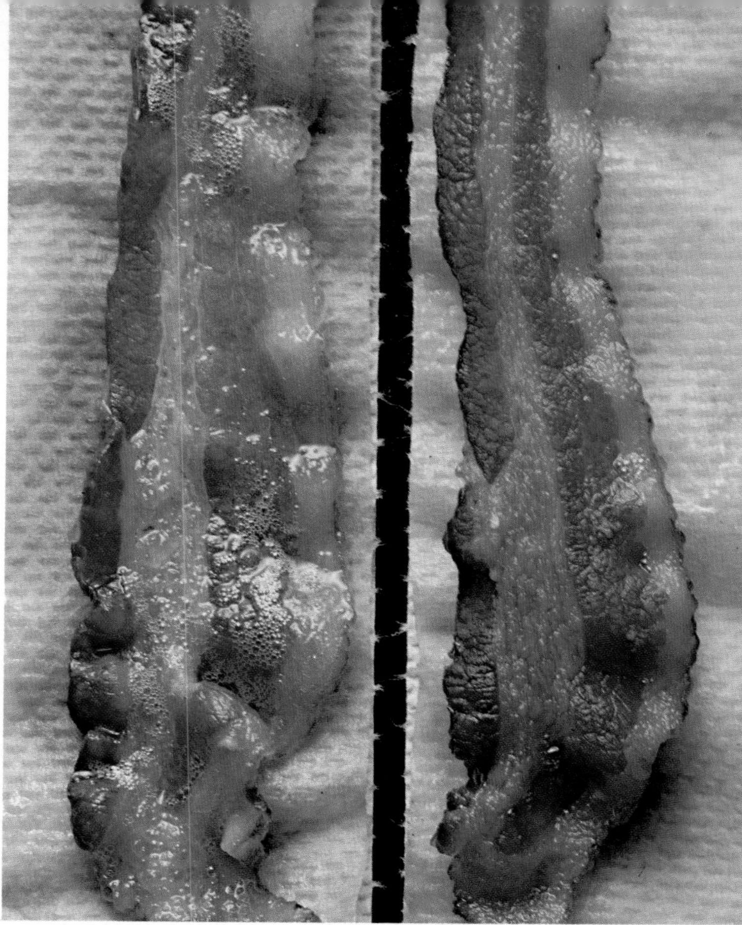

Bacon continues to brown on standing. Left, crisp-cooked bacon as it should look when removed from oven. Right, crisp-cooked bacon after standing 5 minutes.

NOTE: Brown spots on paper towel are due to sugar in the bacon. A high sugar content may also cause bacon to stick to the towel slightly.

HOW TO DEFROST BACON

POWER LEVEL: **Defrost**

4 to 6 Minutes Per Pound

Place unopened package of bacon in oven. Microwave at Defrost for ½ of time. Turn package over. Defrost second ½ of time, just until strips can be separated with a rubber spatula.

HOW TO MICROWAVE BACON

POWER LEVEL: **High**

¾ to 1 Minute Per Slice

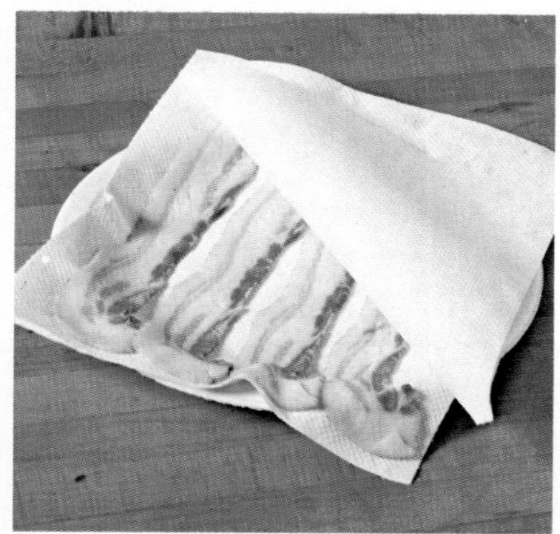

Place two layers of paper towels on paper or pottery plate without metal trim. Arrange bacon on towels and cover with another towel to prevent spatters. Place in oven with strips running from back to front. Microwave at **High** ¾ to 1 minute per slice.

Layer bacon when microwaving more than 6 slices. Place 5 slices of bacon on 2 layers of paper towels in a 13×9×2-in. dish. Cover with a paper towel. Add second layer of bacon. Cover and add more layers as desired. Microwave 4 minutes for each layer of bacon and rotate dish ½ turn after ½ the time. A pound of bacon takes about 15 minutes.

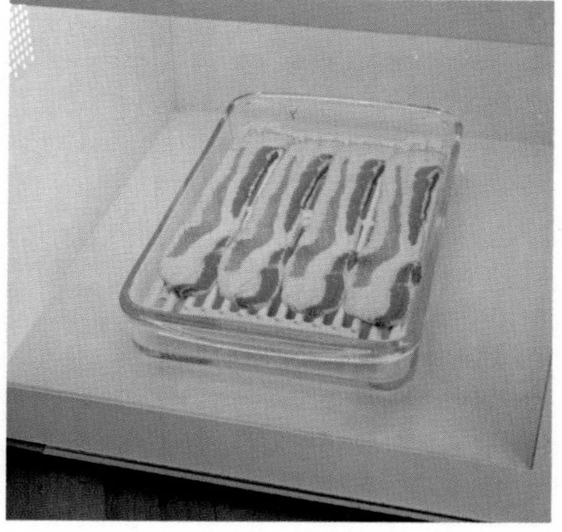

To Save bacon drippings for use in frying, cornbread,or microwave recipes such as wilted lettuce, cabbage or German potato salad, cook bacon on a trivet in a cooking dish. Bacon may also be cooked in a casserole or roasting dish directly in its own fat. As with conventional cooking, remove bacon to paper towel to drain and pour off drippings.

Canadian Bacon

Like most ham, Canadian bacon is precooked and needs only heating to be ready to eat. Whether cooked conventionally or by microwave, Canadian bacon will be dry if it is allowed to cook until brown.

MICROWAVING WHOLE PIECE OF CANADIAN BACON

POWER LEVEL: Medium High
MICROWAVE TIME: 23 to 26 min., total

2 to 3-lb. piece Canadian bacon **¼ cup water**	Remove casing from bacon and arrange in 12×8×2-in. dish. Add water.

Cover tightly with plastic wrap, turning back one corner to vent. **Microwave at Medium High 23 to 26 Minutes,** turning over after 13 minutes. Let bacon stand 10 minutes before serving.

MICROWAVING SLICES OF CANADIAN BACON

Place slices in single layer on dinner plate. Cover with wax paper. Timing below is for thin slices, about ¼-in. thick, such as used for Eggs Benedict, sandwiches or as a breakfast meat.

POWER LEVEL: **High**

SLICES	TIME MINUTES	COMMENTS
2	1 to 1½	No rotation necessary.
4	2 to 2½	Rotate ½ turn after 1 minute.
6 to 8	3½ to 4	Rotate ½ turn after 2 minutes.

Whole Canadian Bacon

Sliced Canadian Bacon

Breakfast Sausage

Breakfast sausage comes in many forms. Each defrosts and cooks differently, but all will be tender, juicy and fully cooked in a very short time. Due to quick cooking, breakfast sausage doesn't brown and, since it is rarely served with a sauce, it will be more attractive if it is brushed with a browning agent before cooking. Use equal parts of brown bouquet sauce and water. If you cook sausage frequently, keep this mixture on hand in a small covered container.

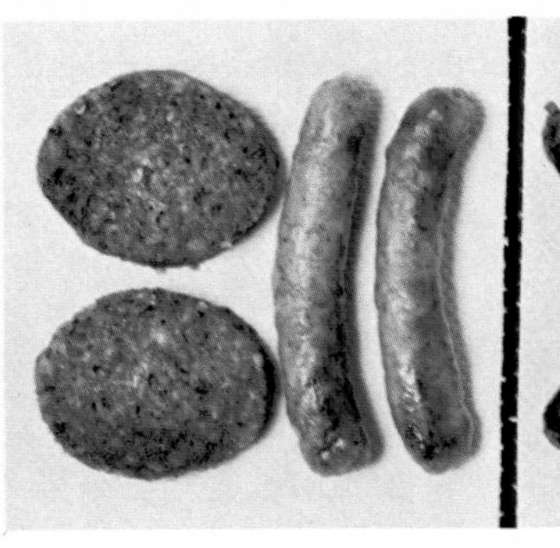

BROWN 'N SEAR SAUSAGE CHART

POWER LEVEL: **High**

Preheat dish 4½ to 5½ minutes.

ITEM	1st SIDE TIME MINUTES	2nd SIDE TIME MINUTES
Pork Sausage, 4 slices ½-in. thick	1 covered	1½ to 2 covered
Pork Sausage Links, 6 to 8 links, uncooked, 8-oz.	1 covered	2 to 2½ covered
Brown 'n Serve, 10 links 8-oz. pkg.	1 covered	1½ to 2 covered

Compare link and patty sausage cooked with and without a browning agent. Both are juicy and flavorful, but sausages cooked with a browning agent have more appetite appeal.

SAUSAGE DEFROSTING & MICROWAVING CHART

The following chart gives specific directions for different types and forms of sausage. Whatever type you are microwaving, a few basic rules are common to all.

Defrost sausage in package, removing any metal closures. When defrosted, sausage should still be cold.

When cooking, select a utensil which is appropriate in size for the amount of sausage you wish to cook: a saucer for 1 or 2 links, a glass pie plate for an 8-oz. package, a roasting dish for a full pound of slices. Add browning agent, if desired, before cooking. Always cover the dish with wax paper to prevent spatters.

DEFROSTING POWER LEVEL: **Defrost**			**MICROWAVING** POWER LEVEL: **High**		
ITEM	TIME MINUTES	COMMENTS	ITEM	TIME MINUTES	COMMENTS
Bulk (1-lb. tray)	8 to 9	Defrost like ground beef, page 66	**4 Patties** (½-lb.)	4 to 5	Rotate dish ½ turn after 1½ minutes.
			8 Patties (1-lb.)	7½ to 8	Rotate dish ½ turn after 2 minutes.
Bulk (1-lb. roll)	4 to 6	Turn over after 1 minute	**4 Patties** (½-lb.)	4 to 5	Rotate dish ½ turn after 1½ minutes.
			8 Patties (1-lb.)	7½ to 8	Rotate dish ½ turn after 2 minutes.
Preformed Patties (12-oz. pkg.)	2 to 3	Turn over after 1 minute	**4 Patties Raw**	2½ to 3½	Rotate dish ½ turn after 1½ minutes.
			8 Patties Raw	4 to 5	Rotate dish ½ turn after 2 minutes.
Preformed Patties Brown 'n Serve (12-oz. pkg.)	2 to 3	Turn over after 1 minute.	**4 Patties Brown 'n Serve**	1 to 1½	No turns.
			8 Patties Brown 'n Serve	2¼ to 2½	Rotate dish ½ turn after 1½ minutes.
Link Sausage Raw (1-lb.)	3 to 4	Turn over after 1 minute	**4 Links**	2 to 3	No turns.
			7 to 8 Links	4 to 5	Rotate dish ½ turn after 2 minutes.
Link Sausage Brown 'n Serve (8-oz.)	3 to 4	Turn over after 1 minute	**4 Links**	1	No turns.
			6 Links	1½ to 2	Rotate dish ½ turn after 1 minute.
			10 Links	2 to 2½	Rotate dish ½ turn after 1 minute.

Add sauces and condiments, such as ketchup, mustard or relish after heating. Saucy spots absorb microwave energy and may toughen the bun.

Franks

Frankfurters are precooked so they only need heating. They react quickly to microwave energy and many beginners overheat them because they can't believe franks will be ready in such a short time.

If you are cooking franks in a main dish casserole, bury them under moist ingredients, such as beans or sauerkraut. If meat is on the bottom, the casserole won't need stirring.

Defrosting. For 1-lb. of franks, place unopened package in oven. **Microwave at Defrost 3 to 5 Minutes,** just until franks can be separated. For ½-lb., cut time in half.

Microwaving. Franks vary in size. Larger ones such as Polish or bratwurst, will take longer than times in chart below. For foot-long hot dogs add ¼ to ½ minute more time, and rotate them once or twice, because they tend to get overdone on the ends.

FRANKS MICROWAVING CHART

When microwaving on microwave ovenproof plate, cover with wax paper. When microwaving in bun, wrap in paper towel. Watch carefully. If ends appear dry, it means they are overdone.

POWER LEVEL: **High**

NO. OF FRANKS	TIME MINUTES	COMMENTS
2	1 to 2	Do not microwave more than 4 franks in buns at once.
4	3 to 4	
6 to 8	4 to 6	Add ½ cup water; rearrange after 2 minutes.
10 (1-lb. pkg.)	7 to 9	Add ¾ cup water; rearrange after 4 minutes.

HOW TO MICROWAVE FRANKS

Franks are prone to pop or explode. You can remedy this by pricking them with a fork, but diagonal slashes are especially attractive.

To Microwave franks on a paper or pottery plate, cover them with wax paper. Use a casserole and additional water to heat more than 6 franks.

To Heat franks right in the buns, place a napkin or paper towel under the bun to absorb moisture. A bun placed directly on a plate or the oven floor gets steamy underneath. To heat more than four, do them in successive batches.

CASSEROLE OF BEANS AND SAUSAGES

The French name for this type of casserole is Cassoulet.

POWER LEVEL: High TEMP:* 160°
APPROX. MICROWAVE TIME: 20 min.

1 lb. Polish sausage diagonally sliced in 1-in. pieces
1 pkg. (8-oz.) brown and serve sausages ..... In 2-qt. casserole place both kinds of sausages.

1 can (16-oz.) kidney beans, drained
1 can (15-oz.) Northern beans, drained
1 can (15-oz.) pinto beans, drained ..... Layer beans evenly over sausage.

1 can (8-oz.) tomato sauce
⅓ cup red cooking wine
2 tablespoons brown sugar
1 tablespoon prepared mustard
1 teaspoon salt
¼ teaspoon garlic powder
⅛ teaspoon pepper ..... In one of the empty cans or small bowl mix together tomato sauce, wine, brown sugar, mustard, salt, garlic powder and pepper. Pour over sausages and beans.

Insert temperature probe so tip rests on center bottom of dish. Cover tightly with plastic wrap, arranging loosely around probe to vent. Attach cable end at receptacle. **Microwave at High. Set Temp, Set 160°.**

When oven signals, stir casserole well and let stand 10 minutes before serving to blend flavors and thicken sauce.

Makes 6 to 8 servings

* On models not equipped with probe use minimum microwave time and check for doneness.

WIENER BEAN POT

POWER LEVEL: High
MICROWAVE TIME: 13 to 15 min., total

2 cans (1-lb. each) pork and beans
⅓ cup chopped onion
¼ cup ketchup
¼ cup water
2 tablespoons brown sugar
1 tablespoon prepared mustard
1 lb. wieners (8 to 10) cut in thirds ..... In 2-qt. casserole stir together beans, onion, ketchup, water, brown sugar and mustard. Add wieners, pushing pieces below surface of beans to prevent overcooking. Cover. **Microwave at High 13 to 15 Minutes,** stirring after 8 minutes, until hot.

Makes 6 to 8 servings

SAUSAGE AND SAUERKRAUT

POWER LEVEL: High
MICROWAVE TIME: 12 to 14 min., total

1 lb. franks (8 to 10) scored, or 1-lb. Polish sausage (Kielbasa) cut in ½-in. pieces
1 can (1-lb.) sauerkraut, rinsed and drained
2 tablespoons instant minced onion
1 teaspoon beef bouillon granules ..... In 2-qt. casserole place meat. Cover with sauerkraut mixed with onions and bouillon. Cover. **Microwave at High 12 to 14 Minutes,** rotating dish ½ turn after 6 minutes, until hot.

Makes 4 to 6 servings

BARBECUED FRANKS

POWER LEVEL: High
MICROWAVE TIME: 9 to 12 min., total

¾ cup ketchup
1 tablespoon Worcestershire sauce
¼ to ½ teaspoon chili powder
1 tablespoon sugar
½ teaspoon salt
Dash liquid pepper seasoning (tabasco)
½ cup water ..... In 2-qt. casserole mix together ketchup, Worcestershire sauce, chili powder, sugar, salt, liquid pepper seasoning and water.

1 lb. franks (8 to 10), scored ..... Place in sauce, pushing pieces below surface to prevent overcooking. Cover.

Microwave at High 9 to 12 Minutes, rearranging franks after 5 minutes. Serve on buns, if desired, with generous amount of sauce over each.

Makes 8 to 10 servings

TAVERN FRANKS

For fuller flavor, prick franks and marinate in beer 3 to 4 hours or overnight before cooking.

POWER LEVEL: High
MICROWAVE TIME: 7 to 9 min., total

1 lb. franks (8 to 10)
1 small onion, thinly sliced
1 can (12-oz.) beer (1½ cups) ..... In 2-qt. casserole place franks. Separate onion into rings and distribute over franks. Pour beer over all. Cover.

Microwave at High 7 to 9 Minutes, redistributing franks so bottom ones are on top after 4 minutes.

Makes 4 to 5 servings

Lamb & Veal

Lamb is naturally juicy and can be prepared in a variety of ways. In addition to the recipes given here, we suggest that you try some of our pork recipes with lamb or use one of the beef marinades, page 84.

Veal is dry because it has no fat marbling. Whether cooked conventionally or microwaved, chops and cutlets should be sliced thinly or pounded to tenderize them. Veal roasts may be microwaved on trivet in cooking dish at Medium with the temperature probe set to 155° (15 to 18 minutes per pound). Let roast stand about 15 minutes to complete cooking and slice thinly. Chunks and pieces of veal which need long slow cooking may be substituted in several of the stew and other main dish recipes.

HOW TO DEFROST CHOPS AND CUTLETS

POWER LEVEL: **Defrost**

4 to 8 Minutes Per Pound

1. Place plastic or paper wrapped package in oven. Microwave at Defrost ½ the minimum total time.
2. Turn package over and defrost second ½ of time.
3. Separate pieces with a table knife and let stand to complete defrosting, or microwave 1 to 2 minutes more.

HOW TO DEFROST ROASTS

POWER LEVEL: **Defrost**

10 to 12 Minutes Per Pound

1. If roast is wrapped in paper or plastic, place the unopened package in microwave oven. (Foil wrapping must be removed before microwaving.)
2. Defrost ½ of total time. Remove paper, place on trivet in dish.
3. Defrost last ½ of time.
4. Let stand 30 minutes before microwaving or conventional cooking.

NOTE: Feel roast for warm areas after each microwaving period. Cover these areas with foil (warmth indicates they have begun to cook).

HOW TO INSERT THE TEMPERATURE PROBE

Insert probe from the side of the roast into the meaty area so tip is in the center under the joint.

CRANBERRY-ORANGE RUBY SAUCE

This sauce complements Microwaved Lamb Roast.

POWER LEVEL: High
MICROWAVE TIME: 4 to 6 min., total

1 can (11-oz.) mandarin oranges
1 can (16-oz.) cranberry sauce

Drain oranges, saving juice. In 1-qt. measuring cup stir together cranberry sauce and 2 tablespoons liquid saved from oranges.

Microwave at High 3 to 4 Minutes, stirring after 1½ minutes.

Stir in drained oranges. **Microwave at High 1 to 2 Minutes** more, until hot and well blended.

Makes about 2½ cups

HOW TO MICROWAVE LAMB ROASTS

POWER LEVEL: **Medium**

9 to 11 Minutes Per Pound for Medium
11 to 13 Minutes Per Pound for Well Done

Microwaving by Temperature: If desired, brush roast with diluted brown bouquet sauce. Place roast fat side up on trivet in 13×9×2-in. dish. Insert temperature probe as directed below. Cover with wax paper. **Microwave at Medium. Set Temp, Set 130°** for medium and **180°** for well done. When oven signals, let stand 10 minutes before carving.

Microwaving by Time: Use minutes per pound, above. When oven signals, remove roast and insert conventional meat thermometer into roast in same location described for temperature probe. Check temperature after about 2 minutes; it should read 130° for medium and 180° for well done. If not, return to microwave oven a few minutes, then check again.

NOTE: Do not place conventional metal meat thermometer in microwave oven.

MANDARIN LAMB CHOPS

POWER LEVEL: Medium High
MICROWAVE TIME: 24 to 27 min., total

4 loin lamb chops, 1 to 1½-in. thick (1½ to 2-lb.) . . In 8-in. square dish arrange chops so thickest meaty areas are to edges. Cover with wax paper. **Microwave at Medium High 12 Minutes.** Drain off fat and turn chops over.

1 can (11-oz.) mandarin oranges, save syrup
¼ cup sugar
½ cup chopped chutney
2 tablespoons lemon juice . . Arrange orange segments over top. Mix ⅓ cup orange syrup with sugar, chutney and lemon juice. Spoon over chops. Recover with wax paper. **Microwave at Medium High 10 to 12 Minutes,** until tender. Remove chops to serving platter.

1 tablespoon cornstarch
2 tablespoons mandarin orange syrup . . . . Mix cornstarch with syrup. Stir into juices in dish. **Microwave at Medium High 2 to 3 Minutes,** stirring once, until thick. Spoon over chops.

Makes 4 servings

VEAL PARMIGIANA

For a meatier entree, substitute veal cutlets for chops.

POWER LEVEL: Medium High
MICROWAVE TIME: 25 to 28 min., total

6 small veal loin chops, ¾-in. thick
1 egg, beaten
1 cup buttery flavored cracker crumbs
1 teaspoon salt
¼ teaspoon pepper
½ cup grated Parmesan cheese . . Coat chops with beaten egg, then with mixture of crumbs, salt, pepper and cheese. In 12×8×2-in. dish, arrange chops so thickest meaty areas are close to edges and "tails" are in center. Cover with wax paper. **Microwave at Medium High 10 Minutes.**

1 cup (4-oz.) shredded Mozzarella or pizza cheese
2 cans (8-oz. each) tomato sauce
1 teaspoon crushed oregano
¼ cup grated Parmesan cheese . . . Turn chops over. Distribute cheese over chops, then mixture of tomato sauce and oregano. Top with Parmesan. Cover. **Microwave at Medium High 15 to 18 Minutes** more, until tender. Let stand, covered, 10 minutes before serving.

Makes 6 servings

BROWN VEAL ROLL UPS

An attractive main dish to serve with rice, mixed green salad and a light dessert, such as sherbet.

POWER LEVEL: High
MICROWAVE TIME: 15½ to 17½ min., total

4 boneless veal cutlets (4-oz. each)
1 can (4½-oz.) deviled ham
1 tablespoon instant minced onion . . Pound cutlets thin, using a wooden mallet or foil covered brick. Mix ham with minced onion and spread over cutlets, just to edge.

1 pkg. (3-oz.) cream cheese . . . . . . Slice cream cheese into 12 narrow strips. Place 3 strips on each cutlet. Roll up firmly. Fasten each roll with a toothpick.

2 tablespoons butter
½ cup fine dry bread crumbs . . . . . Place butter in small glass bowl. **Microwave at High ½ Minute,** until melted. Dip veal rolls in butter, then coat with crumbs. Arrange in 10×6×2-in. dish.

¾ cup water
1 pkg. (1½-oz.) dry mushroom gravy mix
¼ cup cooking sherry or water . . . . In 1-pt. glass measure, combine water, gravy mix and sherry. **Microwave at High 2 Minutes,** stirring after 1 minute. Pour over veal rolls.

Cover with plastic wrap turning back one corner to vent. **Microwave at High 13 to 15 Minutes,** rotating dish ½ turn every 5 minutes, until meat is tender and filling is set.

Makes 4 veal rolls

MICROWAVING LAMB CHOPS IN BROWN 'N SEAR DISH OR BROWNING GRIDDLE

Preheat empty dish or griddle at High. Add chops, cover if Brown 'N Sear Dish is used, and cook first side. Turn chops over, recover dish, cook second side.

POWER LEVEL: **High**

NO. OF CHOPS	PREHEAT MINUTES	1st SIDE MINUTES	2nd SIDE MINUTES
2	5 to 6	3	3 to 4
4	6 to 8	3 to 4	4 to 5
6 (griddle)	8	7 to 8	8 to 9

Poultry

Chicken is one of America's most popular foods and microwaving chicken is one of the best uses of your microwave oven. Chicken microwaves well at High Power and stays juicy and tender. However, juiciness prevents browning because chicken crisps and browns only when the skin dries out enough to change color.

Whole chickens and turkeys up to 12 pounds may be microwaved at Medium High with a minimum of attention. Use the temperature probe, if you have one, for completely carefree microwaving. Standing time is important, because it allows the interior to finish cooking without toughening the delicate breast meat. Directions and recipes for microwaving Cornish hen and duck provide additional variety for this poultry section.

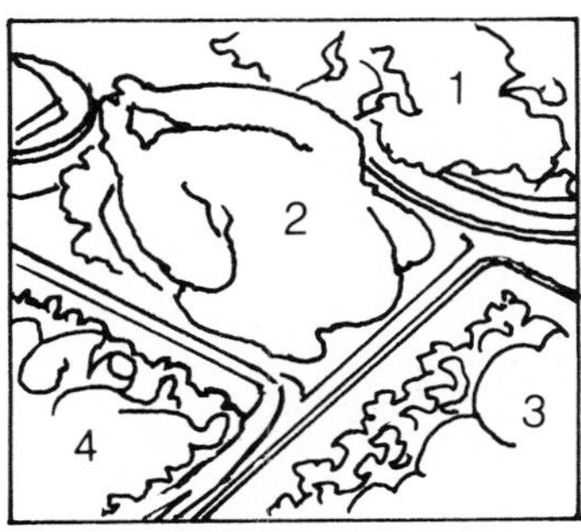

1. Crumb Coated Chicken, page 122
2. Barbecued Stuffed Chicken, page 127
3. Saucy Turkey and Broccoli, page 136
4. Cornish Hen Halves, page 130

Chicken Defrosting

MICROLESSON

Chicken is frozen in many forms, whole or cut-up into halves, quarters or one-of-a-kind pieces, such as breasts or drum sticks. These timings are for one whole or cut-up broiler-fryer, weighing 2½ to 3½ pounds. Several cut-up chickens or a roasting chicken will take longer. Follow directions for turkey when defrosting a large roasting chicken.

HOW TO DEFROST A CUT-UP CHICKEN

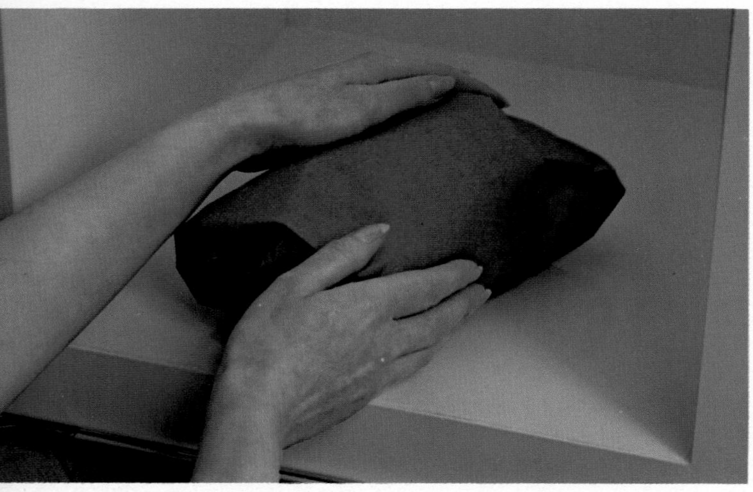

Place wrapped chicken, packaged in paper or plastic, directly on the oven shelf. If chicken is wrapped in foil, unwrap it and place it in a baking dish. Microwave at Defrost for ½ the time.

Unwrap chicken pieces and turn the block over into a baking dish. Defrost for second ½ of time, or until pieces can be separated.

HOW TO DEFROST A WHOLE CHICKEN

Whole chickens are usually frozen in a plastic bag. Remove twist tie, place package on the oven shelf and microwave at Defrost ½ the time. Unwrap chicken and turn it over into cooking dish.

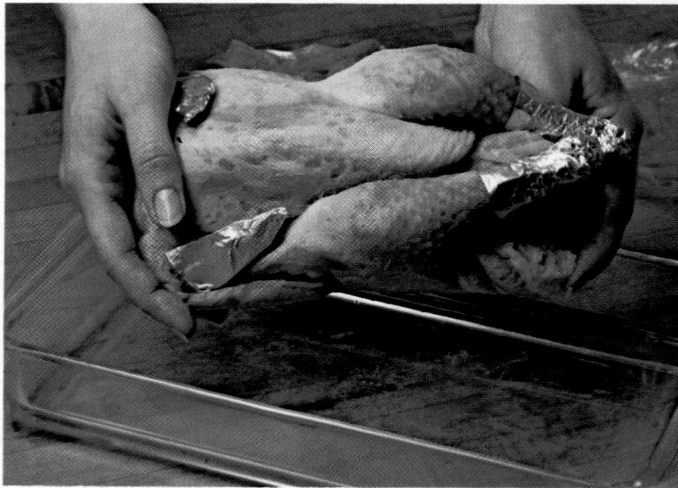

Shield wing tips, tail, ends of legs and any other areas which feel warm or have begun to change color. Microwave for second ½ of time.

With frozen packages of one-of-a-kind pieces, you will need to use your judgement. Bony pieces, such as wings, will take less time than meaty pieces, such as thighs. The defrosting steps also apply to other poultry, such as ducks or cornish game hens. Two cornish hens take about the same amount of time as one chicken.

DEFROST CHART
POWER LEVEL: **Defrost**

ITEM	TIME/MINUTES
Broiler-fryer, cut up (2½ to 3½-lb.)	14 to 16
Broiler-fryer, whole (2½ to 3½-lb.)	18 to 22

Separate chicken pieces and let them stand until defrosted, or if faster defrosting is desired, arrange them in the cooking dish, medium parts to the outside, and microwave 1 to 2 minutes more.

Defrosted chicken will be soft to the touch, very moist and cold, but not frosty. There may be a very small amount of running juice.

Giblets can be loosened but not removed. Chicken should be soft and cool to the touch, with a glistening surface.

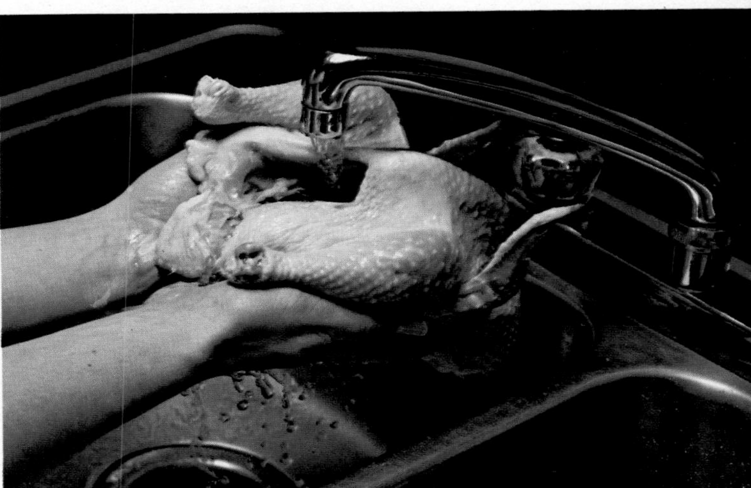

Run Cold Water inside chicken until giblets can be freed. Interior will be cold but not icy.

Chicken Pieces

Chicken is naturally an excellent food for microwaving and illustrates all the advantages of microwave cooking. It is tender, flavorful and juicy. It microwaves rapidly, and takes very little attention during cooking. Don't overcook chicken; it really will be done in the very short cooking periods given in the chart. Because they cook so quickly, chicken pieces do not get brown and crisp. Unless chicken is cooked in a sauce, it will be more attractive if brushed with a browning agent, coated with crumbs, or cooked in a Brown 'N Sear Dish. Plain microwaved chicken is perfect for salads and casseroles.

If you are concerned about calories or cholesterol, skin chicken before cooking, since most of the fat is located directly below the skin. If cooked in a sauce, the flavor will be absorbed by the chicken instead of the skin. Skinned chicken pieces may also be brushed with a browning agent or coated with crumbs, but cannot be cooked in the Brown 'N Sear Dish.

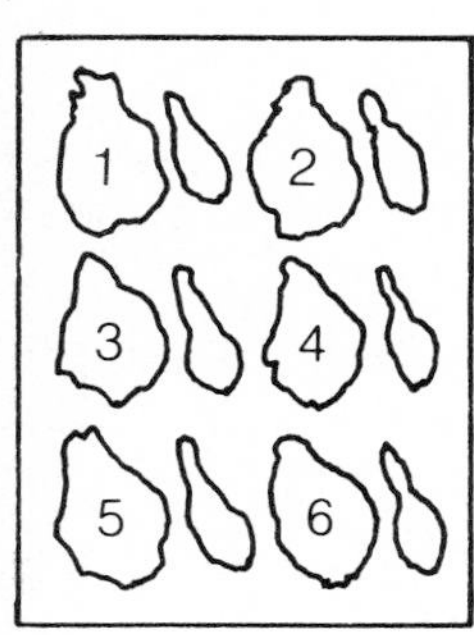

1. Plain microwaved chicken
2. Prepared coating mix
3. Brushed with melted butter, sprinkled with paprika
4. Well seasoned flour in Brown 'N Sear Dish
5. Crushed barbecue potato chips
6. Equal parts brown bouquet sauce and water

HOW TO MICROWAVE CHICKEN PIECES

Use utensils suitable for microwave oven. For a few pieces, use a paper plate or dinner plate. For larger amounts use a suitable size utility dish, such as an 8-in. square, 12×8×2-in., or 13×9×2-in. dish.

Brush chicken pieces with browning agent or sauce before cooking, if desired. Arrange meatiest area toward outside edge of dish.

Cover with wax paper. Microwave according to times given in chart, rotating dish ½ turn where noted. Times given below are for legs, thighs and breasts.

Let stand, covered, about 5 minutes before serving.

POWER LEVEL: **High**

AMOUNT	TIME MINUTES	½ TURN
1 piece	2 to 4	No
2 pieces	4 to 6	No
3 pieces	5 to 7	No
4 pieces	6½ to 10	After 4 minutes
5 pieces	7½ to 12	After 4 minutes
6 pieces	8 to 14	After 5 minutes
1 chicken, 2½ to 3½-lbs., cut up	18 to 22	After 10 minutes

TIPS FOR SUCCESSFUL MICROWAVING

Arrange chicken in baking dish so that the meatiest portions are to the outside of the dish. Brush with browning agent, if desired, or add sauce ingredients.

Cover with wax paper during microwaving. For dryer chicken, uncover during the second ½ of cooking time. For chicken baked in sauce, remove paper after cooking and let stand 5 minutes to glaze and blend flavors.

Test for doneness. Rotate dish ½ turn after ½ the cooking time when microwaving 4 or more pieces. Chicken should be fork tender, with no pinkness next to the bone.

CRUMB-COATED CHICKEN

This has the same appearance and taste as oven fried.

POWER LEVEL: High
MICROWAVE TIME: 18 to 22 min., total

2 eggs
⅓ cup melted butter
1 teaspoon salt
In small bowl beat together eggs, butter and salt.

1½ cups buttery flavored cracker crumbs (about 50)
1 chicken, 2½ to 3½-lb., cut up, skin removed
In shallow dish place crumbs. Coat chicken with crumbs, then egg mixture and crumbs again. In 12×8×2-in. dish arrange chicken with meatiest pieces to outside edges of dish. Cover with wax paper. **Microwave at High 18 to 22 Minutes,** rotating dish ½ turn after 10 minutes.

Makes about 4 servings

SAVORY ONION CHICKEN

POWER LEVEL: High
MICROWAVE TIME: 18 to 22 min., total

1 chicken, 2½ to 3½-lb., cut up
⅓ cup butter, melted
1 pkg. (½ of 2¾-oz. box) dry onion soup mix
Dip chicken in butter. Coat with dry soup mix and arrange in 12×8×2-in. dish, skin side up, with thick meaty pieces to the outside edges of dish. Cover with wax paper. **Microwave at High 18 to 22 Minutes,** until meat is tender. Let stand 5 minutes before serving.

Makes about 4 servings

CHICKEN PARMESAN

Substitute ½ cup bread or corn flake crumbs mixed with ¼ cup grated Parmesan cheese for dry onion soup mix. Sprinkle with paprika before microwaving.

CRUNCHY COATED CHICKEN

Substitute ¾ cup finely crushed cheese cracker crumbs or potato chips (plain or barbecued) for dry onion soup mix.

CHICKEN 'N' DRESSING

For richer flavor, use ¼ cup melted butter for part of chicken broth.

POWER LEVEL: High
MICROWAVE TIME: 18 to 22 min., total

1 pkg. (8-oz.) herb seasoned stuffing mix
½ cup chopped celery
¼ cup minced onion
2 tablespoons chopped pimiento
1 egg
1¾ to 2 cups chicken broth
In 12×8×2-in. dish toss together stuffing mix, celery, onion, pimiento, egg and broth.

1 chicken, 2½ to 3½-lb., cut up
¼ cup butter, melted
Salt
Paprika
Dip chicken pieces into melted butter, place on top of dressing with meaty pieces to the outside edges of dish. Sprinkle with salt and paprika. Cover with wax paper.

Microwave at High 18 to 22 Minutes, rotating dish ½ turn after 10 minutes. Let stand about 5 minutes before serving.

Makes about 4 servings

YOUR FAVORITE SAUCY CHICKEN

For easy chicken creole, use condensed chicken gumbo soup. For "smothered" type chicken, sprinkle with 1 teaspoon instant minced onion, then cover with condensed cream of chicken soup (or use canned chicken gravy). Use other favorite canned soup or ready-to-use canned sauce, or barbecue sauce, if desired.

POWER LEVEL: High
MICROWAVE TIME: 18 to 22 min., total

1 chicken, 2½ to 3½-lb., cut up
In 12×8×2-in. dish arrange chicken skin side up with meatiest pieces to the outside edges of dish.

½ teaspoon salt
1 can (about 10-oz.) condensed soup
Sprinkle chicken with salt. Pour soup over chicken. Cover with wax paper.

Microwave at High 18 to 22 Minutes, rotating dish ½ turn after 10 minutes. Let stand 5 minutes before serving.

Makes about 4 servings

NOT THE SAME OLD CHICKEN

This golden glazed chicken is named for the comments it elicits. It really does taste special.

POWER LEVEL: High
MICROWAVE TIME: 18 to 22 min., total

1 chicken, 2½ to 3½-lb., cut up . . In 12×8×2-in. dish arrange chicken with thickest, meaty pieces to outside edges of dish.

¼ cup mayonnaise
1 pkg. (½ of 2¾-oz. box) dry onion soup mix
½ cup bottled Russian dressing
1 cup apricot-pineapple preserves . . . . . . In small bowl stir together mayonnaise, onion soup mix, dressing and preserves. Spread over chicken, coating each piece. Cover with wax paper.

Microwave at High 18 to 22 Minutes, rotating dish ½ turn after 10 minutes. Allow to stand 5 to 10 minutes before serving, so chicken absorbs flavor of sauce. Serve with rice, if desired.

Makes about 4 servings

ITALIAN CHICKEN

Tastes like pizza and chicken together. Our microwave oven owners have liked this for years.

POWER LEVEL: High
MICROWAVE TIME: 22 to 26 min., total

1 chicken, 2½ to 3½-lb., cut up . . Remove skin from chicken pieces and arrange in lightly greased 12×8×2-in. dish with meatiest pieces to the outside edge of dish.

1 can (10-oz.) condensed tomato soup
1 can (6-oz.) tomato paste
¼ teaspoon onion salt
¼ teaspoon garlic salt
¼ teaspoon oregano
1 can (4-oz.) mushroom pieces, drained . . . . . . In mixing bowl stir together tomato soup, tomato paste, onion salt, garlic salt, oregano and mushrooms. Generously spoon sauce over chicken. **Microwave at High 20 to 22 Minutes,** rotating dish ½ turn after 10 minutes.

2 cups (8-oz.) shredded Mozzarella cheese
¼ cup grated Parmesan cheese . . Sprinkle cheese over chicken. **Microwave at High 2 to 4 Minutes,** until cheese is melted. Let stand about 5 minutes before serving.

Makes about 4 servings

ORIENTAL CHICKEN

An interesting brown raisin wine sauce gives this dish a sweet but savory flavor.

POWER LEVEL: High
MICROWAVE TIME: 11 to 13 min., total

2 chicken breasts split, skinned and boned . . Pierce chicken breasts with cooking fork. Arrange in 3-qt. casserole.

1 tablespoon cornstarch
2 tablespoons brown sugar
¼ teaspoon oregano
1 clove garlic, crushed
2 tablespoons cooking oil
¼ cup soy sauce
¾ cup rose wine
⅓ cup seedless raisins . . . . . . In small bowl combine cornstarch, brown sugar, oregano, garlic, oil, soy sauce, wine and raisins. Pour over chicken. Cover. **Microwave at High 11 to 13 Minutes,** rotating dish ½ turn after 6 minutes. Serve with rice if desired.

Makes 4 servings

FIESTA CHICKEN KIEV

This recipe won $5,000 in a recipe contest exclusively for microwave cooking. Serve Kiev with taco sauce, garnish with lettuce, tomatoes and ripe olives.

POWER LEVEL: High
MICROWAVE TIME: 10 to 12 min., total

4 whole chicken breasts, split, skinned and boned . . . . . . Pound each raw chicken piece with mallet or foil covered brick to flatten.

3 tablespoons butter
3 tablespoons old English-style sharp cheese spread
2 teaspoons instant minced onion
1 teaspoon salt
1 teaspoon monosodium glutamate (accent)
2 tablespoons chopped green chilies . . . In small bowl beat together butter and cheese spread until well blended. Mix in onion, salt, monosodium glutamate and chilies. Place a portion of mixture at one end of each chicken piece, dividing evenly. Roll up each piece, tucking in ends to completely enclose filling. Fasten rolls with toothpicks.

¼ cup butter, melted
1 cup crushed cheddar cheese crackers
1½ tablespoons taco seasoning mix . . . Dip each roll in melted butter to cover, then coat with mixture of crackers and taco seasoning mix. Arrange rolls in 12×8×2-in. dish. Cover with wax paper. **Microwave at High 10 to 12 Minutes,** rotating dish ½ turn after 5 minutes, until done. Let stand about 5 minutes before serving.

Makes 8 servings

HOW TO MICROWAVE A STEWING CHICKEN

Combine in 4-qt. casserole 1 cut up stewing chicken (4 to 5-lb.), 5 cups hot tap water, 1 onion, 1 carrot and 1 celery stem, all coarsely cut up. Add 4 peppercorns, 2 cloves and cover.

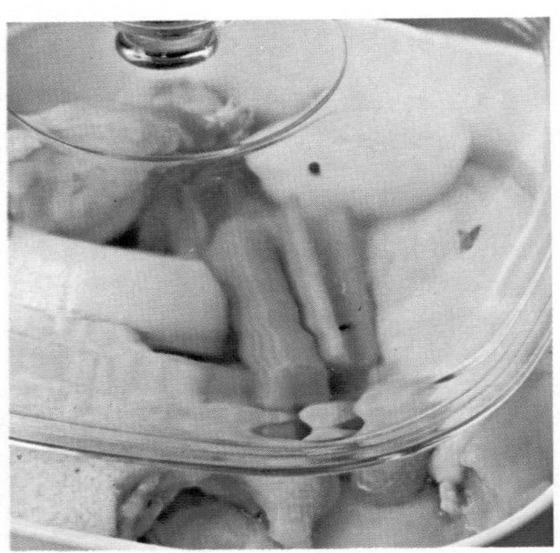

Microwave at High 15 Minutes. Rearrange chicken, bringing bottom pieces to the top. Cover. **Microwave at Medium 2 to 2¼ Hours,** rearranging chicken after 1 hour.

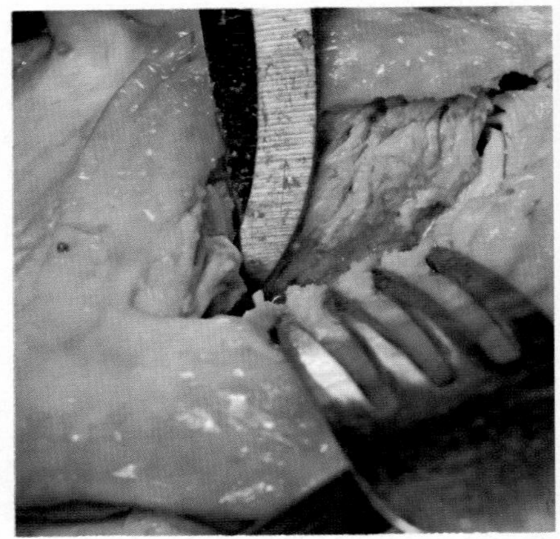

Test for doneness. Chicken should be fork tender. For maximum tenderness, let chicken cool in its broth. Meat will then be easily removed from the bones. To stew a broiler-fryer, microwave 1 to 1½ hours.

CHICKEN A LA KING

The old favorite, creamed chicken, dressed up with colorful pimiento, green pepper and flavorful mushrooms. Serve over toast or in a pastry shell.

POWER LEVEL: High and Medium High
MICROWAVE TIME: 16 to 21 min., total

⅓ cup butter **½ cup unsifted all-purpose flour** **2 cups dairy half & half** **1 cup chicken broth**	In 2-qt. casserole place butter. **Microwave at High 1 Minute,** until melted. Blend in flour. Gradually stir in half & half and broth; mix well. **Microwave at High 8 to 10 Minutes,** stirring with whisk after 4 minutes, until thickened and smooth. Stir well again.
2 cups cubed, cooked chicken **1 jar (4-oz.) sliced pimiento** **1 can (4-oz.) sliced mushrooms, undrained** **½ cup diced green pepper** **1 teaspoon salt** **¼ teaspoon pepper**	Mix in chicken, pimiento, mushrooms, green pepper, salt and pepper. Cover. **Microwave at Medium High 7 to 10 Minutes,** stirring after 5 minutes, until hot. Let stand 5 to 10 minutes before serving, to blend flavors.

Makes 4 servings

MEXICAN CHICKEN CASSEROLE

POWER LEVEL: High TEMP:* 155°
APPROX. MICROWAVE TIME: 15 min.

1 can (10½-oz.) condensed cream of chicken soup **2 tablespoons green chilies, diced** **¼ teaspoon instant minced onion** **½ cup water**	In small mixing bowl place soup, chilies, onion and water. Stir until well blended.
2 large, firm, ripe tomatoes	Slice tomatoes in ½-in. slices.
1 pkg. (6-oz.) corn chips **2 cups diced, cooked chicken, or 2 cans (5-oz. each) boned chicken, diced** **1 cup (4-oz.) shredded cheddar cheese**	In 2-qt. casserole layer ½ of corn chips. Top with 1 cup chicken, then ½ of tomato slices. Pour ½ of soup mixture over chicken; sprinkle with ¾ of cheese, reserving rest for topping after cooking. Repeat layers.

Insert temperature probe so tip is in center of casserole. Attach cable end at receptacle. **Microwave at High. Set Temp, Set 155°.** When oven signals, sprinkle with reserved cheese and let stand 5 minutes before serving.

Makes 6 to 8 servings

* On models not equipped with probe use minimum microwave time and check for doneness.

CHICKEN AND DUMPLINGS

POWER LEVEL: Medium High
MICROWAVE TIME: 30 to 41 min., total

1 chicken, 2½ to 3½-lb., cut up **2 cups hot tap water** **½ cup chopped onion** **½ cup chopped celery** **4 medium carrots, sliced** **2 teaspoons salt** **½ teaspoon pepper**	In 3-qt. casserole place chicken, water, onion, celery, carrots, salt and pepper. Cover. **Microwave at Medium High 15 Minutes.**
¼ cup cornstarch **½ cup cold water**	In small bowl stir together cornstarch and water. Stir into chicken mixture, blending well. Cover. **Microwave at Medium High 10 to 20 Minutes,** until chicken is tender. Spoon Dumplings (below) around edge of dish. **Microwave at Medium High 5 to 6 Minutes,** covered, until puffed and not doughy.

Makes 4 servings

Dumplings: In mixing bowl stir together 1½ cups unsifted all-purpose flour, 1 tablespoon dried parsley flakes, 2 teaspoons baking powder and ½ teaspoon salt. Add ⅔ cup milk, 1 beaten egg and 2 tablespoons cooking oil. Stir with table fork only until flour is moistened.

CHICKEN ENCHILADA CASSEROLE

POWER LEVEL: High
MICROWAVE TIME: 11 to 13 min., total

2½ cups diced, cooked chicken **1 can (15-oz.) evaporated milk** **1 can (10-oz.) condensed cream of chicken soup** **1 pkg. (1¼-oz.) taco seasoning mix** **1 medium onion, chopped** **½ cup chopped celery** **1 can (4-oz.) chopped green chilies, drained** **6 corn tortillas, torn into 1-in. pieces** **¾ cup diced cheddar or longhorn cheese**	In 2-qt. casserole combine chicken, evaporated milk, soup, taco mix, onion, celery, chilies, tortillas and cheese. **Microwave at High 11 to 13 Minutes,** rotating dish ½ turn after 5 minutes.

Makes 4 to 6 servings

BRUNSWICK STEW

If a more highly seasoned stew is desired add about 1 teaspoon Worcestershire sauce and 3 to 5 drops hot pepper (tabasco) sauce.

POWER LEVEL: Medium High and High
MICROWAVE TIME: 50 to 63 min., total

1 chicken, 2½ to 3½-lb., cut up **2 cups water**	In 3-qt. casserole place chicken pieces and water. Cover. **Microwave at Medium High 25 to 30 Minutes,** depending on weight of chicken, until tender. Remove meat from bones discarding skin. Cut meat into pieces and return to broth in casserole.
2 cups diced raw potatoes (2 medium) **½ cup sliced onion (1 small)** **2 teaspoons salt** **¼ teaspoon pepper**	Add potatoes, onion, salt and pepper to casserole. **Microwave at Medium High 15 to 18 Minutes,** stirring after 8 minutes.
½ cup unsifted all-purpose flour **1 can (12-oz.) whole kernel corn, undrained** **1 pkg. (10-oz.) frozen baby lima beans, defrosted** **1 can (16-oz.) tomatoes, drained**	Into small bowl drain liquid from corn and stir in flour, mixing well. Blend into hot mixture. Add corn, lima beans and tomatoes. **Microwave at High 10 to 15 Minutes,** stirring after 5 minutes, until vegetables are hot and sauce is thickened. Let stand 5 to 10 minutes before serving, to blend flavors.

Makes about 8 servings

NOTE: For stronger tomato flavor, use juice from tomatoes for part of water in which chicken is cooked.

TIP: Microwave stewing chicken and prepare any of these casseroles early in the day. Their flavor mellows while standing. Refrigerate them and reheat just before serving.

These saucy dishes make excellent foods for the freezer. Package single servings in cooking pouches and heat as you would frozen convenience entrees.

Whole Chicken

MICROLESSON

When microwaving a whole chicken, be sure to select a young, plump tender bird. The skin should be smooth and have a pale, creamy color tinged with pink. If you are in doubt, choose a broiler-fryer. Avoid chickens with thick, bumpy skin and large amounts of bright yellow fat.

A whole chicken may be microwaved without special attention during cooking time by placing it in a cooking bag. The meat will be tender and moist.

If you do not care to use a cooking bag, or if you prefer a drier surface, microwave chicken covered with wax paper. Turn the chicken over after ½ the time.

Microwaving chicken at Medium High rather than High eliminates excessive handling and foil for shielding.

HOW TO MICROWAVE WHOLE CHICKEN IN A COOKING BAG

POWER LEVEL: **Medium High** **9 to 10 Minutes Per Pound**

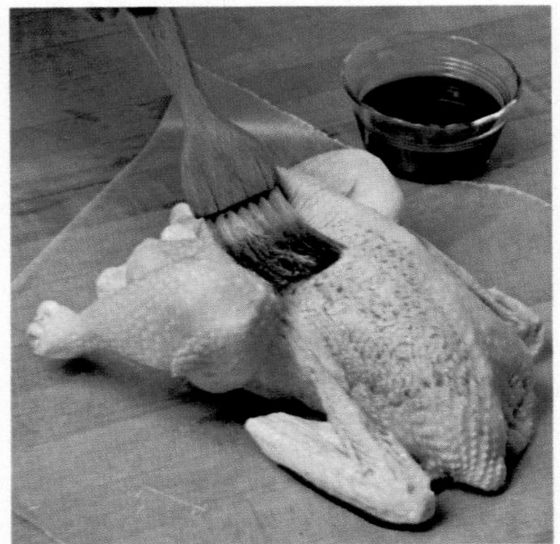

Brush chicken with a mixture of 1 tablespoon bottled brown bouquet sauce and 1 tablespoon melted butter. Cut a ½-in. strip from open end of an oven cooking bag.

Place chicken in bag on a microwave ovenproof platter or baking dish. Add ⅓ cup water, chicken broth or wine. Tie end of bag with plastic strip. Slash bag next to closure.

Insert temperature probe, if you are using it, through the bag into meatiest part of inner thigh, from below the end of and parallel to the leg. Microwave at Medium High to an internal temperature of 190°.

HOW TO MICROWAVE WHOLE CHICKEN WITHOUT A COOKING BAG

Brush chicken with a mixture of 1 tablespoon bottled brown bouquet sauce and 1 tablespoon melted butter. Place breast side down on trivet in cooking dish and cover with wax paper. Microwave at Medium High for ½ the minimum time.

Turn chicken breast side up. Recover with wax paper. Microwave for second ½ of time.

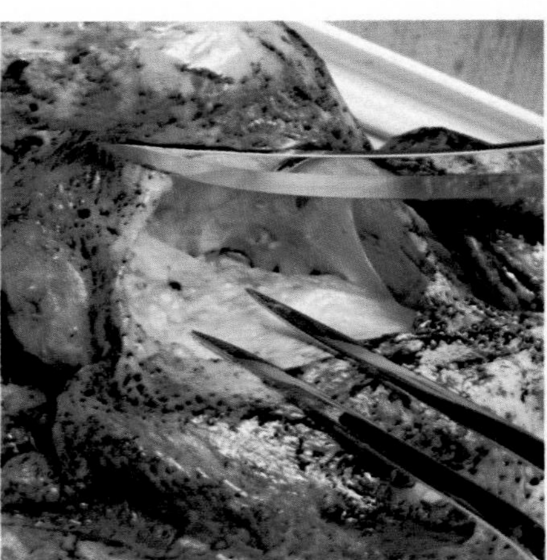

Test for doneness by cutting skin between inner thigh and breast. Meat should show no trace of pink, and juices should run clear.

BARBECUED STUFFED CHICKEN

We have chosen to cook this recipe by time, instead of by temperature, because of the barbecue sauce coating. The time method uses a loose covering of wax paper which allows steam to escape away from the surface of the bird. As the skin cooks, the barbecue sauce dries to form a beautiful showy glaze.

This stuffing makes delicious use of stale bread. Or, for Southern style, try the cornbread variation. Stuffings made from top of range stuffing mix or dried herb seasoned stuffing mix may also be used.

POWER LEVEL: Medium High
MICROWAVE TIME: 30 to 35 min., total

4 cups day-old ½-in. bread cubes or crumbled cornbread
¼ cup minced onion
½ cup minced celery
1 teaspoon salt
1 teaspoon poultry seasoning
¼ teaspoon pepper
⅓ cup melted butter
⅔ cup chicken broth

In large bowl toss together bread, onion, celery, salt, poultry seasoning, pepper, butter and chicken broth to make stuffing.

1 whole broiler-fryer, about 3-lb.
Bottled barbecue sauce

Fill body cavity of chicken with stuffing. Tie wings flat to body with string around chicken; tie legs together. Brush all areas with barbecue sauce.

On trivet in 12×8×2-in. dish place chicken with breast side down. Cover with wax paper. **Microwave at Medium High 30 to 35 Minutes,** turning chicken breast side up and brushing with barbecue sauce after 15 minutes. Chicken is done when no trace of pink shows in meat when cut is made between inner thigh and breast. Let chicken stand 10 minutes before serving.

Makes 2 to 4 servings

TIP: Serve plain microwaved whole chicken with Cranberry Sauce, page 137, chutney, pepper relish or Apple Cider Sauce (below).

APPLE CIDER SAUCE

Good with ham or chicken.

POWER LEVEL: High
MICROWAVE TIME: 5 to 7 min., total

2 cups apple cider
⅓ cup cornstarch
½ cup seedless raisins
1 tablespoon lemon juice

In 1-qt. measuring cup measure cider. Stir in cornstarch until thoroughly mixed. Add raisins and lemon juice. **Microwave at High 5 to 7 Minutes,** stirring every 1½ minutes, until clear and thickened.

Makes about 2¼ cups

Chicken Teriyaki

CHICKEN TERIYAKI

POWER LEVEL: Medium High and High TEMP:* 190°
APPROX. MICROWAVE TIME: 24 to 30 min.

¼ cup soy sauce
⅓ cup honey
⅓ cup sherry

In small cooking bag, mix soy sauce, honey and sherry.

1 whole broiler-fryer, about 3-lb.

Add chicken to bag and tie open end securely with plastic strip cut from open end of bag.

Turn chicken on its side and place in 12×8×2-in. dish. Marinate in refrigerator 1 to 2 hours, turning chicken over after ½ of time. To microwave, place bird breast side up in dish. Slash bag near closure. Insert temperature probe as shown at left. **Microwave at Medium High. Set Temp, Set 190°.** When oven signals, remove chicken. Prepare Teriyaki Sauce (below) and finish chicken as described in sauce recipe.

Makes about 4 servings

* On models not equipped with probe use minimum microwave time and check for doneness.

Teriyaki Sauce: In 1-pt. glass measuring cup stir together 1 tablespoon water and 2 tablespoons cornstarch. Cut off one corner of cooking bag with scissors and drain juices into cup. **Microwave at High 2 to 3 Minutes,** until thick and clear, stirring after 1 minute. After 10 minutes, remove chicken from bag to serving platter. Pour sauce over chicken just before serving.

Chicken Liver Pate

Chicken Livers & Giblets

Chicken livers may be sauteed in the Brown 'N Sear Dish, or microwaved in liquid at Medium before they are used in other dishes.

Prick giblets with a fork before microwaving. As with conventional cooking, giblets tend to pop, but the effect is more noticeable when they are microwaved.

Poultry Giblet Gravy may be located on page 172.

SAUTEED CHICKEN LIVERS

POWER LEVEL: High
MICROWAVE TIME: 8 to 10 min., total

1 tablespoon butter
½ lb. chicken livers

Preheat Brown 'N Sear Dish (uncovered), or griddle. **Microwave at High 3 to 4 Minutes.** Add butter, then livers. **Microwave at High 5 to 6 Minutes,** turning over after 3 minutes, until crisp and tender.

Makes 2 servings

CHICKEN LIVER PATE

Finely chopped pieces of onion add nice texture to this creamy spread. Garnish with sieved hard-poached egg, ripe olives and additional chopped onion. Serve with crackers and, if desired, butter to spread over crackers before adding the pate.

POWER LEVEL: Medium
MICROWAVE TIME: 18 to 22 min., total

1 lb. chicken livers
1 cup water

In 2-qt. casserole place livers. Prick each liver with fork. Add water. Cover. **Microwave at Medium 18 to 22 Minutes,** stirring after 10 minutes, until tender. Drain livers, place in container of electric blender. Whir until evenly blended.

⅓ cup soft butter
1 tablespoon finely chopped onion
1 tablespoon lemon juice
1 tablespoon brandy
½ teaspoon salt
½ teaspoon dry mustard
¼ teaspoon thyme
3 to 4 drops liquid pepper seasoning

In small mixing bowl stir together butter, onion, juice, brandy, salt, mustard, thyme and pepper seasoning, to blend. Mix in livers well. Pack into well greased 1½ to 2 cup mold. Chill thoroughly, then turn out onto serving plate. Garnish and serve with crackers.

Makes about 1½ cups

Poultry Convenience Foods

Canned convenience foods, or foods frozen in metal trays, should be removed from their containers to suitable microwave plates or casseroles. Small boil-in-bag pouches (about 5 to 10-oz.) can be placed directly in the oven. Slit or pierce the top of the pouch before microwaving and open carefully after heating to avoid burns from steam. Large boil-in-bags may be placed in a serving dish. When contents are partially defrosted, open the bag, slide food into the dish and stir before continuing to microwave.

Chicken Gravy and Main Dishes such as barbecue chicken, chicken a la king, chicken and dumplings, creamed chicken, croquettes, escalloped chicken with noodles, fried chicken, pieces or slices in gravy, stew and turkey tetrazzini may be microwaved according to chart below.

POWER LEVEL: **High**

CANNED AMOUNT	TIME MINUTES	COMMENTS
7½ to 10½-oz.	2 to 4	Cover. Stir after 2 minutes and before serving, or use temperature probe set for 150°.
14 to 24-oz.	4 to 6	Cover. Stir after 2 minutes and before serving, or use temperature probe set for 150°.

FROZEN AMOUNT	TIME MINUTES	COMMENTS
5 to 6½-oz. pouch	3 to 4	Slit pouch before microwaving.
12-oz.	7 to 9	Cover. Stir after 6 minutes.
16 to 17-oz.	11 to 14	Cover. Stir or turn over after 8 minutes.
Chicken Croquettes (12-oz. pkg.)	4 to 6	Pierce sauce pouch with fork. Place with food on plate. Cover with wax paper. Rotate dish ½ turn after 2 minutes.
Fried Chicken 2 pieces	2 to 4	Follow procedure below. Some brands of frozen fried chicken are not fully cooked. If label does not state "fully cooked", check for doneness.
Fried Chicken 1 lb., 6 pieces	6 to 7	
Fried Chicken 2 lb., 10 pieces	8 to 10	

HOW TO MICROWAVE FROZEN FRIED CHICKEN

Arrange chicken pieces in a single layer on a microwave ovenproof platter or cooking dish with meatiest parts to the outside.

Cover with wax paper. Microwave at High for ½ the heating time shown on chart above.

Rotate platter ½ turn. Microwave for second ½ of time. If package label does not state "fully cooked", check for doneness by cutting through meat to bone. Pinkness indicates more cooking is needed.

Stuffed Cornish Hens

Cornish Hens

Delicate Cornish Hens need some extra attention during defrosting or they may start to cook. We recommend defrosting in 3 steps rather than 2.

Cornish Hens are naturally tender, especially when microwaved. Because they cook so quickly, the unevenness of browning is particularily noticeable.

Plain microwaved Cornish Hen in background contrasts with a hen brushed with teriyaki sauce before microwaving. Teriyaki sauce gives a more golden color than brown bouquet sauce.

CORNISH HENS FAR EAST STYLE

POWER LEVEL: High
MICROWAVE TIME: 18 to 20 min., total

2 cornish hens, about 1-lb. each, defrosted	Split hens in halves, using kitchen shears or a sharp knife. Place in 12×8×2-in. dish, skin side down.
¼ cup soy sauce **¼ cup sherry wine** **¼ cup pineapple juice** **1 clove garlic, crushed or ⅛ teaspoon garlic powder** **½ teaspoon curry powder** **¼ teaspoon dry mustard**	In small bowl mix together soy sauce, sherry, pineapple juice, garlic, curry powder and mustard. Stir to blend well and pour over meat in dish. Refrigerate 4 to 6 hours, or overnight.

To cook, turn skin side up and baste with marinade. Cover dish with wax paper. **Microwave at High 8 Minutes.** Brush with marinade and rotate dish ½ turn. Recover. **Microwave at High 10 to 12 Minutes** more, until meat is tender. Serve immediately.

Makes 2 to 4 servings

HOW TO DEFROST CORNISH HENS

POWER LEVEL: **Defrost**

10 to 14 Minutes Per Pound

1. Place unopened packages in oven. (Metal closure need not be removed.) Microwave at Defrost for ⅓ the total defrosting time.
2. Turn packages over. Microwave for ⅓ the time.
3. Unwrap and shield ends of legs with foil. Microwave for last ⅓ of time. If giblets do not move freely, run cold water into cavities.

MICROWAVING CORNISH HENS, Halved

POWER LEVEL: **High**

9 to 10 Minutes Per Pound

1. Brush halves with browning sauce. Place in cooking dish, skin side up. Cover with wax paper. Microwave at High for ½ the cooking time.
2. Rotate dish ½ turn. Microwave for second ½ of time. Hen is done if juices run clear when inner thigh is pierced with a fork.

MICROWAVING CORNISH HENS, Whole

POWER LEVEL: **High**

6 to 8 Minutes Per Pound

1. Stuff hens*, if desired. Brush with browning sauce. Place breast side down in suitable cooking dish. Cover with wax paper. Microwave for ½ the cooking time.
2. Turn breast side up. Microwave for second ½ of time. Let stand 10 minutes. Hen is done when leg moves freely and juices run clear when inner thigh is pierced with a fork.

*Rice is an excellent stuffing for Cornish Hens. For each hen, use about ½ cup cooked rice (white and/or wild), well-buttered and seasoned.

Duckling

Duckling with Colorful Marmalade Sauce

Like other poultry, duckling microwaves juicy and tender in a very short time. Since duckling is so fatty, browning sauce is not brushed on before the first half of cooking because it will not adhere to the skin. After the duckling has rendered some of its fat, you may brush it with browning sauce or, if you prefer, after microwaving broil it under a conventional broiler to crisp and brown the thick skin. This rich meat is traditionally served with a fruit sauce or glaze.

HOW TO DEFROST DUCKLING

POWER LEVEL: **Defrost**

4 to 6 Minutes Per Pound

1. Place plastic wrapped duckling in oven. (Metal closure need not be removed.) Microwave at Defrost for ½ the time.
2. Unwrap duckling and turn over into cooking dish. Shield wings, tail, ends of legs and any other warm areas with foil. Defrost for second ½ of time.
3. Run cold water into cavity until giblets can be removed. For step-by-step photographs, see *How To Defrost A Whole Chicken,* page 118.

MICROWAVING DUCKLING

POWER LEVEL: **High**

7 to 8 Minutes Per Pound

1. Shield wings, tail and ends of legs with foil. Place duckling breast side down on trivet in a 12×8×2-in. dish. Microwave at High for ½ the cooking time.
2. Remove foil and turn breast side up. With a kitchen fork, prick skin of breast and legs to release fat. Baste duckling with drippings, then drain fat from dish. Brush with browning or barbecue sauce, if desired.
3. Microwave for second ½ of the time. Duckling is done when the last drops of juice drained from the cavity run clear, without a trace of pink.

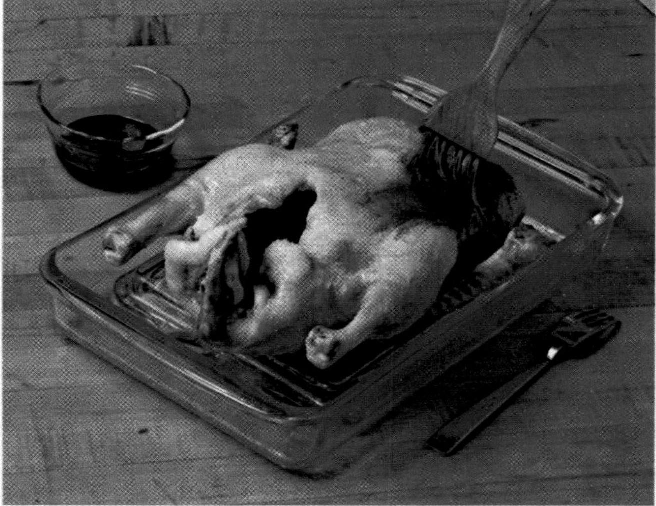

Prick skin of breast and legs with a kitchen fork after first ½ of cooking time. Brush with diluted brown bouquet sauce, if desired. For a crisp skin, omit sauce and, after microwaving, broil under a conventional broiler until crisp and brown.

Turkey Defrosting

MICROLESSON

Shape as well as size influences defrosting. A broad breasted, meaty turkey takes longer to defrost than a streamlined one of the same weight. The breast may also need more shielding because it is higher in the oven and closer to the source of microwave energy.

These directions are for defrosting turkeys weighing up to 12 pounds. Larger turkeys may be defrosted using the same method, but allowing turkey to stand 30 minutes after each ¼ of defrosting time. A 5-in. strip of foil is needed on the top of these large birds during each defrosting period to prevent over-defrosting.

If you wish to start defrosting a large turkey the day before you plan to roast it, defrost for ¾ the time, letting turkey stand between each ¼ period. Then place turkey in refrigerator overnight to complete defrosting.

HOW TO DEFROST TURKEY

POWER LEVEL: **Defrost**

10 to 12 Minutes Per Pound

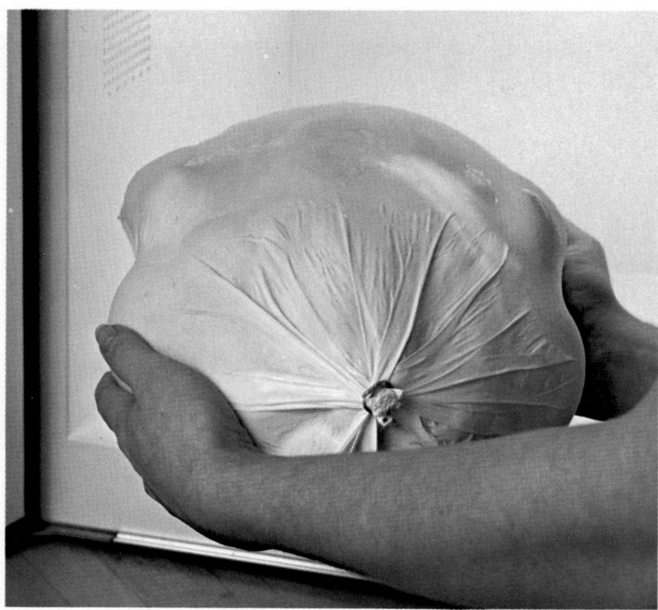

Place unwrapped turkey, breast side down, in oven. It is not necessary to remove the metal closure because of the great mass of food. Microwave at Defrost for ¼ the time. Rotate turkey ½ turn, so legs point to opposite side of the oven. Microwave for ¼ the time.

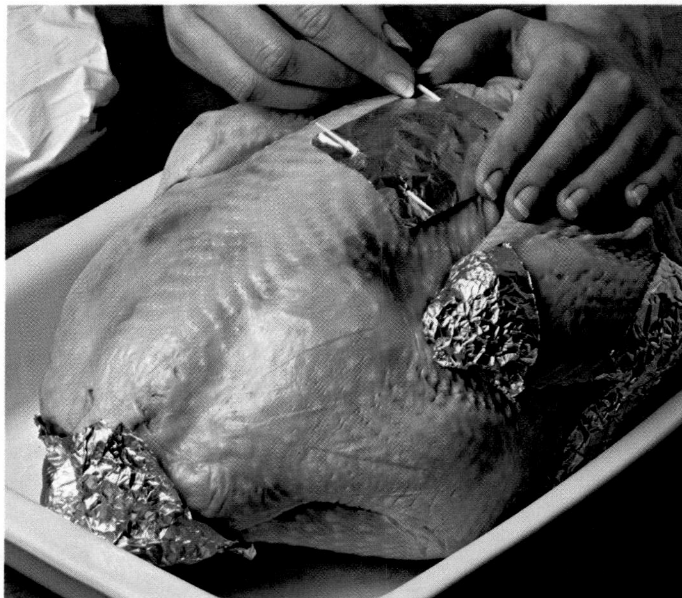

Unwrap turkey and place it in a cooking dish. Shield legs, wing tips and any warm or brown areas, with foil. Secure with wooden picks.

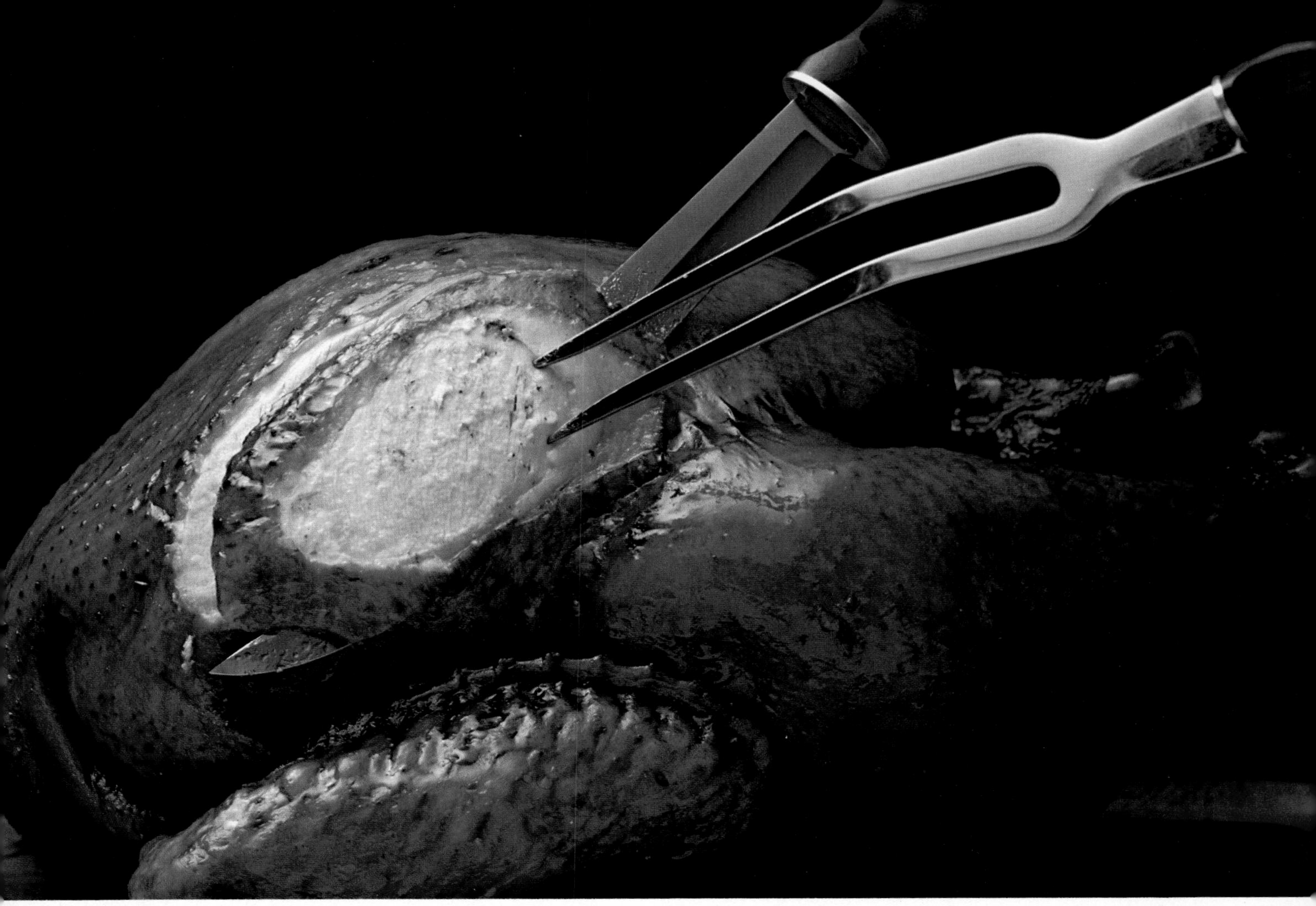

Microwaved Turkey

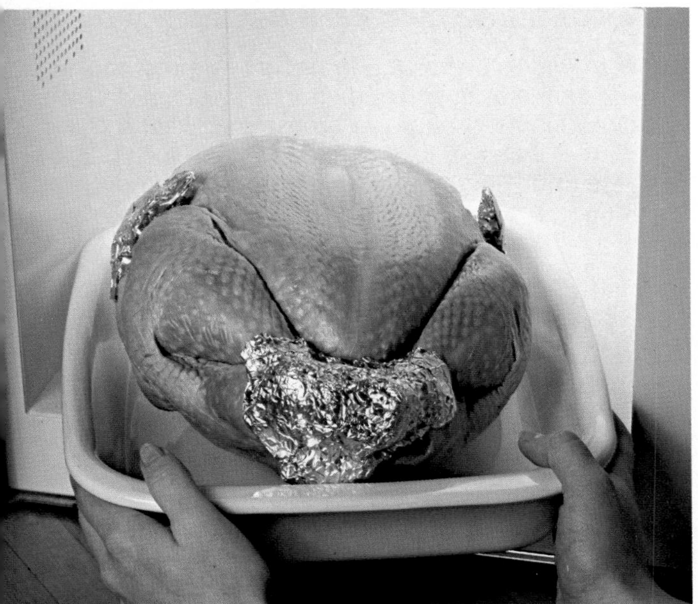

Turn breast side up and defrost for ¼ of time. Check breast for warm spots and shield if necessary. Rotate dish ½ turn, so legs point to opposite side of the oven. Microwave for final ¼ of time.

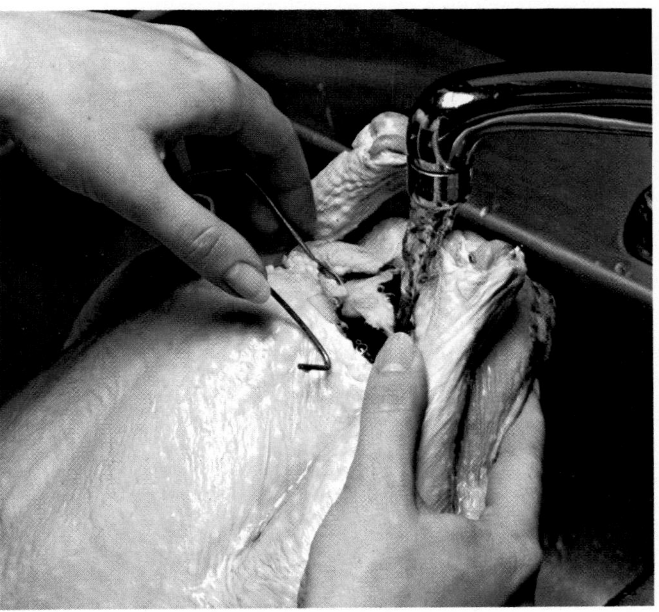

Remove metal clamp from legs. Run cold water into breast and neck cavities until giblets and neck can be removed. Turkey should feel soft and cool with a glistening surface. Interior should be cold and slightly icy.

Turkey

HOW TO MICROWAVE TURKEY IN A COOKING BAG

POWER LEVEL: **Medium**

11 to 13 Minutes Per Pound

MICROLESSON

Turkeys weighing 6 to 12 pounds may be microwaved in two ways. For a moist turkey, needing no attention during cooking, use an ovenproof cooking bag.

If you do not care to use a cooking bag, or prefer turkey with a drier surface, microwave turkey in a roasting dish covered with wax paper. This method requires some attention, since you start the turkey breast side down and turn it over to finish microwaving. While dry-roasted turkeys develop some browning, you may want to use a browning sauce for even color.

If your oven is equipped with a temperature probe, be sure to use it when microwaving turkey. The oven will sig-

Brush turkey with a mixture of 2 tablespoons brown bouquet sauce and 2 tablespoons water or melted butter. When using butter mixture, dry turkey thoroughly before brushing, or sauce will not cling to bird.

Cut ½-in. wide strip from open end of ovenproof cooking bag. Place turkey in bag and arrange in a roasting dish. Lightly oil inside of bag over breast to prevent sticking. Add ½ cup water, chicken broth or wine. Close bag by tying the open end securely with the plastic strip. Slash bag near closure.

HOW TO MICROWAVE TURKEY WITHOUT A COOKING BAG

Brush turkey with browning sauce as directed above. Place turkey in roasting dish, breast side down. Cover with wax paper. Insert temperature probe, if you are using it, as shown above. Set Temp, Set 120°, or Microwave at Medium for ½ the cooking time.

When oven signals, or after ½ the time, turn turkey, breast side up. Recover with wax paper and microwave second ½ of time to an internal temperature of 190°. Let stand 20 minutes before carving.

Insert meat thermometer, when not using probe, after minimum cooking time. Follow directions for probe placement and allow 2 minutes for an accurate reading. If turkey has not reached 190°, remove thermometer and return turkey to oven for a few more minutes.

Do not put conventional metal meat thermometer in microwave oven.

Standing Time of 20 minutes allows the interior of the turkey to finish roasting without overcooking the tender breast meat.

nal when turkey has reached 190°. Let turkey stand 20 minutes after microwaving, before serving.

When microwaving turkey by time, check for doneness after the minimum cooking time. You may have to reset your timer to complete the cooking cycle.

Do not use a trivet when microwaving turkey. A trivet raises turkey closer to top of oven, where microwave energy is released. Overcooking on top can result.

TIP: *On turkey over 6 inches high, areas next to breastbone are vulnerable to overcooking. To prevent overcooking on these high-breasted birds, shield breastbone area from neck cavity to tip of breastbone with strip of aluminum foil (5 inches long and 2 inches wide) before putting bird into cooking bag.*

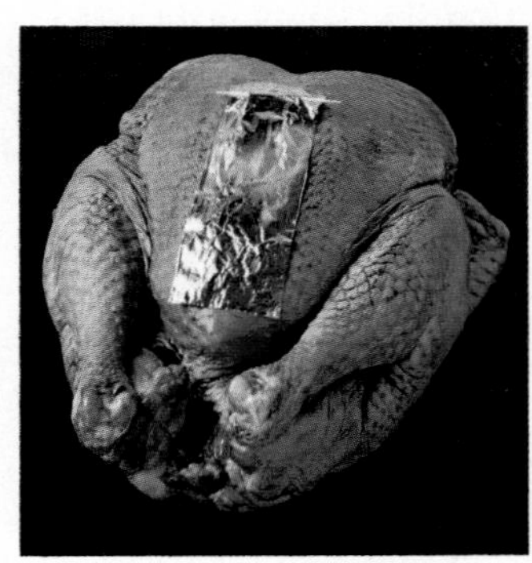

Insert temperature probe, if you are using one, through the bag into the meatiest part of the inner thigh. Position the probe below the end of, and parallel to the leg. Microwave at Medium. Set Temp, Set 190°. If not using the probe, microwave for minimum time and check with a meat thermometer.

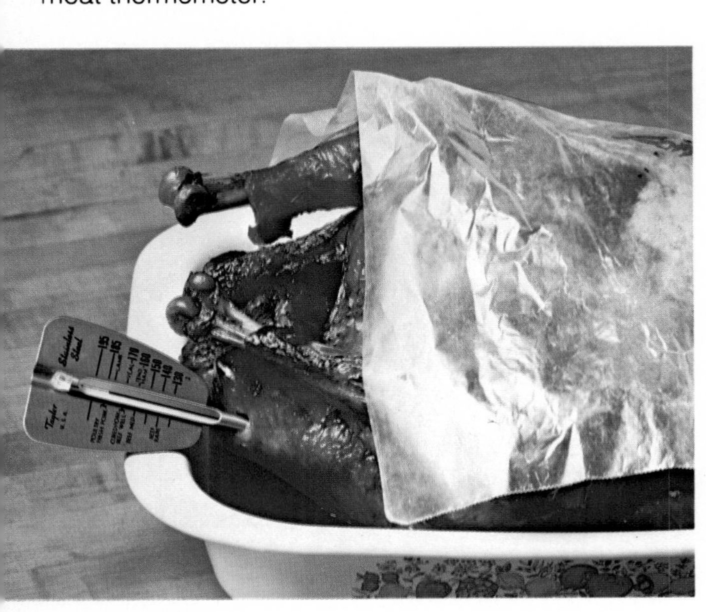

Fat Free Gravy can be made from drippings in cooking bag. Hold bag over a 1-qt. measure and strainer. Fat will rise to top of juices. Cut a small slit in bottom of bag and let only the light brown juice run into measure. Quickly remove bag with remaining yellow fat to cooking dish.

STUFFING SUGGESTIONS FOR TURKEY

Use one of the following suggestions for stuffing, packing lightly into body cavity. Microwave as illustrated on this page.

Savory Stuffing: For 8 to 10-lb. bird, toss together: 8 cups day-old bread cubes, ½ cup minced onion, 1 cup minced celery, 2 teaspoons salt, 2 teaspoons poultry seasoning, ¼ teaspoon pepper, ⅔ cup melted butter and 1 cup chicken broth.

Range Top Stuffing Mix: Prepare as package directs.

Prepared Seasoned Stuffing Mix: Follow package directions.

SAVORY TURKEY SQUARES

POWER LEVEL: Medium High
MICROWAVE TIME: 26 to 30 min., total

3 cups cooked, chopped turkey
2 cups day-old bread cubes
½ cup minced celery
¼ cup minced onion
2 tablespoons chopped pimiento
1 tablespoon lemon juice
½ teaspoon salt
¼ teaspoon pepper
⅔ cup milk
½ cup chicken broth
3 eggs, slightly beaten

In large mixing bowl mix together turkey, bread cubes, celery, onion, pimiento, lemon juice, salt, pepper, milk, broth and eggs. Pour into 12×8×2-in. dish. Cover with wax paper. **Microwave at Medium High 26 to 30 Minutes,** rotating dish ½ turn after 15 minutes, until set but still slightly soft in center. Let stand 5 to 10 minutes to firm before serving.

Makes 6 to 8 servings

HOT TURKEY AND CHEESE SANDWICHES

These are known in the South as "Hot Browns", created at a once-famous hotel in Louisville.

POWER LEVEL: Medium High
MICROWAVE TIME: 9½ to 12 min., total

4 strips bacon — On paper plate lined with double thickness paper towels, arrange bacon. Cover with single thickness paper towel. **Microwave at Medium High 2½ to 3 Minutes,** until only partially cooked.

4 slices toast
8 to 12 large slices turkey breast
4 slices tomato (¼-in. thick)
1 recipe Cheese Sauce, page 173
¼ cup Parmesan cheese

In 2 (7 to 9-in.) oval au gratin dishes, divide toast, arranging to cover bottoms of dishes. Place 4 to 6 large slices turkey in each dish and top each with 2 tomato slices. Divide cheese sauce over sandwiches. Sprinkle tops of sandwiches with Parmesan cheese. Arrange 2 slices partially-cooked bacon over each sandwich.

Place dishes side by side in microwave oven. Cover with wax paper. **Microwave at Medium High 7 to 9 Minutes,** rearranging dishes after 4 minutes, until hot.

Makes 2 sandwiches

SAUCY TURKEY AND BROCCOLI

Called Turkey Divan when made with the traditional Mornay Sauce. This makes a very nice luncheon or supper dish. A salad of tomato slices is a colorful accompaniment.

POWER LEVEL: High
MICROWAVE TIME: 6 to 8 min., total

1 bunch (about 1¼-lb.) broccoli, cut in spears — Microwave broccoli according to directions, page 188 Drain. In 12×8×2-in. dish or microwave ovenproof platter arrange attractively.

8 large slices cooked turkey
1 recipe Mornay Sauce, or Cheese Sauce, both page 173

Layer turkey slices over broccoli. Cover with sauce. **Microwave at High 6 to 8 Minutes,** rotating dish ½ turn after 5 minutes.

Makes 4 servings

TURKEY GOULASH

The 2 tablespoons paprika gives a distinctive mellow flavor.

POWER LEVEL: High
MICROWAVE TIME: 12 to 15 min., total

¼ cup butter
2 large onions, thinly sliced
1 clove garlic, minced

In 2-qt. casserole place butter, onions and garlic. **Microwave at High 5 to 6 Minutes,** stirring after 3 minutes, until onion is limp.

3 cups cooked, cubed turkey
1½ cups turkey or chicken broth
1 can (8-oz.) tomato sauce
2 tablespoons paprika
1½ teaspoons salt
¼ teaspoon pepper

Add turkey, broth, tomato sauce, paprika, salt and pepper. Cover. **Microwave at High 7 to 9 Minutes,** stirring after 4 minutes, until hot.

1 cup (8-oz.) dairy sour cream — Stir sour cream into hot mixture just before serving. Serve over rice or noodles.

Makes 6 servings

TURKEY TETRAZZINI

POWER LEVEL: High
MICROWAVE TIME: 24 to 28 min., total

1 pkg. (7-oz.) spaghetti	Cook spaghetti (see chart, page 179), except **Microwave 9 Minutes.** Drain. Place in greased 12×8×2-in. dish.
¼ cup butter **1 can (4-oz.) sliced mushrooms, drained** **1 small onion, chopped** **1½ teaspoons lemon juice**	In 2-qt. casserole place butter, mushrooms, onion and lemon juice. **Microwave at High 2 to 3 Minutes,** stirring after 1 minute.
⅓ cup flour **1 tablespoon salt** **½ teaspoon paprika** **⅛ teaspoon nutmeg** **2 cups turkey or chicken broth**	Stir in flour, salt, paprika and nutmeg, until smooth. **Microwave at High 1 Minute.** Stir well. Gradually stir in broth. **Microwave at High 5 to 6 Minutes,** stirring after 3 minutes, until thickened.
½ cup dairy half & half **2½ cups cooked, cubed turkey** **½ cup Parmesan cheese** **Paprika**	Mix in half & half and turkey. Pour over spaghetti. Sprinkle with cheese and paprika. **Microwave at High 7 to 9 Minutes,** rotating dish ½ turn after 4 minutes, until hot.

Makes 4 to 6 servings

TURKEY CONVENIENCE FOODS

Foods frozen in metal trays should be removed to suitable microwave plates or casseroles. Small boil-in-bag pouches (5 to 10-oz.) can be placed directly in the oven. Slit or pierce the top of the pouch before microwaving and open carefully after heating. Large boil-in-bags may be placed in a serving dish. When contents are partially defrosted, open the bag, slide the food into the dish and stir before continuing to microwave.

TURKEY CONVENIENCE CHART

POWER LEVEL: **High**

ITEM	TIME MINUTES	COMMENTS
Gravy & Sliced Turkey, Frozen (5-oz. pkg.)	3 to 4	Make 1-in. slit in top of pouch with sharp knife.
Turkey Tetrazzini, Frozen (12-oz. pkg.)	7 to 9	Place food in 1-qt. casserole. Cover. Stir after 6 minutes.

HOW TO MICROWAVE TURKEY PARTS

POWER LEVEL: **Medium High**

Turkey pieces, except whole bone-in breasts, cook best by time, rather than temperature, due to their uneven shape.

For color, brush with equal parts brown bouquet sauce and melted butter or water, or use teriyaki sauce or barbecue sauce.

To microwave by time, place turkey skin side down in appropriate size roasting dish without trivet. Add no water (except frozen roast, see below). Cover as indicated below. Turn over after ½ of microwaving time.

To microwave turkey breast by temperature, insert temperature probe from side into center of thickest meaty area. Set at 170°. (NOTE: Breast cooks to lower finished temperature than whole turkey.)

After microwaving, let stand 10 to 20 minutes before slicing. Special directions are given for frozen packaged turkey roasts.

ITEM	MINUTES PER LB.	COMMENTS
Frozen Packaged Turkey Roasts (2 to 4-lb.)	18 to 20	Add ½ cup water. Can be microwaved from frozen without defrosting. Cover with plastic wrap. Turn over after ½ of time.
Turkey Legs **Turkey Quarters** **Turkey Halves**	12 to 14	Must be defrosted before microwaving to cook evenly. Defrost like frozen whole turkey, page 132. Cover with wax paper. Turn over after ½ of time. Brush again with sauce.
Whole Turkey Breast	9 to 11	Microwave with temperature probe in cooking bag (see directions for whole turkey, page 134 .) Do not brush with barbecue sauce when using cooking bag. Insert temperature probe as described above and microwave to 170°.

CRANBERRY SAUCE

This sauce is so compatible with turkey, it has become a traditional accompaniment.

POWER LEVEL: High
MICROWAVE TIME: 18 to 20 min., total

2 cups sugar **½ cup water** **1 lb. fresh or frozen cranberries**	In 3-qt. casserole stir together sugar, water and cranberries. Cover. **Microwave at High 18 to 20 Minutes,** stirring every 6 minutes. Serve warm or cold.

Makes 3 to 4 cups

Fish & Seafood

Fish and seafood are naturally tender and require minimal cooking to preserve their delicate flavor and texture. The speed and moisture retention of microwaving are decided advantages in cooking them.

Overcooking dries and toughens fish. We recommend that many seafoods, especially the meatier types, be cooked until the outer areas appear opaque but the centers are still slightly translucent. These areas will finish cooking as the seafood stands, while the outer areas remain tender.

1. Lobster Thermidor, page 158
2. Stuffed Whole Fish, page 148
3. Microwaved Shrimp in the Shell, page 152
4. Fillets in Lemon Butter, page 145

MICROLESSON

Fish defrosts rapidly. It is naturally delicate and tender, so care should be taken not to toughen it by over-defrosting. Remove fish from the microwave oven while it is still slightly icy.

HOW TO DEFROST FILLETS AND STEAKS

DEFROSTING CHART

POWER LEVEL: **Defrost**

ITEM	1st SIDE TIME MINUTES	2nd SIDE TIME MINUTES
Fillets, 1-lb.	4	4 to 6
Steaks, 6-oz. - 1	2	None
Steaks, 6-oz. - 2	2	1 to 2

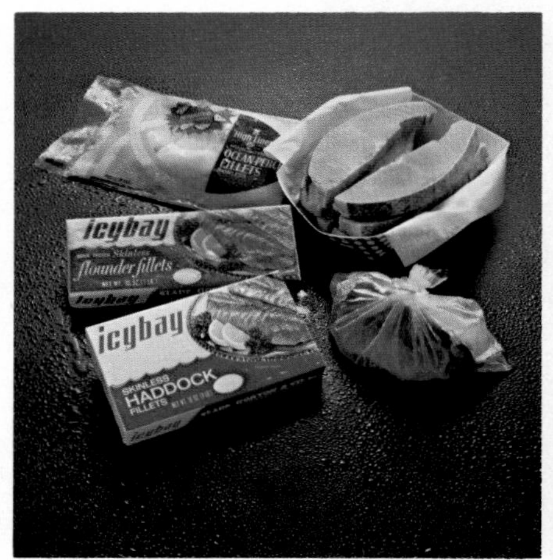

Shape of package, as well as its weight influences defrosting time. Thick fillets or bulky packages take longer than flat packages of the same weight.

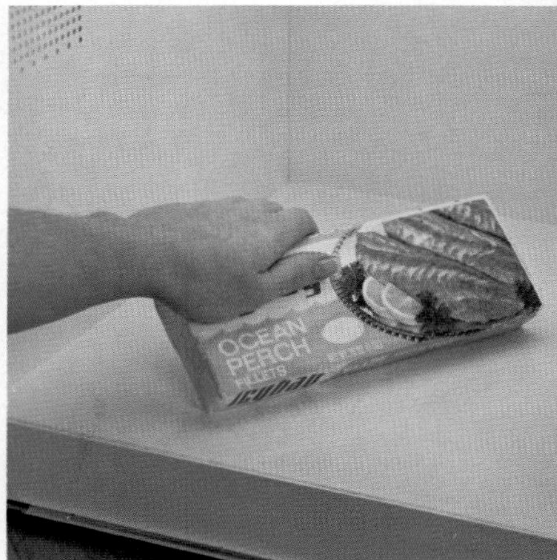

Place unopened paper or plastic package directly on oven floor. Fillets frozen at home in a bag of water should be placed in a dish to avoid leakage.

HOW TO DEFROST WHOLE FISH

DEFROSTING CHART

POWER LEVEL: **Defrost**

ITEM	1st SIDE TIME MINUTES	2nd SIDE TIME MINUTES
1 - 8 to 10-oz. Fish	2	2 to 4
2 - 8 to 10-oz. Fish	4	6 to 8
1 - 3 to 4-lb. Fish	8	12 to 14

Shape of fish, as well as weight, determines defrosting time. A short, thick fish may take longer to defrost than a long, thin one of the same weight.

Arrange fish in a cooking dish large enough to hold it easily. Microwave at Defrost for first part of time.

If you or a family member like to fish, freeze your catch for fresh-tasting fish all year 'round. Seal fillets or steaks in a plastic bag with a small amount of water and freeze. Clean whole fish, then dip them in water and freeze on a baking dish. The icy coating will protect fish from freezer burn. Package for freezing after icy coating forms.

When defrosting home frozen fish, use a cooking dish to collect water as it melts.

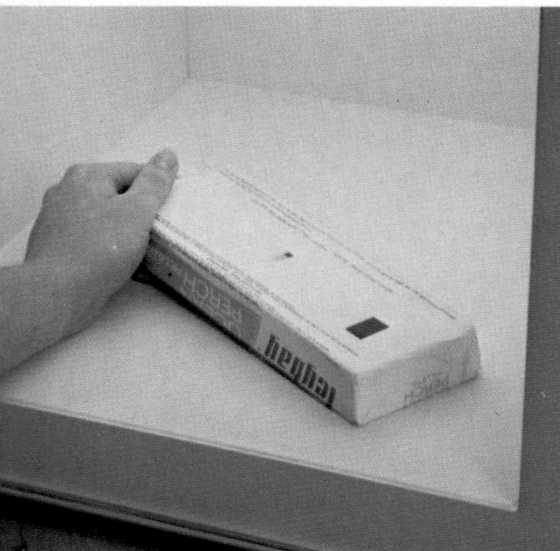

Turn package over so that the side which was closest to the back of the oven is brought to the front. Rotate ¼ turn.

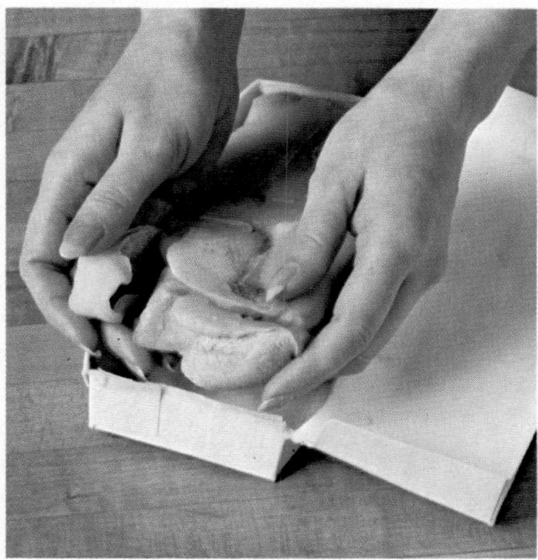

Check after minimum defrosting time. Corners should not feel warm, although outer pieces may have started to loosen.

Hold fillets under cold running water until they can be separated.

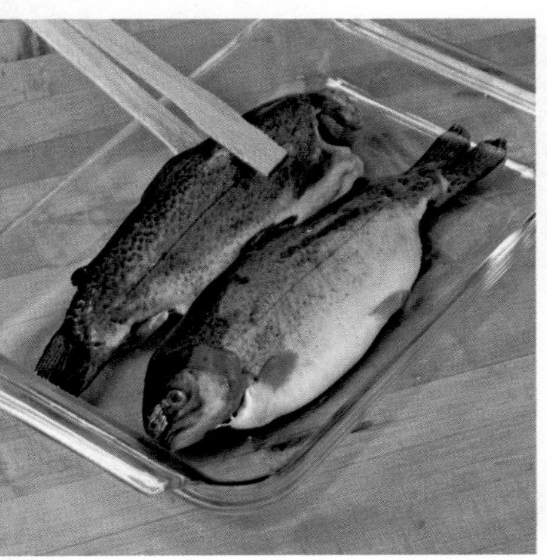

Turn fish over. Microwave for second part of minimum time.

Test fish. It should feel cold and pliable and may still be slightly icy in the cavity.

Rinse cavity with cold running water to complete defrosting.

Fish Fillets & Steaks

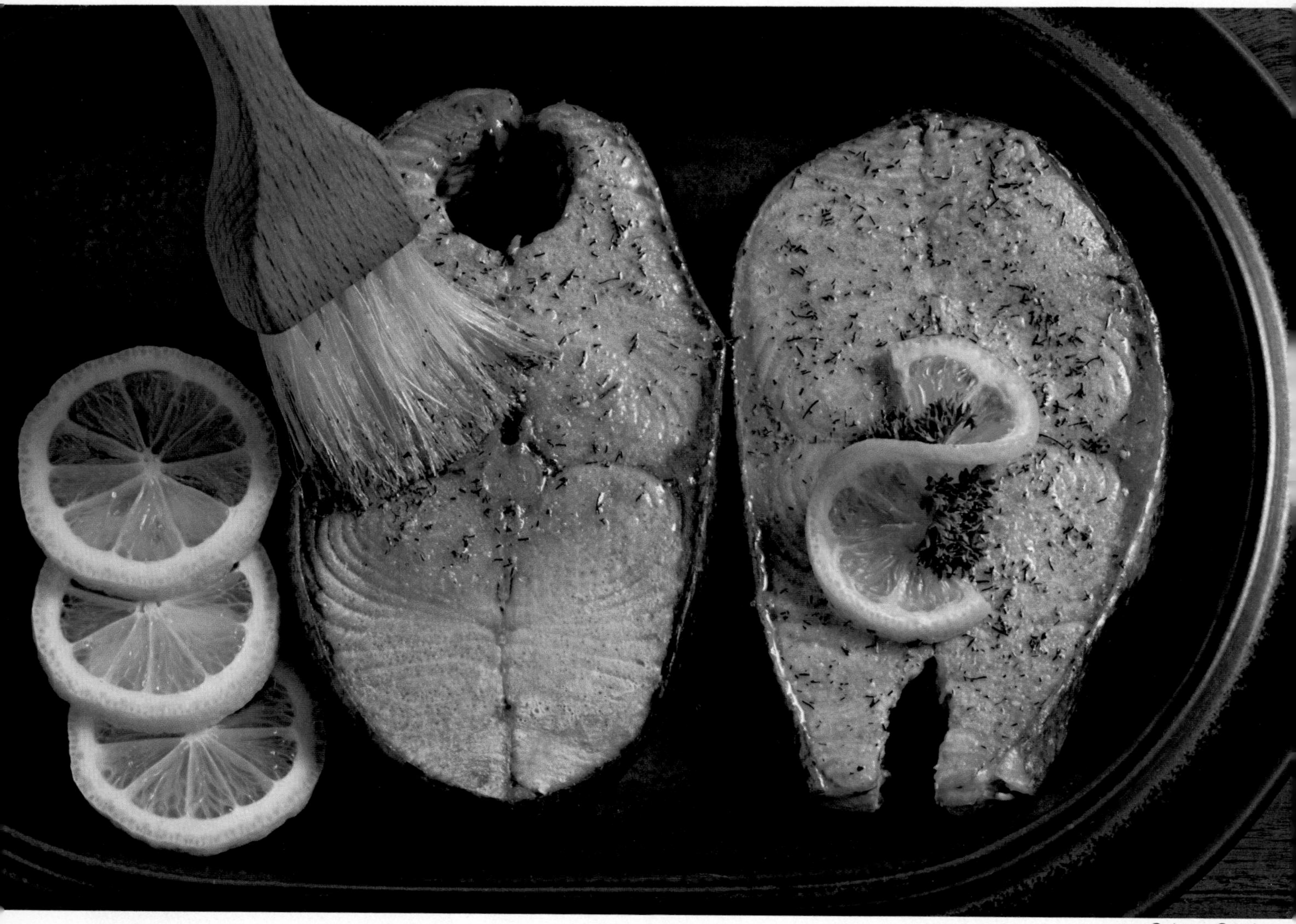

Salmon Steaks

MICROLESSON

Fillets of steak may be microwaved in several ways to produce a variety of dishes. Microwave them in a sauce for rich flavor. Steam or poach them for a delicate, but simple dish. Smother partially cooked fillet in crumbs and cream for scalloped fish. Whether cooked conventionally or microwaved, juices of salmon or halibut steaks coagulate on the surface of the fish. To eliminate this, before microwaving, line the dish with a paper towel to absorb excess juices, then turn over to serve. Flounder, which is extremely moist, should be microwaved on a trivet.

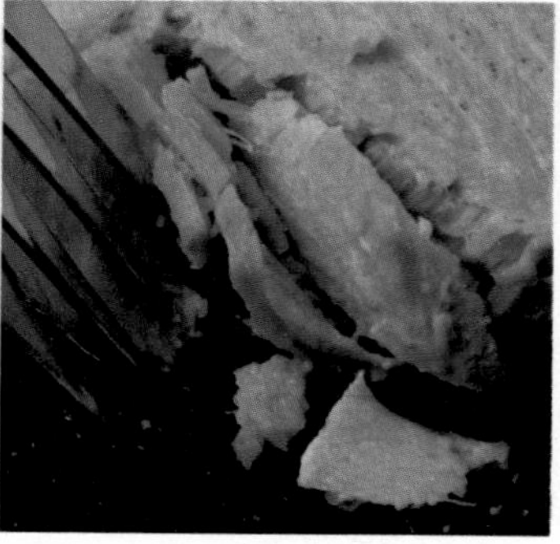

Fish is done when flesh flakes easily with a fork. Center should still be slightly translucent.

HOW TO MICROWAVE FILLETS IN SAUCE

Arrange fillets in a cooking dish, thickest parts to outside of dish.

Pour sauce on fillets. Cover with wax paper. Microwave for ½ of time.

Rotate dish ½ turn and microwave until fish flakes easily.

HOW TO MICROWAVE STEAMED FISH

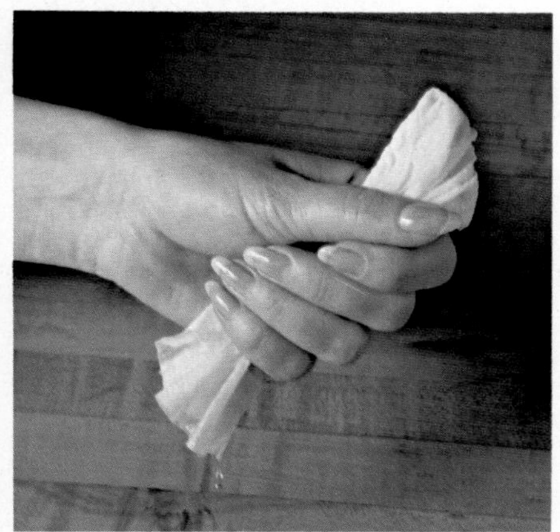

Dampen a paper towel with water. No additional moisture is needed. Arrange fish in dish with meatiest parts to the outside.

Cover with dampened towel. Microwave for ½ of time. Rotate dish ½ turn and finish steaming, or remove towel and scallop fish if desired.

Scallop fish by spreading crumbs over fillets and pouring in cream. Return to oven and microwave second ½ of time.

HOW TO MICROWAVE FISH STEAKS

Brush steaks with lemon-butter mixture. (If desired, line dish with paper towel before placing fish in it.)

Cover tightly with plastic wrap, turning back corner to vent. Microwave for ½ the time.

Turn steaks over and recover, or, if paper towel was not used, rotate dish ½ turn. Complete cooking.

FROZEN FISH FILLETS WITH SEASONED COATING MIX

Very moist result. Cook these on a microwave trivet for drier, firmer fish.

POWER LEVEL: High
MICROWAVE TIME: 6 to 8 min., total

1 lb. fish fillets, defrosted
1 pkg. (2-oz.) seasoned coating mix for fish

Separate fish fillets and coat with seasoned coating mix. Arrange in 12×8×2-in. dish with thickest meaty areas to outside edges of dish. Cover with wax paper. **Microwave at High 6 to 8 Minutes,** rotating dish ½ turn after 4 minutes, until fish flakes with fork.

Makes about 4 servings

FILLETS IN CREAMY WINE SAUCE

A dinner party dish. This French wine and cream sauce is sometimes called Bercy Sauce.

POWER LEVEL: High
MICROWAVE TIME: 11 to 14 min., total

1 tablespoon butter
2 tablespoons minced green onions
1 lb. sole or flounder fillets, defrosted and cut into serving pieces
1½ cups sliced fresh mushrooms
¾ cup dry white wine, such as Sauterne

In 12×8×2-in. dish place butter. **Microwave at High ½ Minute,** until melted. Spread butter over bottom of dish and sprinkle with onions. Arrange fillets over onions and cover with mushrooms. Pour wine over top. **Microwave at High 7 to 9 Minutes,** rotating dish ¼ turn every 3 minutes, or until fish flakes with a fork. Remove fish to microwave ovenproof platter and cover to keep warm while cooking sauce.

2 tablespoons flour
¼ cup heavy cream
1 teaspoon salt
⅛ teaspoon pepper

In 1-qt. casserole combine flour, cream, salt and pepper, until smooth. Carefully drain hot liquid from fish into cream mixture and stir well. **Microwave at High 2 to 3 Minutes,** stirring sauce every minute.

½ teaspoon lemon juice
¾ cup shredded Swiss cheese

Stir lemon juice into sauce. Pour sauce over fish and sprinkle cheese on top. **Microwave at High 2 Minutes** more, until cheese has melted. Garnish with parsley sprigs.

Makes about 4 servings

SCALLOPED FISH OR SCALLOPS

POWER LEVEL: High
MICROWAVE TIME: 7 to 9 min., total

1 lb. white fish fillets (flounder or sole) or scallops

On microwave ovenproof platter or 9-in. pie plate place fish fillets or scallops with thickest, meaty areas to outside edges of dish. Cover with paper towel which has been completely dampened, with most of water squeezed out. **Microwave at High 4 Minutes.**

½ cup (¼-lb.) butter
1 cup soft bread crumbs
1 cup saltine cracker crumbs

Remove platter from oven and let stand covered with paper towel while preparing buttered crumbs. In 1-qt. glass measure place butter. **Microwave at High 1 Minute,** or until melted. Add bread and cracker crumbs. Mix with fork.

1 teaspoon salt
⅛ teaspoon freshly ground pepper
⅓ cup milk or cream

Remove paper towel from fish and sprinkle evenly with salt and pepper, then buttered crumbs. Pour milk evenly over top. **Microwave at High 2 to 4 Minutes** more, until fish flakes easily with a fork or scallops are tender but not overcooked.

Makes 4 servings

NOTE: Leftover scalloped seafood may be used as a good omelet filling.

Complimentary sauces for fish and seafood include Dill Butter, or Herbed Butter, page175; Hollandaise Sauce, page 174; or, use the microwave oven to prepare Clarified Butter.

Clarified Butter: In 1-pt. measuring cup place ½ cup (¼-lb.) butter. **Microwave at High 2 Minutes,** until boiling. The clear layer which floats to top is clarified butter and may be poured off into a serving container.

Fish Creole

FILLETS IN LEMON BUTTER

POWER LEVEL: High
MICROWAVE TIME: 10 to 13 min., total

1 lb. firm fish fillets such as sole or haddock **½ to 1 teaspoon salt** **⅛ teaspoon pepper**	In 12×8×2-in. dish, arrange fillets with thickest, meaty areas to outside edges of dish. Sprinkle with salt and pepper.
½ cup (¼-lb.) butter **½ cup chopped fresh parsley** **1 tablespoon lemon juice** **½ cup buttery flavored cracker crumbs** **½ teaspoon paprika**	In 1-qt. casserole place butter. **Microwave at High 1 to 2 Minutes,** until melted. Blend in parsley and lemon juice and pour over fish. Top with crumbs, then sprinkle on paprika.

Microwave at High 9 to 11 Minutes, rotating dish ½ turn after 5 minutes, until fish flakes easily with fork.

Makes 4 servings

FISH CREOLE (A Low Calorie Recipe)

POWER LEVEL: High
MICROWAVE TIME: 8 to 10 min., total

1 lb. sole or haddock fillets, defrosted	Rinse fish and pat dry with paper towels. In 12×8×2-in. dish arrange fish with thickest pieces to outside edges of dish.
1 can (8-oz.) tomato sauce **1 can (2-oz.) sliced mushrooms, drained** **½ green pepper, diced** **1 stalk celery, diagonally sliced** **3 tablespoons water** **1½ tablespoons instant minced onion** **1 teaspoon chicken bouillon granules**	In 1-qt. glass measure stir together tomato sauce, mushrooms, green pepper, celery, water, minced onion and bouillon. Pour evenly over fish. Cover tightly with plastic wrap, turning back one corner to vent. **Microwave at High 8 to 10 Minutes,** rotating dish ½ turn after 4 minutes, until fish flakes easily with fork. Let stand about 5 minutes before serving, to blend flavors.

Makes about 4 servings

SALMON STEAKS

POWER LEVEL: High
MICROWAVE TIME: 8 to 9 min., total

4 (½-in. thick) salmon steaks (1-lb.)
2 tablespoons melted butter
2 teaspoons lemon juice
½ teaspoon dill weed

In paper towel lined 12×8×2-in. dish place steaks. Brush with melted butter mixed with lemon juice. Sprinkle with dill if desired. Cover dish with wax paper.

Microwave at High 8 to 9 Minutes, rotating dish ½ turn after 3 minutes. When done, fish will flake easily with fork. Turn fish over onto serving plate. (Paper towel absorbs juices for best appearance of fish.) Garnish top of steaks with sprinkling of paprika or parsley and additional melted butter, if desired.

Makes 4 servings

FOR 2 SALMON STEAKS: Use half of all ingredients and place fish in 8-in. square dish. Cover with wax paper. **Microwave at High 4 to 5 Minutes;** no turns necessary.

Salmon With Cucumber Sauce: Cook 4 salmon steaks as directed above, but omit dill weed. Cook to minimum time, then spread over the tops a mixture of: ½ cup dairy sour cream, ⅓ to ½ cup shredded or chopped cucumber (¼ medium cucumber), 1 teaspoon chopped parsley, ½ teaspoon chopped chives, 1 teaspoon lemon juice and ¼ teaspoon salt. **Microwave at High 1 to 2 Minutes** more before serving.

ROUND SALMON LOAF

Round shape is best for fish loaves, just as it is for meat loaves.

POWER LEVEL: High
MICROWAVE TIME: 9 to 11 min., total

1 egg
1 cup milk
¼ cup melted butter
3 slices soft bread, cubed
½ teaspoon salt
2 cans (1-lb. each) red salmon, bone and skin removed, if necessary

In large mixing bowl beat egg slightly and mix with milk, butter, bread cubes, salt and salmon, blending well. Pack firmly in greased 9-in. pie plate. Cover with wax paper. **Microwave at High 9 to 11 Minutes,** rotating dish ½ turn after 5 minutes. Let stand 10 minutes before slicing. Serve with Dill Butter, page 174, if desired.

Makes 6 to 8 servings

COLORFUL CREAMED TUNA

POWER LEVEL: High
MICROWAVE TIME: 11 to 15 min., total

2 tablespoons butter
¼ cup chopped onion
¼ cup chopped green pepper

In 2-qt. casserole place butter, onion and green pepper. **Microwave at High 2 to 3 Minutes,** stirring every minute.

1 can (2-oz.) mushrooms
1 can (10-oz.) cream of celery soup
1 can (6½-oz.) tuna, drained
½ teaspoon salt
⅛ teaspoon pepper

Drain mushrooms, reserving 2 tablespoons juice. Add mushrooms and reserved juice to casserole along with soup, tuna, salt and pepper. Cover. **Microwave at High 7 to 9 Minutes,** stirring after 4 minutes.

2 tomatoes, cut in wedges

Add tomatoes. Cover. **Microwave at High 2 to 3 Minutes** more, until hot. Serve over rice.

Makes 3 to 4 servings

HOT TUNA SALAD

A good dish for entertaining. Can be made ahead of time and reheated before serving. Shrimp or crab might also be used in place of tuna. Try this in a hot patty shell for a treat.

POWER LEVEL: Medium High
MICROWAVE TIME: 10 to 13 min., total

2 cans (7-oz. each) tuna, drained
2 cups chopped celery
2 cups croutons, divided
1 cup mayonnaise
½ cup whole almonds or cashews
1 tablespoon finely chopped onion
1 tablespoon lemon juice
½ teaspoon salt

In 1½-qt. casserole mix together tuna, celery, 1 cup croutons, mayonnaise, almonds, onion, lemon juice and salt. Cover. **Microwave at Medium High 9 to 11 Minutes,** stirring after 5 minutes, until hot.

½ cup shredded cheddar or Swiss cheese

Sprinkle with cheese and remaining 1 cup croutons, **Microwave at Medium High 1 to 2 Minutes,** until cheese melts.

Makes 6 servings

TUNA NOODLE CASSEROLE

POWER LEVEL: High
MICROWAVE TIME: 31 to 36 min., total

1 pkg. (8-oz.) fine egg noodles	Microwave noodles (see chart, page 179), except cook 10 minutes.
3 tablespoons butter **1 clove garlic, minced** **½ cup finely chopped green onions** **½ teaspoon salt** **⅛ teaspoon pepper**	In 3-qt. casserole place butter, garlic, onion, salt and pepper. **Microwave at High 2 to 3 Minutes,** stirring after 1 minute, until onion is softened.
¼ cup unsifted all-purpose flour **1½ cups milk**	Stir in flour until smooth. Gradually stir in milk. **Microwave at High 4 to 6 Minutes,** stirring every 2 minutes, until smooth and thickened.
2 cans (7-oz. each) tuna, drained	Gently stir tuna and noodles into sauce. Cover. **Microwave at High 15 to 17 Minutes,** stirring after 8 minutes, until hot.
⅓ cup cracker crumbs **2 tablespoons minced parsley** **2 tablespoons melted butter**	In small bowl, mix together crumbs, parsley and butter. Sprinkle over casserole before serving.

Makes 6 to 8 servings

Tuna Wedges

SCALLOPED TUNA AND CHIPS

Cook by time, or use the temperature probe set at 150°.

POWER LEVEL: High
MICROWAVE TIME: 15 to 17 min., total

1 can (10½-oz.) condensed cream of celery soup **1 can (7 to 8-oz.) mushrooms, stems and pieces** **1 teaspoon instant minced onion** **1 tablespoon chopped parsley** **1 cup milk** **1 tablespoon lemon juice**	Mix soup, undrained mushrooms, onion, parsley, milk and lemon juice.
1 pkg. (5-oz.) potato chips, crushed (3 cups) **2 cans (7-oz. each) tuna, drained and flaked**	In 2-qt. greased casserole layer 1 cup crushed chips, ½ of tuna, ½ of soup mixture. Repeat layers and top with potato chips. **Microwave at High 15 to 17 Minutes,** until bubbly.

Makes 6 servings

TUNA WEDGES

A tuna loaf, microwaved in a round shape. Garnish with tomato slices and sprinkle with grated cheese if desired.

POWER LEVEL: High
MICROWAVE TIME: 10 to 12 min., total

2 eggs **1½ cups cooked rice** **6 green onions, finely chopped** **2 cans (7-oz.) solid pack tuna**	In large mixing bowl beat eggs with fork. Add rice, onions and undrained tuna. Mix well.
½ cup (¼-lb.) butter **¼ teaspoon thyme** **1 cup fine dry bread crumbs**	In small glass bowl place butter. **Microwave at High 1 Minute,** until melted. Add to tuna along with thyme and crumbs. Mix well.

Spread mixture evenly in lightly greased 9-in. pie plate. Cover with wax paper. **Microwave at High 9 to 11 Minutes,** rotating dish ½ turn after 5 minutes. Serve in wedges.

Makes about 6 servings

Whole Fish

Whole fish makes a dramatic presentation. Microwaving is a superior way of preparing them. With a tight cover fish steam in their own natural moisture and are delicate and juicy.

For a baked appearance, brush with browning sauce and butter. For poached color, use lemon-butter sauce.

Although the head is not eaten, it should be shielded with foil to maintain its appearance for serving. The eye, which turns white during cooking, can be covered with an olive slice.

HOW TO INSERT THE TEMPERATURE PROBE

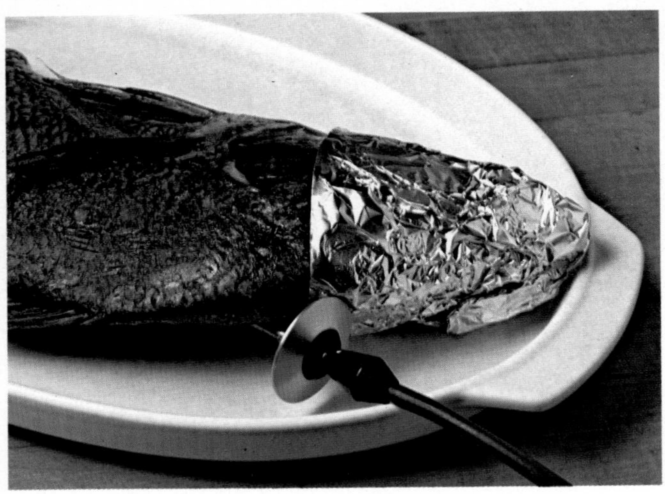

Insert Probe from just above the gill into the meatiest area, parallel to the backbone. Probe should be on the side of the fish closest to the dish.

HOW TO MICROWAVE A WHOLE FISH BY TEMPERATURE (Striped Bass, Snapper, etc. 2½ to 4 pounds)

Brush entire fish with a mixture of 1 tablespoon bottled bouquet sauce and 1 tablespoon water, then with melted butter; or brush with lemon-butter sauce. Add stuffing, such as Vegetable Stuffing (below, right) if desired.

Insert temperature probe; place the fish in a baking dish with the probe on the side of the fish closest to the dish.

Shield the head and thin tail area with foil, making sure that the foil on the head is no closer than ¾-in. from the probe disc.

Cover the dish tightly with plastic wrap, arranging loosely around probe to vent. Attach cable end at receptacle. **Microwave at High. Set Temp, Set 170°.**

STUFFED RED SNAPPER

POWER LEVEL: High
MICROWAVE TIME: 9 to 11 min., total

1 red snapper (1½ to 2½-lb.), cleaned and gutted **Vegetable Stuffing (right)** **2 tablespoons bottled brown bouquet sauce** **¼ cup butter, melted**	Place fish on microwave-type platter or in 12×8×2-in. dish. Stuff cavity with Vegetable Stuffing. Brush all areas with mixture of brown bouquet sauce and butter.

Cover head and thin tail end with strips of aluminum foil. Cover platter or dish with plastic wrap, turning back one corner to vent. **Microwave at High 9 to 11 Minutes,** until fish flakes easily with fork. While letting stand 5 minutes, brush again with butter, if desired. Place cross-cut slice of pimiento-stuffed olive in eye cavity.

Makes about 2 servings

HOW TO MICROWAVE A WHOLE FISH BY TIME

POWER LEVEL: **High**
5 to 7 Minutes Per Pound

Brush fish with sauce as directed in the recipe.

Shield head and thin tail area with foil.

Cover tightly with plastic wrap, turning back one corner to vent.

Rainbow Trout

VEGETABLE STUFFING

½ cup (¼-lb.) butter, melted **½ cup finely chopped onion** **½ cup finely grated carrots** **½ cup chopped raw mushrooms** **¼ cup finely minced parsley** **½ cup fine dry bread crumbs** **1 egg, beaten** **1 tablespoon lemon juice** **1 teaspoon salt** **⅛ teaspoon pepper**	In 2-qt. casserole place butter, onion, carrots, mushrooms, parsley, bread crumbs, egg, lemon juice, salt and pepper. Toss to mix well. Pack lightly into fish.

Makes about 2 cups

RAINBOW TROUT

POWER LEVEL: High
MICROWAVE TIME: See Recipe

Trout (8 to 10-oz. each)	In 12×8×2-in. dish arrange 1 to 2 trout which have been cleaned and gutted.
For each fish: **2 tablespoons lemon juice** **¼ cup butter, melted**	Brush fish with mixture of lemon juice and butter.

Cover head and tail areas with strips of aluminum foil. Cover cooking dish with plastic wrap, turning back one corner to vent. **Microwave at High** according to times below. When done, fish flakes easily with fork. Let stand 5 minutes and serve with rest of lemon butter.

NO. OF TROUT	TIME/MINUTES
1	5 to 6
2	8 to 9

Place cross-cut slice of pimiento-stuffed olive in eye cavity.

Defrosting Shellfish

MICROLESSON

POWER LEVEL: **Defrost**

HOW TO DEFROST SMALL LOOSE PIECES OF SHELLFISH

TYPE	TIME MINUTES
Crab Fingers (1-lb.)	7 to 8
Scallops (1-lb.)	7 to 8
Shrimp (1-lb.)	7 to 8

HOW TO DEFROST SHELLFISH FROZEN IN BLOCKS

TYPE	TIME MINUTES
Crab Meat (6-oz. pkg.)	4 to 5
Crab Meat (2 6-oz. pkgs.)	6 to 7
Crab Meat (1-lb. can)	14 to 16
Oysters (12-oz. can)	8 to 10
Oysters (3 12-oz. cans)	18 to 20
Scallops (1-lb. pkg.)	8 to 10

HOW TO DEFROST LARGE SHELLFISH

TYPE	TIME MINUTES
Crab Legs (8 to 10-oz.) 1 to 2	5 to 7
Crab Legs (8 to 10-oz.) 3 to 4	10 to 12
Lobster Tails (6 to 9-oz.) 1 to 2	5 to 7
Lobster Tails (6 to 9-oz.) 3 to 4	10 to 12
Lobster Tails (12 to 16-oz.) 1 to 2	8 to 10
Whole Lobster or Crab (1½-lb.)	16 to 18 (approx. 12 min. per pound)

Small pieces of loose-packed shellfish, such as shrimp, scallops or crab fingers, are easiest to defrost, since they can be spread out in a single layer and absorb microwave energy evenly. Check at minimum time because they defrost rapidly.

Blocks of shellfish, such as crab meat and scallops, frozen in paper packages, can be defrosted in the package. Turn over after ½ of time. Oysters and crab meat frozen in cans must be removed to a casserole. Break up these dense blocks as soon as possible.

Large pieces such as lobster, lobster tails, whole crab or large crab legs should be turned over after ½ of time. If thinner areas feel warm, shield them with foil. Remove large shellfish from the oven while still slightly icy and allow them to stand a few minutes.

Spread shellfish loosely in a baking dish so they are in a single layer. Microwave at **Defrost** for half the time.

Rearrange pieces and defrost for second half of time.

Test after minimum defrosting time. Shellfish should feel cool and soft, and still be translucent.

Place block in a casserole and cover. Microwave at **Defrost** for half the time.

Turn block over and break it up with a fork. Center may still be firm. Microwave for second half of time, breaking off pieces as they loosen.

Pieces should be loose and still feel icy. Let stand to complete defrosting.

Arrange shellfish in a baking dish with the light underside up. Paper towels hold tails upright. Microwave at **Defrost** for half the time.

Turn over, so that the back or darker side is up. Defrost for second half of time.

Defrosted shellfish should be flexible and transparent and feel cool.

Small Shellfish

Steaming is the classic method for cooking shellfish. In the microwave oven most shellfish steam without water in a cooking dish covered tightly with plastic wrap. A dampened paper towel provides sufficient steam for scallops. Clams steam in their shells. Whole lobster needs some water because of its size. We recommend cooking unpeeled shrimp in water with bay leaf and vinegar to reduce cooking odors.

When Done most shellfish turns from translucent to opaque. Remove clams from oven as soon as shells open partially.

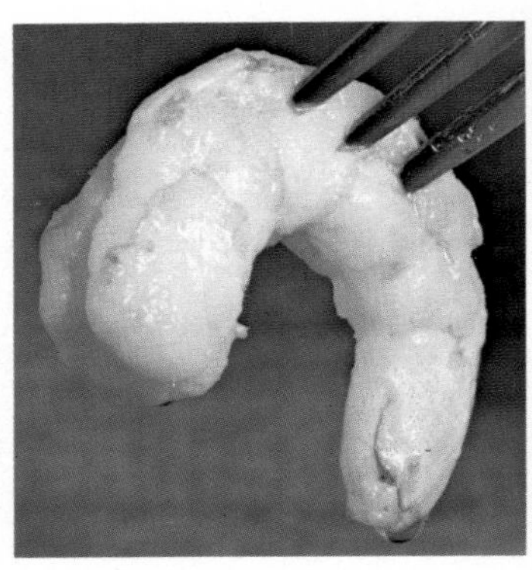

TIPS FOR MICROWAVING SMALL SHELLFISH

Small Shellfish such as scallops, shrimp, oysters or clams, are cooked on a pie plate or shallow dish. Cover tightly with plastic wrap.

Arrange cleaned and deveined shrimp in a ring. Cover tightly with plastic wrap, turning back 2-in. to vent. Cook clams in a ring with hinged side out. Rotate dish ½ turn after ½ time.

A Damp paper towel helps steam scallops. The ring arrangement is not necessary for even cooking. Rotate dish ½ turn after ½ time.

SMALL SHELLFISH CHART

POWER LEVEL: **High**

TYPE	TIME MINUTES
Clams (3 to 5-oz.) 6	3 to 5
Scallops (1-lb.)	5 to 7
Shrimp, peeled (1-lb.)	5
Shrimp, unpeeled (1 to 2-lb.) with 2½ cups water, 1 bay leaf, 1 tablespoon vinegar, in 2-qt. casserole.	6 to 10

Cook scallops and peeled shrimp as directed under the photographs above. When cooking clams, follow the directions given under shrimp. Clams will be partially opened when done. (Tightly closed shells contain bad clams and should be discarded.)

JIFFY SHRIMP CURRY

POWER LEVEL: High
MICROWAVE TIME: 7 to 8 min., total

1 can (10½-oz.) condensed cream of shrimp soup **1 tablespoon butter** **2 tablespoons instant minced onion** **1 teaspoon curry powder** **1 cup (8-oz.) dairy sour cream**	In 1½-qt. casserole combine soup, butter, onion, curry powder and sour cream. **Microwave at High 5 Minutes,** uncovered, or until sauce bubbles around edges.
2 cans (4½-oz. each) shrimp, drained and rinsed **Chopped egg or crumbled bacon (optional)**	Stir in shrimp. **Microwave at High 2 or 3 Minutes,** until hot. Garnish with egg or bacon, if desired.

Makes 4 to 6 servings

SHRIMP GUMBO

For spicy flavor, tie 1 to 2 teaspoons crab boil (found in condiment section of supermarket) in a cheesecloth bag and add along with shrimp. For bright color accent, save out about 1/4 of green pepper to stir into finished gumbo.

POWER LEVEL: High and Medium High
MICROWAVE TIME: 32 to 34 min., total

1 medium onion, sliced (about 1/2 cup) **1/4 cup butter (use bacon fat, if desired)**	In 3-qt. casserole place onion and butter. **Microwave at High 3 Minutes,** stirring after 2 minutes, until onion is limp.
2 tablespoons cornstarch **1 cup water** **2 cans (16-oz. each) stewed tomatoes** **1 cup diced green pepper (2 medium)** **2 cloves garlic, crushed** **2 teaspoons salt** **1 teaspoon ground nutmeg** **1/4 teaspoon pepper** **1 pound raw shrimp, shelled, deveined** **2 pkgs. (10-oz. each) frozen okra, defrosted, cut into 1-in. pieces**	In small bowl stir together cornstarch and water. Add to onion along with tomatoes, green pepper, garlic, salt, nutmeg, pepper, shrimp and okra. Stir well. Cover. **Microwave at Medium High 29 to 31 Minutes,** stirring and recovering after 1/2 of time.

Makes 6 to 8 servings

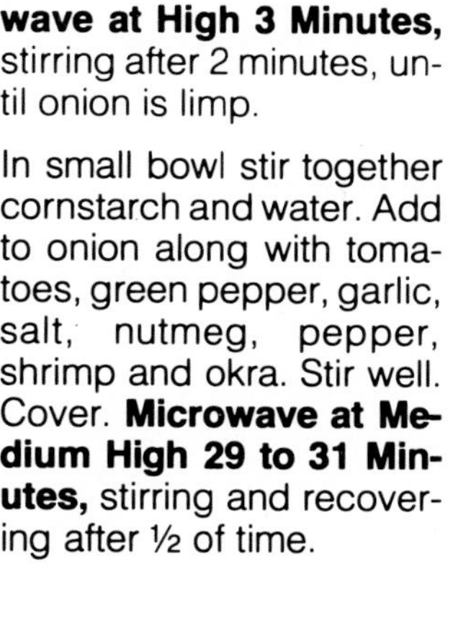
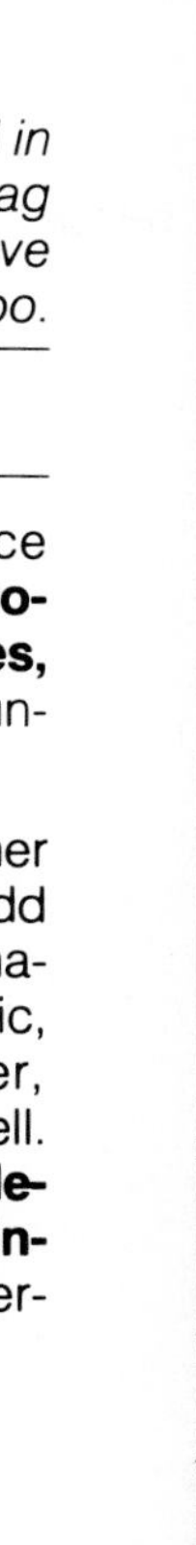

Shrimp Gumbo

CREAMY SHRIMP AND RICE

POWER LEVEL: High
MICROWAVE TIME: 31 to 33 min., total

1 1/2 cups uncooked long grain rice **3 1/2 cups water**	In 3-qt. casserole place rice and water. Cover. **Microwave at High 20 Minutes,** stirring and recovering after 10 minutes.
1/2 cup chopped onion **1/2 cup chopped green pepper** **2 cups (16-oz.) dairy sour cream** **1 cup milk** **1/2 teaspoon salt** **1/8 teaspoon pepper** **2 cups cooked shrimp**	Add onion, green pepper, sour cream, milk, salt, pepper and shrimp. Stir well; then smooth top. **Microwave at High 10 to 12 Minutes,** stirring after 6 minutes, until hot.
1 cup (4-oz.) shredded cheddar cheese	Sprinkle cheese over top. **Microwave at High 1 Minute,** until melted.

Makes 6 to 8 servings

SHRIMP IN PARMESAN BUTTER

POWER LEVEL: High
MICROWAVE TIME: 7 1/4 to 8 1/4 min., total

36 large raw shrimp, peeled and deveined	"Butterfly" shrimp by cutting each piece lengthwise halfway through and separating the 2 sides to form thin, flat piece of shrimp.
1 cup (1/2-lb.) butter **3 tablespoons capers, including liquid** **2 cloves garlic, minced** **2 tablespoons lemon juice**	In 1-qt. measure place butter. **Microwave at High 1 1/4 Minutes,** until melted. Stir in capers, garlic and lemon juice. Pour 2/3 of butter in 12×8×2-in. dish. Arrange shrimp in sauce.
1 cup (4-oz.) grated Parmesan cheese	Top with cheese, then remaining butter. Cover with wax paper.

Microwave at High 6 to 7 Minutes, rotating dish 1/2 turn after 3 minutes, until shrimp is opaque and firm.

Makes 3 to 4 servings

SHERRIED SHRIMP ROCKEFELLER

This won $5,000 in a recent microwave recipe contest.

POWER LEVEL: Defrost and High
MICROWAVE TIME: 30 to 33 min., total

2 pkgs. (10-oz. each) frozen chopped spinach
1 lb. medium to large raw shrimp, peeled, deveined
In 10-in. square casserole or 12×8×2-in. dish place unwrapped, frozen blocks of spinach. **Microwave at Defrost 10 Minutes.** Break up blocks. **Microwave at High 3 to 4 Minutes** more, until just completely thawed. With hands, squeeze out as much juice as possible. Spread over bottom of casserole. Distribute shrimp evenly over spinach.

1 can (10½-oz.) condensed cream of shrimp soup
1 cup (4-oz.) shredded sharp cheddar cheese
3 tablespoons cooking sherry
In 1-qt. glass measure stir together undiluted soup, cheese and sherry. **Microwave at High 4 Minutes,** stirring after 2 minutes, until cheese is melted. Set aside while preparing crumb topping.

2 medium slices fresh bread
3 tablespoons butter
Break bread in tiny bits or coarsely crumb in blender. Place in small glass bowl and add butter.

Microwave at High 1 Minute, stirring after ½ minute, until butter is distributed among crumbs. Pour hot sauce over casserole and distribute crumbs over top. Sprinkle with paprika, if desired.

Microwave at High 12 to 14 Minutes, uncovered, rotating dish ½ turn after 5 minutes. Let stand, covered, 5 minutes before serving.

Makes 4 servings

SWEET AND SOUR SHRIMP

Garnish with chopped bacon and green onion slices.

POWER LEVEL: High
MICROWAVE TIME: 6 to 8 min., total

1 recipe Sweet and Sour Sauce, page 174
1 lb. cleaned and cooked shrimp
1 can (8-oz.) pineapple slices
Stir together Sweet and Sour Sauce, shrimp and drained pineapple slices. **Microwave at High 6 to 8 Minutes,** stirring gently after 3 minutes.

Makes 4 to 5 servings

SHRIMP NEWBURG

POWER LEVEL: High and Medium
MICROWAVE TIME: 14 to 19 min., total

¼ cup butter
¼ cup chopped green onion
1 jar (4-oz.) sliced mushrooms, drained
In 2-qt. casserole place butter, onion and mushrooms. **Microwave at High 2 to 3 Minutes,** until bubbly.

2 tablespoons flour
½ teaspoon salt
Stir in flour and salt. **Microwave at High 1 Minute,** to blend.

1¼ cup milk
Stir in milk. **Microwave at High 5 to 6 Minutes,** stirring after 3 minutes.

¼ cup sherry
2 egg yolks
Stir in sherry. Stir small amount of sauce into yolks. Add yolk mixture to sauce; stir well. **Microwave at Medium 2 to 3 Minutes,** stirring after 1 minute.

12 oz. frozen cooked shrimp, defrosted
Stir in shrimp. **Microwave at Medium 4 to 6 Minutes,** stirring after 2 minutes, until heated through.

Makes about 4 servings

JAMBALAYA

POWER LEVEL: High
MICROWAVE TIME: 14 to 17 min., total

2 cups diced cooked ham
½ cup chopped green pepper
½ cup chopped onion
1 garlic clove, minced
2 tablespoons butter
In 2-qt. casserole place ham, green pepper, onion, garlic and butter. **Microwave at High 6 to 7 Minutes** or until vegetables are tender.

1 can (10¾-oz.) condensed tomato soup
⅓ cup water
½ cup shrimp, or 1 can (4½-oz.), drained
1 medium bay leaf, crushed
¼ teaspoon crushed oregano
⅛ teaspoon salt
Dash pepper
Stir in soup, water, shrimp, bay leaf, oregano, salt and pepper. **Microwave at High 4 Minutes.**

1½ cups cooked rice
Stir in rice. **Microwave at High 4 to 6 Minutes** more, or until bubbly.

Makes 4 servings

SCALLOPED OYSTERS

POWER LEVEL: High
MICROWAVE TIME: 13 to 15 min., total

3 cans (12-oz. each) frozen oysters, thawed (about 4 cups) ..... Drain oysters, reserving 1/4 cup liquid.

3/4 cup butter, melted
2 cups fine soda cracker crumbs (about 40 small squares)
1 teaspoon salt
1/8 teaspoon pepper
1/8 teaspoon nutmeg ..... In small mixing bowl mix together butter and crumbs. In 10×6×2-in. dish layer 1/3 of crumb mixture, 1/2 of drained oysters, 1/2 of seasonings, then 1/3 of remaining crumbs, rest of oysters, seasonings and crumbs.

1/4 cup milk .... Mix milk with oyster liquid and pour evenly over top.

With knife, poke 3 to 4 holes through layers so liquid goes to bottom. **Microwave at High 7 Minutes.** Sprinkle with 1/4 cup parsley. Rotate dish 1/2 turn. **Microwave 6 to 8 Minutes,** until oysters are firm when pierced with fork.

Makes about 6 servings

CRAB IMPERIAL

POWER LEVEL: High and Medium High
MICROWAVE TIME: 12 1/2 to 15 min., total

2 tablespoons butter
2 tablespoons flour
1 teaspoon salt
3/4 teaspoon pepper
1 teaspoon dry mustard ..... In 1 1/2-qt. casserole place butter. **Microwave at High 1/2 Minute,** until melted. Stir in flour, salt, pepper and mustard until smooth. **Microwave at High 1 Minute.**

1 cup dairy half & half
1 teaspoon lemon juice
2 teaspoons Worcestershire sauce
2 tablespoons minced green pepper
2 tablespoons minced pimiento ... Very slowly stir in half & half until mixture is smooth. Add lemon juice, Worcestershire sauce, green pepper and pimiento. **Microwave at High 3 to 3 1/2 Minutes,** until thickened, stirring every minute.

1 egg, beaten .... Stir a little hot mixture into egg, then add egg to rest of sauce. **Microwave at Medium High 2 Minutes.**

1 lb. lump crabmeat
1/2 cup fine dry bread crumbs
1/4 cup melted butter .... Drain crab. Remove shells or cartilage. Stir sauce into crab. Divide mixture into 6 to 8 shells or ramekins. Combine crumbs and butter. Divide over top. **Microwave at Medium High 6 to 8 Minutes,** rearrange after 3 minutes, until heated.

Makes 6 to 8 servings

COQUILLE ST. JACQUES

The classic creamed scallop dish. Large scallop shells are natural microwave utensils for this.

POWER LEVEL: High, Medium and Medium High
MICROWAVE TIME: 17 to 22 min., total

3 tablespoons butter
1 jar (4-oz.) sliced mushrooms
2 green onions, sliced
1/4 cup chopped celery ..... In 2-qt. casserole place butter, mushrooms, onions and celery. **Microwave at High 2 to 3 Minutes,** stirring after 1 minute.

2 tablespoons flour
1/2 teaspoon salt
1/4 teaspoon thyme
1 tablespoon pimiento, chopped
1/3 cup white wine
1 lb. raw scallops ..... Stir in flour, salt, thyme and pimiento well, then wine and scallops, stirring again. **Microwave at High 5 to 6 Minutes,** stirring after 3 minutes, until thickened.

1/4 cup dairy half & half
1 egg yolk, beaten ... Stir in half & half and egg yolk. **Microwave at Medium 3 to 4 Minutes,** stirring after 2 minutes.

Divide mixture among 4 scallop shells. Top with Crumb Mixture (below). Cover with wax paper. **Microwave at Medium High 7 to 9 Minutes,** rearranging after 4 minutes, until hot.

Makes 4 servings

Crumb Mixture: In small bowl, place 2 tablespoons butter. **Microwave at High 1/4 to 1/2 Minute,** until melted. Stir in 1/4 cup fine dry bread crumbs and 2 tablespoons Parmesan cheese.

Crab Imperial

Large Shellfish

MICROLESSON

Arrange large shellfish in the cooking dish so that the light colored underside is up during the first half of the cooking period. Because of its size, a whole lobster needs a small amount of water for added steam. Lobster tails and crab legs steam in their own natural moisture. When done, lobster and lobster tails should still be slightly translucent in the center. Cooking will be completed during standing time.

LARGE SHELLFISH CHART POWER LEVEL: **High**

TYPE	TIME MINUTES	TYPE	TIME MINUTES
Crab Legs (8 to 10-oz.) 1	3 to 4	**Lobster Tails** (8 to 10-oz.) 2	5½ to 6
Crab Legs (8 to 10-oz.) 2	5 to 6	**Lobster Tails** (8 to 10-oz.) 4	9 to 11
Crab Legs (8 to 10-oz.) 4	9 to 11	**Lobster Tails** (12 to 16-oz.) 1	5 to 6
Lobster Tails (8 to 10-oz.) 1	3 to 4	**Whole Lobster** (1½-lb.)	9 to 11

HOW TO MICROWAVE LOBSTER TAILS AND CRAB LEGS

Arrange lobster tails in baking dish with under side up. (No water added.) Cover tightly with plastic wrap, turning back corner to vent. Microwave at High for half the time.

Remove tails from dish. Cut through back of shell and meat, leaving undershell intact.

Spread to expose meat. Loosen meat from shell with fingers.

Brush lobster meat with mixture of 1 tablespoon melted butter and 1 tablespoon lemon juice. Cover and microwave second half of time. Meat should still be slightly translucent in the center. Let stand 5 minutes.

Arrange crab legs in baking dish with light colored side up. (No water added.) Cover tightly with plastic wrap, turning back corner to vent. Microwave at High for half the time.

Turn over, so that dark side is up. Cover and continue microwaving until flesh at ends of legs is opaque. Let stand 5 minutes.

Microwaved Whole Lobster

HOW TO MICROWAVE A WHOLE LOBSTER

Plunge the tip of a heavy knife into live lobster between the head and first segment to sever the spinal cord, which kills lobster. Lobster may show signs of movement for few minutes.

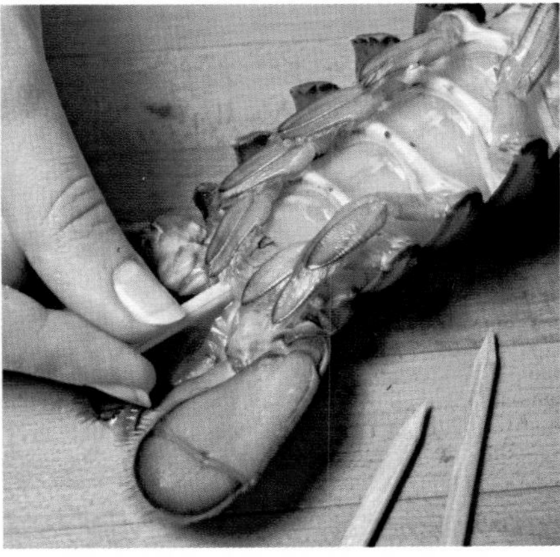

Peg the tail to prevent curling by inserting a wooden skewer lengthwise through the meat. At this time, or after lobster is cooked, cut through the undershell of the body and remove the intestinal vein and small sack below the head, if desired.

Arrange lobster in a baking dish with the back down and add ½ cup hot water. Cover tightly with plastic wrap, turning back a corner to vent. **Microwave at High 9 to 11 Minutes,** turning over after 6 minutes.

LOBSTER THERMIDOR

An enriched version of creamed lobster. It is often served in the shells of the lobster tails from which the meat was removed.

POWER LEVEL: High and Medium
MICROWAVE TIME: 15¼ to 19½ min., total

2 tablespoons butter
1 can (3-oz.) mushroom slices, drained
2 tablespoons chopped onion
In 1½-qt. casserole place butter, mushrooms and onions. **Microwave at High 3 Minutes,** stirring after 2 minutes.

2 tablespoons flour
¼ teaspoon salt
⅛ teaspoon pepper
⅛ teaspoon paprika
Stir in flour, salt, pepper and paprika until smooth. **Microwave at High 1 Minute.**

¼ cup chicken broth
½ cup dairy half & half
Slowly stir in broth and half & half. **Microwave at High 3 to 4 Minutes,** stirring after 2 minutes, until thickened.

1 egg yolk, beaten
2 tablespoons sherry
2 cups cooked lobster
Stir part of hot mixture into egg yolk, then add egg to rest of hot mixture. Stir in sherry. **Microwave at Medium 3 to 4 Minutes,** stirring after 2 minutes. Stir in lobster.

Refill 4 tail shells of lobster with creamed mixture, or use 4 large scallop shells or au gratin dishes if desired. Cover with Crumb Mixture (below). Cover with wax paper. **Microwave at High 5 to 7 Minutes,** rearranging after 3 minutes, until heated through.

Makes 4 servings

Crumb Mixture: In small bowl, place 2 tablespoons butter. **Microwave at High ¼ to ½ Minute,** until melted. Stir in ¼ cup fine dry bread crumbs and 2 tablespoons Parmesan cheese.

MIXED SEAFOOD CASSEROLE

POWER LEVEL: High and Medium High
MICROWAVE TIME: 33 to 39 min., total

3 cups fresh bread cubes (3 medium slices bread)
In 12×8×2-in. dish place bread cubes. **Microwave at High 4 to 5 Minutes,** stirring every 2 minutes, until crisp. Remove about half of cubes and save for top layer.

2 cups mixed seafood or 2 cans (7-oz.) tuna, shrimp or crab*
1 cup chopped onion
1 cup chopped celery
½ cup mayonnaise
In large mixing bowl mix together seafood, onion, celery and mayonnaise. Spread over bread cubes in dish. Cover seafood mixture with remaining half of bread cubes.

2 eggs
1 cup milk
1 can (10-oz.) condensed cream of mushroom soup
In small bowl beat eggs well and mix in milk and soup. Pour over casserole. **Microwave at Medium High 28 to 32 Minutes,** rotating dish ½ turn after 15 minutes, until set but still slightly soft in center.

1 cup (4-oz.) shredded cheddar cheese
Paprika
Sprinkle top with cheese, then paprika. **Microwave at Medium High 1 to 2 Minutes,** until cheese is melted. Let stand 5 to 10 minutes before serving.

Makes 6 to 8 servings

*Canned tuna can be undrained, but canned shrimp or crab should be drained.

FISH AND SHELLFISH CONVENIENCE CHART

POWER LEVEL: **High**

All these frozen seafood entrees can be heated to serving temperature at High.

ITEM	TIME MINUTES	COMMENTS
Alaska King Crab Newburg (6½-oz. pouch)	3 to 5	Puncture pouch with fork to vent.
Deviled Crabs (6-oz. pkg.)	3 to 4	Will not be crisp.
Fish 'N' Chips (14-oz. pkg.)	7 to 9	Distribute evenly in large dish. Will not be crisp.
Fish Fillets With Crumb Coating (8-oz. pkg.)	4½ to 6	Distribute evenly in dish and rotate ½ turn after 3 minutes. Will not be crisp.
Fish Sticks (9-oz. pkg.)	4½ to 6	Distribute evenly in dish and rotate ½ turn after 3 minutes. Will not be crisp.
Shrimp Croquettes (12-oz. pkg.)	4 to 6	Pierce sauce pouch with fork and place with food on plate. Cover with wax paper. Rotate dish ½ turn after 2 minutes.
Shrimp Newburg (6½-oz. pkg.)	4 to 6	Puncture top with fork to vent.
Tuna Noodle Casserole (11½-oz. pkg.)	7 to 9	Place in 1-qt. casserole with cover. Stir after 5 minutes and before serving.

Eggs & Cheese

Eggs

MICROLESSON

Eggs are versatile; they can be prepared in a variety of ways, each with its own character. Although omelets and poached eggs are both eggs, they are completely different. Here we present the basic ways of cooking eggs. All but one microwave well. Do not try to hard boil eggs in the microwave oven. They expand during cooking and burst the shell.

HOW TO MICROWAVE SCRAMBLED EGGS

Place 1 teaspoon butter per egg in a glass measure or casserole. Microwave at High until melted.

Scramble eggs with the melted butter and 1 tablespoon milk per egg.

Place in oven. Estimate ¾ minute per egg and microwave at High for ½ of total time.

HOW TO MICROWAVE BASIC EGGS

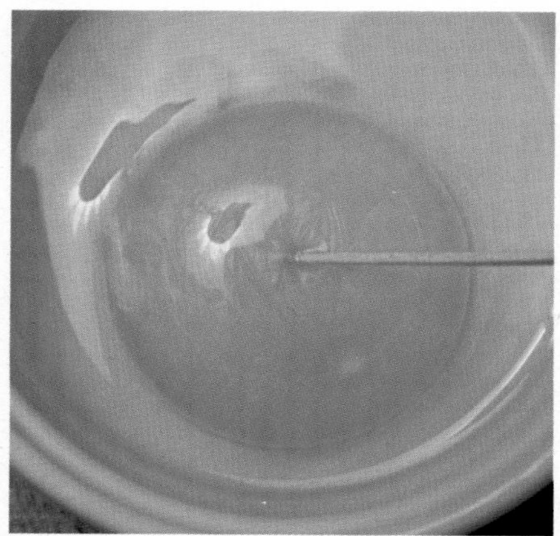

Puncture membrane of yolk to prevent bursting when microwaving shirred or poached eggs.

Microwave shirred eggs in buttered custard cups. Puncture membrane and cover with plastic wrap. Microwave 1 minute per egg at Medium Power, rotating ½ turn after ½ minute.

Poach eggs by microwaving 2 cups hot tap water 5 to 6 minutes at High, until boiling. Break eggs onto plate; puncture membrane. Swirl boiling water with spoon; slip in eggs gently. Cover. Microwave at Medium 1 minute per egg; ¾ minute per egg for more than 1 egg. Let stand in water a few minutes.

Eggs microwave rapidly, and since they are a delicate food, toughen when overcooked. The yolks, which have a higher fat content, cook faster than the whites. Poach eggs at Medium Power to allow the whites time to set without toughening the edges or overcooking the yolks.

When yolks and whites are mixed together, eggs may be cooked at higher power settings. Omelets, which need time to set, are cooked at Medium, while scrambled eggs, which are stirred, are microwaved at High. Scrambled eggs are one of the foods which microwave better than they cook conventionally. Not only do they take less time and need less stirring, but they are fluffier and greater in volume. For easy clean up, scrambled eggs may be microwaved in plastic-coated paper bowl.

Stir set portions from the outside to the center. Repeat 1 or 2 times during remaining cooking period.

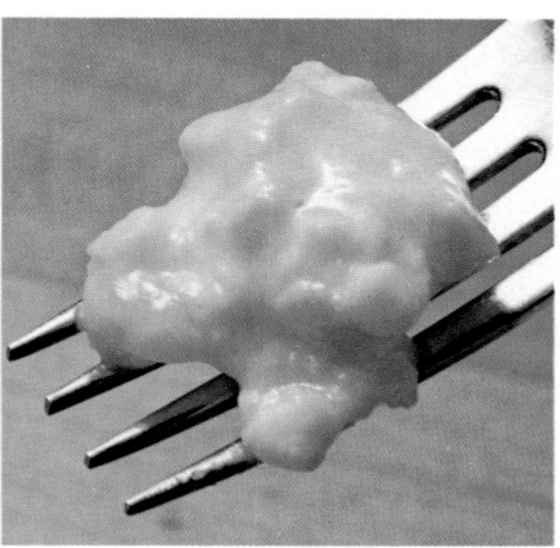

When Done, eggs should be just past the runny stage.

After Standing 1 or 2 minutes, eggs will be set.

Fry eggs in the Brown 'N Sear Dish. Preheat dish at High 1 minute per egg. Add ½ tablespoon butter per egg. Break eggs into dish, cover and microwave ¾ minute per egg, or to desired doneness.

Puffy Omelets are microwaved in a pie plate and folded over a filling. See recipes on next page.

Never attempt to hard-cook eggs or reheat eggs in shells.

JELLY OMELET

POWER LEVEL: High and Medium
MICROWAVE TIME: 6 to 7 min., total

¼ to ⅓ cup strawberry or currant jelly . . . In custard cup place jelly. **Microwave at High 1 Minute,** until jelly is soft and can be stirred smooth. Set aside.

3 eggs, separated
2 tablespoons water . . . In largest mixer bowl beat egg whites at highest speed of mixer, until soft peaks form. Then, in smaller bowl, using same beaters, beat yolks and water. Gently pour yolk mixture over beaten whites. Fold together carefully.

1 tablespoon butter . . . In 9-in. pie plate place butter. **Microwave at High 1 Minute,** swirl to coat dish.

Carefully pour egg mixture into pie plate. **Microwave at Medium 4 to 5 Minutes,** rotating dish ¼ turn every minute, until set but still glossy on top. Spoon jelly over half of omelet. Quickly run spatula or turner around sides and bottom of dish. Fold plain half of omelet over jelly half. Gently slide onto serving plate. If desired, sprinkle cinnamon-sugar over omelet before serving.

Makes 1 to 2 servings

FRENCH OMELET

French omelets need a hot pan surface to cook properly. This one, made in the Brown 'N Sear Dish, looks best when rolled to form a cylinder; it does not fold easily. Do not use a browning griddle because egg mixture runs into the grease well. This recipe serves 1 to 2 people. For more than 2 omelets we recommend the range top.

POWER LEVEL: High
MICROWAVE TIME: 5 to 5½ min., total

2 tablespoons butter
3 eggs, well beaten
Salt
Pepper . . . Preheat empty, uncovered Brown 'N Sear Dish. **Microwave at High 3 Minutes.** Immediately add butter and tip dish to melt. Stir in eggs. **Microwave at High 2 to 2½ Minutes,** stirring well every ½ minute, until almost set. Do not stir last ½ minute to allow eggs to set into solid layer. Remove from oven. Immediately tip dish and roll up into cylindrical-shape omelet.

Makes 1 to 2 servings

PUFFY CHEESE OMELET

POWER LEVEL: High and Medium
MICROWAVE TIME: 7½ to 10 min., total

3 eggs, separated
⅓ cup mayonnaise
2 tablespoons water . . . In largest mixer bowl beat egg whites at highest speed of mixer, until soft peaks form. Then in smaller bowl, using same beaters, beat yolks, mayonnaise and water. Gently pour yolk mixture over beaten whites. Fold together carefully.

2 tablespoons butter . . . In 9-in. pie plate place butter. **Microwave at High 1 Minute,** swirl to coat dish. Carefully pour egg mixture into pie plate. **Microwave at Medium 6 to 8 Minutes,** rotating dish ½ turn after 3 minutes, until set but still glossy on top.

½ cup finely shredded cheddar cheese . . . Sprinkle cheese over omelet.

Microwave at Medium ½ to 1 Minute, until cheese is slightly melted. Quickly run spatula or turner around sides and bottom of dish. Fold half of omelet over the other half. Gently slide onto serving plate. Sprinkle with chives, if desired.

Makes 1 to 2 servings

EGGS AND COTTAGE CHEESE SCRAMBLE

This brunch dish has a rich but delicate flavor. Add the cottage cheese at the last minute to melt it slightly.

POWER LEVEL: High
MICROWAVE TIME: 9½ to 12 min., total

3 tablespoons butter
¼ cup finely chopped green onions . . . In 3-qt. casserole place butter and onions. **Microwave at High 2 Minutes.** Stir.

9 eggs
1½ cups diced, cooked ham or other firm pre-cooked meat such as salami or dried beef . . . Add eggs to casserole and beat well. Stir in meat. **Microwave at High 7 to 9 Minutes,** stirring every ½ minute.

½ cup creamed cottage cheese . . . Stir in cottage cheese. **Microwave at High ½ to 1 Minute,** just until cottage cheese is slightly melted. Do not overmelt, or cheese becomes runny.

Makes 6 servings

EGGS BENEDICT

POWER LEVEL: High and Medium
MICROWAVE TIME: 13 to 14 min., total

4 poached eggs (page 160)	Poach eggs and allow to stand as directed.
2 egg yolks **1 tablespoon lemon juice** **½ teaspoon dry mustard** **⅛ teaspoon salt** **½ cup (¼-lb.) butter**	While eggs are standing, make Hollandaise sauce. In container of electric blender measure egg yolks, lemon juice, mustard and salt. In 1-qt. glass measure place butter. **Microwave at High 1 Minute** until hot and bubbly. Turn electric blender to highest speed and gradually add butter, blending until creamy and thickened.
8 thin slices (¼-in. thick) Canadian bacon	Just before serving, microwave Canadian bacon which has been arranged in single layer on microwave ovenproof plate. **Microwave at High 4 Minutes,** rotating dish ½ turn after 2 minutes.
4 English muffins, split and toasted*	Assemble Eggs Benedict by arranging 2 slices of Canadian bacon, then a poached egg over each of 4 English muffin halves. Top eggs with Hollandaise Sauce. Butter remaining muffin halves and serve as accompaniment. Decorate with parsley if desired.

Makes 4 servings

*Or, if desired, use only 2 English muffins and divide eggs and sauce among the 4 halves. Serve 2 halves per serving.

EGGS BENEDICT VARIATIONS FOR BRUNCH

Sausage and Eggs: Substitute thin sausage patties (see Sausage Chart, page 111) for Canadian bacon. Substitute Cheese Sauce (see recipe page 173), if desired, for Hollandise.

Ham and Eggs: Substitute thin slices cooked ham for Canadian bacon. Substitute Bearnaise Sauce (see recipe page 174), if desired, for Hollandaise.

Poultry and Eggs: Substitute thin slices cooked chicken or poultry for Canadian bacon. Substitute Curry Sauce (see recipe page 173), if desired, for Hollandaise.

Eggs Benedict

POACHED EGGS WITH SPANISH SAUCE

These are known as Huevos Rancheros in the Southwestern United States.

POWER LEVEL: High and Medium
MICROWAVE TIME: 16 to 19 min., total

⅓ cup finely chopped onions **⅓ cup finely chopped green pepper** **1 clove garlic, crushed** **2 tablespoons cooking oil**	In 1-qt. casserole stir together onion, green pepper, garlic and oil. **Microwave at High 3 to 4 Minutes,** until onion is tender.
1 can (16-oz.) tomatoes, drained **1 to 2 teaspoons chili powder** **¼ teaspoon salt** **⅛ teaspoon pepper** **⅛ teaspoon oregano**	Add tomatoes, chili powder, salt, pepper and oregano. **Microwave at High 5 to 7 Minutes,** stirring after 3 minutes, until thickened and hot.
4 poached eggs (page 160) **¼ to ½ cup shredded cheddar cheese**	Place poached eggs on serving plates. Spoon sauce over eggs. Sprinkle with cheese.

Makes 2 to 4 servings

Quiche

Quiche is simple farm-style food which has earned a gourmet reputation because it tastes so good. A quiche is a pie shell filled with chopped cooked meat, cheese and a creamy custard. Substitute about ½ cup seafood for the bacon, and any firm cheese for the Swiss, if desired. In the province of Lorraine, French farmers use bacon, cheese and onions. Quiche is so versatile that wedges make a hearty supper, while small pieces provide a distinctive appetizer.

Microwaved quiche differs from conventionally baked because the milk or cream is heated before the custard is prepared. The warm filling microwaves more evenly, allowing the center to set without overcooking the edges. With microwaving, you have tender custard in about half the time.

HOW TO MICROWAVE QUICHE LORRAINE

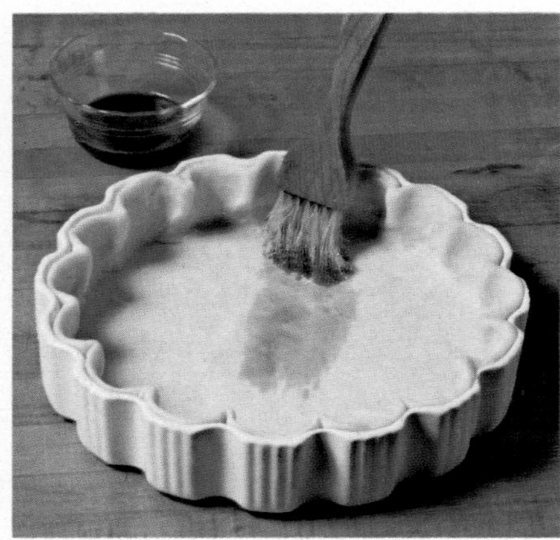

Brush pastry with a mixture of 1 egg yolk and 1 teaspoon Worcestershire sauce. Microwave at High, rotating dish ½ turn after about ½ time.

Fill pastry with crumbled cooked bacon, grated cheese and green onions. Pour in hot custard mixture. Microwave at Medium High, rotating dish ½ turn after about ½ of time.

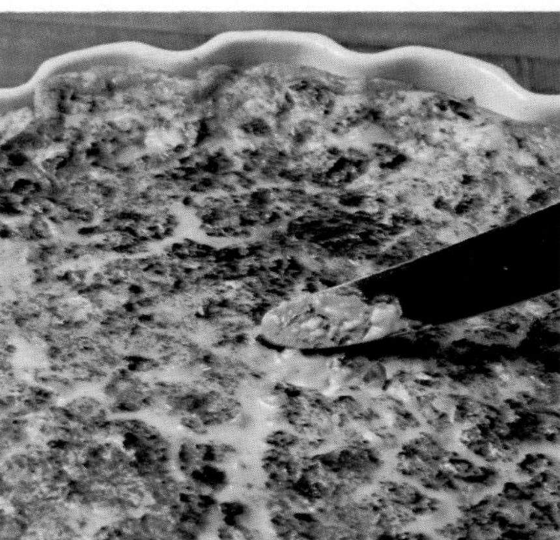

Metal Knife inserted in the center will come out coated with partially cooked custard when quiche is done. Center will set during the 5 minutes of standing time.

CLASSIC QUICHE LORRAINE

POWER LEVEL: Medium High
MICROWAVE TIME: 14 to 18 min., total

6 strips crisp cooked bacon, crumbled **½ cup grated Swiss cheese** **3 green onions, chopped** **1 Quiche Pastry**	Reserve 2 tablespoons each of bacon and cheese and 1 tablespoon onion. Sprinkle remaining bacon, cheese and onion over bottom of microwaved Quiche Pastry (right).
1½ tablespoons flour **¼ teaspoon salt** **¼ teaspoon nutmeg** **Dash cayenne** **1 cup milk** **1 cup whipping cream**	In 1-qt. measure mix flour, salt, nutmeg and cayenne. Gradually stir in milk and cream. **Microwave at Medium High 7 to 8 Minutes.** Stir every 2 minutes.
4 eggs	In 1-qt. casserole beat eggs. Stir in hot liquid.

Microwave at Medium High 1 to 2 Minutes, stirring every ½ minute, until thick. Pour into pastry. Top with bacon, cheese, onion and, if desired, paprika. **Microwave at Medium High 6 to 8 Minutes,** rotating dish ¼ turn every 2 minutes, until almost set. Let stand 5 minutes.

Makes 1 (9-in.) quiche, about 6 servings

QUICHE PASTRY

POWER LEVEL: High
MICROWAVE TIME: 4 to 6 min., total

1 cup unsifted all-purpose flour **½ teaspoon salt** **3 tablespoons shortening** **3 tablespoons cold butter**	In small mixing bowl stir together flour and salt. With pastry blender, cut in shortening until it has the appearance of cornmeal. Cut in butter until particles form the size of peas.
2½ tablespoons cold water	Sprinkle mixture with cold water. Blend lightly with fingers until dough holds together and can be formed into ball. Roll out to fit 9-in. quiche dish.
1 egg yolk **1 teaspoon Worcestershire sauce**	Brush pastry with mixture of egg yolk and Worcestershire sauce.

Microwave at High 4 to 6 Minutes, rotating dish ½ turn after 2½ minutes.

Makes 1 (9-in.) quiche pastry

GOLDEN ONION QUICHE

POWER LEVEL: High and Medium
MICROWAVE TIME: 16 to 18 min., total

1 commercially frozen pie crust **Worcestershire sauce (about 2 teaspoons)**	Remove pastry from foil pan to glass 8-in. pie plate. **Microwave at High 1 Minute,** until softened. With fingers, press firmly in pie plate. Brush inside with Worcestershire sauce. Prick pastry. **Microwave at High 4 Minutes,** rotating plate ½ turn after 2 minutes.
1 cup (4-oz.) shredded Mozzarella or pizza cheese	Sprinkle cheese over bottom of pie shell.
3 eggs **½ cup whipping cream** **3 drops hot pepper sauce (tabasco)**	With fork, beat together eggs, cream and hot pepper sauce. Pour over cheese in pie shell.
1 can (3-oz.) French fried onions	With sharp knife, cut through onions in can to chop medium fine. Pour over top and lightly press down.
1 tablespoon dried or frozen chives	Sprinkle chives over top.

Microwave at Medium 11 to 13 Minutes, rotating pie ½ turn after 6 minutes. Let stand about 5 minutes to firm slightly before serving.

Makes 1 (8-in.) pie, about 6 servings

Golden Onion Quiche and its variations have been favorites with our customers ever since Medium Power was available. It is easy to make because it starts with convenience ingredients.

VARIATIONS:

BACON AND CHEESE QUICHE

Follow recipe for Golden Onion Quiche (left) except sprinkle 4 slices crisp-microwaved bacon, crumbled over cheese before adding custard mixture. Substitute shredded Swiss cheese for Mozzarella, if desired.

HAM AND CHEESE QUICHE

Follow recipe for Golden Onion Quiche (left), except substitute sharp cheddar cheese for Mozzarella. Before adding filling, spread 1 can (4-oz.) deviled ham over bottom of microwaved pastry crust. Then add cheese and rest of filling ingredients. **Microwave at Medium 12 to 15 Minutes.**

GREEN CHILIES QUICHE

Especially appropriate cut in small wedges and served as an appetizer.

Follow recipe for Golden Onion Quiche (left) except sprinkle 2 tablespoons chopped green chilies over cheese before adding custard mixture.

Golden Onion Quiche

Souffles

Souffles must be specially formulated for microwaving, so you cannot adapt conventional recipes. Because it cooks so quickly, a microwaved souffle needs to be stabilized. For this reason we use evaporated milk in making the cream sauce base.

A microwaved souffle rises very high because it does not form a crust. It requires a larger dish than conventionally baked. A 2½-qt. souffle dish is the minimum size for a 6-egg souffle. Souffles can be microwaved only with a combination of Low and Medium Power and should be rotated frequently.

When done, the souffle will be dry on top with a creamy meringue in the center. Traditionally, this creamy center is served as a "sauce". See page 201 for Spinach Souffle, a vegetable variation of Cheese Souffle.

CHEESE SOUFFLE

POWER LEVEL: High, Low and Medium
MICROWAVE TIME: 27 to 32 min., total

¼ cup flour
¾ teaspoon salt
½ teaspoon dry mustard
⅛ teaspoon paprika
1 can (13-oz.) evaporated milk
In 1½-qt. casserole blend together flour, salt, mustard and paprika. Stir in evaporated milk. **Microwave at High 4 to 6 Minutes,** stirring every 2 minutes, until thickened.

2 cups (8-oz.) sharp cheddar cheese
Stir cheese into hot sauce. **Microwave at High 1 to 2 Minutes,** until smooth.

6 eggs, separated
1 teaspoon cream of tartar
In large mixer bowl beat egg whites with cream of tartar until stiff but not dry. Set aside and, using same beaters, beat yolks in medium mixer bowl until thick and lemon colored.

Slowly pour cheese mixture over beaten yolks, beating until well combined. Gently pour over beaten egg whites, fold together gently just until blended. Pour into ungreased 2½-qt. souffle dish. **Microwave at Low 10 Minutes,** rotating dish ¼ turn every 5 minutes. **Microwave at Medium 12 to 14 Minutes** more, rotating dish ¼ turn every 5 minutes, until puffed top edges are beginning to appear dry and souffle has "set" appearance. Serve immediately.

Makes 6 to 8 servings

PARMESAN AND CHEDDAR CHEESE SOUFFLE

This combination gives a distinctive sharp cheese flavor to the souffle.

Prepare Cheese Souffle (above), except substitute 1 cup Parmesan cheese for 1 cup of the sharp cheddar.

CHOCOLATE SOUFFLE

This tastes like fluffy chocolate pudding. A crack may appear on top, and is normal with this souffle.

POWER LEVEL: High, Low and Medium
MICROWAVE TIME: 28 to 30 min., total

¼ cup cocoa
¼ cup flour
½ cup sugar
1 teaspoon salt
2 cans (5-oz. each) evaporated milk
In 1-qt. measure mix cocoa, flour, sugar and salt to blend. Add milk and stir smooth. **Microwave at High 6 Minutes,** stirring after 2 minutes, then after each additional minute.

¼ cup butter
Stir butter into hot mixture.

6 eggs, separated
¾ teaspoon cream of tartar
½ cup sugar
In large mixer bowl beat egg whites with cream of tartar until foamy. Gradually add sugar, beating to a stiff, glossy meringue.

With same beaters, beat egg yolks in medium mixer bowl until thick and lemon colored. Add chocolate mixture, beat smooth. Gently pour chocolate mixture over meringue, fold together gently, just until blended. Pour into ungreased 3 qt. souffle dish. **Microwave at Low 10 Minutes,** rotating dish ¼ turn every 5 minutes. **Microwave at Medium 12 to 14 Minutes** more, rotating dish ¼ turn every 5 minutes, until puffed top edges begin to appear dry and souffle has "set" appearance. Serve immediately.

Makes 6 to 8 servings

CHOCOLATE CREAM CHEESE SOUFFLE

Prepare Chocolate Souffle (above), except add 1 pkg. (8-oz.) softened cream cheese along with butter. Stir smooth; continue as in recipe. Instead of time given in recipe above, **Microwave at Low 10 Minutes** and **at Medium 16 to 18 Minutes.** This souffle has a less airy, but firm and stable consistency.

TIPS FOR MICROWAVING A SOUFFLE

Beat egg whites until stiff but not dry. Set aside, and with the same beaters, beat egg yolks until thick and lemon colored. Mix yolks with prepared cheese sauce.

Fold egg-cheese mixture into whites, using a rubber spatula to cut down to bottom of dish, move across the bottom, and lift the egg whites up over top of sauce.

Pour into souffle dish. Rotate dish every 5 minutes. Microwave at Low 10 minutes, then Microwave at Medium 12 to 14 minutes, until top appears dry.

Cheese Souffle

Melted Cheese Sandwich

Cheese

Natural cheese reacts to microwaving much as it does to conventional cooking, but faster. Because of its high fat content it melts quickly and tends to become stringy when overcooked. Where cheese must be cooked for more than a few moments, layer it between other ingredients and use Medium Power, or use process cheese, which is less apt to become stringy. Many cheese dishes make good appetizers. Try our selection of cheese fondues next time you entertain.

MELTED CHEESE SANDWICH

POWER LEVEL: Medium High
MICROWAVE TIME: 4 min., total

2 slices bread	In conventional toaster, toast bread. At the same time, preheat empty and uncovered Brown 'N Sear Dish at **Medium High 3 Minutes.**
Butter **2 slices processed cheese**	When toasted, assemble sandwich and butter outside surfaces. Place in Brown 'N Sear Dish. **Microwave at Medium High ½ Minute** per side.

Makes 1 sandwich

TIPS FOR MICROWAVING CHEESE

Cubed process cheese combines with cooked macaroni and evaporated milk for a quick and easy casserole. To use natural cheese, fold cooked macaroni into homemade cheese sauce.

Add cheese toppings to vegetables, casseroles and hamburgers after cooking. Heat from the food melts the cheese. Shredded cheese on pizza and nachos is microwaved a few seconds to melt it.

CHEESE FONDUE WITH NATURAL CHEESE

It is important to whisk or stir the fondue every minute after the cheese is added, and to cook only until melted. The kirsch, while a classic ingredient, is optional.

POWER LEVEL: High and Medium
MICROWAVE TIME: 7 to 8 min., total

1 cup dry white wine
2 tablespoons kirsch

In 2-qt. microwave oven-proof fondue pot or casserole place wine and kirsch. **Microwave at High 4 Minutes,** until very hot.

2½ cups (10-oz.) shredded natural gruyere cheese
2½ cups (10-oz.) shredded natural baby Swiss cheese
3 tablespoons flour
⅛ teaspoon pepper
Dash nutmeg (optional)

Toss cheeses with flour, pepper and nutmeg, until cheese is well coated. When wine is very hot, whisk or stir in cheese quickly. Cover. **Microwave at Medium 3 to 4 Minutes,** stir briskly every minute, until cheese is just melted. Serve immediately with cubes of crusty French bread for dipping.

Makes about 4 servings

CHEESE FONDUE WITH PROCESSED CHEESE

Processed cheese gives the fondue a very smooth, even texture.

Follow recipe above, except substitute processed gruyere and Swiss cheeses for the natural cheeses. Or, as an alternate, use 5 cups (20-oz.) shredded Swiss cheese and omit gruyere.

QUICK AND EASY FONDUE

This recipe can easily be doubled or tripled to use as a party dip for crackers or the traditional bread cubes. Increase time about 2 minutes.

POWER LEVEL: High
MICROWAVE TIME: 3 to 4 min., total

1 can (10-oz.) condensed cream of shrimp soup
1 roll (6-oz.) process garlic cheese, cubed

In 1-qt. casserole stir together soup and cheese cubes. **Microwave at High 3 to 4 Minutes,** stirring after 2 minutes, until cheese is melted.

Makes about 2 to 3 servings

Cheese Fondue

CHEESE SANDWICH CASSEROLE

POWER LEVEL: Medium
MICROWAVE TIME: 9 to 12 min., total

4 slices bread
Butter
2 cups (8-oz.) shredded cheddar cheese

Spread each bread slice with butter. In 10×6×2-in. dish place 2 slices bread, butter side up. Top with 1 cup cheese. Repeat layers.

2 eggs
1 cup dairy half & half
2 tablespoons butter, melted
½ teaspoon salt
½ teaspoon dry mustard
¼ teaspoon paprika
Dash cayenne pepper

In mixing bowl beat eggs. Blend in half & half, butter, salt, mustard, paprika and cayenne pepper. Pour over sandwiches. Cover with wax paper. **Microwave at Medium 9 to 12 Minutes,** rotate dish ¼ turn every 3 minutes. Let stand 5 minutes before serving.

Makes 2 or 4 servings

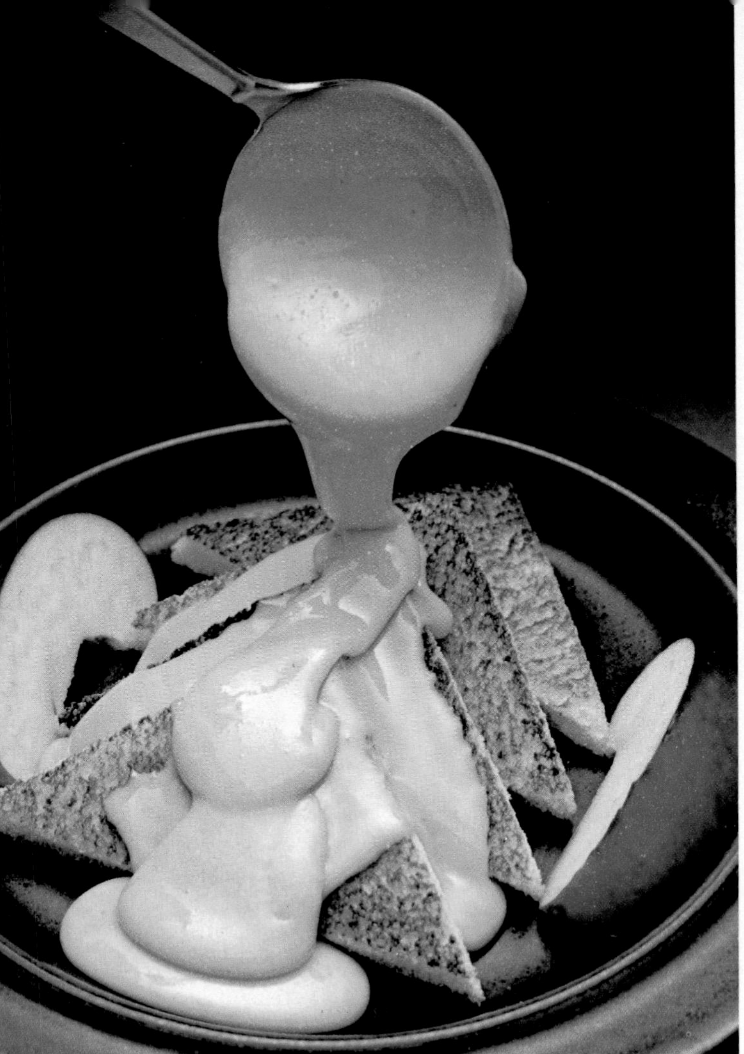

Cheese Rarebit

CHEESE RAREBIT

Rarebit is a rich cheese sauce traditionally served over toast points or other types of toasted bread.

POWER LEVEL: High and Medium
MICROWAVE TIME: 7 to 10 min., total

8 oz. pasturized processed cheese, diced
1 tablespoon butter .... In 1-qt. casserole place cheese and butter. **Microwave at High 2 to 3 Minutes,** stirring every minute, until melted and cheese can be stirred smooth.

¼ teaspoon salt
¼ teaspoon dry mustard
½ teaspoon Worcestershire sauce
Dash cayenne pepper
¼ cup dairy half & half
1 egg yolk, beaten .... Add salt, mustard, Worcestershire sauce and cayenne pepper. Quickly stir in half & half and egg yolk. **Microwave at Medium 5 to 7 Minutes,** stirring every minute, until hot.

Makes 3 to 4 servings

CHEESE ENCHILADAS

POWER LEVEL: High
MICROWAVE TIME: 12½ to 15¾ min., total

1 lb. ricotta cheese (2 cups)
1 egg
1 cup chopped green onions
2 tablespoons chopped green chilies
1 teaspoon cumin
1 cup (4-oz.) shredded Jack cheese ...... In mixing bowl stir together ricotta, egg, onions, chillies, cumin and Jack cheese.

8 fresh corn or flour tortillas, (about 6-in diameter) or, 10 to 12 canned tortillas (5-in. diameter) ...... Wrap tortillas in towel. **Microwave at High ½ to ¾ Minute,** until pliable. Divide filling among tortillas. Roll up each one tightly.

1 can (10-oz.) enchilada sauce .. In lightly greased 12×8×2-in. dish place rolls, seam side down. Pour sauce over rolls. **Microwave at High 11 to 13 Minutes,** until filling begins to bubble.

2 cups (8-oz.) shredded cheddar cheese ... Cover with cheddar cheese. **Microwave at High 1 to 2 Minutes,** until cheese is almost melted.

Sour cream and chopped green onions .... Garnish with sour cream and green onions.

Makes 4 generous servings

There are many references to cheese and cheese recipes in other sections of this book; including:

Cream Cheese Dips, page 52
Cheese Crock, page 54
Crab Swiss Crisps, page 54
Soft Smokey Cheese Ball, page 54
Mushroom Stuffings, page 58
Cheese Souffle, page 166
Spaghetti and Cheese Casserole, page 178
Macaroni and Cheese, page 178
Lasagna, page 180
Cheese Grits Casserole, page 183
Cheezy Broccoli, page 194
Zippy Zucchini, page 203
Cheesecake, page 250

CHEESE PIE WITH HAMBURGER CRUST

POWER LEVEL: High and Medium
MICROWAVE TIME: 14 to 16 min., total

1 egg
½ cup milk
2 cups fresh bread, cubed (3 slices)
In large mixing bowl beat egg slightly. Add milk and bread. Toss lightly, then let stand few minutes, until most of liquid is absorbed.

½ lb. ground chuck beef
1 teaspoon Worcestershire sauce
1 teaspoon salt
¼ teaspoon thyme
¼ teaspoon dried parsley
1¼ cups sliced green onions, including tops, divided
To bread mixture add beef, Worcestershire sauce, salt, thyme, parsley and ¼ cup onions. Mix lightly until combined. Spoon into 9-in. pie plate and spread to line bottom and sides of plate. Sprinkle remaining green onions over crust.

3 eggs
1 cup (4-oz.) shredded Swiss cheese
3 to 4 drops liquid pepper seasoning (tabasco)
½ teaspoon salt
⅓ cup milk
Paprika
In same bowl beat eggs until foamy. Stir in cheese, liquid pepper seasoning, salt and milk. Pour over green onions in meat crust. Sprinkle lightly with paprika.

Microwave at High 5 Minutes, then rotate dish ¼ turn. **Microwave at Medium 9 to 11 Minutes,** rotating dish ¼ turn after 5 minutes. Center will be soft but set when done.

Makes 6 to 8 servings

MICROWAVE CHEESE TOPPINGS

The following toppings may be prepared to garnish favorite vegetables or casseroles.

Cheese Topping for Vegetables: In small mixing bowl place 1 jar or pkg. (8-oz.) processed cheddar cheese food. **Microwave at Medium High 3 to 4 Minutes,** stirring after 2 minutes, until cheese is melted and can be stirred smooth. For thinner topping, add 1 to 2 tablespoons milk, beer or tomato juice. Add chopped parsley and/or garlic salt for more color or flavor.

Cheese Topping for Casseroles: In small mixing bowl place ¼ cup butter. **Microwave at High ½ to 1 Minute,** until melted. Stir in ½ cup fine dry bread or cracker crumbs, ¼ cup Parmesan cheese and ¼ teaspoon paprika. **Microwave at Medium High 2 to 3 Minutes,** stirring after 1 minute.

CHEESE PUDDING

This interesting casserole is a good substitute for potatoes, rice or pasta in a full course menu. Or serve it as a luncheon or supper dish, along with a salad.

POWER LEVEL: High, Medium and Medium High
MICROWAVE TIME: 21¼ to 26½ min., total

2 cups water
4 eggs
Poach eggs hard; into 1½-qt. casserole pour water. **Microwave at High 5 to 6 Minutes,** until boiling. Break eggs into saucer and puncture membrane around yolk with toothpick. **Microwave at Medium 5 to 6 Minutes,** until yolks begin to harden. Let stand several minutes in water. Remove and grate or chop finely.

1 cup buttery flavored cracker crumbs
2 cups (double recipe) thick White Sauce, page 173
2 cups (8-oz.) shredded cheddar cheese
2 jars (4-oz.) sliced pimiento, drained
Into 8-in. square dish place ½ of cracker crumbs. Cover with ½ of white sauce, ½ of cheese, ½ of pimiento and ½ of eggs. Repeat layers. Cover with Buttered Crumbs (below). **Microwave at Medium High 10 to 12 Minutes,** rotating dish ½ turn after 5 minutes, until heated through.

Makes about 8 servings

Buttered Crumbs: In 1 cup measure place 2 tablespoons butter. **Microwave at High ¼ to ½ Minute,** until melted. Add ½ cup fine dry bread crumbs. **Microwave at Medium High 1 to 2 Minutes,** until browned.

EGGS & CHEESE CONVENIENCE CHART

ITEM	POWER LEVEL	TIME MINUTES	COMMENTS
Egg Substitute (egg beaters) (8-oz. carton)	Defrost	4 to 4½	Time 3 minutes, turn over after 1½ minutes. Open carton and stir every ½ minute until smooth.
Cheese Souffle (12-oz. pkg.)	Defrost	10 to 14	To Defrost: Place in 8-in. pie plate. Stir.
	Medium High	9 to 11	To Cook: Divide between 3 or 4 buttered custard cups; 6 or 7-oz. Rearrange after 4 minutes. Souffles are done when center is set.
Welsh Rarebit (10-oz. pkg.)	High	5 to 6	Stir every 2 minutes.

Poultry Giblet Gravy

Gravies & Main Dish Sauces

Gravies and sauces microwave easily because there is no scorching or lumping or constant stirring. They save time in cooking and clean-up, too. Make them right in the cup you use for measuring or in the microwave oven-proof sauce boat you use for serving.

Main Dish Sauces found in other sections include:

Kentucky Bourbon Sauce, page 107
Cranberry Orange Ruby Sauce, page 114
Apple Cider Sauce, page 127
Cranberry Sauce, page 137
Clarified Butter, page 144

POULTRY GIBLET GRAVY

POWER LEVEL: Medium and High
MICROWAVE TIME: 21 to 29 min., total

Giblets from a 3-lb. chicken **1 cup water**	In 1-qt. casserole place giblets. Prick each giblet several times with fork. Add water. Cover. **Microwave at Medium 16 to 20 Minutes,** stirring after 10 minutes, until tender. Chop medium fine.
¼ cup poultry drippings **¼ cup flour** **½ teaspoon salt** **¼ teaspoon celery salt** **Dash pepper**	In separate 1-qt. casserole place drippings. **Microwave at High 1 to 2 Minutes,** until hot. Stir in flour, salt, celery salt and pepper until smooth.
Broth from giblets plus water to make 1¼ cups	Gradually stir in broth until well blended. **Microwave at High 2 to 4 Minutes,** stirring every minute. Add chopped giblets. **Microwave at High 2 to 3 Minutes** more, stirring every minute, until thickened.

Makes about 1½ cups

TIPS FOR MICROWAVING GRAVIES AND SAUCES

Use More flour or cornstarch to thicken microwaved gravies and sauces, since they will not reduce by evaporation.

Combine flour, butter and salt in a glass measure when making White Sauce. Microwave until butter melts and bubbles. Stir and microwave 1 minute more to cook flour.

Stir occasionally to bring cooked portions from the outside of the measure to the center. Use a wire whisk or table fork for a smooth sauce with minimum stirring.

MILK GRAVY

Be sure to use a 1-qt. utensil to prevent boilover. These proportions are for gravy which runs easily from spoon. For thicker gravy, which mounds from spoon, use ⅓ cup flour.

POWER LEVEL: High
MICROWAVE TIME: 7 to 10 min., total

¼ cup chicken or beef drippings **¼ cup flour** **¼ teaspoon salt** **1¼ cups milk**	In 1-qt. glass measure, measure drippings. **Microwave at High 1 to 2 Minutes,** until hot. Add flour and salt. Stir well. Stir in milk slowly. **Microwave at High 6 to 8 Minutes,** stirring every minute.

Makes about 1½ cups

VARIATIONS:

Cream Gravy: Prepare Milk Gravy as above, except, instead of 1¼ cups milk, use ⅔ cup milk and ⅔ cup whipping cream.

Brown Gravy: Prepare Milk Gravy or Cream Gravy as above, using beef or lamb drippings and adding ½ teaspoon brown bouquet sauce.

BASIC WHITE SAUCE

POWER LEVEL: High
MICROWAVE TIME: 5½ to 6½ min., total

2 tablespoons butter **2 tablespoons flour** **½ teaspoon salt**	In 1-qt. glass measure place butter, flour and salt. **Microwave at High 2 Minutes** stirring after 1 minute.
1 cup milk	Gradually stir in milk. **Microwave at High 3½ to 4½ Minutes,** stirring every minute until thick and bubbly.

Makes 1 cup

VARIATIONS:

Cheese Sauce: To finished sauce, add 1 cup (4-oz.) shredded sharp cheese and a dash of cayenne pepper. **Microwave at High 1 to 2 Minutes,** to melt cheese.

Mornay Sauce: To finished sauce, add ½ cup shredded Swiss, gruyere or Parmesan cheese, 1 teaspoon lemon juice and a dash of cayenne pepper.

Curry Sauce: Add 2 to 3 teaspoons curry powder along with flour. Microwave as above.

Dill Sauce: To finished sauce, add 2 teaspoons dill weed and 1 teaspoon lemon juice.

Horseradish Sauce: To finished sauce, add 1 to 2 teaspoons cream style horseradish.

Thick White Sauce: Use 3 tablespoons flour instead of 2 tablespoons.

Asparagus with White Sauce

HOLLANDAISE SAUCE FOR MICROWAVERS

We have tried many recipes for microwaving Hollandaise Sauce, even the "never-fail" ones, and our recommendation is to use the blender method. The microwave oven helps you by rapidly melting the butter.

You can reheat leftover Hollandaise successfully at Low Power for 1/4 to 1/2 minute. Stir and let the sauce stand before continuing to reheat; it is so delicate that it can curdle easily even upon reheating if you set the timer for too long.

POWER LEVEL: High
MICROWAVE TIME: 1 to 2 min., total

2 egg yolks **1 tablespoon lemon juice** **1/2 teaspoon dry mustard** **1/8 teaspoon salt**	Into container of electric blender place yolks, juice, mustard and salt.
1/2 cup (1/4-lb.) butter	In glass measuring cup place butter. **Microwave at High 1 to 2 Minutes,** until hot and bubbly. Turn electric blender to highest speed and gradually add butter, mixing well until Hollandaise is creamy and thickened.

Makes about 1/2 cup

SWEET AND SOUR SAUCE

This piquant sauce is so versatile that it goes with just about every type of meat, poultry and seafood. It's very good with hamburgers, especially if you increase garlic to 1 clove. The 10 drops liquid pepper seasoning gives it zip.

POWER LEVEL: High
MICROWAVE TIME: 5 to 7 min., total

1/2 cup sugar **2 tablespoons cornstarch** **1/4 cup cold water**	In 1 1/2-qt. casserole stir together sugar, cornstarch and water, until well blended.
1 can (8-oz.) crushed pineapple **1/2 cup chopped green pepper** **1/4 cup (4-oz. can) chopped pimiento** **1/2 clove garlic, mashed** **1/2 cup cider vinegar** **2 tablespoons soy sauce** **10 drops liquid pepper seasoning (tabasco)**	Stir in pineapple, pepper, pimiento, garlic, vinegar, soy sauce and pepper seasoning. **Microwave at High 5 to 7 Minutes,** stirring every 2 minutes, until clear and thickened. Let sauce stand 5 to 10 minutes, to develop flavor, before serving.

Makes about 1 3/4 cups

BEARNAISE SAUCE

Serve this sauce over steaks, poached eggs on toast, or microwaved green vegetables.

POWER LEVEL: High
MICROWAVE TIME: 1 to 2 min., total

4 egg yolks **1 teaspoon instant minced onion** **1 teaspoon tarragon vinegar** **1 teaspoon white wine**	In blender container place yolks, onion, vinegar and wine.
1/2 cup (1/4-lb.) butter	In glass measure place butter. **Microwave at High 1 to 2 Minutes,** until hot and bubbly. Turn electric blender to highest speed and gradually add butter, mixing until sauce is creamy and thickened.

Makes about 1/2 cup

WHIPPED BUTTERS

Savory garnishes for sliced, roasted meats or plain vegetables.

POWER LEVEL: Low
MICROWAVE TIME: ½ to ¾ min., total

1. In small glass mixer bowl place ½ cup butter. **Microwave at Low ½ to ¾ Minute,** until softened.
2. Add ingredients from one of the variations.
3. Whip with electric mixer at high speed, until fluffy.

Makes ½ cup

VARIATIONS:

Herbed Butter: Add 2 teaspoons minced parsley, 2 teaspoons lemon juice, ¼ teaspoon thyme, ¼ teaspoon salt and ¼ teaspoon pepper.

Parsley Garlic Butter: Add ½ cup minced parsley, 2 cloves minced garlic, 2 teaspoons minced onion, 2 teaspoons lemon juice and 1 teaspoon dry mustard.

Dill Butter: Add 4 teaspoons dill weed, ½ teaspoon salt, ⅛ teaspoon pepper and 2 hard cooked egg yolks, sieved. To hard cook egg yolks: Place yolks in 6-oz. custard cup. Add 1 tablespoon water. Cover with plastic wrap. **Microwave at Medium 1 Minute.** Let stand a few minutes, then remove from water to cool.

COLORFUL MARMALADE SAUCE

This bright sauce looks and tastes good over duck, chicken, turkey and ham. It serves as a glaze as well as a sauce. Use sweet, not bitter, orange marmalade.

POWER LEVEL: High
MICROWAVE TIME: 5 to 7 min., total

1 cup sweet orange marmalade **1 can (8-oz.) tomato sauce** **2 tablespoons chopped onion** **1½ teaspoons soy sauce** **1 teaspoon ground ginger** **½ cup sliced almonds**	In 1½-qt. casserole combine marmalade, tomato sauce, onion, soy sauce, ginger and almonds. **Microwave at High 5 to 7 Minutes,** stirring every 2 minutes, until hot and well combined.

Makes about 2 cups

LEMON BUTTER SAUCE

A favorite sauce for fish and fish loaves, and for some vegetables, such as asparagus and broccoli.

POWER LEVEL: High
MICROWAVE TIME: ½ to 1 Minute

¼ cup butter	In 1-cup glass measure place butter. **Microwave at High ½ to 1 Minute,** until melted.
1 tablespoon fresh lemon juice **1 tablespoon snipped parsley** **Dash pepper**	Stir lemon juice, parsley and pepper into melted butter. Keep warm.

Makes about ¼ cup

ALMOND BUTTER SAUCE

POWER LEVEL: High
MICROWAVE TIME: 6 to 7 min., total

¼ cup slivered almonds **½ cup (¼-lb.) butter, divided**	In 9-in. pie plate place almonds and 1 teaspoon butter. **Microwave at High 5 to 6 Minutes,** stirring every 2 minutes, until toasted. Add remaining butter. **Microwave at High 1 Minute,** until melted.
½ teaspoon seasoned salt	Stir in seasoned salt. Serve warm.

Makes ½ cup

RAISIN SAUCE

Traditionally served with ham or pork.

POWER LEVEL: High
MICROWAVE TIME: 4 to 6 min., total

½ cup brown sugar (packed) **2 tablespoons cornstarch** **1½ teaspoons mustard** **⅛ teaspoon cloves**	In 1-qt. measuring cup or casserole blend together brown sugar, cornstarch, mustard and cloves, until well combined.
1 cup water or apple cider **2 tablespoons lemon juice** **¼ cup raisins** **2 tablespoons butter**	Stir in water and lemon juice until smooth. Add raisins and butter. **Microwave at High 4 to 6 Minutes,** stirring every 2 minutes, until clear and thickened.

Makes about 1¼ cups

CLAM SAUCE

This is a popular sauce for spaghetti or other pasta. If possible, buy a green (spinach) pasta to serve with this clear sauce.

POWER LEVEL: High
MICROWAVE TIME: 7 to 8 min., total

2 tablespoons olive oil
3 cloves garlic, minced
¼ teaspoon salt

In 1-qt. casserole place oil, garlic and salt. **Microwave at High 3 Minutes,** until softened.

2 cans (6.5-oz. each) minced clams
¼ cup water
1 tablespoon cornstarch
¼ cup minced parsley

Drain clams, reserving juice. Set aside. Stir together water and cornstarch. Add to garlic along with clam juice and parsley. **Microwave at High 3 Minutes,** stirring after 2 minutes, until thickened. Stir in clams. **Microwave at High 1 to 2 Minutes,** until hot.

Makes about 2 cups

BARBECUE SAUCE

The traditional sauce to use when cooking ribs and chicken. Or, slice leftover beef or pork into barbecue sauce and serve warm as an entree or sandwich filling.

POWER LEVEL: High
MICROWAVE TIME: 5 to 6 min., total

1 cup chili sauce
½ cup water
¼ cup lemon juice
1 tablespoon cooking oil
2 tablespoons brown sugar (packed)
½ teaspoon salt
¼ teaspoon paprika
¼ teaspoon liquid pepper seasoning (tabasco)
1 tablespoon Worcestershire sauce

In 1-qt. casserole thoroughly combine chili sauce, water, lemon juice, cooking oil, brown sugar, salt, paprika, pepper seasoning and Worcestershire sauce. Cover. **Microwave at High 5 to 7 Minutes,** stirring after 3 minutes, until hot. Use as desired.

Makes 2 cups

CLASSIC ITALIAN SAUCE

Complements pasta, meatballs, meat slices and cooked chicken pieces.

POWER LEVEL: High
MICROWAVE TIME: 15 to 18 min., total

1 large onion, chopped
3 tablespoons olive or cooking oil
3 cloves garlic, minced

In 3-qt. casserole place onion, oil and garlic. **Microwave at High 3 to 4 Minutes,** stirring after 2 minutes, until onion is limp.

2 cans (15-oz. each) tomato sauce
2 cans (6-oz. each) tomato paste
⅔ cup burgundy, beef broth or tomato juice
2 tablespoons brown sugar
2 teaspoons Worcestershire sauce
1 teaspoon oregano
1 teaspoon basil
1 teaspoon salt
½ teaspoon pepper

Add tomato sauce, tomato paste, wine, broth or juice, brown sugar, Worcestershire sauce, oregano, basil, salt and pepper. Mix together well. Cover. **Microwave at High 12 to 14 Minutes,** stirring after 6 minutes, until very hot.

Makes about 2 quarts

Italian Sauce With Meat: Add 2-lb. ground chuck beef, crumbled, seasoned and cooked.

Italian Sauce With Mushrooms: Add 2-lb. fresh mushrooms, sliced and sauteed.

MUSHROOM SAUCE

This is elegant for steaks or chops.

POWER LEVEL: Medium High
MICROWAVE TIME: 6 to 7 min., total

2 cups sliced fresh mushrooms
¼ cup butter

In 1-qt. casserole place mushrooms and butter. Cover. **Microwave at Medium High 3 Minutes.**

¼ cup water
¼ cup sherry wine or additional water
1 tablespoon cornstarch
⅛ teaspoon salt

Mix together water, sherry, cornstarch and salt. Gradually stir into mushrooms. Cover. **Microwave at Medium High 3 to 4 Minutes,** stirring after 2 minutes, until thickened.

Makes about 2 cups

Pasta, Rice
& Cereal

Among microwave cooks and microwave cookbooks, pasta and rice are a controversial subject. They take about the same time to soften, whether you cook them by microwave or conventionally. Advocates of microwaved pasta insist that they have a better flavor and firm, "al dente" texture. Other people prefer to cook them conventionally because this leaves the microwave oven free to cook the sauce or main dish.

Both sides agree that microwaving is a perfect way to reheat pasta and rice. Reheated conventionally, pasta and rice will dry out unless you add more water, which overcooks them. Tightly covered with plastic wrap, pasta and rice reheat to "fresh cooked" flavor and texture. Undercook pasta and rice 3 to 5 minutes if you are using it in a casserole which requires further cooking.

Many of our recipes in the main dish sections call for quick-cooking rice, because regular rice will not be cooked in the short times needed for the other ingredients. Make this same substitution in adapting your own recipes.

For sauces try Italian Sauce and variations, page 176, with spaghetti; Clam Sauce, page 176, with linguine; Flavored Butters, page 175, with noodles or rice.

SPAGHETTI-CHEESE CASSEROLE

As a garnish, save out a few olive slices from sauce to decorate top.

POWER LEVEL: High
MICROWAVE TIME: 21 to 26 min., total

1 pkg. (7-oz.) spaghetti	Cook spaghetti (see chart at right), except **Microwave 9 Minutes.**
1 can (10½-oz.) condensed cream of mushroom soup **½ cup milk** **1 teaspoon instant minced onion** **⅛ teaspoon pepper** **½ cup sliced stuffed olives**	In small bowl mix soup, milk, onion, pepper and olives.
2 cups (8-oz.) cheddar cheese, cubed	In greased 1½-qt. casserole alternate layers of spaghetti, cheese and soup mixture. **Microwave at High 9 to 12 Minutes,** rotating dish ½ turn after 4 minutes.

Makes 4 to 6 servings

NOTE: This casserole is a good meat accompaniment or makes a nice luncheon dish, served with sliced tomato salad.

CREAMY MACARONI AND CHEESE

POWER LEVEL: High and Medium High
MICROWAVE TIME: 23 to 27 min., total

1 pkg. (7-oz.) elbow macaroni	Cook macaroni (see chart at right), except **Microwave 10 Minutes.** Drain well and return to same casserole.
¼ cup butter	In 1-qt. measure place butter. **Microwave at High ½ to 1 Minute,** to melt.
6 tablespoons flour **1 teaspoon salt** **2 cups milk**	Blend in flour and salt. Stir in milk until smooth. **Microwave at High 5½ to 6 Minutes,** stirring with table fork every minute, until thickened.
2 cups (8-oz.) grated sharp cheddar cheese	Stir in cheese until completely melted.

Stir sauce into drained macaroni, mixing well. **Microwave at Medium High 7 to 10 Minutes,** stirring every 3 minutes. If desired, sprinkle top with paprika or buttered crumbs before serving.

Makes 6 to 8 servings

QUICK AND EASY MACARONI AND CHEESE

A family-type favorite. For added zip, stir in a few drops Worcestershire sauce.

POWER LEVEL: High
MICROWAVE TIME: 16 to 18 min., total

1 pkg. (7-oz.) elbow macaroni	Cook macaroni (see chart at right), except **Microwave 10 Minutes.**
1 block pkg. (1-lb.) pasteurized process cheese spread **1 can (5⅓-oz.) evaporated milk**	Cut cheese into cubes. Into 3-qt. casserole place cheese with macaroni and milk. Toss together until cheese is distributed.

Microwave at High 6 to 8 Minutes, stirring after 3 minutes, until cheese is melted and mixture bubbles. Stir to blend.

Makes 6 to 8 servings

HOW TO MICROWAVE PASTA & RICE

Combine pasta or rice with very hot tap water and salt in the recommended cooking dish. Add oil if needed.

Cover tightly with casserole cover or plastic wrap, turned back at edge 2-in. to vent. Microwave at High Power.

Stir or rearrange after ½ the time. Recover and continue microwaving. Drain immediately.

PASTA & RICE MICROWAVING CHART

POWER LEVEL: **High**

FOOD TYPE	AMOUNT	UTENSIL	WATER SALT & OIL	TIME MINUTES	GENERAL DIRECTIONS
Macaroni	6 to 8-oz. pkg.	2-qt. casserole	3 cups water 2 teaspoons salt	15 to 18	Stir after 10 minutes.
Rotini	16-oz. pkg.	3-qt. casserole	6 cups water 1 teaspoon salt	13 to 16	Stir after 10 minutes. Check rotini after 10 minutes as this cooks faster than other types.
Spaghetti or Linguine	16-oz. pkg.	13×9×2-in. dish	6 to 7 cups water 1 tablespoon salt 1 tablespoon oil	16 to 19	Rearrange after 10 minutes.
Spaghetti or Linguine	7-oz. pkg.	13×9×2-in. dish	6 to 7 cups water ½ teaspoon salt 1 tablespoon oil	12 to 14	Rearrange after 8 minutes.
Egg Noodles, Narrow	3 cups or 6-oz.	8-in. square dish	3 cups water 1 teaspoon salt	13 to 16	Time is the same for spinach or regular.
Egg Noodles, Wide	8-oz.	3-qt. casserole	8 cups water 1 teaspoon salt 1 teaspoon oil	23 to 25	Stir after 10 minutes.
Lasagna	16-oz. pkg.	13×9×2-in. dish	Cover with water placing ½ teaspoon salt in bottom of dish 1 tablespoon oil	14 to 16	Rearrange after 7 minutes.
Lasagna	½ pkg.	13×9×2-in. dish	Cover with water placing ½ teaspoon salt in bottom of dish 1 tablespoon oil	11 to 13	Rearrange after 6 minutes.
Manicotti	10 to 12 pieces, about 5-oz. pkg.	12×8×2-in. dish	Brush with oil first then cover with water	22 to 25	Using fork turn over every 5 minutes to prevent sticking.
Long Grain Rice	1 cup	3-qt. casserole	2¼ cups water 1 teaspoon salt	18 to 21	Stir after 10 minutes.
Minute Rice	1½ cups	2-qt. casserole	1½ cups water ½ teaspoon salt	4 to 6	Stir after 2 minutes.
Rice-Vermicelli Mixes	8-oz. pkg.	2-qt. casserole	Follow package directions	18 to 22	Stir every 6 minutes. Let stand 5 minutes before serving.

CHEESE STUFFED MANICOTTI

Add cooked meatballs or sausages for an even heartier dish.

POWER LEVEL: High
MICROWAVE TIME: 35 to 38 min., total

10 manicotti	Cook manicotti (see chart, page 179), except **Microwave 20 Minutes.**
1 pkg. (6-oz.) sliced Mozzarella cheese **2 cups (1-pt.) ricotta cheese** **½ cup romano cheese** **1 can (7¾-oz.) spinach, drained** **½ teaspoon garlic powder** **½ teaspoon salt** **¼ teaspoon pepper**	Dice cheese into ½-in. cubes before separating slices. Reserve about ⅓ cup for topping. Combine rest of Mozzarella with ricotta, romano, spinach, garlic, salt and pepper. Stuff cooked manicotti with cheese filling. Rearrange in 12×8×2-in. dish.
1 can (15-oz.) tomato sauce **Marjoram**	Pour tomato sauce over top. Sprinkle with cheese and marjoram. Cover with wax paper.

Microwave at High 15 to 18 Minutes, rotating dish ½ turn after 8 minutes.

Makes 4 servings

NOODLES ROMANOFF

A traditional combination of noodles, cheese and sour cream.

POWER LEVEL: High
MICROWAVE TIME: 19 to 21 min., total

1 pkg. (7 to 8-oz.) narrow noodles	Cook noodles (see chart, page 179), except **Microwave 9 Minutes.** Place cooked noodles in 3-qt. casserole.
1 cup cottage cheese **1 cup (8-oz.) dairy sour cream** **¼ cup chopped stuffed olives** **1 teaspoon instant minced onion** **½ teaspoon salt** **½ teaspoon Worcestershire sauce** **Dash liquid pepper seasoning (tabasco)**	Add cheese, sour cream, olives, onion, salt, Worcestershire sauce and liquid pepper. Mix well. Cover. **Microwave at High 8 Minutes,** stirring after 4 minutes, until hot.
1 cup (4-oz.) shredded sharp cheese	Sprinkle cheese on top. **Microwave at High 2 to 4 Minutes** more, uncovered.

Makes 6 servings

LASAGNA

POWER LEVEL: High
MICROWAVE TIME: 28 to 34 min., total

½ pkg. (½-lb.) lasagna noodles	Cook noodles (see chart, page 179), except **Microwave 8 Minutes.**
2 cans (8-oz. each) tomato sauce **1 can (6-oz.) tomato paste** **1 tablespoon leaf oregano** **2 teaspoons basil** **½ teaspoon salt** **¼ teaspoon garlic powder or 1 garlic clove, minced**	In large bowl mix together tomato sauce, tomato paste, oregano, basil, salt and garlic. Spread ½ cup sauce over bottom of 12×8×2-in. dish.
1 lb. ground chuck beef cooked, drained	Mix beef with remaining sauce.
2 cups (1-pt.) small curd cottage cheese **1 egg** **1 tablespoon dried parsley flakes** **½ teaspoon salt** **1 pkg. (6-oz.) sliced Mozzarella cheese**	In small bowl mix together cottage cheese, egg, parsley and salt. Layer 3 noodles, half of cottage cheese mixture, half of Mozzarella cheese, half of tomato sauce in dish. Repeat layers.
½ cup grated Parmesan cheese	Sprinkle Parmesan cheese over top. Cover with wax paper.

Microwave at High 20 to 26 Minutes, rotating dish ¼ turn every 8 minutes. Letting lasagna stand about 10 minutes helps it hold shape when cutting.

Makes 6 to 8 servings

NOTE: Lasagna may be made and refrigerated. Add about 4 to 6 minutes to total cooking time.

VARIATIONS:

Meat: Substitute bulk pork sausage, cooked and drained, for ground chuck; or instead of bulk sausage use 2 pkg. (8-oz. each) brown and serve sausages, diced. (When brown and serve sausages are substituted no precooking is needed. Sausages heat as assembled casserole microwaves.) Or substitute Italian sausages, diced in same way as brown and serve sausages.

Cheese: Substitute ricotta cheese for cottage cheese and provolone cheese for Mozzarella, and, if desired, romano cheese for Parmesan.

Lasagna With Hard Cooked Eggs: Hard cook eggs in shell on range top, not in microwave oven. Layer slices of 3 or 4 hard cooked eggs over first layer of cottage cheese mixture. Eggs give an especially rich flavor to lasagna.

PASTA & RICE CONVENIENCE CHART

Canned or frozen pasta and rice should be removed from metal containers, placed in a casserole or dish of appropriate size and covered. Check at minimum time.

POWER LEVEL: **High**

ITEM	TIME MINUTES	COMMENTS
CANNED Or use temperature probe and dial 150°.		
Macaroni & Cheese, Ravioli, Spaghetti, Spanish Rice, (12 to 15-oz.)	3 to 5	Stir after ½ time and before serving.
Lasagna (40-oz.)	9 to 11	Stir after ½ time and before serving.
FROZEN		
Rice Dishes (10-oz. pouch)	6 to 8	Puncture pouch and flex after ½ time.
Macaroni & Cheese, Macaroni & Beef, (8-oz. pkg.)	5 to 6	Stir after 3 minutes.
Macaroni & Cheese Stuffed Shells, Spaghetti & Meatballs (11 to 14-oz.)	8 to 12	Stir after ½ time and before serving.
Macaroni & Cheese (2-lb.)	15 to 22	Stir after ½ time and before serving.
Lasagna (3-lb. 8-oz.)	33 to 37	Rotate dish ½ turn every 10 minutes. Let stand 5 to 10 minutes before serving.

JIFFY SPANISH RICE

POWER LEVEL: High
MICROWAVE TIME: 13 to 17 min., total

1 lb. ground chuck beef
1 cup packaged precooked (minute) rice
1 can (1-lb. 12-oz.) tomatoes, undrained, cut up
1 tablespoon instant minced onion
1 to 2 tablespoons chili powder
2 teaspoons salt
⅛ teaspoon pepper

In 3-qt. casserole crumble beef. **Microwave at High 5 to 6 Minutes,** stirring after 3 minutes. Drain. Add rice, tomatoes, onion, chili powder, salt and pepper. Cover. **Microwave at High 8 to 11 Minutes,** stirring after 4 minutes. Stir well. Let stand, covered, about 5 to 10 minutes before serving.

Makes 4 to 6 servings

RIPE OLIVE RISOTTO

Risotto means rice casserole. This combination is colorful with olives and pimiento.

POWER LEVEL: High
MICROWAVE TIME: 22 to 24 min., total

¼ cup butter or cooking oil
1 cup finely chopped onion
⅓ cup chopped celery
1 cup uncooked long grain rice
2 cups chicken bouillon
1 teaspoon salt
¼ teaspoon pepper

In 2-qt. casserole combine butter, onion, celery, rice, bouillon, salt and pepper. Cover. **Microwave at High 20 Minutes,** stirring after 10 minutes.

½ cup chopped ripe olives
1 can (4-oz.) mushroom stems and pieces, drained
1 jar (2-oz.) pimiento strips
¼ cup grated Parmesan cheese

Add olives, mushrooms, pimiento and cheese. Stir to mix well. **Microwave at High 2 to 4 Minutes.** Stir before serving.

Makes 6 to 8 servings

SAVORY TOMATO RICE

This casserole is very juicy immediately after microwaving. Stir and let stand uncovered a few minutes before serving. Very good with pork or chicken.

POWER LEVEL: High
MICROWAVE TIME: 23 to 25 min., total

4 strips bacon, cooked and crumbled
1 can (1-lb.) tomatoes, undrained, cut up
½ cup uncooked long grain rice
½ cup chili sauce
¼ cup finely chopped green pepper
2 tablespoons instant minced onion
1 teaspoon brown sugar
1 teaspoon salt
⅛ teaspoon pepper
½ teaspoon Worcestershire sauce
2 cups hot tap water

In 2-qt. casserole place bacon, tomatoes, rice, chili sauce, green pepper, onion, brown sugar, salt, pepper, Worcestershire sauce and water. Mix well. Cover. **Microwave at High 23 to 25 Minutes,** stirring every 8 minutes, until hot and rice is done.

Makes 4 to 6 servings

Cereals microwave in a simple, 1-step process. You don't have to boil the water first, or stir frequently during cooking. Microwaved cereals are easy to clean up since the cereal does not stick to the cooking dish. Family members can microwave single servings of instant cereal in paper bowls. There'll be no dirty dishes in the sink after breakfast.

HOW TO MICROWAVE CEREALS

Mix cereal and hottest tap water in a bowl large enough to prevent boilover. Microwave at High, uncovered.

Stir half way through the cooking time. For softer cereal, let stand a few minutes after microwaving.

CEREAL MICROWAVING CHART

POWER LEVEL: **High**

TYPE CEREAL	NO. OF SERVINGS	INGREDIENTS WATER	SALT	CEREAL	CONTAINER	TIME MINUTES
Oatmeal, Quick*	1	¾ cup	¼ teaspoon	⅓ cup	16-oz. cereal bowl	1 to 2
	2	1½ cups	½ teaspoon	⅔ cup	1½-qt. casserole	2 to 3
	4	3 cups	¾ teaspoon	1⅓ cups	2-qt. casserole	5 to 6
	6	4 cups	1 teaspoon	2 cups	3-qt. casserole	7 to 8
Oatmeal, Old-fashioned	1	¾ cup	¼ teaspoon	⅓ cup	1-qt. casserole	3 to 5
	2	1½ cups	½ teaspoon	⅔ cup	2-qt. casserole	6 to 7
	4	3 cups	¾ teaspoon	1⅓ cups	3-qt. casserole	8 to 9
	6	4 cups	1 teaspoon	2 cups	3-qt. casserole	10 to 11
Cornmeal	1	⅔ cup	¼ teaspoon	3 tablespoons	16-oz. cereal bowl	1½ to 2
	2	1⅓ cups	½ teaspoon	⅓ cup	1½-qt. casserole	2½ to 3
	4	2⅔ cups	¾ teaspoon	⅔ cup	2-qt. casserole	3½ to 4
	6	4 cups	1 teaspoon	1 cup	2-qt. casserole	4½ to 5
Grits, Quick*	1	¾ cup	Dash	3 tablespoons	16-oz. cereal bowl	3 to 4
	2	1⅓ cups	¼ teaspoon	⅓ cup	1½-qt. casserole	6 to 7
	4	2⅔ cups	¾ teaspoon	⅔ cup	2-qt. casserole	8 to 9
	6	4 cups	1 teaspoon	1 cup	2-qt. casserole	10 to 11
Cream of Wheat	1	1 cup	⅛ teaspoon	2½ tablespoons	1-qt. casserole	3 to 4
	2	1¾ cups	¼ teaspoon	⅓ cup	2-qt. casserole	5 to 6
	4	3½ cups	½ teaspoon	⅔ cup	3-qt. casserole	7 to 8
	6	5 cups	1 teaspoon	1 cup	3-qt. casserole	9 to 10
Cream of Rice	1	¾ cup	Dash	3 tablespoons	16-oz. cereal bowl	1½ to 2
	2	1⅓ cups	¼ teaspoon	⅓ cup	1½-qt. casserole	2 to 3
	4	2⅔ cups	½ teaspoon	⅔ cup	2-qt. casserole	3½ to 4½
	6	4 cups	1 teaspoon	1 cup	2-qt. casserole	6 to 7

*Single servings of instant oatmeal or grits (about 1-oz. pkg.): Follow package directions for amount of water. **Microwave at High ½ to 1 Minute.**

Old-Fashioned Oatmeal

GRITS AND CHEESE CASSEROLE

POWER LEVEL: High
MICROWAVE TIME: 28 to 33 min., total

4 cups hot tap water **1 cup quick grits** **1 teaspoon salt**	In 3-qt. casserole place water, grits and salt. **Microwave at High 10 to 12 Minutes,** stirring after 5 minutes.
6 tablespoons butter, sliced **8 oz. pasteurized processed cheese* cut into cubes**	Add butter and cheese to grits. Mix well. **Microwave at High 1 to 2 Minutes,** until melted, stirring well.
2 eggs, beaten **Milk** **½ teaspoon garlic powder** **Dash hot pepper sauce (tabasco)**	In 1-cup measure beat eggs and fill to 1 cup line with milk. Add garlic powder and pepper sauce. Quickly stir into grits. Pour into well greased 12×8×2-in. dish.
1 cup coarsely crushed corn flakes **2 tablespoons butter** **Paprika**	Sprinkle corn flakes over top. Dot with butter. Sprinkle with paprika. **Microwave at High 17 to 19 Minutes,** rotating dish ½ turn after 9 minutes, until set. Serve in squares. Especially good with ham.

Makes 8 to 10 servings

*1 roll (5-oz.) garlic cheese may be substituted for processed cheese and garlic powder. Reduce final cooking time by about 2 minutes.

MOLASSES CORNMEAL PUDDING

Known as Indian Pudding in the New England states. Serve with vanilla ice cream, cream or hard sauce.

POWER LEVEL: High and Medium High
MICROWAVE TIME: 33 to 35 min., total

3 cups milk **⅔ cup dark molasses**	In 2-qt. casserole stir together milk and molasses. **Microwave at High 5 Minutes.**
⅔ cup yellow cornmeal **⅓ cup sugar** **1 teaspoon salt** **¾ teaspoon cinnamon** **¾ teaspoon nutmeg** **¼ cup butter**	In small bowl mix together cornmeal, sugar, salt, cinnamon and nutmeg. Gradually stir into hot milk mixture. Add butter. Cover. **Microwave at High 14 Minutes,** stirring every 2 to 3 minutes, until smooth and thickened. (If a softer consistency is preferred add 1 cup milk at this time.) **Microwave at Medium High 12 to 14 Minutes** more until consistency of cornmeal mush. Let stand about 10 minutes before serving.

Makes about 8 servings

Vegetables

With microwaving, vegetables are not only an essential part of the meal, they're one of the best parts. Fresh, frozen or canned, microwaved vegetables retain their attractive color, fresh taste and natural texture. Since you add only a small amount of water, just enough to produce steam, you don't drain off flavor and nutrients before serving.

Vegetables with a high natural moisture content will taste more like themselves than you've ever experienced before. Until you taste microwaved corn on the cob, you'll never realize how much good corn taste you discarded with the cooking water.

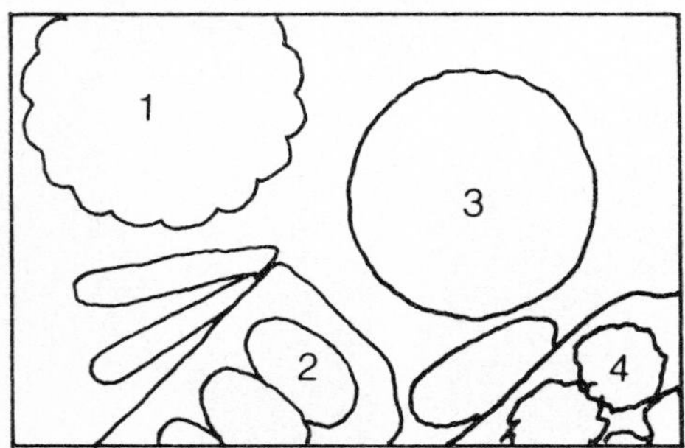

1. Fresh Broccoli, page 188
2. Twice Baked Potatoes, page 200
3. Squash Combo, page 201
4. Tomato Halves Au Gratin, page 202

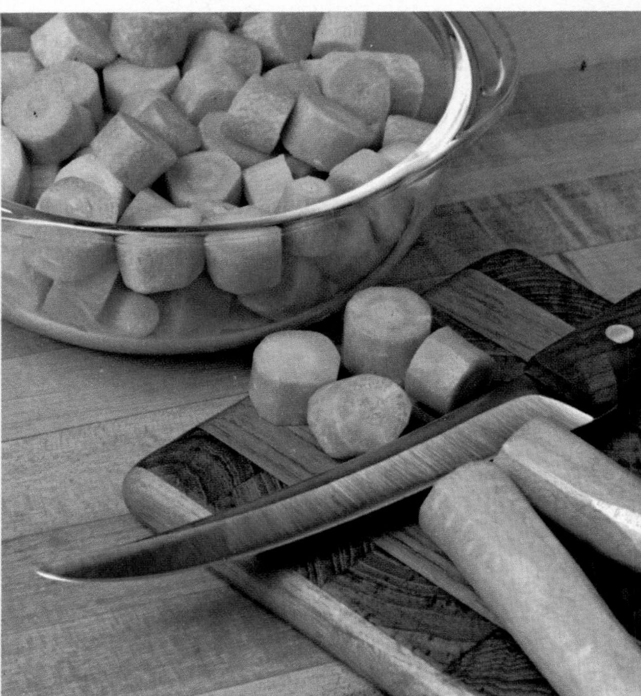

Small Pieces cook faster than large ones. Cut vegetables, such as carrots, to uniform size. Unless otherwise directed, vegetables should be tightly covered.

MICROLESSON:

Vegetables should be tightly covered. Vegetables cooked in their skins, such as potatoes, are already so tightly covered, that they should be pricked with a fork before cooking to release excess steam.

Salt vegetables after cooking, or put salt in the casserole with the water before adding vegetables. Salting the tops of vegetables before microwaving causes darkened, dried-out spots.

Vegetables continue to cook after they are removed from the microwave oven, even in the time it takes to serve them. Many of our instructions include standing time to finish cooking and develop flavors. Our recipes are timed for tender texture. If you prefer crisper vegetables, reduce cooking time a minute or two. For very soft texture, increase the time.

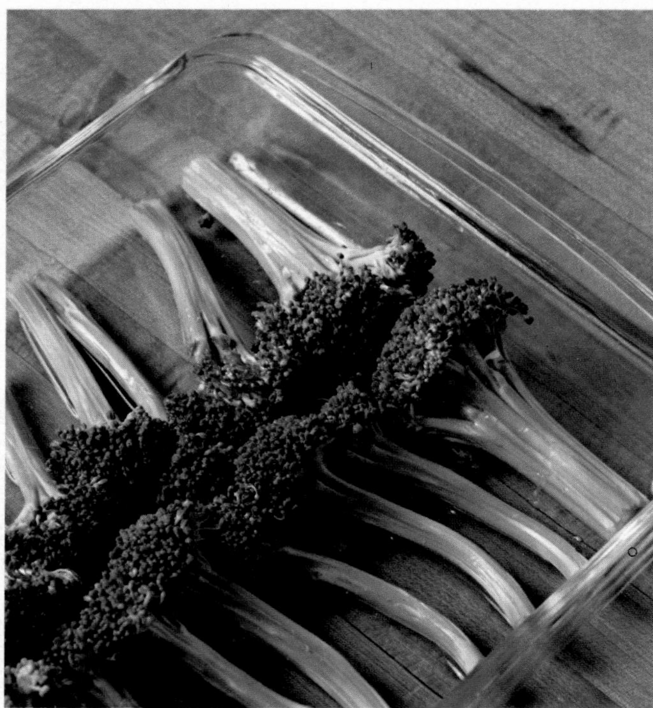

Large or Uneven Pieces should be arranged with thinner or more tender portions toward the center of the dish. Rotate dish ½ turn half way through cooking time.

Stir Vegetables, either fresh or frozen, ½ to ⅓ through the cooking time. This helps distribute heat. Rotate dish or turn over vegetables too large to stir.

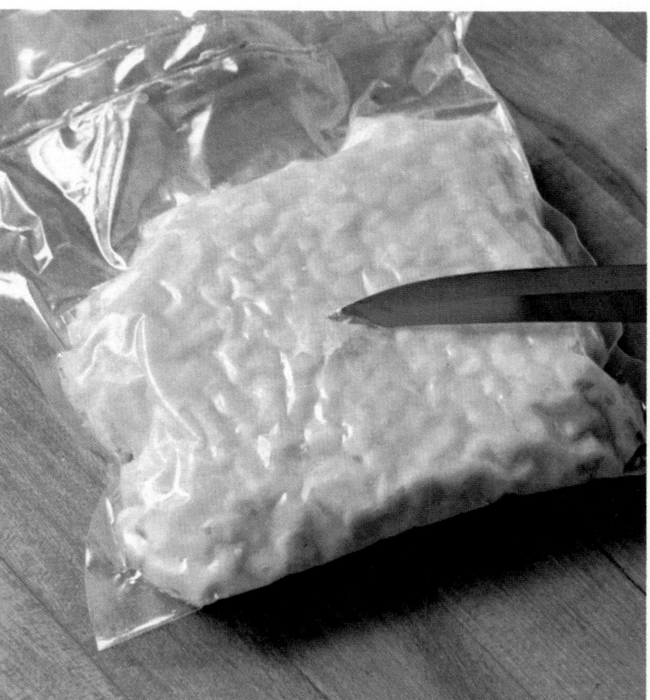

Frozen Vegetables may be heated in pouch, package or freezer container. Puncture pouch before heating, and flex half way through cooking to distribute heat.

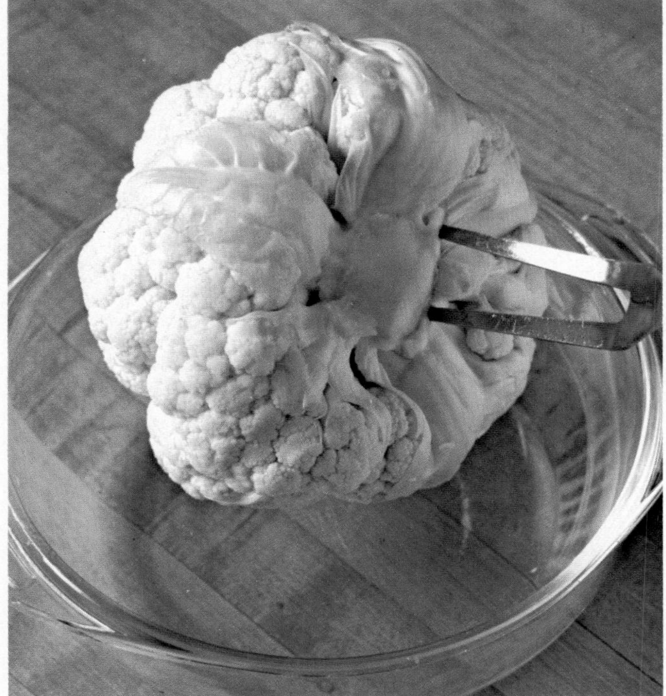

Whole or Chunky vegetables should be turned over half way through cooking time. Pierce vegetables cooked in skins, such as potatoes or squash, with fork.

Canned or Cooked vegetables reheat without flavor loss. With temperature probe, include small amount of liquid. Place probe tip in center of dish and heat to 150°.

VEGETABLE MICROWAVING CHART

FRESH FROZEN

VEGETABLE	AMOUNT	PROCEDURE	POWER LEVEL	TIME MINUTES	COMMENTS
Artichokes Fresh	4 medium	Prepare by discarding tough outer leaves. Snip tips with scissors and cut off stems. In 3-qt. casserole place 1 cup water and ½ teaspoon salt. Add artichokes. Cover. Rotate dish ½ turn after 7 minutes. Test for doneness: At minimum time, try to pull a leaf from whole artichoke. If it comes away freely, artichoke is done.	High	14 to 15	Drain artichokes upside down before serving. Curry mayonnaise is easy accompaniment; mix 1 cup mayonnaise with 1 to 2 teaspoons curry powder. Artichokes are eaten by pulling off leaves and, with teeth, scraping tender green inner leaf; cut heart into chunks and eat.
Asparagus Fresh Cuts	1 lb. (3 cups, cut into 1 to 2-in. pieces)	In 2-qt. casserole place ¼ cup water and ½ teaspoon salt; add asparagus. Cover. Stir asparagus every 3 minutes.	High	9 to 11	If pieces are longer than 4-in. lengths microwave at Medium following technique below.
Asparagus Fresh Spears	1 lb.	In 10×6×2-in. dish place ¼ cup water and ¼ teaspoon salt. Add asparagus, arranging thicker pieces to outside of dish with tender tops to center. Cover dish with plastic wrap turning back corner to vent. Rotate dish ½ turn after 5 min.	Medium High	15 to 17	Larger, more mature stem ends should be peeled.
Asparagus Frozen Spears	10-oz. pkg.	In 1-qt. casserole place ½ teaspoon salt and asparagus spears. Cover. Rearrange asparagus after 4 minutes.	High	8 to 10	No water is needed with this frozen vegetable.
Beans Fresh Green & Wax	1 lb. cut in half	In 1½-qt. casserole place ½ cup water and ½ teaspoon salt. Add beans. Cover. Stir beans after 7 minutes.	High	15 to 17	Tenderness in beans varies. Test beans after 15 minutes to determine if more cooking is needed.
Beans Frozen French Cut Green & Wax	10-oz. pkg. (about 2 cups)	In 1-qt. casserole place 2 tablespoons water and ½ teaspoon salt. Add beans. Stir beans after 5 minutes.	High	10 to 12	For 2 packages or about 4 cups frozen beans microwave 15 to 18 minutes.
Beans Frozen Lima	10-oz. pkg. (about 2 cups)	In 1-qt. casserole place ¼ cup water and ½ teaspoon salt. Add limas. Stir beans after 4 minutes.	High	7 to 8	For 2 packages or about 4 cups frozen limas microwave 10 to 12 minutes.
Beets Fresh Whole	1 bunch (5 medium)	In 2-qt. casserole place ½ cup water and ½ teaspoon salt; add beets. Cover. Stir beets after 11 minutes.	High	22 to 25	After cooking, skins peel easily. Slice or dice and season.
Broccoli Fresh Spears	1 bunch (1¼ to 1½ lb.)	In 13×9×2-in. dish place ¼ cup water and ½ teaspoon salt. Arrange broccoli spears with stalks to outside of dish and flowerets in center. Cover with plastic wrap, turning back one corner to vent. Rotate dish ½ turn after 6 minutes.	Medium High	15 to 17	Larger, more mature stalks should be peeled. As an alternate arrangement place in circular dish, flowers to center, stalks to edges.
Broccoli Fresh Cut	1 bunch (1¼ to 1½ lb.) cut into 1-in. pieces	In 2-qt. casserole place ½ cup water and ½ teaspoon salt. Add broccoli. Cover. Stir broccoli after 6 minutes.	High	12 to 14	Broccoli cooks most evenly cut in 1-in. pieces.
Broccoli Frozen Chopped	10-oz. pkg. (about 2 cups)	In 1-qt. casserole place 2 tablespoons water and ½ teaspoon salt. Add broccoli. Cover. Break up and stir broccoli after 7 minutes.	High	8 to 10	For 2 packages or about 4 cups frozen broccoli microwave 12 to 15 minutes.

VEGETABLE	AMOUNT	PROCEDURE	POWER LEVEL	TIME MINUTES	COMMENTS
Broccoli Frozen Spears	10-oz. pkg.	In 1-qt. casserole place 3 tablespoons water and ½ teaspoon salt. Add broccoli. Cover. Rearrange broccoli after 4 minutes.	High	8 to 10	Broccoli should be rearranged carefully to avoid breaking tender flower tips.
Brussels Sprouts Fresh	1 lb.	In 1½-qt. casserole, place ¼ cup water and ½ teaspoon salt. Add brussels sprouts. Cover. Stir brussels sprouts after 4 minutes.	High	7 to 9	Trim dry or old outer leaves and cut extra-large sprouts in half before cooking.
Brussels Sprouts Frozen	10-oz. pkg. (1½ to 2 cups)	In 1-qt. casserole place 2 tablespoons water and ½ teaspoon salt. Add brussels sprouts. Cover. Stir brussels sprouts after 4 minutes.	High	8 to 10	For 2 packages or about 3 to 4 cups frozen brussels sprouts microwave 12 to 15 minutes.
Cabbage Fresh Chopped	1 medium head (about 2 lbs.)	In 1½ or 2-qt. casserole place ¼ cup water and ½ teaspoon salt. Add cabbage. Stir cabbage after 5 minutes.	High	9 to 11	Use large enough casserole so cabbage fits loosely.
Cabbage Fresh Wedges	1 medium head (about 2 lbs.)	In 2 or 3-qt. casserole place ¼ cup water and ½ teaspoon salt. Add cabbage. Cover. Rearrange cabbage after 7 minutes.	High	13 to 15	Use large enough casserole so cabbage fits loosely.
Carrots Fresh Whole	1 to 2 lb. (see time column)	In 1½-qt. casserole place ½ cup water and ¼ teaspoon salt; add carrots. Cover. Rearrange carrots after half of time.	High	1 lb. - 12 to 14 2 lb. - 18 to 20	Size of carrots affects cooking time; larger carrots take longer time.
Carrots Fresh Sliced	1 lb. (6 to 8 carrots)	In 1½-qt. casserole place ¼ cup water and ½ teaspoon salt; add slices. Cover. Stir carrots after 7 minutes.	High	12 to 14	Cut slices about ½-in. thick. Old carrots take longer to cook. Diagonally sliced carrots reduce cooking time by about 2 minutes.
Carrots Frozen Sliced	10-oz. pkg. (about 2 cups)	In 1-qt. casserole place 2 tablespoons water and ½ teaspoon salt. Add carrots. Stir carrots after 4 minutes.	High	8 to 10	
Carrots & Peas Frozen	10-oz. pkg. (about 2 cups)	In 1-qt. casserole place 2 tablespoons water and ½ teaspoon salt. Add vegetables. Cover. Stir carrots and peas after 3 minutes.	High	5 to 7	For 2 packages or about 4 cups microwave about 8 to 11 minutes.
Cauliflower Fresh Whole	1 medium head (about 1½ lb.)	In 1½-qt. casserole place ½ cup water and ¼ teaspoon salt. Place cauliflower stem side down. Cover. Turn cauliflower over after 7 minutes.	Medium High	13 to 17	Let stand about 5 minutes before serving. If desired, surround on platter with French style green beans.
Cauliflower Fresh Flowerets	1 medium head (about 1½ lb.) cut into flowerets	In 1½-qt. casserole place ½ cup water and ¼ teaspoon salt; add flowerets. Cover. Stir cauliflower after 6 minutes.	High	12 to 14	
Cauliflower Frozen Flowerets	10-oz. pkg. (about 1½ cups)	In 1-qt. casserole place 2 tablespoons water and ½ teaspoon salt. Add flowerets. Stir cauliflower after 4 minutes.	High	8 to 9	For 2 packages or about 3 cups flowerets microwave 12 to 14 minutes.
Celery Fresh	4 cups ½-in. slices	In 2-qt. casserole place ¼ cup water and ¼ teaspoon salt; add celery. Cover. Stir celery after 6 minutes.	High	11 to 13	Celery is crisp-tender when cooked.

VEGETABLE	AMOUNT	PROCEDURE	POWER LEVEL	TIME MINUTES	COMMENTS
Corn Frozen Kernel	10-oz. pkg. (about 2 cups)	In 1-qt. casserole place 2 tablespoons water and ½ teaspoon salt; add corn. Stir corn after 3 minutes.	High	5 to 7	For 2 packages or about 4 cups microwave 9 to 11 minutes.
Corn on the Cob Fresh	1 to 5 ears (see time column)	In 2 or 3-qt. casserole place corn. If corn is in husk, use no water; if corn has been husked, add ¼ cup water. Cover. If ears are stacked in casserole rearrange after half of time.	High	3 to 4 per ear	For convenience and freshest flavor, microwave corn in husk.
Corn on the Cob Frozen	1 to 6 ears (see time column)	In 2 or 3-qt. casserole place corn. (No additional water needed.) Cover tightly with lid or plastic wrap. Turn over after half of time. Let stand 5 minutes after microwaving.	High	1 ear 5 to 6 min., over 1 ear 3 to 4 min. per ear	Corn should lay flat in dish. Use oblong glass casserole if necessary.
Eggplant Fresh	1 medium (about 1 lb.) 4 cups cubed	In 2-qt. casserole place 2 tablespoons water and ¼ teaspoon salt; add peeled, diced eggplant. Cover. Stir eggplant after 3 minutes.	High	5 to 6	If peeled, cubed vegetable is prepared ahead of cooking; cover with salted water to retain color and flavor.
Mushrooms Fresh Sliced	½ to 1 lb. (see time column)	In 1½-qt. casserole place 2 tablespoons butter or water for each ½ lb. mushrooms. Add mushrooms. Cover. Stir mushrooms after half of time.	High	½ lb. - 2 to 4 1 lb. - 4 to 6	Don't overcook. As soon as color begins to darken remove from oven and let stand a few minutes before serving. If mushrooms are thinly sliced they will take minimum time.
Onions Fresh	4 to 8 medium quartered	In 1 or 2-qt. casserole place ½ cup water and ½ teaspoon salt; add onions. Cover. Stir onions after half of time.	High	4 onions - 10 to 12 8 onions - 14 to 16	Timing gives tender but not mushy onions.
Okra Frozen Whole	10-oz. pkg.	In 1-qt. casserole place 2 tablespoons water and ½ teaspoon salt; add okra. Cover. Rearrange after 4 minutes.	High	7 to 9	
Parsnips Fresh	1 lb. (2 to 3 cups cubed)	In 1½-qt. casserole place ¼ cup water and ¼ teaspoon salt; add peeled, cubed parsnips. Cover. Stir parsnips after 4 minutes.	High	8 to 10	Age of parsnips affects microwaving time.
Peas Fresh Shelled	2 lb.	In 1-qt. casserole place ¼ cup water and ½ teaspoon salt; add peas. Cover. Stir peas after 6 minutes. After microwaving, add 1 tablespoon butter and let stand 5 minutes.	High*	12 to 14	*Fresh young peas microwave best at High. Mature peas (yellow color, some sprouts) should be microwaved at Low Power for longer time.
Peas Frozen Shelled	10-oz. pkg. (about 2 cups)	In 1-qt. casserole place 2 tablespoons water and ½ teaspoon salt; add peas. Cover. Stir peas after 3 minutes.	High	5 to 6	For 2 packages or about 4 cups microwave 8 to 10 minutes.
Peas & Onions Frozen	10-oz. pkg. (about 2 cups)	In 1-qt. casserole place 2 tablespoons water and ½ teaspoon salt; add peas and onions. Cover. Stir peas and onions after 3 minutes.	High	6 to 8	For 2 packages or about 4 cups microwave 9 to 12 minutes.
Potatoes Fresh Whole Sweet or White	6 to 8-oz. each (see time column)	Pierce with cooking fork. Place on paper towel on shelf of microwave oven, 1-in. apart. Turn potatoes over and rearrange after half of time.	High	1 - 4 to 6 2 - 6 to 8 3 - 8 to 12 4 - 12 to 16 5 - 16 to 20	Potatoes may still feel firm when done; let stand to soften. Dry or old potatoes do not microwave well whole. Peel and dice them before microwaving.

See page 11 for step-by-step picture directions.

NOTE: When microwaving more than 2 potatoes, moisture can collect in oven. This does not harm food or oven and will evaporate (or may be wiped with cloth) when door is opened. Cook potatoes just until done. Excessive cooking dehydrates them.

VEGETABLE	AMOUNT	PROCEDURE	POWER LEVEL	TIME MINUTES	COMMENTS
Potatoes Fresh Cubed White	4 potatoes (6 to 8-oz. each)	Peel potatoes and cut into small pieces (1-in. cubes). Place in 2-qt. casserole with ½ cup water. Cover. Stir potatoes after 6 minutes.	High	12 to 14	Drain potatoes and mash with electric mixer, adding 1 teaspoon salt, ¾ cup milk and 2 tablespoons butter.
Spinach Fresh	10 to 16-oz. washed	In 2-qt. casserole place ¼ teaspoon salt; add washed spinach (no extra water needed). Cover. Stir spinach after 4 minutes.	High	7 to 9	Water which clings to leaves is enough moisture to create steam for cooking.
Spinach Frozen Chopped & Leaf	10-oz. pkg.	In 1-qt. casserole place 3 tablespoons water and ½ teaspoon salt. Add spinach. Break up and stir well after 5 minutes.	High	7 to 8	
Squash Fresh Summer & Yellow	1 lb. sliced or cubed	In 1½-qt. casserole place ¼ cup water and ½ teaspoon salt; add squash. Cover. Stir squash after 5 minutes.	High	10 to 12	If desired, add 2 tablespoons butter to water before microwaving.
Squash Fresh Winter (Acorn or Butternut)	1 to 2 squash (about 1 lb. each)	Cut in half and remove fibrous membranes. In 8-in. square dish or 12×8×2-in. oblong dish, place squash cut side down. Cover with wax paper. Turn cut side up and brush with butter (sprinkle with brown sugar if desired) after 8 minutes.	High	10 to 15	Wax paper cover is best to hold right amount of steam.
Squash Frozen Summer	10-oz. pkg. (about 1½ cups)	In 1-qt. casserole place ½ teaspoon salt and squash (no extra water needed). Cover. Stir squash after 3 minutes.	High	5 to 7	Ice crystals in frozen squash provide enough moisture for microwaving. For 2 packages or about 3 cups microwave 8 to 11 minutes.
Succotash Frozen	10-oz. pkg. (about 2 cups)	In 1-qt. casserole place 2 tablespoons water and ½ teaspoon salt; add succotash. Cover. Stir succotash after 4 minutes.	High	8 to 9	For 2 packages or 4 cups frozen succotash microwave 12 to 14 minutes.
Turnips Fresh	1 lb. cubed (2 to 3 medium)	In 1½-qt. casserole place 3 tablespoons water and ¼ teaspoon salt; add peeled cubed turnips. Cover. Stir turnips after 5 minutes.	High	10 to 12	If desired, turnips can be mashed with added butter after microwaving.
Vegetables, Mixed Frozen	10-oz. pkg. (about 2 cups)	In 1-qt. casserole place 2 tablespoons water and ½ teaspoon salt; add vegetables. Cover. Stir vegetables after 5 minutes.	High	9 to 10	Lima beans are last vegetable to cook; check them for tenderness. Stir and let stand 5 minutes before serving. For 2 packages or 4 cups frozen mixed vegetables microwave 14 to 16 minutes.
Zucchini Fresh	1 lb. sliced or cubed	In 1½-qt. casserole place ¼ cup water and ½ teaspoon salt; add zucchini. Cover. Stir zucchini after 5 minutes.	High	10 to 12	If desired, add 2 tablespoons butter to water before microwaving.

VEGETABLE SUMMARY: Always add salt to water before adding vegetable. Times here are for just-tender texture. Reduce time a minute or two for crisp-tender; increase time for very soft texture. Remember to allow standing time of 3 to 5 minutes after cooking, if possible. If you cook more, or less, vegetables than described in the chart, be sure to adjust the time accordingly.

VEGETABLE CONVENIENCE FOODS

VEGETABLE	PROCEDURE	POWER LEVEL	TIME MINUTES
Breaded Vegetables 7-oz. pkg., Frozen	Place on plate suitable for microwaving. Cook uncovered. Rotate dish ½ turn after 2 minutes. Breading will not be crisp. Cook conventionally for crispness.	High	3 to 4
Canned Vegetables	Place vegetables in serving dish suitable for microwave oven. Use about ½ cup liquid. Cover dish with plastic wrap. As a general rule, when heating more than 2 cups of vegetables, check at about half of cooking time. Stir or rearrange to shorten total cooking time. Or use temperature probe set to 150°.	High	8 to 9-oz. - 1½ to 2½ 15 to 17-oz. - 3½ to 4½ 28 to 32-oz. - 5 to 7
Casserole, Vegetable 8 to 10-oz. pkg., Frozen	Place in 1-qt. casserole. Cover. Stir after 4 minutes.	High	5 to 7
Casserole, Vegetable 11 to 12-oz. pkg., Frozen	Place in 1-qt. casserole. Cover. Stir after 4 minutes.	High	7 to 9
Potatoes Baked, Stuffed, Frozen	Examine potatoes to see that mashed filling is encased in potato skin, NOT FOIL. Place potato(es) on plate suitable for microwave oven. Cover with wax paper. Rotate dish ½ turn after half of cooking time.	High	1 - 3 to 4 2 - 5 to 6 3 - 7 to 8 4 - 8 to 9
Potatoes Canned German Potato Salad 15½-oz. can	Place food in 1-qt. casserole. Cover. Stir after 2 minutes. Stir before serving. At minimum time food is warm; at maximum time, hot.	High	2 to 4
Potatoes Instant Mashed	Use utensil size and amounts of water, milk, butter and salt on package. Cover. After heating, briskly stir in potatoes, adding extra 1 to 2 tablespoons dry mix.	High (Or heat liquid with temperature probe set to 200°.)	5
Souffle 11-oz. pkg., Frozen	To Defrost: Place food in 8-in. pie plate. Stir. To Cook: Divide equally between 3 or 4 buttered custard cups (6 or 7-oz.). Rearrange after 4 minutes. Souffles are done when center is set. Invert on serving plate.	Low Medium High	9 to 11 9 to 11

COOKING DRIED BEANS AND PEAS

POWER LEVEL: High and Medium
MICROWAVE TIME: See Recipe

1. Place specified amount of beans and water in casserole. Cover.
2. **Microwave at High** to bring to boil, then **Microwave at Medium** until tender. Cooking time depends on variety and amounts. See recommendations below.

GREAT NORTHERN BEANS

1 pkg. (12-oz.) rinsed beans (2 cups)
6 cups water
1 small onion
½ carrot
½ stalk celery
4 strips cooked bacon, crumbled
2 teaspoons salt
¼ teaspoon pepper

In 3-qt. casserole place beans, water, onion, carrot, celery, bacon, salt and pepper. Cover. **Microwave at High 20 Minutes.** Stir. Recover. **Microwave at Medium 1 Hour 30 Minutes to 1 Hour 40 Minutes,** until tender. Stir every 45 minutes.

For Ranch Style Beans: Remove celery and carrot. Stir in 2 tablespoons brown sugar, 1 tablespoon dark molasses and ½ teaspoon dry mustard. Cover. **Microwave at Medium High 20 to 30 Minutes.** Stir after 10 minutes.

Makes 8 to 10 servings

PINTO BEANS

1 pkg. (1-lb.) beans, rinsed
4 cups water
1 ham hock
1 small onion, sliced

In 3-qt. casserole place beans, water, ham hock and onion. Cover. **Microwave at High 30 Minutes,** stirring after ½ time. **Microwave at Medium 1 Hour 40 Minutes to 1 Hour 50 Minutes,** until tender. Stir every 45 minutes.

For "Let's Eat" Bean Soup: Remove ham hock. Cut meat into small pieces and return to casserole. Add water to thin soup as desired. Cover. Microwave to heat.

Makes 6 to 8 servings

SPLIT PEAS

1 cup split peas
4 cups water
1 ham hock
1 rib celery, cut in half
1 small onion, sliced
1 tablespoon lemon juice

In 3-qt. casserole place peas, water, ham hock, celery, onion and lemon juice. Cover. **Microwave at High 15 Minutes.** Stir well. **Microwave at Medium 60 to 70 Minutes,** until tender, stirring every ½ hour.

For Split Pea Soup: Dice meat from ham hock. Slice celery. Return to dish. Stir in 1 cup water. Cover. **Microwave at Medium 5 to 10 Minutes,** until hot.

Makes 6 to 8 servings

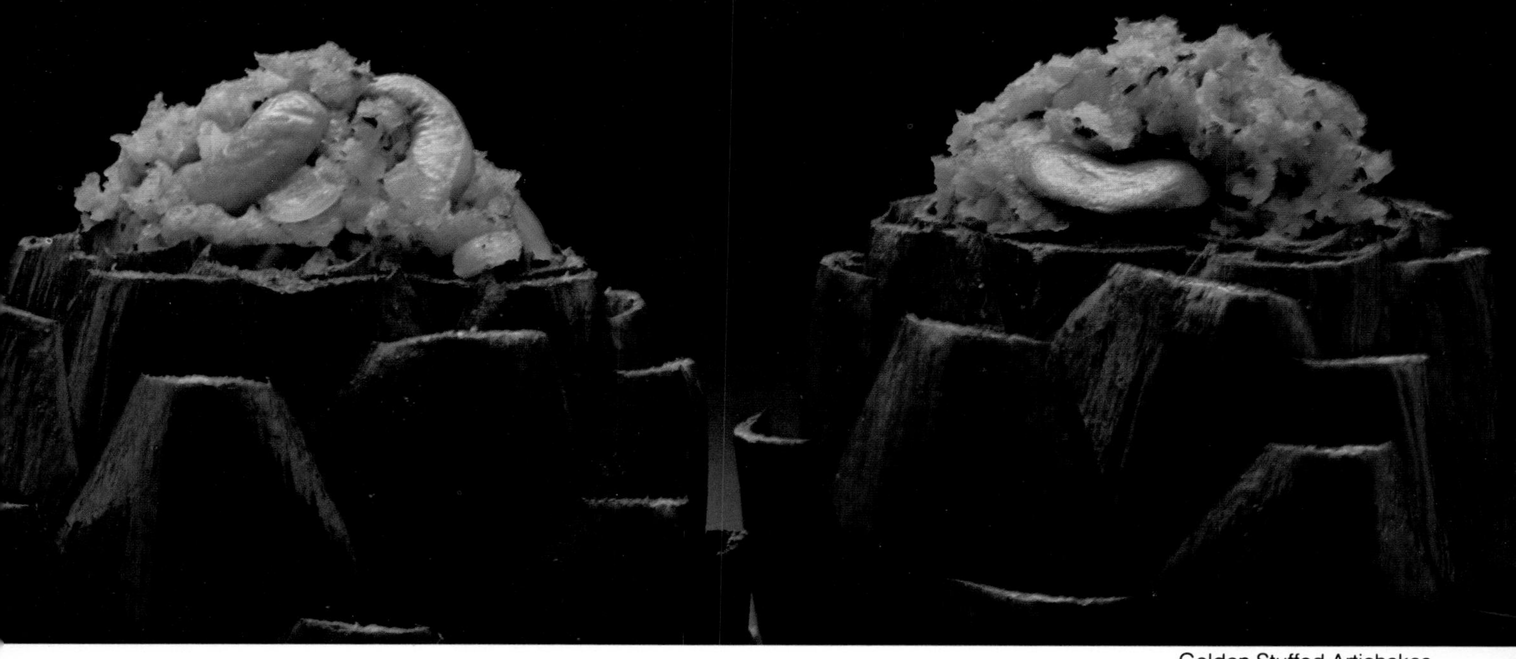

Golden Stuffed Artichokes

GOLDEN STUFFED ARTICHOKES

POWER LEVEL: High
MICROWAVE TIME: 27 to 31 min., total

4 medium artichokes
1 cup water
½ teaspoon salt
. . . Prepare artichokes by discarding the tough outer leaves. Snip tips off with scissors and cut off stems. In 3-qt. casserole place artichokes with salted water. Cover. **Microwave at High 14 to 15 Minutes,** rotating dish ½ turn after 7 minutes. Remove and place artichokes upside down to partially cool.

1 pkg. (6-oz.) chicken flavor top-of-range type stuffing mix with crumbs
1½ cups water
¼ cup butter
. . . In 1½-qt. casserole, combine vegetable seasoning packet from stuffing mix, water and butter. Cover. **Microwave at High 4 to 5 Minutes.** Stir crumbs into mixture just to moisten. Cover and let stand.

2 small carrots, grated
1 small onion, diced
1 tablespoon olive oil
1 pkg. (3¼-oz.) cashews, salted
. . . In 1-qt. casserole combine carrots, onion and oil. Cover. **Microwave at High 5 Minutes,** until vegetables are soft. Add these vegetables to bread stuffing along with cashews.

Force the center of each artichoke open to form a well. Remove the center leaves and the choke (the choke is the fuzzy, purple-tinged area covering the heart, or base of the artichoke) with a spoon. Stuff artichokes with cashew-carrot stuffing. Rearrange in 3-qt. casserole. **Microwave at High 4 to 6 Minutes,** uncovered, until heated.

Makes 4 stuffed artichokes

POPULAR GREEN BEAN CASSEROLE

POWER LEVEL: Low and High TEMP:* 170°
APPROX. MICROWAVE TIME: 12 to 15 min.

3 pkgs. (10-oz. each) frozen French-style green beans
. . . Defrost beans by placing packages in single layer in microwave oven. **Microwave at Low 10 to 12 Minutes,** turning over and rearranging packages every 2 to 3 minutes.

1 can (10-oz.) cream of mushroom soup
½ cup milk
1 jar (2-oz.) pimiento, sliced and drained
. . . Separate beans into 1½-qt. casserole. Mix with canned soup, milk and pimiento to blend well.

1 can (3-oz.) French fried onions
. . . Arrange onions in a ring around edge of dish.

Insert temperature probe so tip rests on center bottom of dish. Cover with plastic wrap, arranging loosely around probe to vent. Attach cable end at receptacle. **Microwave at High. Set Temp, Set 170°.** When oven signals let stand, covered, about 10 minutes before serving. Toss to mix, if desired.

Makes about 8 servings

* On models not equipped with probe use minimum microwave time and check for doneness.

Popular Green Bean Casserole

Hot Bean Salad

HOT BEAN SALAD

This sweet-sour bean salad tastes even better when made in advance. Reheat before serving.

POWER LEVEL: High
MICROWAVE TIME: 12 to 14 min., total

4 strips bacon .... Using scissors, snip bacon strips into small pieces into 2-qt. casserole. **Microwave at High 3 to 4 Minutes,** stirring after 2 minutes. With slotted spoon, remove cooked bacon pieces to paper towels to drain.

½ cup sugar
1 tablespoon cornstarch
1 teaspoon salt
¼ teaspoon pepper
⅔ cup vinegar
.... To bacon drippings in casserole, add sugar and cornstarch, blending well. Stir in salt, pepper and vinegar. **Microwave at High 3 to 4 Minutes,** until thick.

1 can (1-lb.) cut green beans, drained
1 can (1-lb.) cut wax beans, drained
1 can (15-oz.) red kidney beans, drained
1 onion, sliced
... Add drained beans and onion slices to sauce in casserole, stirring well. Cover. **Microwave at High 6 Minutes,** stirring after 3 minutes. Let compote stand 10 minutes before serving to blend flavors. Sprinkle cooked bacon pieces over top and serve.

Makes 8 to 10 first course servings or 4 to 5 servings as vegetable

CHEEZY BROCCOLI

POWER LEVEL: High
MICROWAVE TIME: See Recipe

2 pkgs. (10-oz. each) frozen chopped broccoli ..... Place unopened packages of broccoli on end in microwave oven. **Microwave at High 4 to 5 Minutes,** turning over after 2 minutes. Set aside.

2 cups packaged precooked (minute) rice
2 cans (10¾-oz. each) cream of chicken soup
1 cup milk
1 jar (16-oz.) pasteurized processed cheese food
1 tablespoon salt
½ teaspoon pepper
.... In 3-qt. casserole combine rice, soup, milk, cheese, salt, pepper. **Microwave at High 2 to 4 Minutes,** until cheese melts and can be blended easily.

½ cup chopped onion
1 cup chopped celery
1 can (6-oz.) water chestnuts, drained and sliced
.... To cheese mixture, add onion, celery, water chestnuts and broccoli. Stir thoroughly. Divide evenly between 2 lightly greased 10×6×2-in. dishes. Microwave one dish at a time. **Microwave at High 12 to 14 Minutes,** rotating dish ½ turn after 5 minutes. Let stand 5 minutes before serving.

Makes 12 servings

NOTE: For convenience, freeze one dish of broccoli. When cooking from the frozen state, unwrap, **Microwave at High 18 to 21 Minutes,** rotating dish ½ turn every 5 minutes.

SWEET-SOUR BEETS

POWER LEVEL: High
MICROWAVE TIME: 18 to 22 min., total

1 medium bunch beets (about 1-lb.)
1 cup warm tap water
. . . Wash and remove tops from beets. Place in 1½-qt. casserole with water. Cover. **Microwave at High 10 to 12 Minutes,** until fork tender. Place beets in cold water. Peel and quarter.

2 tablespoons butter
2 tablespoons cider vinegar
2 tablespoons sugar
. . . . . Return beets to casserole. Add butter, vinegar and sugar. Cover. **Microwave at High 8 to 10 Minutes,** stirring after 5 minutes.

Makes 3 to 4 servings

CABBAGE PATCH CASSEROLE

If you prefer, you may substitute 2 cups homemade Cheese Sauce, page 173, for the diluted cheese soup in this recipe.

POWER LEVEL: High
MICROWAVE TIME: 20 to 24 min., total

1 medium head cabbage
2 tablespoons water
½ teaspoon salt
. . . . Chop cabbage into small pieces. Place in 2-qt. casserole along with water and salt. **Microwave at High 10 to 12 Minutes,** rearranging cabbage after 5 minutes. Drain off liquid.

4 strips bacon
. . . . Separate and place strips of bacon on a double thickness of paper towels which have been placed on a paper or pottery plate. Cover with single layer of paper towel. **Microwave at High 4 Minutes.** Crumble.

1 can (10¾-oz.) condensed cheddar cheese soup
½ cup milk
. . . . Mix together crumbled bacon, soup and milk until well blended. Pour over cooked cabbage and mix thoroughly. Cover. **Microwave at High 5 to 6 Minutes.** Stir.

1 can (3-oz.) French fried onions
. . . . . Sprinkle onions over top of casserole. **Microwave at High 1 to 2 Minutes** more, uncovered, until lightly bubbling around edges.

Makes 6 servings

HARVARD BEETS

POWER LEVEL: High
MICROWAVE TIME: 18 to 24 min., total

1 medium bunch beets (about 1-lb.)
1 cup warm tap water
. . . Wash and remove tops from beets. Place beets and water in 1½-qt. casserole. Cover. **Microwave at High 10 to 12 Minutes,** until fork tender. Remove beets from oven and place in cool water. Peel and slice or cube as desired.

1 tablespoon cornstarch
1 tablespoon sugar
¾ teaspoon salt
Dash pepper
⅔ cup water
¼ cup vinegar
. . . . In same 1½-qt. casserole stir together cornstarch, sugar, salt, pepper, water and vinegar. **Microwave at High 3 to 4 Minutes,** until thickened, stirring after 2 minutes. Add beets and **Microwave at High 5 to 8 Minutes,** until hot, or, if desired, serve cold.

Makes 4 servings

COLORFUL CARROT RING

POWER LEVEL: High and Medium High
MICROWAVE TIME: 26 to 32 min., total

½ cup water*
½ teaspoon salt
2 lbs. carrots, peeled
. . . . In 3-qt. casserole place water, salt and carrots. Cover. **Microwave at High 18 to 20 Minutes,** rearranging after 9 minutes, until tender. Drain. Press carrots through coarse sieve with back of wooden spoon, or for more coarse texture run through meat grinder.

¼ cup softened butter
2 egg yolks
2 tablespoons brown sugar (packed)
1 teaspoon salt
½ teaspoon pepper
. . . To the sieved carrots add butter, egg yolks, brown sugar, salt and pepper. Generously butter 1-qt. casserole. Place small drinking glass (3-in. or less diameter, 4 to 5-in. high) in center of dish. Pack carrot mixture evenly around glass. Cover with plastic wrap, turning one edge back slightly to vent.

Microwave at Medium High 8 to 12 Minutes, until hot. Let stand 5 minutes to set, then invert on serving plate. Garnish with chopped parsley and cooked, crumbled bacon if deisred.

*½ teaspoon chicken bouillon granules may be added for additional flavor.

Makes 4 to 6 servings

SUNDAY GLAZED CARROTS

POWER LEVEL: High
MICROWAVE TIME: 11 to 15 min., total

1 lb., about 6 to 8 medium carrots
2 tablespoons butter
¼ cup brown sugar (packed)

Wash and cut carrots into ½-in. diagonal slices. Place in 1-qt. casserole with butter and brown sugar. Cover. **Microwave at High 9 to 11 Minutes,** stirring after 5 minutes.

2 tablespoons cold water
1½ teaspoons cornstarch
¼ cup pecans, coarsely chopped (optional)

Mix water and cornstarch until smooth. Stir into carrot mixture. Add pecans. Cover. **Microwave at High 2 to 4 Minutes,** until thickened. Stir before serving.

Makes 3 to 4 servings

TO DOUBLE THIS RECIPE: Use 2-qt. casserole and double the ingredients. Microwave the carrots 15 minutes, stirring after 7 minutes. Add thickening and microwave 4 to 6 minutes more.

Sunday Glazed Carrots

CREAMY CAULIFLOWER

POWER LEVEL: High
MICROWAVE TIME: 16 to 19 min., total

½ teaspoon salt
2 tablespoons water
2 pkgs. (10-oz. each) frozen cauliflower

In 2-qt. casserole place salt and water. Add cauliflower. **Microwave at High 5 to 7 Minutes,** until just done. Place in strainer or colander to drain.

1 tablespoon butter, softened
1 tablespoon flour
½ cup milk
1 cup small curd cottage cheese
½ cup shredded cheddar cheese
1 tablespoon chopped pimiento
½ teaspoon salt
⅛ teaspoon pepper

In same 2-qt. casserole, stir to mix butter and flour. Stir in milk, cheeses, pimiento and seasonings. **Microwave at High 6 Minutes,** stirring after 3 minutes, until cheese melts and mixture thickens.

½ cup crushed corn flakes
½ teaspoon paprika
½ teaspoon dill weed

Mix cauliflower gently into sauce and sprinkle top with corn flakes mixed with paprika and dill weed. **Microwave at High 5 to 6 Minutes,** until hot.

Makes 6 servings

CAULIFLOWER AU GRATIN

For convenience, this recipe uses herb-seasoned stuffing mix, but you may substitute coarse bread crumbs dried in the microwave oven.

POWER LEVEL: High
MICROWAVE TIME: 9 to 11 min., total

1 pkg. (10-oz.) frozen cauliflower
2 tablespoons water
½ teaspoon salt

In 1½-qt. casserole place cauliflower in water and salt. **Microwave at High 8 to 9 Minutes,** stirring after 4 minutes. Drain off liquid from dish.

¼ cup herb-seasoned stuffing mix
½ cup shredded mild cheese

Sprinkle stuffing mix, then cheese, over cauliflower. **Microwave at High 1 to 2 Minutes,** uncovered, until cheese melts.

Makes 2 to 3 servings

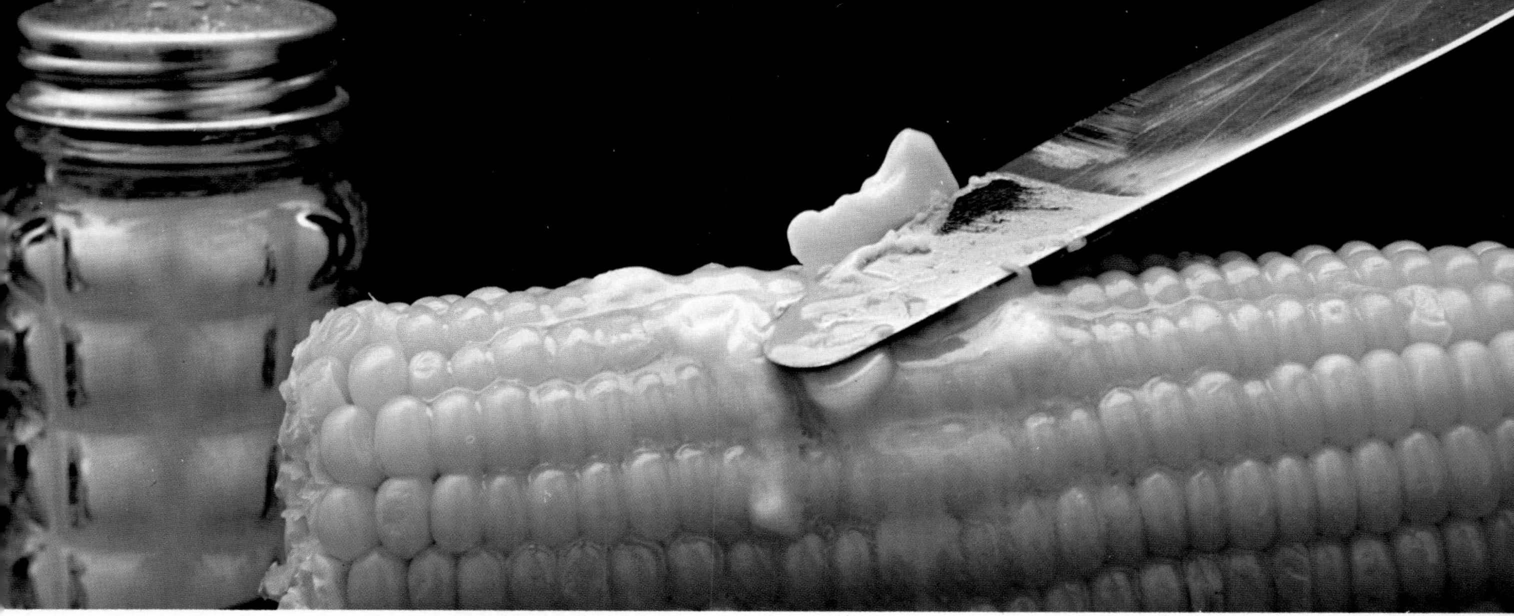

Corn on the cob is a microwave specialty, see page 190.

CELERY AND PEAS, BRAISED

POWER LEVEL: High
MICROWAVE TIME: 12 to 14 min., total

2 cups celery slices, ¼-in. thick
⅓ cup chopped onion
2 tablespoons butter
2 tablespoons water
½ teaspoon salt
In 2-qt. casserole combine vegetables, butter, water and salt. Cover. **Microwave at High 6 Minutes.** Stir.

1 package (10-oz.) frozen peas
Add peas. Cover. **Microwave at High 6 to 8 Minutes,** stirring after 4 minutes.

Makes 6 servings

CORN PUDDING

POWER LEVEL: Medium High
MICROWAVE TIME: 18 to 21 min., total

1 egg
½ cup milk
1 tablespoon sugar
1 can (16-oz.) cream-style corn
¾ cup crushed crackers
2 tablespoons butter, cut in pieces
Place egg in 1½-qt. casserole and beat well with fork. Stir in milk, sugar, corn, crackers and butter. **Microwave at Medium High 7 Minutes** and stir well.

Paprika
Sprinkle with paprika. **Microwave at Medium High 11 to 14 Minutes,** rotating dish ¼ turn after 5 minutes. When done, center will be just barely set.

Makes 4 servings

SOUTHERN STUFFED EGGPLANT

POWER LEVEL: High
MICROWAVE TIME: 13 to 18 min., total

1 medium eggplant
2 tablespoons water
Cut eggplant in half. Scoop out insides leaving outer shell intact. Dice the scooped-out eggplant into 2-qt. casserole. Add water. Cover. **Microwave at High 5 to 6 Minutes,** stirring after 3 minutes.

¼ cup chopped onion
2 tablespoons butter
2 teaspoons chopped parsley
1 can (10½-oz.) condensed cream of mushroom soup
¼ teaspoon salt
⅛ teaspoon pepper
1 teaspoon Worcestershire sauce
½ cup butter-cracker crumbs
½ cup coarsely chopped salted peanuts, if desired
In 1½-qt. casserole, place onion, butter and parsley. **Microwave at High 2 to 3 Minutes,** until onion is softened. Add to eggplant with soup, salt, pepper, Worcestershire sauce, crumbs and peanuts; blend well. Evenly divide filling between the 2 shells. Place in 12×8×2-in. dish.

½ cup water
Add water to dish. Cover with plastic wrap, turning back one corner to vent. **Microwave at High 5 to 7 Minutes,** rotating dish ½ turn after 3 minutes, until hot.

¼ cup butter-cracker crumbs
Paprika
Sprinkle crumbs and paprika over top. **Microwave at High 1 to 2 Minutes,** until bubbly.

Makes 4 servings

EGGPLANT ITALIANO

This hearty vegetable casserole goes well with plain meats such as roasts, lamb, ham or chicken.

POWER LEVEL: High
MICROWAVE TIME: 15 to 18 min., total

1 medium eggplant	Pare eggplant; slice ⅛-in. thick.
2 cans (8-oz. each) tomato sauce **1 to 2 teaspoons oregano** **½ cup shredded sharp cheese, optional**	Spread 2 tablespoons tomato sauce in bottom of 2-qt. casserole. Layer half of eggplant, 1 can tomato sauce, half of oregano and half of sharp cheese. Repeat layers. Cover. **Microwave at High 14 to 16 Minutes,** rotating dish ¼ turn after 8 minutes.
1 pkg. (6-oz.) mozzarella cheese, sliced	Add mozzarella cheese. **Microwave at High 1 to 2 Minutes,** until cheese has melted.

Makes 4 to 6 servings

WILTED LETTUCE SALAD

POWER LEVEL: High
MICROWAVE TIME: 5 to 6 min., total

3 strips bacon	With scissors, snip bacon into 1-in. pieces into 3-qt. casserole. **Microwave at High 3 Minutes,** until crisp. With slotted spoon, remove bacon to paper towels to drain.
¼ cup vinegar **2 teaspoons sugar** **¼ teaspoon salt** **⅛ teaspoon pepper** **⅛ teaspoon crushed dried tarragon** **¼ cup chopped celery** **1 tablespoon sliced green onion**	To drippings in casserole add vinegar, sugar, salt, pepper and tarragon. **Microwave at High 2 to 3 Minutes** to boil. Stir in celery and onion.
1 medium head of lettuce, torn (about 8 cups total) **2 medium oranges, sectioned, each section seeded and cut in half***	Gradually add lettuce to hot dressing, tossing to coat each piece, just until slightly wilted. Add orange segments and crisp bacon pieces and toss again lightly. Serve immediately.

Makes 8 to 10 servings

*Or substitute 1 can (11-oz.) Mandarin oranges, drained.

LIMA BEAN SPECIAL

POWER LEVEL: High
MICROWAVE TIME: 14 to 15 min., total

4 strips bacon	Place bacon on 2 thicknesses of paper towels in 2-qt. casserole. Cover with paper towel. **Microwave at High about 4 Minutes** until crisp. Drain off fat; crumble bacon and reserve.
1 pkg. (10-oz.) frozen lima beans **½ cup chopped unpared red apple** **¼ cup green pepper** **½ cup water** **¼ teaspoon salt** **¼ teaspoon crushed rosemary**	In same 2-qt. casserole, combine beans, apple, green pepper, water, salt and rosemary. Cover. **Microwave at High 10 to 11 Minutes** stirring after 5 minutes. Stir in reserved bacon before serving.

Makes 4 servings

ZESTY SEASONED ONIONS

Using this recipe as a guide, try garnishing onions with different herb and cheese combinations, bacon crumbles, crushed crackers or potato chips.

POWER LEVEL: High
MICROWAVE TIME: See Recipe

Large whole onions	Wash and halve onions. Arrange in dish suggested below, depending on number of onions.
For each onion **1 tablespoon steak sauce** **1 tablespoon Worcestershire sauce** **1 to 2 drops tabasco sauce** **1 tablespoon butter** **¼ teaspoon garlic salt** **1 teaspoon Parmesan cheese**	Sprinkle seasonings over onion halves. **Microwave at High** according to chart below.

AMOUNT	DISH	TIME MINUTES
1 (2 halves)	1-qt. casserole (covered)	4 to 5
2 (4 halves)	1½-qt. casserole (covered)	8 to 9
3 (6 halves)	2-qt. casserole (covered)	11 to 13

NOTE: A good side dish with roasted or broiled meats.

HOT GERMAN POTATO SALAD

POWER LEVEL: High
MICROWAVE TIME: 19 to 22 min., total

4 medium potatoes . . . . .Wash and pierce potatoes through with fork. Place on paper towel in microwave oven. **Microwave at High 10 to 12 Minutes,** turning over and rearranging after 4 minutes, or until tender. Remove from oven, cool slightly, peel potatoes and cut in ⅛-in. slices to make about 4 cups.

6 strips bacon . . . . In 2-qt. casserole cut bacon in small pieces. Cover with paper towel. **Microwave at High about 6 Minutes,** stirring after 3 minutes, until crisp. With slotted spoon remove bacon to paper towels to drain. Set aside.

2 tablespoons flour
¼ cup sugar
1½ teaspoons salt
½ teaspoon celery seed
⅛ teaspoon pepper . . . . .Stir flour, sugar and seasonings into bacon fat until smooth. **Microwave at High 1 to 2 Minutes,** until bubbly, stirring after 1 minute.

1 cup water
½ cup vinegar . . . . .Add water and vinegar to flour mixture. **Microwave at High 4 Minutes,** until mixture boils and thickens, stirring after 1 minute. Remove from oven and stir smooth. Add potatoes and bacon; stir gently so potatoes hold their shape. Cover casserole and let stand until ready to serve.

Makes 4 to 6 servings

TIP: Not all potatoes are suitable for baking. Dry or old potatoes do not bake well, either conventionally or by microwaving, and are best peeled, cubed and cooked with water.

Hot German Potato Salad

GREEN AND GOLD POTATO CASSEROLE

POWER LEVEL: High
MICROWAVE TIME: 17½ to 21 min., total

3 or 4 large potatoes
2 large onions . . . .Peel potatoes and onions. Slice in ¼-in. slices. Layer in 2-qt. casserole.

3 tablespoons butter
1½ cups hot tap water
2 teaspoons instant chicken bouillon seasoning or 2 chicken bouillon cubes . . .Dot butter over top. Then pour over the hot water mixed with the chicken bouillon. Cover. **Microwave at High 17 to 20 Minutes,** until potatoes are tender, stirring after 10 minutes.

¼ cup shredded sharp cheese
1 teaspoon minced parsley . .Uncover casserole and sprinkle with cheese and parsley. **Microwave at High ½ to 1 Minute,** uncovered, or until cheese melts.

Makes 6 to 8 servings

SCALLOPED POTATOES

If desired, sprinkle top with paprika and/or ½ cup shredded sharp cheese after cooking. Cheese melts as casserole stands.

POWER LEVEL: High
MICROWAVE TIME: 25½ to 29½ min., total

3 tablespoons butter
2 tablespoons flour
1 teaspoon salt
¼ teaspoon pepper
3 cups milk
. . .Place butter in 1-qt. measuring cup. **Microwave at High ½ Minute,** or until melted. Blend in flour and seasonings. Gradually stir in milk. **Microwave at High 8 to 10 Minutes,** stirring every 3 minutes.

3½ to 4 cups thinly sliced white potatoes (about 3 medium)
2 tablespoons minced onion
. . .Layer half of potatoes, onion and sauce in greased 2-qt. casserole. Repeat layers. Cover.

Microwave at High 17 to 19 Minutes, stirring after 10 minutes. Remove from oven and let stand 5 minutes before serving.

Makes 4 to 6 servings

TWICE BAKED POTATOES

POWER LEVEL: High
MICROWAVE TIME: See Recipe

Potatoes . . .Microwave desired number of potatoes according to chart, page 190. Slice the top from each potato. With teaspoon, remove center of potatoes to mixing bowl, leaving shells intact.

For each potato
2 tablespoons butter
2 tablespoons sour cream
¼ teaspoon salt
Dash pepper
. . .Add to mixing bowl butter, sour cream, salt and pepper. Mix with electric mixer until smooth. Divide potato mixture evenly among shells, mounding, if necessary. Sprinkle with chives if desired. Place potatoes on plate suitable for microwave oven. Potatoes may be refrigerated at this point if desired.

If potatoes are microwaved immediately, **Microwave at High 1 Minute** per potato. If more than 2 potatoes are microwaved at one time, arrange in a circle and rotate dish ½ turn after half of time.

If potatoes are microwaved from refrigerator temperature, increase time for each potato by ½ minute.

POTATO-CHEESE HURRY UP

POWER LEVEL: High
MICROWAVE TIME: 9 to 11 min., total

1 can (10½-oz.) condensed cream of celery soup
½ cup chopped onions
½ cup shredded cheddar cheese
¼ teaspoon dill weed
1 teaspoon salt
¼ teaspoon pepper
. . .Mix together soup, onions, cheese, dill weed, salt and pepper in 1½-qt. casserole.

2 cans (1-lb. each) sliced white potatoes, drained . . .Add potatoes and mix thoroughly. **Microwave at High 9 to 11 Minutes,** stirring after 5 minutes.

2 tablespoons grated Parmesan cheese . . .Sprinkle cheese on top before serving.

Makes 4 to 6 servings

EGGPLANT-VEGETABLE CASSEROLE

This casserole, known as Ratatouille in Southern France, combines eggplant, green pepper, onion, zucchini and tomato in the classic seasonings of Provence.

POWER LEVEL: High and Medium
MICROWAVE TIME: 18 to 22 min., total

1 medium eggplant, peeled and cut into ½-in. cubes
1 large green pepper, cut into strips
1 large onion, thickly sliced
3 tablespoons olive or cooking oil
1 clove garlic, finely chopped
. . .In 3-qt. casserole, mix together eggplant, green pepper, onion, oil and garlic. Cover. **Microwave at High 5 to 6 Minutes,** or until onions are transparent.

2 medium zucchini sliced ¼-in. thick . . .Stir in zucchini and cover. **Microwave at High 5 to 6 Minutes.**

2 to 3 large tomatoes, peeled (if desired) and cut in wedges or 1 can (16-oz.) tomato wedges, drained
2 teaspoons minced parsley
1 teaspoon basil
1 teaspoon salt
⅛ teaspoon pepper
1 bay leaf
. . .Gently stir in tomatoes, parsley, basil, salt, pepper and bay leaf. **Microwave at Medium 8 to 10 Minutes,** or until vegetables are barely tender.

Makes 6 to 8 servings

SPINACH-CHEESE SOUFFLE

Souffles designed for conventional baking cannot be adapted to microwaving without changing the recipe. One of the "success ingredients" in this recipe is the evaporated milk.

POWER LEVEL: Defrost, High and Medium
MICROWAVE TIME: 33 to 41 min., total

1 pkg. (10-oz.) frozen chopped spinach . . . Microwave spinach in package. **Microwave at Defrost 8 to 10 Minutes,** turning over after 4 minutes, until no ice remains. Remove spinach from package. With hands, squeeze out all juice and set aside.

¼ cup flour
¾ teaspoon salt
½ teaspoon dry mustard
⅛ teaspoon paprika
1 can (13-oz.) evaporated milk (1⅔ cups)
. . . In 1½-qt. casserole, blend together flour, salt, mustard and paprika. Stir in evaporated milk. **Microwave at High 4 to 6 Minutes,** until thickened, stirring every 2 minutes.

1 cup (4-oz.) sharp cheddar cheese . . . Stir cheese and squeezed-out spinach into hot sauce. **Microwave at High 1 to 2 Minutes,** until cheese melts.

6 eggs, separated
1 teaspoon cream of tartar
. . . Beat egg whites with cream of tartar until stiff but not dry. Set aside and, using same beater, beat yolks until thick and lemon colored. Slowly pour spinach-cheese mixture over beaten egg yolks, beating constantly until well combined. Gently pour over beaten egg whites and fold together gently just until blended. Pour into ungreased 2½-qt. souffle dish. **Microwave at Medium 20 to 23 Minutes,** rotating dish ¼ turn every 5 minutes, until puffed top edges are beginning to appear dry and souffle has "set" appearance.

Makes 6 to 8 servings

NOTE: Center of souffle will remain creamy.

SQUASH COMBO

POWER LEVEL: See Recipe TEMP:* 200°
APPROX. MICROWAVE TIME: 12 to 15 min.

1 lb. zucchini squash (4 medium)
1 lb. yellow squash (4 medium)
1 jar (2-oz.) pimiento
2 tablespoons water
2 tablespoons butter
. . . Wash squash and cut into chunks, alternating yellow and zucchini into 2-qt. casserole. Arrange undrained pimiento strips over top. Add water and dot with butter.

Insert temperature probe so tip rests on center bottom of dish. Cover with plastic wrap, arranging loosely around probe to vent. Attach cable end at receptacle. **Microwave at High. Set Temp, Set 200°.** When oven signals, let squash stand, covered, about 10 minutes before serving. Toss to mix, if desired.

Makes 6 to 8 servings

* On models not equipped with probe use minimum microwave time and check for doneness.

PECAN CRISP SQUASH

Squash is easy to cut into halves if microwaved 1 to 2 minutes at High. Let stand a few minutes before cutting.

POWER LEVEL: High
MICROWAVE TIME: 12 to 14 min., total

2 acorn squash (about 1 lb. each) . . . Cut squash in half lengthwise. Remove seeds and fibrous membranes. Place cut side down in 12×8×2-in. dish. Cover with plastic wrap turning back one corner to vent. **Microwave at High 6 Minutes,** rotating dish ¼ turn after 3 minutes.

⅔ cup butter-cracker crumbs
⅓ cup coarsely chopped pecans
⅓ cup butter, melted
3 tablespoons brown sugar (packed)
½ teaspoon salt
¼ teaspoon nutmeg
. . . While squash is cooking, toss together crumbs, pecans, butter, brown sugar, salt and nutmeg.

After squash has cooked 6 minutes, turn cut-side-up and divide filling among the 4 halves. Recover with plastic wrap and **Microwave at High 6 to 8 Minutes,** until squash is tender. Remove plastic wrap and let stand 5 minutes until serving.

Makes 4 servings

NOTE: Recipe may be doubled for a party. Microwave squash in 13×9×2-in. dish, cut side down, about 10 minutes; turn over and fill. Recover. Finish microwaving 9 to 12 minutes more.

YELLOW SQUASHEROLE

POWER LEVEL: High and Medium
MICROWAVE TIME: 16½ to 21 min., total

2 tablespoons butter
¼ cup buttery flavored cracker crumbs
¼ cup chopped pecans

In 1-qt. casserole place butter. **Microwave at High ½ to 1 Minute** until melted. Add crumbs and pecans. **Microwave at High 2 Minutes,** stirring after 1 minute. Pour crumbs onto wax paper and set aside.

¼ cup water
½ teaspoon salt
1 lb. yellow squash, sliced

In same casserole, place water, salt and squash. Cover. **Microwave at High 8 to 10 Minutes,** stirring after 4 minutes, until tender. Drain.

¼ cup mayonnaise
1 egg, beaten
½ cup shredded cheddar cheese
2 tablespoons butter, melted
1½ teaspoons sugar
¼ to ½ teaspoon instant minced onion

Mix together mayonnaise, egg, cheese, butter, sugar and onion. Pour over squash, mixing well. **Microwave at Medium 4 Minutes.** Stir, then add crumb topping. **Microwave at Medium 2 to 4 Minutes** more until center is set. Let Stand 5 Minutes before serving.

Makes about 4 servings

TOMATO PEPPER QUICKIE

POWER LEVEL: High
MICROWAVE TIME: 8 to 9 min., total

2 medium green peppers, cut into chunks
1 medium onion
½ teaspoon basil
1 teaspoon salt
2 tablespoons water

In 1-qt. casserole place green pepper. Cut onion into ¼-in. slices, separate into rings and lay on top of green pepper. Sprinkle on seasonings. Add water. Cover. **Microwave at High 6 Minutes,** stirring after 3 minutes.

2 medium ripe tomatoes or 1 can (1-lb.) tomato wedges, drained

Cut tomatoes into ¾-in. wedges and arrange over casserole. Cover. **Microwave at High 2 to 3 Minutes** more, until tomatoes are just heated.

Makes 4 servings

TOMATO HALVES AU GRATIN

For a simple version of this recipe, sprinkle tomato halves with Butter Crumb Topping (right), and microwave as directed below.

POWER LEVEL: High
MICROWAVE TIME: See Recipe

Tomatoes

Wash and halve tomatoes. Arrange in dish suggested below, or in microwave ovenproof pottery plate of suitable size.

For each tomato half:
½ teaspoon instant minced onion
½ teaspoon sugar
½ teaspoon sweet basil
¼ teaspoon salt
Dash pepper
1 tablespoon crushed potato or corn chips
1 tablespoon shredded cheddar cheese

Sprinkle each tomato half with seasonings. **Microwave at High** according to times below. Time may vary due to size and variety of tomato.

NUMBER OF TOMATOES	DISH	TIME MINUTES
2 halves	1-qt. casserole	2 to 2½
4 halves*	2-qt. casserole	3 to 4
6 or 8 halves*	12×8×2-in. dish	5 to 6

*Rotate dish ½ turn after half of cooking time.

YAMS HAWAIIAN STYLE

POWER LEVEL: High
MICROWAVE TIME: 6 to 8 min., total

2 cans (1-lb. 2-oz. each) yams or sweet potatoes, drained
1 can (8½-oz.) crushed pineapple
½ cup (¼-lb.) melted butter
¼ cup granulated sugar
1 teaspoon cinnamon

Slice yams into ½-in. thick pieces. Combine with pineapple, butter, sugar and cinnamon in 2-qt. casserole. **Microwave at High 4 Minutes.** Stir.

½ cup coarsely chopped pecans
¼ cup light brown sugar (packed)

Sprinkle top with pecans and brown sugar. **Microwave at High 2 to 4 Minutes.** If dish is not hot and topping not melted after 2 minutes, rotate dish ¼ turn, continue to microwave.

Makes 6 to 8 servings

NOTE: If desired, yams may be mashed with the next 4 ingredients, then cooked. Finish with brown sugar-nut topping and continue to microwave as above.

BUTTER CRUMB TOPPING FOR VEGETABLES

POWER LEVEL: Medium High
MICROWAVE TIME: 3 to 4½ min., total

¼ cup butter . . . . In small mixing bowl place butter. **Microwave at Medium High 1 to 1½ Minutes,** until melted. Add crumbs and dill weed, mixing well with butter. **Microwave at Medium High 2 to 3 Minutes** more, stirring after 1 minute.
1 cup fine dry bread crumbs
¼ to ½ teaspoon dill weed or other desired seasoning

Makes 1 cup topping

NOTE: Butter Crumb Topping is good with cauliflower, asparagus, broccoli and tomatoes.

TOSSED VEGETABLE DRESSING

This unusual tossed vegetable dressing combines crunchy, quick cooked vegetables tossed with savory croutons. As a bonus, each serving is only about 87 calories. Toss just before serving.

POWER LEVEL: High
MICROWAVE TIME: 8½ to 10½ min., total

2 chicken bouillon cubes . . . . . . In 3-qt. casserole, place bouillon cubes and water. **Microwave at High ¼ Minute.** Stir to blend.
1 tablespoon water

2 tablespoons butter . . . Add butter, salt and pepper. **Microwave at High ¼ Minute** more to melt and blend.
1 teaspoon salt
¼ teaspoon pepper

2 eggs, well beaten . . . . . Quickly whisk eggs into hot mixture. Then toss in vegetables to mix well. Cover dish tightly with plastic wrap turning one edge back slightly to vent. **Microwave at High 8 to 10 Minutes** stirring mixture after 4 minutes. Vegetables should be just crisp-tender.
1½ cups finely grated carrots
1 cup finely chopped onions
2½ cups (8-oz.) sliced fresh mushrooms
¾ cup finely chopped parsley, slightly packed down in cup

1 pkg. (6-oz.) seasoned croutons . . . . Remove vegetables from oven and toss in croutons. To retain best crispy texture of dressing, serve immediately.

Makes 12 (½-cup) servings

ZIPPY ZUCCHINI

Covering the custard mixture during the first 8 to 10 minutes of microwaving helps it cook evenly and shortens the total time.

POWER LEVEL: High and Medium High
MICROWAVE TIME: 15 to 17 min., total

4 cups zucchini, cut into chunks (2 medium) . . . Place zucchini and onion in 10×6×2-in. dish. Cover with plastic wrap, turning one edge back slightly to vent. **Microwave at High 7 Minutes.** Drain.
½ medium onion, thinly sliced

4 eggs, beaten . . . . In large bowl mix together eggs, cheese, pimiento, salt and pepper. Add zucchini and onions, stirring well. Grease dish in which vegetables were cooked. Pour mixture into dish and cover with paper towel. **Microwave at Medium High 8 to 10 Minutes,** stirring and removing paper towel after 4 minutes, until center is set.
1½ cups (6-oz.) shredded cheddar cheese
1 jar (2-oz.) pimiento, drained
½ teaspoon salt
⅛ teaspoon pepper

Makes 4 servings

Zippy Zucchini

Blanching Vegetables

For those who like to freeze fresh vegetables while they are in season, highest in quality and lowest in price, the microwave oven is a great help. It's especially useful to home gardeners, since vegetable crops do not ripen uniformly. You can pick vegetables as they reach the peak of flavor, even if you have only a few servings. Minutes after the vegetables are picked, you'll have them blanched and ready-to-freeze, without spending all day in a steamy kitchen, handling heavy pots of boiling water.

HOW TO BLANCH AND FREEZE VEGETABLES

Prepare vegetables (wash, peel, slice or dice) as you would for regular cooking. Measure 1 quart or 1 pound of vegetables into the recommended casserole. Add water, as given in the chart. DO NOT ADD SALT. Cover the casserole.

Set Power at High. Microwave for half the minimum time and stir. Recover the casserole and microwave for second half of minimum time. Stir again.

Check for Doneness. Vegetables should have an evenly bright color throughout. If all the vegetables are not evenly bright, recover the casserole and cook to maximum time. Drain vegetables.

POWER LEVEL: **High**

VEGETABLE	AMOUNT	CASSEROLE SIZE	WATER	MINUTES
Asparagus	1-lb. cut into 1 to 2-in pieces	2-qt.	¼ cup	3 to 4
Beans, Green or Wax	1-lb.	1½-qt.	½ cup	4 to 6
Broccoli (1-in. cuts)	1 bunch 1¼ to 1½ lb.	2-qt.	½ cup	4 to 5½
Carrots	1-lb. sliced	1½-qt.	¼ cup	4 to 6
Cauliflower	1 head, cut into flowerets	2-qt.	½ cup	4 to 5½
Corn on the Cob*				

*Special Directions for Corn On The Cob

For most even blanching, cut corn off the cob before blanching. Blanch corn cut from 4 ears at a time. Place cut corn in 1-qt. casserole. Add ¼ cup water. Cover. Cook 4 to 5 minutes, stirring after 2 minutes. Cool by setting casserole in ice water, stirring occasionally until cool.

Cooking Frozen Blanched Vegetables

A 1-pint container holds about the same amount of vegetables as a 10-ounce package of commercially frozen vegetables. To cook this amount, follow directions on the Vegetable Cooking Chart, page 188. If you package vegetables in smaller or larger amounts, adjust the casserole size, amount of water and cooking time proportionately.

DO NOT OVER-COOK. Home-frozen vegetables taste best when cooked to crisp-tender. Cook for a minimum time, then let stand, covered, an additional 5 to 10 minutes to finish softening and develop flavor.

Plunge vegetables into ice water immediately, to prevent further cooking. Spread them on paper towels and blot with additional towels to absorb excess moisture.

Package in freezing containers or boil-in-bag pouches. Label packages with type of vegetable, amount and date. Freeze.

To loose-pack vegetables in larger containers or bags, spread individual pieces on a cookie sheet. Place in freezer until vegetables are frozen; then place loose pieces in containers. Seal, label and freeze.

POWER LEVEL: **High**

VEGETABLE	AMOUNT	CASSEROLE SIZE	WATER	MINUTES
Onions	4 medium quartered	1-qt.	½ cup	3 to 4½
Parsnips	1-lb. cubed	1½-qt.	¼ cup	2½ to 4
Peas	2-lb. shelled	1-qt.	¼ cup	3½ to 5
Spinach	1-lb. washed	2-qt.	None	2½ to 3½
Squash, Summer, Yellow	1-lb. sliced or cubed	1½-qt.	¼ cup	3 to 4½
Turnips	1-lb. cubed	1½-qt.	¼ cup	3 to 4½
Zucchini	1-lb. sliced or cubed	1½-qt.	¼ cup	3 to 4½

For vegetables not given on the chart, refer to the Vegetable Cooking Chart, page 188. Follow directions for fresh vegetables, but DO NOT ADD SALT. Blanching time will be ¼ to ⅓ the regular cooking time. Stir, test and cool as directed in blanching steps.

Breads

Quick breads really are quick with microwaving. Whether you start from scratch or use a mix, you'll have fresh, hot muffins, breads or coffee cakes in minutes. Microwaved quick breads have an even texture and greater volume than conventionally baked, but they do not brown. Use batters with color, such as corn, bran or spice bread, or a topping. For "up-side-down" breads, butter the baking dish and coat the bottom and sides with topping. Savory or sweet toppings add eye appeal as well.

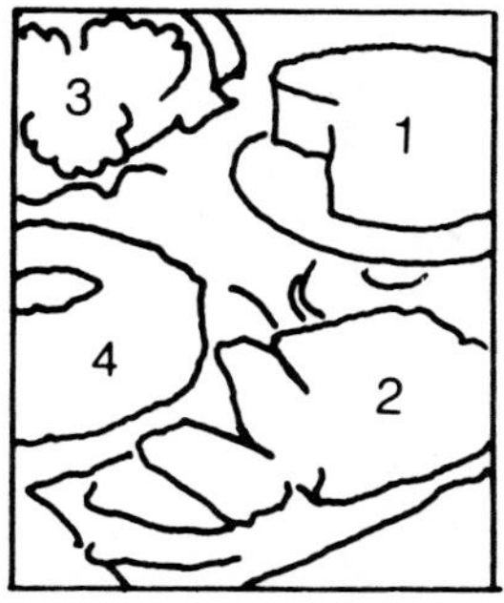

1. Cornbread Ring, page 210
2. Savory Cheese Bread, page 215
3. Bran Nut Muffins, page, 209
4. Stacked Maple Nut Rings, page 212

Savory Toppings on microwaved quick breads are shown below in comparison with conventional and microwaved breads without toppings. See Quick Bread Toppings, next page.

Conventional | Microwaved | Crushed French Fried Onions | Crumbled Bacon & Shredded Cheddar Cheese | Sauteed Onions & Green Pepper With Paprika | Taco Seasoning Mix

Sweet Toppings on microwaved quick breads are shown below in comparison with conventional and microwaved breads without toppings. See Quick Bread Toppings, next page.

Conventional | Microwaved | Nut-Crunch Topping | Microwaved Toasted Coconut | Cinnamon & Sugar | Chopped Nuts

HOW TO MICROWAVE MUFFINS

Cupcaker, especially designed for microwaving, assures good shape and even cooking for muffins and cupcakes; or, make your own muffin cups.

Cut The Tops from paper hot drink cups, leaving 1-in. sides. Line each with a fluted paper baking cup. Arrange in a ring on a flat plate.

Fill Cups half full. Microwaved muffins rise higher than conventionally baked. Rotate ½ turn half way through the cooking time.

Test after minimum time. A wooden pick inserted in center comes out clean. Muffins will appear barely set; there may be moist spots on the surface.

FLUFFY MUFFINS

Select a topping (at right) to add color to top of muffins. This versatile quick bread batter is also used for Simple Coffee Cake, page 211.

POWER LEVEL: Medium High
MICROWAVE TIME: See Recipe

2 cups unsifted all-purpose flour **½ cup sugar** **3 teaspoons baking powder** **½ teaspoon salt**	In mixing bowl stir flour with sugar, baking powder and salt. Make a well in center of dry mixture.
2 eggs, beaten **½ cup cooking oil** **½ cup milk**	Combine eggs, oil and milk. Add all at once to dry ingredients and stir just to moisten. Fill paper lined microwave containers ½ full; see comments. Cook according to chart below. Muffins are done when toothpick stuck in center comes out clean.

MUFFINS	TIME MINUTES	COMMENTS
1	½ to 1	For best shape use microwave cupcaker or make reusable "homemade muffin supports" by cutting down paper hot drink cups. Check for doneness at minimum time. Redistribute after ½ of cooking time. If using cupcaker, rotate ½ turn. Rich, thick batters may take longest time.
2	1 to 1¾	
3	1½ to 2¼	
4	2 to 3	
5	2½ to 3½	
6	3 to 5	

Makes about 14 muffins

FLUFFY MUFFINS VARIATIONS

Fold ½ cup raisins or rinsed, drained blueberries into batter (top with cinnamon sugar); or add ½ cup shredded cheese (top with bacon-cheese topping); or add ½ cup chopped nuts (top with toasted coconut).

SAVORY OR SWEET TOPPINGS FOR MICROWAVED MUFFINS & BREADS

Before microwaving, sprinkle suggested toppings over 12 muffins or a bread ring made with muffin or cornbread batter. Microwave as for Cornbread (page 210) or Muffins (left).

SAVORY TOPPINGS:

Onion: Crush ½ can (3-oz.) French fried onions.

Bacon-Cheese: Microwave 3 slices bacon until very crisp; crumble finely. Mix with ⅓ cup grated sharp cheddar cheese.

Onion-Green Pepper: Saute ¼ cup each of chopped vegetables in 1 teaspoon butter 3 to 4 minutes at High. Sprinkle with paprika.

Taco Seasoning Mix: Use ½ pkg. (1¼-oz.)

SWEET TOPPINGS:

Nut Crunch: Cut together with pastry blender: ¼ cup flour, 2 tablespoons brown sugar, 2 tablespoons butter and ¼ cup chopped nuts.

Microwaved Coconut: Spread 1 pkg. (4-oz.) shredded coconut in 9-in. pie plate. Microwave 5 to 6 minutes stirring after 2 minutes and then every minute.

Cinnamon, Sugar or Chopped Nuts: Use about ⅓ cup.

BRAN NUT MUFFINS

POWER LEVEL: Medium High
MICROWAVE TIME: See Recipe

2 cups unsifted all-purpose flour **1 cup sugar** **5 teaspoons baking powder** **1½ teaspoons salt** **2 cups whole bran cereal** **1 cup chopped nuts (or raisins)**	In large mixing bowl stir together flour, sugar, baking powder, salt, bran and nuts or raisins.
2 eggs **1½ cups milk** **½ cup cooking oil**	Combine eggs, milk and oil. Stir into dry mixture just until all flour is dampened. Fill paper lined muffin cups ½ full.
¼ cup crushed bran cereal or chopped nuts	Sprinkle muffins with cereal or nuts. **Microwave at Medium High,** using same directions as Fluffy Muffins.

Makes about 24 muffins

BRAN NUT BREAD VARIATION

Prepare batter for Bran Nut Muffins. Pour into well greased 10-in. microwave fluted ring mold. **Microwave at Medium High 14 to 16 Minutes,** rotating dish ½ turn after 6 minutes, until toothpick stuck into center comes out clean. Let stand 5 minutes, then turn out onto cooling rack. Serve warm or cool.

Makes 1 (10-in.) fluted ring

APPLESAUCE GINGER GEMS

POWER LEVEL: Medium High
MICROWAVE TIME: See Recipe

1 pkg. (about 14-oz.) gingerbread mix **Applesauce** **Egg, if package directs**	In mixing bowl prepare gingerbread batter as package directs, except substitute applesauce for amount of water called for on package. Add egg if package directs.

Microwave at Medium High, using same directions as Fluffy Muffins. Because this is a very moist batter, maximum time will probably be required. If desired, sprinkle tops of muffins with cinnamon and drizzle with Simple Glaze before serving.

Makes about 2 dozen

APPLESAUCE GINGER BREAD VARIATION

Prepare batter for Ginger Gems. Divide evenly between 2 greased 8×4×3-in. dishes. Microwave one loaf at a time. **Microwave at Medium High 5 to 6 Minutes,** rotating dish ½ turn after 3 minutes, until toothpick stuck in center comes out clean.

Makes 2 (8×4×3-in.) loaves

Blueberry Fluffy Muffins

PUMPKIN GEMS

Gems is an old-fashioned word for small muffins or cupcakes. These muffins keep very well if tightly covered.

POWER LEVEL: Medium High
MICROWAVE TIME: See Recipe

1⅓ cups sugar **⅓ cup shortening** **2 eggs** **1 cup mashed pumpkin**	In large mixing bowl beat together sugar, shortening and eggs. Stir in pumpkin.
1⅓ cups unsifted all-purpose flour **1 teaspoon baking soda** **¼ teaspoon baking powder** **¾ teaspoon salt** **½ teaspoon cinnamon** **½ teaspoon nutmeg**	Stir together flour, soda, baking powder, salt, cinnamon and nutmeg. Add to pumpkin mixture, stirring well.
½ teaspoon vanilla **⅓ cup water** **½ cup chopped nuts**	Mix in vanilla, water and nuts.

Microwave at Medium High, using same directions as Fluffy Muffins. Because this is a very moist batter, maximum time will probably be required. If desired, sprinkle tops of muffins with cinnamon and drizzle with Simple Glaze before serving.

Makes about 25 gems

Simple Glaze: Stir together ½ cup sifted confectioners sugar, 1 to 2 tablespoons milk or hot water, ¼ teaspoon vanilla extract and ⅛ teaspoon salt.

BASIC NUT BREAD

To vary this recipe, add 1 cup chopped dates or cranberries. Best shape is attained when baked in microwave fluted ring mold.

POWER LEVEL: Medium High
MICROWAVE TIME: See Recipe

2½ cups unsifted all-purpose flour
1 cup sugar
3 teaspoons baking powder
1 teaspoon salt
In large mixing bowl stir together flour, sugar, baking powder and salt.

1¼ cups milk
1 egg
3 tablespoons cooking oil
1¼ cups finely chopped nuts, divided
Measure milk into 1-pt. glass measure. Add egg and oil. Beat well. Add to flour mixture along with 1 cup nuts. Stir until flour is moistened. Generously grease 10-in. microwave fluted ring mold. Dust with ¼ cup nuts. Pour batter into prepared mold.

Microwave at Medium High 11 to 13 Minutes, rotating dish ¼ turn every 4 minutes, until toothpick stuck into center comes out clean. Let stand 5 minutes; then turn out onto cooling rack. Serve warm or cool.

Makes 1 (10-in.) fluted ring

To microwave 2 (8×4×3-in.) loaves, divide batter evenly between 2 greased 8×4×3-in. dishes. Sprinkle remaining ¼ cup nuts over breads. Microwave one loaf at a time. **Microwave at Medium High 6 to 8 Minutes,** rotating dish ¼ turn every 2 minutes, until toothpick stuck into center comes out clean.

NUT BREAD FROM A MIX

POWER LEVEL: Medium High
MICROWAVE TIME: 9 to 12 min., total

1. Make batter as directed on package, using greased 9×5×3-in. dish.
2. Sprinkle batter with ¼ cup finely chopped nuts.
3. **Microwave at Medium High 9 to 12 Minutes,** rotating dish ½ turn after 5 minutes. Bread is done when toothpick inserted in center comes out clean. Top surface appears different from conventionally baked.

Makes 1 (9×5×3-in.) loaf.

CORNBREAD RING

POWER LEVEL: High and Medium
MICROWAVE TIME: 8 to 10 min., total

1 cup yellow corn meal
1 cup unsifted all-purpose flour
2 tablespoons sugar
4 teaspoons baking powder
½ teaspoon salt
In large mixing bowl, stir together cornmeal, flour, sugar, baking powder and salt.

1 egg
1 cup milk
½ cup cooking oil
Add egg, milk and cooking oil. Beat until smooth, about 1 minute.

½ cup finely crushed French fried onions (about ½ of 3-oz. can)
1 tablespoon Parmesan cheese
Place onions and cheese in well-greased 8-in. round dish. Tilt to coat all sides, reserving excess crumbs. Place a small drinking glass (3-in. or less diameter, 4 to 5-in. high) in center of dish. Pour batter around glass and sprinkle with reserved crumbs.

Microwave at Medium 5 Minutes. Rotate dish ½ turn. **Microwave at High 3 to 5 Minutes** more, until toothpick stuck in center comes out clean. Turn out on cooling rack or serving plate. Serve warm.

Makes 1 (8-in.) ring

TRADITIONAL STEAMED BROWN BREAD

POWER LEVEL: Medium
MICROWAVE TIME: 19 to 21 min., per loaf

1¼ cups cornmeal
1¼ cups whole wheat flour
1¼ cups rye flour
1 tablespoon baking soda
1 teaspoon salt
Stir together cornmeal, whole wheat flour, rye flour, baking soda and salt.

1 cup dark molasses
2½ cups buttermilk
1¼ cups raisins
Stir in molasses, buttermilk and raisins thoroughly. Pour into 2 greased 9×5×3-in. loaf dishes.

Cover each dish tightly with plastic wrap so bread steams as it cooks. Microwave one dish at a time. **Microwave at Medium 19 to 21 Minutes,** rotating dish ¼ turn every 6 minutes. Unmold and let stand 10 minutes before slicing.

Makes 2 (9×5×3-in.) loaves

Coffee Cakes

Coffee cakes may be microwaved in a round dish, rather than a ring. The richer, sweeter batter cooks evenly, so there will be no depression in the center. Like other quick breads, coffee cakes do not brown, and need a colorful topping or simple icing to give them a finished appearance.

EVERYDAY COFFEE CAKE

Biscuit mix recipe.

POWER LEVEL: High
MICROWAVE TIME: 5 to 7 min., total

1½ cups buttermilk biscuit mix
¼ cup sugar
In mixing bowl stir together biscuit mix and sugar.

½ cup milk
1 egg
2 tablespoons cooking oil
Add milk, egg and oil. Beat by hand, mixing well. Pour into greased 8-in. round dish.

⅓ cup buttermilk biscuit mix
⅓ cup brown sugar (packed)
2 tablespoons butter
1 teaspoon cinnamon
¼ cup chopped nuts
Blend biscuit mix, brown sugar, butter and cinnamon until crumbly. Sprinkle over batter and sprinkle with nuts. **Microwave at High 5 to 7 Minutes,** rotating dish ½ turn after 3 minutes. Cool 15 minutes; drizzle with Fine Glaze. Serve warm.

Fine Glaze: Stir together ¾ cup confectioners sugar and 1 tablespoon milk. From tip of spoon, drizzle glaze over cake in spoke fashion.

Makes 1 (8-in. round) cake

Coffee Cakes microwave very quickly, and should be checked for doneness after the minimum cooking time. The cake is done when a wooden pick inserted in the center comes out clean. There may be some doughiness on the outside, which will disappear on standing. Drizzle icing or glaze over the cake to finish.

Stacked Maple Nut Rings, page 212

SIMPLE COFFEE CAKE

Scratch recipe.

POWER LEVEL: High
MICROWAVE TIME: 5 to 7 min., total

2 cups unsifted all-purpose flour
½ cup sugar
3 teaspoons baking powder
½ teaspoon salt
In mixing bowl stir flour with sugar, baking powder and salt. Make a well in center of dry mixture.

2 eggs, beaten
½ cup cooking oil
½ cup milk
Combine eggs, oil and milk. Add all at once to dry ingredients and stir just to moisten.

Pour into greased 8-in. round dish and sprinkle with Topping (below). **Microwave at High 5 to 7 Minutes,** rotating dish ½ turn after 3 minutes. Cool 15 minutes; if desired, drizzle with Fine Glaze (left).

Makes 1 (8-in. round) coffee cake

Topping: Blend 2 tablespoons flour, 1 tablespoon cinnamon, 1 tablespoon cocoa, ⅓ cup sugar and ¼ cup cold butter until crumbly.

MAPLE-NUT RING

POWER LEVEL: Medium
MICROWAVE TIME: 8 to 10 min., total

1/3 cup finely chopped walnuts
2 tablespoons brown sugar (packed)
2 tablespoons sugar
1 teaspoon cinnamon
. . . . Invert 6-oz. custard cup in center of lightly greased 8-in. round dish. In small bowl, mix together walnuts, brown sugar, sugar and cinnamon.

1/4 cup maple syrup
1 roll (10-oz.) refrigerated buttermilk biscuits
. . . . Place maple syrup in small bowl. Coat each biscuit with syrup, then sugar-nut mixture. Arrange in circle in prepared dish, overlapping edges.

Microwave at Medium 8 to 10 Minutes, rotating dish 1/2 turn after 4 minutes. Let cool 5 minutes. Remove custard cup and invert onto serving plate. Sprinkle with any remaining sugar-nut mixture. Serve warm.

Makes 1 (8-in.) ring

STACKED MAPLE-NUT RINGS

Make two rings, inverting one over the other. Drizzle with confectioners sugar glaze made by mixing 1 cup confectioners sugar and 1 to 2 tablespoons milk.

CHERRY CARAMEL RING

POWER LEVEL: High and Medium
MICROWAVE TIME: 8 1/2 to 10 3/4 min., total

1/4 cup butter
. . . . Place butter in 8-in. round dish. **Microwave at High 1/2 to 3/4 Minute,** until melted.

1/2 cup brown sugar (packed)
2 tablespoons light corn syrup
1/2 cup pecan halves
1/4 cup maraschino cherries, quartered
. . . . Sprinkle sugar over butter and add corn syrup. Stir well with fork. Place drinking glass in center of dish. Sprinkle with pecans and cherries.

1 roll (10-oz.) refrigerated buttermilk biscuits
. . . . Arrange biscuits over mixture in dish in petal shape, squeezing to fit, if necessary. **Microwave at Medium 6 to 8 Minutes,** rotating dish 1/2 turn after 3 minutes. Remove glass and invert onto serving plate. Let dish stand over rolls a few minutes so remaining syrup in dish may drizzle over rolls. Serve warm.

Makes 1 (8-in.) ring

HOW TO MICROWAVE A CARAMEL BISCUIT RING

Prepare topping in bottom of improvised tube pan made by placing a drinking glass about 4-in. high or inverted 6-oz. custard cup, in an 8-in. dish.

Arrange biscuits over topping and around glass center.

Inverted onto a serving plate, the ring has a rich caramel-colored syrup over the top and sides, although the bottoms of the biscuits are not brown.

CONVENIENCE BREADS

One of the best uses for the microwave oven is defrosting frozen convenience breads and warming bakery products. The Defrost setting provides rapid defrosting and warming, yet keeps breads tender.

Coffeecakes packaged in foil should be removed from the container. If the cardboard cover is not foil-lined it may be used as a plate under cake. Other breads may be placed on pottery or paper plates before heating.

Metal Twist Ties must be removed before package of rolls or bread is placed in oven. Under some conditions, metal twist ties can cause package to catch fire.

CONVENIENCE BREADS DEFROSTING AND WARMING CHART

POWER LEVEL: **Defrost**

ITEM	TIME MINUTES	COMMENTS
DEFROSTING		
Bread or Buns (1-lb. pkg.)	3 to 4	Turn over after 2 minutes.
Heat & Serve Rolls (7-oz. pkg.)	2 to 3	Rotate ½ turn after 1 minute.
Coffee Cake (11 to 13-oz. pkg.)	5½ to 6	Rotate ½ turn after 3 minutes.
Coffee Cake (6½-oz. pkg.)	2 to 3	No turn needed.
Coffee Ring (10-oz. pkg.)	3½ to 4	Rotate ½ turn after 2 minutes.
Sweet Rolls, Crumb Cakes, Pull-aparts (8¾ to 12-oz. pkg.)	2½ to 3½	Rotate ½ turn after 1½ minutes.
Doughnuts (1 to 3)	½ to 1	No turn needed.
Doughnuts (4 to 6)	1 to 2	No turn needed.
Doughnuts (1 box of 12 glazed)	2 to 3	Rotate ½ turn after 1 minute.
French Toast (2 slices)	5½ to 6½	Rotate ½ turn after 3 minutes.
French Toast (4 slices)	9 to 10	Rotate ½ turn after 5 minutes.
WARMING (room temperature)		
Dinner Rolls (1 to 3)	½ to 1½	No turn needed.
Dinner Rolls (4 to 6)	1½ to 2½	No turn needed.
Doughnuts	1 to 2	Rotate more than 6.

Cherry Caramel Ring

Breads/Yeast

The microwave oven can be used to defrost frozen yeast bread and, if you wish, to cook the dough. However, its appearance will not be the same as if it were conventionally baked.

Breads cooked in the microwave oven do not brown or develop a crust as they do conventionally because there is no hot air in the oven to dry out the surfaces. Microwaved bread raises higher during cooking than conventionally baked bread, because it does not have a firm crust to prevent it from rising too much. For this reason bread must be microwaved in a larger loaf dish and carefully cooked to avoid forming large air pockets which collapse and cause uneven shape. When properly microwaved, breads look set and dry on top and, when touched, the surface springs back. Toppings provide a colorful finished appearance.

Toppings on microwaved breads made from frozen dough are shown at the left in comparison with conventional and microwaved breads without toppings. From the top: Conventional, Microwaved, Taco Seasoning Mix with Cornmeal, Toasted Sesame Seeds, Cinnamon Sugar, Crushed Canned Onion Rings.

Toast Sesame Seeds in a small bowl or 10-oz. custard cup, using 1 teaspoon of butter and 1 jar (2¾-oz.) seeds. **Microwave at High 4 to 5 Minutes,** stirring every minute, until toasted.

HOW TO DEFROST FROZEN BREAD DOUGH

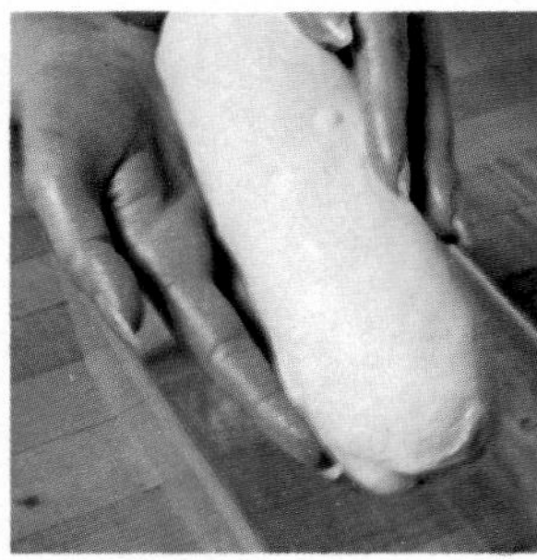

Place frozen bread in 9×5×3-in. loaf dish containing 1 tablespoon softened butter. Turn loaf to coat dish and bread with butter. (For conventional baking use 8×4×3-in. dish.)

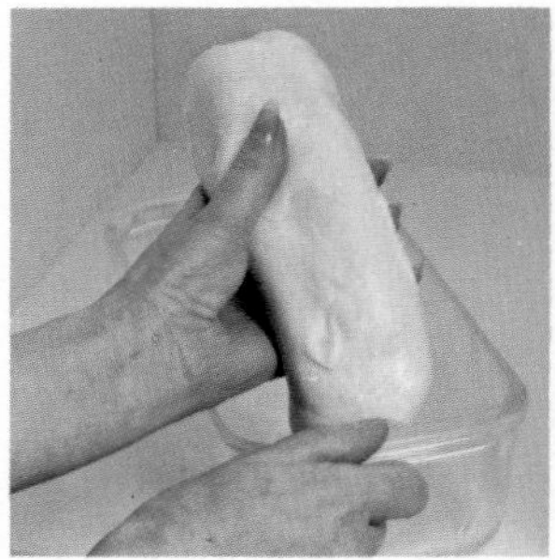

Defrost for a total time of 4 minutes, turning loaf over and rotating dish ¼ turn every ¾ minute. Let rise 2 hours in a warm place until double. Top of loaf should be about 1-in. below top of dish.

After defrosting and proofing frozen bread dough **Microwave at Medium 10 to 12 Minutes,** rotating loaf ½ turn after 5 minutes.

Savory Cheese Bread, created especially for microwaving contains butter and cheese for richness. A topping adds color and flavor. Low shape provides maximum exposure to microwave energy for even cooking.

SAVORY CHEESE BREAD

POWER LEVEL: Medium
MICROWAVE TIME: 10 to 12 min. per loaf

2¾ cups unsifted all-purpose flour **2 tablespoons sugar** **½ teaspoon salt** **½ cup (¼-lb.) butter**	In large mixing bowl place flour, sugar, salt and butter. Cut through mixture with pastry blender until mixture resembles coarse meal.
1 pkg. (¼-oz.) active dry yeast **¼ cup warm water** **1 cup milk** **1 egg, beaten**	Dissolve yeast in warm water. Add to crumbly mixture along with milk and egg. Beat with spoon until well blended.
1 pkg. (½ of 2¾-oz. box) dry onion soup mix **1 cup (4-oz. pkg.) shredded cheddar cheese**	Mix together 2 tablespoons onion soup mix and ¼ cup shredded cheese. Set aside. Add remaining soup mix and cheese to batter. Stir well.

Divide batter evenly between 2 well greased 8×4×3-in. dishes. Sprinkle loaves with reserved cheese mixture. Cover lightly and let rise in warm place 1½ to 2 hours, just until dough is slightly puffy.

Microwave one loaf at a time. **Microwave at Medium 10 to 12 Minutes,** rotating dish ½ turn after 5 minutes. Let stand in dish 5 minutes.

Carefully remove breads to cooling rack. Serve warm or cool.

Makes 2 (8×4×3-in.) loaves

NO-KNEAD OATMEAL BREAD

POWER LEVEL: Medium
MICROWAVE TIME: 10 to 12 min. per loaf

2 pkg. (¼-oz. each) active dry yeast **½ cup warm water**	Dissolve yeast in warm water. Set aside.
1½ cups boiling water **⅓ cup shortening** **1 cup quick oatmeal** **½ cup light molasses** **1 tablespoon salt**	In large bowl, combine boiling water, shortening, oatmeal, molasses and salt. Cool to lukewarm.
6 cups unsifted all-purpose flour **2 eggs, slightly beaten**	Stir in well 2 cups flour and eggs. Add yeast and beat well. Add flour, 2 cups at a time, mixing well after each addition. Beat smooth, about 10 minutes. Grease top lightly. Cover tightly with plastic wrap. Refrigerate 2 hours or overnight.
2 tablespoons wheat germ or ¼ cup quick oatmeal	Shape 2 loaves. Place in greased 9×5×3-in. dishes. Sprinkle with wheat germ or oatmeal.

Cover with plastic wrap. Let rise in warm place until double, about 2 hours. Microwave one loaf at a time. **Microwave at Medium 10 to 12 Minutes,** rotating dish ½ turn after 5 minutes. Let stand 5 minutes. Turn out of dish. Cool on wire racks.

Makes 2 (9×5×3-in.) loaves

Desserts

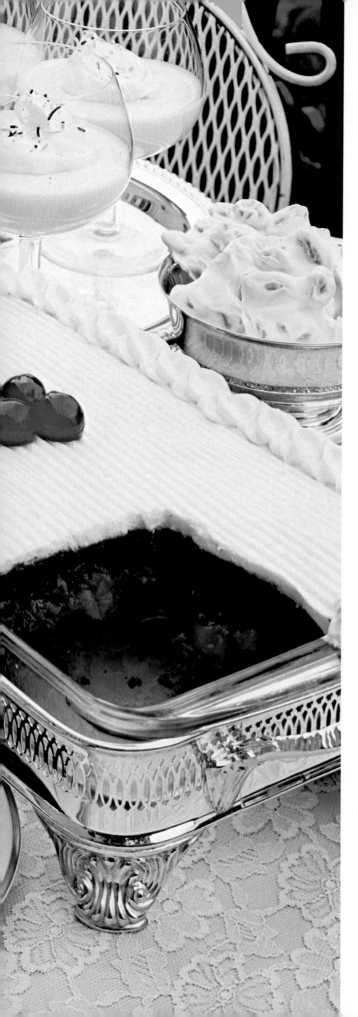

Your microwave oven can help you prepare almost any dessert, both those you have baked in your conventional oven and those you have cooked on the range top. Candies, custards, puddings, fruits and frosting are usually easier to microwave than they are to cook on your range top. Microwave energy is absorbed from all surfaces, the top and sides as well as the bottom, so less stirring is needed to heat them evenly.

Baked desserts are likely to appear different when microwaved. Brownies, bars and dark batters such as gingerbread or chocolate cake are the exceptions.

Pastries and cakes do not brown, but because they are served with fillings or toppings, the difference will not be apparent when they are served. What will impress you is the time saved by microwaving them.

1. Pecan Sponge Roll, page 249
2. Layered Fudge, page 219
3. Rainbow Pretzels, page 222
4. Floating Islands, page 230
5. White Chocolate Nut Bark, page 221
6. Black Forest Trifle, page 232

HOW TO MICROWAVE PEANUT BRITTLE

Stir well to combine sugar and corn syrup. Stirring this mixture helps it to microwave evenly. Add peanuts, stirring well. Stir again when adding butter and vanilla.

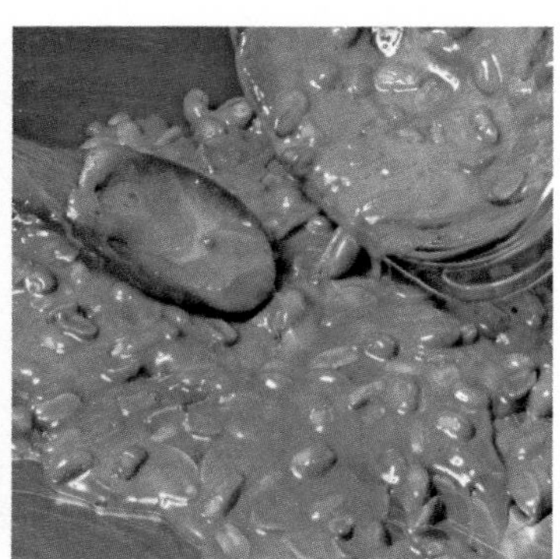

Stir in baking soda until mixture is light and foamy. Spread out quickly on greased cookie sheet. When cool, flex sheet to remove.

Munching Peanut Brittle

Candies

Candies demonstrate many of the advantages of microwaving. Chocolate and caramelized mixtures which require careful attention and constant stirring by old-fashioned methods, microwave with occasional stirring.

MUNCHING PEANUT BRITTLE

This is the same old-fashioned recipe which required constant stirring in a black iron skillet. Stir only 4 times when microwaving.

POWER LEVEL: High
MICROWAVE TIME: 8 to 11 min., total

1 cup sugar **½ cup white corn syrup**	In 1½-qt. casserole stir together sugar and syrup. **Microwave at High 4 Minutes.**
1 cup roasted, salted peanuts	Stir in peanuts. **Microwave at High 3 to 5 Minutes,** until light brown.
1 teaspoon butter **1 teaspoon vanilla extract**	Add butter and vanilla to syrup, blending well. **Microwave at High 1 to 2 Minutes** more. Peanuts will be lightly browned and syrup very hot.
1 teaspoon baking soda	Add baking soda and gently stir until light and foamy.

Pour mixture onto lightly greased cookie sheet, or unbuttered non-stick coated cookie sheet. Let cool ½ to 1 hour. When cool, break into small pieces and store in airtight container.

Makes about 1 pound

NOTE: If raw peanuts are used add, before microwaving, to the sugar-syrup mixture, along with ⅛ teaspoon salt.

ALMOND BRITTLE

Substitute 1 jar (7-oz.) dry roasted almonds for peanuts and 1 teaspoon almond extract for vanilla. Omit butter and add 1 cup (4-oz.) shredded coconut with 1 teaspoon almond extract.

PECAN OR CASHEW BRITTLE

Omit peanuts and add 1 cup pecan halves or 1 jar (7-oz.) dry-roasted cashews.

REAL CHOCOLATE FUDGE

POWER LEVEL: High and Medium High
MICROWAVE TIME: 20 to 22 min., total

2 cups sugar
1/8 teaspoon salt
3/4 cup milk
2 squares (2-oz.) unsweetened chocolate
1/4 cup butter

In 3-qt. casserole stir together sugar, salt and milk, mixing well. Add chocolate and butter. Cover. **Microwave at High 6 Minutes,** until hot and bubbly. Stir very well. **Microwave at Medium High 14 to 16 Minutes,** uncovered. Stir well every 5 minutes. When sufficiently cooked, a few drops of mixture will form a soft ball in cup of cold water. (Candy thermometer reads 235°.)

2 teaspoons vanilla

Let candy stand without stirring, at room temperature, until lukewarm.* Add vanilla, beat with spoon or mixer until it begins to thicken and loses its gloss.

1/2 cup chopped nuts (optional)

Quickly stir in nuts and pour into 8×4×3-in. loaf dish which has been lined with wax paper (or use buttered plate). Cut when set.

Makes about 1 pound

*Or place bowl in a pan of cool water or place in refrigerator until lukewarm.

REAL PEANUT BUTTER FUDGE

Make Real Chocolate Fudge as above, except substitute 1/3 cup crunchy peanut butter for chocolate and butter. If desired, use coarsely chopped salted peanuts for nuts in recipe, or omit nuts altogether.

LAYERED FUDGE

Prepare 2 (8-in.) loaf dishes by lining with wax paper. Prepare Real Chocolate Fudge and divide between the 2 dishes. Let set in refrigerator while preparing Real Peanut Butter Fudge. Divide evenly over chocolate fudge. Refrigerate until firm. Cut into squares. (Wiping knife with damp cloth between cuts best shows layered effect.)

For Shapely Square Pieces line loaf dish with wax paper. Use a 14×12-in. strip of wax paper (wax paper is 12-in. wide so cut 14-in. off roll); fold in half. Fit the 7-in. side on longest sides and bottom of loaf dish, leaving about 1-in. "handles" at each edge. When fudge is hardened, loosen fudge at narrow edges of loaf dish and lift out fudge in one piece using wax paper "handles". Pull off wax paper and, with sharp knife, cut into squares.

HOW TO MICROWAVE FUDGE

Combine first 5 ingredients in large bowl to prevent overboiling. Stir very well when mixture is hot and chocolate melted. Then stir every 5 minutes.

Soft ball will form from a small amount of mixture dropped into very cold water when fudge is sufficiently cooked. Line dish with 14×12-in folded strip of wax paper. Use long ends to lift out fudge when set.

Real Chocolate Fudge

2-MINUTE FUDGE

POWER LEVEL: High
MICROWAVE TIME: 2 min., total

1 box (1-lb.) confectioners sugar
½ cup cocoa
¼ teaspoon salt
¼ cup milk
1 tablespoon vanilla extract
½ cup (¼-lb.) butter

In 1½-qt. casserole stir sugar, cocoa, salt, milk and vanilla together until partially blended (mixture is too stiff to thoroughly blend in all of dry ingredients). Put butter over top in center of dish. **Microwave at High 2 Minutes,** or until milk feels warm on bottom of dish. Stir vigorously until smooth. If all butter has not melted in cooking, it will as mixture is stirred.

1 cup chopped nuts

Blend in nuts. Pour into wax paper lined (see page 219) 8×4×3-in. dish. Chill 1 hour in refrigerator or 20 to 30 minutes in freezer. Cut into squares.

Makes about 36 squares

COFFEE FONDANT

Prepare 2-Minute Fudge as above, except, omit cocoa and substitute 1 tablespoon instant coffee granules dissolved in 2 tablespoons milk. Before fondant sets, press "chocolate shot" decors into top.

TOFFEE HEATH SQUARES

POWER LEVEL: High
MICROWAVE TIME: 5 to 6 min., total

1 cup chopped nuts

Sprinkle nuts over bottom of buttered 8-in. square dish.

1 cup brown sugar (packed)
⅓ cup butter
3 tablespoons water

In 1½-qt. casserole place brown sugar, butter and water. **Microwave at High 5 to 6 Minutes,** stirring after 2 minutes, until thick. Stir well; quickly spread over chopped nuts.

½ cup semi-sweet chocolate pieces

Sprinkle chocolate pieces over toffee. Cover dish so heat melts chocolate. Let stand 5 minutes. Spread chocolate evenly over top. Refrigerate to set. Turn out of dish and break into pieces to serve.

Makes about 1 pound

BROWN SUGAR FUDGE

Its old-fashioned name is Penuche. When done just right, it is soft and creamy. Overcooked, it can be dry and crumbly. It has same soft ball test as fudge, page 219

POWER LEVEL: High
MICROWAVE TIME: 17 to 19 min., total

2 cups light brown sugar (packed)
1 cup whipping cream
1 cup maple syrup

In 3-qt. casserole stir together brown sugar, cream and syrup. **Microwave at High 17 to 19 Minutes,** stirring well after 7 minutes. When cooked, a few drops of the syrup will form a soft ball when dropped into a cup of cold water.

2 cups chopped walnuts

Let stand until lukewarm, then beat with electric mixer 10 to 12 minutes, until mixture becomes creamy. Add nuts and stir well. Pour into buttered 8-in. square dish. Refrigerate until set.

Makes about 36 squares

MARSHMALLOW CRISP

POWER LEVEL: High
MICROWAVE TIME: 2½ to 3 min., total

¼ cup butter
1 pkg. (10-oz.) large marshmallows* (about 40)
5 cups crispy rice cereal

In 3-qt. casserole place butter. **Microwave at High 1 Minute** to melt. Add marshmallows. Cover. **Microwave at High 2½ to 3 Minutes.** Remove from oven and stir until butter is melted and marshmallows are well blended. Add cereal. Stir until well coated.

Press warm mixture evenly and firmly into lightly buttered 12×8×2-in. dish. Use wax paper or buttered spatula to press firmly into an even layer. Cut into squares when cool.

Makes 24 (2-in.) squares

*Or use 4 cups miniature marshmallows or 1 jar (9-oz.) marshmallow cream (about 2 cups).

VARIATIONS:

Peanut: Add 1 cup whole or chopped peanuts, or stir ¼ cup peanut butter into marshmallow mixture just before adding cereal.

Chocolate Dot: After cereal has been stirred into marshmallow mixture, quickly stir in 1 pkg. (6-oz.) semi-sweet chocolate pieces.

HOW TO MELT CHOCOLATE

Chocolate Bits may be melted in a paper bowl. Cover with plastic wrap and Microwave at Medium or Low. For 6-oz. pkg. (1 cup) microwave 3 to 4 minutes, until bits are glossy but hold their shape. They smooth out when stirred. Chocolate burns easily, so check at minimum time.

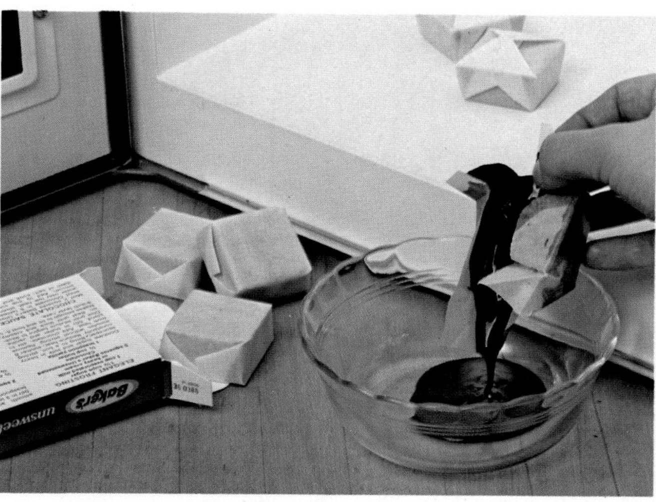

Chocolate Squares can be melted in paper wrappers, seam side up. Microwave up to 3 squares at Medium or Low about 2 to 3 minutes per square (1-oz.). For 4 to 6 squares, allow ¾ to 1¼ minute per square. Melt until square feels soft. Beyond this point, chocolate will scorch or burn.

CHOCOLATE NUT BARK

POWER LEVEL: Medium or Low
MICROWAVE TIME: 5 to 7 min., total

1 pkg. (12-oz.) semi-sweet or milk chocolate, broken or in squares ...... In 1-qt. casserole place chocolate. Cover. **Microwave at Medium or Low 5 to 7 Minutes.** Stir well.

1 cup whole toasted almonds or coarsely chopped Brazil nuts ...... Stir nuts into chocolate. Place a piece of wax paper on small cookie sheet. Spread chocolate mixture in a thin layer over wax paper. Refrigerate until firm, about 1 hour. Break into pieces.

Makes about ¾ pound

VARIATIONS:

1. Use 16-oz. white chocolate and melt in 1½-qt. casserole 5 to 6 minutes. Good with whole almonds in above recipe.
2. Any number of variations of chocolate and other ingredients are good: Cashews and semi-sweet chocolate, raisins and milk chocolate, even other dried fruits such as apricots and white chocolate. Candied cherries with white or milk chocolate are colorful for Christmas. Milk chocolate and peanuts is an all-time favorite combination.

ROCKY ROAD CANDY

POWER LEVEL: Medium or Low
MICROWAVE TIME: 5 to 7 min., total

1 pkg. (12-oz.) semi-sweet chocolate pieces
¼ cup butter ..... In 2-qt. casserole place chocolate and butter. Cover. **Microwave at Medium or Low 5 to 7 Minutes,** until chocolate and butter can be stirred smooth.

1 pkg. (10-oz.) miniature marshmallows
½ cup chopped nuts .... Add marshmallows and nuts blending well. Spread evenly in greased 8-in. square dish or pan. Refrigerate until firm. Cut in squares.

Makes about 25 squares

CHOCOLATE RAISIN NUT CLUSTERS

POWER LEVEL: Low
MICROWAVE TIME: 4 to 5 min., total

1 pkg. (6-oz.) semi-sweet chocolate bits
1 cup salted jumbo peanuts
1 cup seedless raisins ...... In 1½-qt. casserole place chocolate, peanuts and raisins. Cover. **Microwave at Low 4 to 5 Minutes,** or until chocolate is melted.

Stir mixture until chocolate covers peanuts and raisins. Drop by teaspoonfuls onto wax paper. Chill until firm.

Makes about 24 pieces

S'MORES

POWER LEVEL: High
MICROWAVE TIME: ¼ min., per S'More

2 graham cracker squares
½ plain chocolate bar (1.15-oz.)
1 large marshmallow
. . . . .On paper napkin place 1 graham cracker square. Top with chocolate and marshmallow. **Microwave at High ¼ Minute,** or until marshmallow puffs. Place remaining cracker over top and eat like a sandwich.

Makes 1 S'More

RAINBOW PRETZELS

POWER LEVEL: Medium
MICROWAVE TIME: 3 to 4 min., total

½ lb. white chocolate
2 tablespoons white corn syrup
2 tablespoons butter
1 tablespoon water
. . . . .In 1-qt. casserole place chocolate, syrup, butter and water. Cover. **Microwave at Medium 3 to 4 Minutes,** until melted. Stir well, until smooth.

Food coloring . . . . .Prepare up to 2 colors of Rainbow Pretzels per batch. Tint with food coloring as desired.

Miniature pretzel twists . . . . . . .Dip "mini-size" pretzels into mixture, removing excess. Place on cooling rack over wax paper to dry.

Makes about 1 cup, or enough to cover about 50 to 60 miniature pretzels

NOTE: If mixture becomes firm, **Microwave at Medium ½ to 1 Minute,** stirring smooth and adding a few drops of water if necessary.

CHOCOLATE CHOW MEIN "HAYSTACKS"

POWER LEVEL: Medium or Low
MICROWAVE TIME: 4 to 5½ min., total

1 pkg. (6-oz.) semi-sweet chocolate pieces . . . . .In 3-qt. casserole or large bowl place chocolate pieces. Cover with lid or plastic wrap. **Microwave at Medium or Low 4 to 5½ Minutes,** until melted.

1 can (3-oz.) chow mein noodles . .Stir chocolate smooth. Add noodles and, using 2 forks, toss to coat well. On strips of foil or wax paper form into 1½-in. clusters. Cool to set.

Makes about 24 1½-in. "Haystacks"

CHOCOLATE COVERED RUM BALLS

Some people call these "rumbles". Stale, unfrosted cake, finely crumbled, is even better than wafer crumbs.

POWER LEVEL: Low
MICROWAVE TIME: 5 to 6 min., total

2 cups fine vanilla wafer crumbs
1 cup finely chopped nuts
¼ cup butter, melted
¼ cup rum
. . . . . . .In mixing bowl place crumbs, nuts, butter and rum. Stir together well. Shape mixture into 1-in. balls. Refrigerate while melting chocolate.

6 squares semi-sweet chocolate . . . .In 1-qt. casserole place chocolate. Cover. **Microwave at Low 5 to 6 Minutes,** until melted. Stir.

Dip balls into chocolate, coating well but removing excess chocolate. Excess chocolate can be removed by holding dipped ball on a fork and tapping on side of dish so excess chocolate drops into dish. Place on wax paper lined cookie sheet and refrigerate until set.

Makes about 36 rum balls

CHOCOLATE FONDUE

POWER LEVEL: Medium
MICROWAVE TIME: 8 to 10 min., total

4 squares (1-oz. each) unsweetened or semi-sweet chocolate (see note)
1 cup (8-oz.) dairy half & half
. . .In 1-qt. casserole place chocolate and half & half. **Microwave at Medium 5 to 6 Minutes,** or until chocolate melts. Stir well.

1 cup sugar
½ teaspoon vanilla extract
. . . . .Add sugar and vanilla. **Microwave at Medium 3 to 4 Minutes,** or until sugar is dissolved.

Serve immediately or transfer mixture to fondue pot. Serve with marshmallows, apple, pear, banana or pineapple chunks, strawberries, cherries, ladyfingers, cubes of firm pound cake or angel food cake, or cookies.

Makes 2 cups of fondue

NOTE: If you plan to use sweet dippers such as marshmallows or cookies, use unsweetened chocolate in fondue. If you plan to use fruits, use semi-sweet chocolate in fondue. To eat, spear the "dipper" on a fork and dip into fondue. Let excess drip off into pot, then eat. Kids will enjoy dipping firm cookies into fondue with their fingers.

Fruit Desserts

Fruits microwave tender but still crisp, retain their fresh flavor, texture, color and shape. One reason for the flavor retention of microwaved fruit is the shorter cooking time. Another is that fruit is microwaved with little or no water, which intensifies the flavor of both fruit and juice.

DEFROSTING CHART

Properly defrosted fruit should be cold, firm and slightly icy for best flavor and texture. Remove any metal or foil from package and, if necessary, place fruit in a casserole. Be sure to check at minimum time and break up with a fork. Flex package to speed defrosting of fruit frozen in plastic pouches.

TYPE	POWER LEVEL	TIME MINUTES
Fruit (10 to 16-oz. pkg.)	Defrost	5 to 10
Fruit, plastic pouch (1 to 2 10-oz. pkgs.)	Defrost	5 to 8
Escalloped Apples (12-oz. pkg.)	High	6 to 8, covered

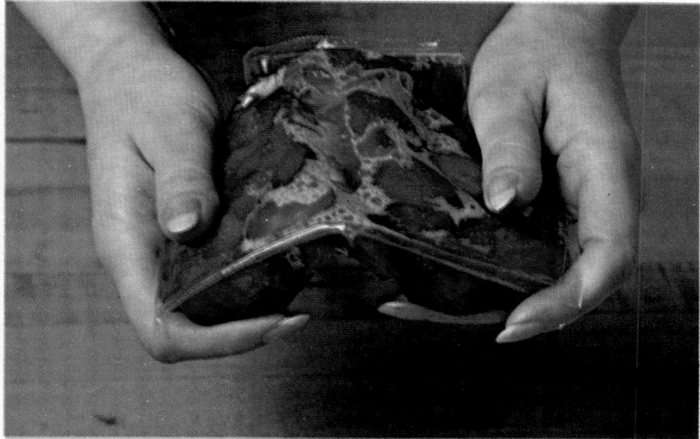

Defrosted fruit will be cold, firm and slightly icy. Pouch will be flexible and juices liquid.

Pound Cake

QUICK STRAWBERRIES AND POUND CAKE DESSERT

Three separate defrostings make one good and easy assembled dessert.

POWER LEVEL: Defrost
MICROWAVE TIME: 9 to 12 min., total

1 frozen, baked, pound cake (about 12-oz.), unfrosted . . . Place cake on microwave ovenproof plate or board. **Microwave at Defrost 2 Minutes.** Let stand while defrosting berries.

2 pkg. (10-oz. each) frozen strawberries in plastic pouch . . . . . . Place unopened packages on microwave oven shelf. **Microwave at Defrost 5 to 8 Minutes,** removing from boxes and flexing packages after 3 minutes.

1 pkg. (9-oz.) commercially frozen whipped topping . . . . Place topping container on microwave oven shelf. **Microwave at Defrost 2 Minutes,** turning over after 1 minute.

To serve, slice cake and serve slices topped with strawberries and whipped topping.

Makes 6 to 8 servings

Baked Apple

BAKED APPLES OR PEARS

The chart below is a good guide to time but because fruit varies, time may vary too. Small, juicy apples and pears cook faster than larger, drier ones.

POWER LEVEL: High
MICROWAVE TIME: See Recipe

Large whole apples or pears* .... Core apples or pears. Slit through skin around center of each fruit to prevent bursting. Arrange in casserole, see chart below.

For each fruit:
2 tablespoons brown sugar
⅛ teaspoon cinnamon
1 teaspoon butter
2 tablespoons water .... Fill each fruit core with brown sugar, cinnamon and butter. Pour total amount of water around fruit. Cover casserole. **Microwave at High** according to chart below.

*Peel pears before microwaving.

NO. OF FRUIT	CASSEROLE SIZE	TIME MINUTES
1	1-qt.	2 to 4
2	1½-qt.	4 to 5½
3	2-qt.	6 to 8
4	2-qt.	9 to 10

APPLESAUCE

POWER LEVEL: High
MICROWAVE TIME: 7 to 8 min., total

6 apples, pared, cored and quartered
¼ cup water ... In 2-qt. casserole place apples with water. Cover. **Microwave at High 7 to 8 Minutes,** until fork-tender.

⅓ cup sugar
⅛ teaspoon salt
⅛ teaspoon cinnamon, nutmeg or cloves (optional) .... Into blender container, place apple mixture, sugar, salt and spices, if desired. Blend until smooth.

Makes 3 to 4 cups

If blender is unavailable, mash with potato masher or put apples through ricer.

STREUSELED APPLES

Known conventionally as Apple Crisp. Vary this recipe by substituting other fresh or canned fruits for apples.

POWER LEVEL: High
MICROWAVE TIME: 9 to 12 min., total

6 cups sliced, peeled apples
¾ cup brown sugar (packed) .... In 8-in. square dish place apples and sugar.

½ cup unsifted all-purpose flour
⅓ cup brown sugar (packed)
⅓ cup quick-cooking oats
¼ cup butter
½ teaspoon cinnamon .... With pastry blender mix flour, sugar, oats, butter and cinnamon until crumbly. Sprinkle over top of apples.

Microwave at High 9 to 12 Minutes, rotating dish ½ turn after 5 minutes. Let stand few minutes before serving.

Makes 6 to 8 servings

STEWED PEARS OR APPLES

Juice bubbles up high. Be sure to use large casserole.

POWER LEVEL: High
MICROWAVE TIME: 9 to 10 min., total

¾ cup sugar
¼ cup light corn syrup
6 pears or apples, pared, cored, halved .... In 3-qt. casserole mix together sugar and syrup. Gently mix in fruit.

Cover. **Microwave at High 9 to 10 Minutes,** stirring gently after 5 minutes.

Makes 3 to 6 servings

BUTTERSCOTCH BANANAS

POWER LEVEL: High
MICROWAVE TIME: 5 to 7 min., total

½ cup brown sugar (packed)
¼ cup rum
¼ cup butter
In 1½-qt. casserole stir together brown sugar and rum. Add butter. Cover. **Microwave at High 4 to 5 Minutes,** stirring after 2 minutes, until sugar is dissolved.

2 large ripe, firm bananas
Cut bananas lengthwise, then crosswise so there are 8 pieces. Add to syrup, stirring to coat each piece. **Microwave at High 1 to 2 Minutes,** until hot. Serve over ice cream.

Makes 4 servings

CHERRIES JUBILEE

POWER LEVEL: High
MICROWAVE TIME: 5½ to 6½ min., total

2 cans (16-oz. each) dark sweet cherries
3 tablespoons cornstarch
1 tablespoon lemon juice
1 teaspoon grated lemon rind
¾ cup sugar
Into 2-qt. casserole drain cherry syrup. Stir in cornstarch, lemon juice, rind and sugar. **Microwave at High 5 to 6 Minutes,** stirring after 3 minutes, until sauce begins to thicken. Add cherries, stirring well.

½ cup brandy
Measure brandy into glass measure. **Microwave at High ½ Minute.**

Pour 1 tablespoon heated brandy into metal tablespoon and remaining brandy over top of cherries. Ignite brandy in the tablespoon and pour over cherries. When flame has subsided, serve over ice cream.

Makes 8 to 10 servings

STEWED DRIED FRUIT

POWER LEVEL: High
MICROWAVE TIME: 8 to 11 min., total

1 pkg. (12 to 16-oz.) dried apricots or prunes
¼ cup sugar (optional)
2 cups water
In 1½-qt. casserole place fruit, sugar (if desired), and water. Cover. **Microwave at High 8 to 11 Minutes,** until tender. Serve warm or cold.

Makes about 6 to 8 servings

EASY FRUIT PUDDING

POWER LEVEL: High
MICROWAVE TIME: 15 to 17 min., total

1 can (20 to 22-oz.) cherry, blueberry, apple or other prepared fruit pie filling
Spread pie filling in 8-in. square dish. **Microwave at High 4 Minutes,** stirring after 2 minutes, until heated through.

1 box (about 9-oz.) 1-layer cake mix (white, yellow or spice)
¼ cup cold butter, thinly sliced
Sprinkle dry cake mix evenly over fruit. Distribute butter slices over top.

2 tablespoons sugar mixed with 1 teaspoon cinnamon, or, ¼ cup finely chopped nuts
Sprinkle cinnamon sugar or chopped nuts evenly over top.

Microwave at High 11 to 13 Minutes, rotating dish ½ turn after 6 minutes. Serve warm with ice cream, if desired.

Makes 6 servings

ALL SEASONS FRUIT COMPOTE

This is a tangy, rather than sweet, fruit compote. It may also be served as a meat accompaniment.

POWER LEVEL: High TEMP:* 160°
APPROX. MICROWAVE TIME: 14 to 16 min.

1 pkg. (12-oz.) dried apricots
1 can (1-lb.) sliced peaches, drained
1 can (16-oz.) pitted bing cherries, undrained
¾ cup brown sugar (packed)
½ cup orange juice
1 tablespoon grated orange peel
¼ cup lemon juice
1 tablespoon grated lemon peel
In 2-qt. casserole place apricots and peaches. Drain cherry juice into small bowl. Add cherries to other fruit. To cherry juice add brown sugar, orange juice and peel, lemon juice and peel. Stir well. Pour over fruit. Insert temperature probe so tip is in center of food. Cover with plastic wrap, arranging loosely around probe to vent.

Attach cable end at receptable. **Microwave at High. Set Temp, Set 160°.**

When oven signals, remove from oven and stir. Recover compote and chill overnight. Serve with garnish of sour cream, or omit garnish and serve with meat.

Makes 8 to 10 servings

* On models not equipped with probe use minimum microwave time and check for doneness.

FLAMING PEACHES

POWER LEVEL: High
MICROWAVE TIME: 4¼ to 5¾ min., total

4 large fresh peaches, or 1 can (29-oz.) peach halves . . . Peel and halve peaches and remove pits. In 10×6×2-in. dish place peaches cut side up. For canned fruit, drain syrup, reserving 1 tablespoon.

¼ cup apricot jam
3 tablespoons sugar
1 tablespoon peach syrup or water
2 teaspoons lemon juice . . . In 1-cup glass measure place jam, sugar, syrup and juice. **Microwave at High 1 to 1½ Minutes,** or until sugar dissolves. Mix well. Pour over peaches.

8 teaspoons currant jelly
8 tablespoons macaroon crumbs . . . Place 1 teaspoon currant jelly and 1 tablespoon macaroon crumbs on each peach half. **Microwave at High 3 to 4 Minutes.**

¼ cup brandy . . . Measure brandy into 1-cup glass measuring cup and **Microwave at High ¼ Minute.** Remove 1 metal tablespoonful. Pour rest of brandy over peaches. Ignite brandy in spoon and pour over peaches to flame. Serve peaches hot with ice cream if desired.

Makes 8 servings

STRAWBERRIES HAWAIIAN

Serve as a sauce for ice cream and pineapple chunks.

POWER LEVEL: High
MICROWAVE TIME: 8½ to 9½ min., total

1 pkg. (10-oz.) frozen sliced strawberries
½ cup red currant jelly . . . In 1½-qt. casserole place berries. **Microwave at High 2½ to 3½ Minutes,** until defrosted. Mash with spoon. Add jelly. Cover. **Microwave at High 4 Minutes,** or until boiling.

2 tablespoons cornstarch
2 tablespoons rum or syrup from canned pineapple . . . Mix cornstarch with rum or syrup. Add to hot strawberries. Stir well. Cover. **Microwave at High 2 Minutes** more, until thick.

Makes about 1½ cups

COLD LIME SOUFFLE

To prepare limes, first grate the rind, then squeeze out the juice. This souffle mixture also makes an excellent chiffon pie filling and the lime version here is often known as Key Lime Pie when piled into a 9-in. shell.

POWER LEVEL: Medium High
MICROWAVE TIME: 6 to 8 min., total

1½ tablespoons gelatin
½ cup sugar
4 egg yolks
½ cup fresh lime juice (5 limes) . . . In 1-qt. measure stir together gelatin and sugar. Beat in egg yolks and lime juice. **Microwave at Medium High 6 to 8 Minutes,** until hot and well blended, stirring every 2 minutes.

2 tablespoons grated lime peel
5 drops green food coloring . . . To hot mixture, add lime peel and food coloring. Stir well. Cool mixture. While mixture is cooling, prepare souffle dish (see below).

6 egg whites
½ cup sugar
1¼ cups whipping cream . . . When mixture is cool, beat egg whites, adding sugar gradually, to make soft meringue. Also beat whipping cream to soft peaks.

Fold cool lime mixture gently into soft meringue. Then lightly fold in whipped cream. Pile mixture into prepared souffle dish and chill until set, at least 3 hours. Remove wax paper collar. Garnish sides with chopped pistachio nuts (¼ to ½ cup needed).

Makes about 8 servings

To prepare souffle dish: Place a strip of double thick (folded) wax paper around edge of 1-qt. souffle dish so wax paper collar rises about 3-in. above edge of dish. Secure wax paper with tape. This technique allows mixture to be piled into dish above the rim. When souffle is set, paper collar is easily removed and souffle appears to have "risen" above edge of dish.

CARAMEL APPLES

POWER LEVEL: High
MICROWAVE TIME: 2 to 3 min., total

½ of 14-oz. pkg. caramels (about 25)
1 tablespoon water . . . In 1-pt. glass measure place unwrapped caramels and water. **Microwave at High 2 to 3 Minutes,** until mixture can be stirred smooth.

4 apples
4 wooden sticks (usually come with caramels) . . . Insert sticks into stem ends of apples. Dip one apple at a time into caramel, coating evenly. Repeat. Place apples on buttered wax paper, stick side up, to set.

Makes 4 apples

Fruit-Filled Pineapple

FRUIT-FILLED PINEAPPLE

POWER LEVEL: High TEMP:* 120°
APPROX. MICROWAVE TIME: 10 to 12 min.

1 medium fresh pineapple	Cut pineapple, including leafy crown, in half lengthwise. Cut out fruit, leaving outside shell intact. Remove woody core; cut remaining fruit in chunks.
1 cup (3 to 4-oz.) shredded coconut **½ cup toasted sliced almonds** **1 can (11-oz.) mandarin orange sections, drained** **½ cup maraschino cherries without stems, drained** **½ cup sweet orange marmalade**	Toss pineapple chunks with coconut, almonds, oranges, cherries and marmalade. Place pineapple shells in 13×9×2-in. dish or on serving plate suitable for microwave oven. Fill shells with fruit mixture. Insert temperature probe so tip is in center of one of pineapple halves. Cover with wax paper. Attach cable end at receptacle. **Microwave at High. Set Temp, Set 120°.**
¼ cup light rum	Measure rum into glass measure. **Microwave at High ¼ Minute.** Remove 1 metal tablespoonful. Pour rest of rum over pineapple. Ignite rum in spoon and pour over pineapple to flame.

Makes 6 servings

* On models not equipped with probe use minimum microwave time and check for doneness.

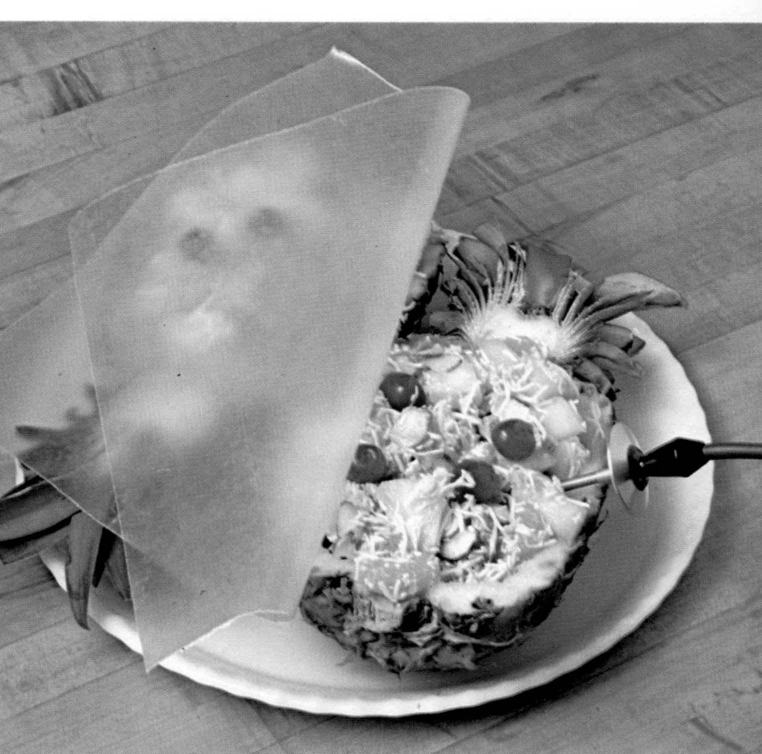

The Temperature Probe, dialed to 120°, will signal when the pineapple is warm enough to develop flavor and be flamed.

Custards & Puddings

Custards and puddings are a microwave specialty. Conventionally baked custard must be set in a pan of water, which provides moisture to prevent drying and browning. On the range top you must stir custard or pudding constantly to keep it free from lumps. Delicate custard microwaves smooth and creamy with a minimum of stirring and the microwave oven does not dry or brown it. The variety of custards and puddings extends from simple desserts to dramatic looking presentations.

1. Caramel Flan, right
2. Bavarian Cream, page 231
3. Cup Custard, below
4. English Trifle, page 232

BASIC CASSEROLE CUSTARD

POWER LEVEL: High and Low
MICROWAVE TIME: 14 to 17 min., total

3 eggs
¼ cup sugar
1 teaspoon vanilla
⅛ teaspoon salt
In 1½ qt. casserole beat eggs, sugar, vanilla, and salt with table fork, until very well blended and sugar is dissolved.

1½ cups milk
Place milk in glass measure. **Microwave at High 4 Minutes,** until scalded. Gradually add to egg mixture, stirring well.

Cover with casserole lid. **Microwave at Low 10 to 13 Minutes,** rotating dish ¼ turn every 3 minutes, until set. Sprinkle top with nutmeg before serving, if desired.

NOTE: Covering with casserole lid is important for success. Cool before serving.

Makes 4 to 6 servings.

Cup Custards: Prepare custard mixture as above except pour into 4 (6-oz.) custard cups. Place in circle on shelf in microwave oven. **Microwave at Low 11 to 13 Minutes,** rearranging every 3 minutes. If some custards are done before others, remove those and continue cooking until all custards are cooked.

CARAMEL FLAN

POWER LEVEL: High and Low
MICROWAVE TIME: 20 to 25 min., total

½ cup water
½ cup sugar
In 1-pt. glass measure place water and sugar, stirring well. **Microwave at High 10 to 12 Minutes,** until light but rich brown. (Do not let syrup get too dark before taking from oven; it continues to cook after it has been microwaved.) Pour ¾ of caramel syrup into 1½-qt. casserole and quickly rotate casserole to coat bottom and about half way up sides with caramel. Let cool to harden before adding custard. Drizzle remaining ¼ of syrup in fine ribbons onto ungreased cookie sheet to harden.

1 recipe Basic Casserole Custard
Prepare custard in small mixing bowl. Pour or strain mixture into caramel lined casserole. Cover with casserole lid.

Microwave at Low 10 to 13 Minutes, rotating dish ¼ turn every 3 minutes, until set. Chill thoroughly. Unmold onto serving plate which has shallow rim. Crush the syrup which has hardened into a brittle and sprinkle in a wreath shape over top of flan.

NOTE: Covering with casserole lid is important for success.

Makes 4 to 6 servings.

Dramatic Caramel Flan is Basic Custard strained into a caramel-lined casserole. After microwaving, garnish it with crushed caramel brittle, on the right.

FLOATING ISLANDS

POWER LEVEL: High, Medium High and Medium
MICROWAVE TIME: 11 to 16 min., total

1/3 cup sugar
3 tablespoons cornstarch
1/4 teaspoon salt
2 3/4 cups milk
2 drops yellow food color (optional)

In 2-qt. casserole blend together sugar, cornstarch and salt until well mixed. Add milk and food coloring, stirring until well blended. **Microwave at High 8 to 10 Minutes,** stirring every 3 minutes until smooth and slightly thickened.

2 egg yolks, well beaten

Stir a small amount of hot pudding quickly into yolks. Return egg mixture to hot pudding, mixing well. **Microwave at Medium High 2 to 4 Minutes,** stirring after 1 minute, until slightly thickened.

2 egg whites
1/4 cup sugar

Beat egg whites until foamy, on high speed of mixer.

Gradually add sugar, beating to a stiff glossy meringue. Drop meringue immediately in 8 to 10 mounds over hot pudding. **Microwave at Medium 1 to 2 Minutes** to set meringues slightly. Chill before serving.

Makes 6 to 8 servings

BASIC BREAD PUDDING

POWER LEVEL: High and Medium High
MICROWAVE TIME: 13 to 16 min., total

4 cups bread cubes lightly packed into cup (4 to 5 slices)
1/2 cup brown sugar (packed)
1/4 teaspoon salt
1/2 cup raisins (optional)

Spread bread cubes evenly in 8-in. round dish. Sprinkle evenly with brown sugar and salt, then raisins.

2 cups milk
1/4 cup butter
2 eggs, beaten

Measure milk into 1-qt. measuring cup. Add butter. **Microwave at High 4 Minutes,** until butter is melted and milk is warm. Rapidly stir in eggs with a fork and mix well. Pour over bread cubes in dish.

Microwave at Medium High 9 to 12 Minutes, rotating dish 1/2 turn after 6 minutes. When cooked, center may still be slightly soft but it will set up as pudding cools. Serve warm or chilled.

Makes about 6 servings

TWO WAYS TO MICROWAVE INDIVIDUAL MERINGUES

On Pudding. The traditional way to serve Floating Islands is to drop mounds of meringue over hot pudding. **Microwave at Medium 1 to 2 Minutes.** Serve with small, crisp cookies, if desired.

On Brown Paper. For best shape cook pudding for maximum time and microwave meringues separately. Place sheet of brown wrapping paper on a flat cookie sheet and drop 6 to 8 mounds of meringue in a circle on paper. Slide paper from cookie sheet into oven. **Microwave at Medium 1 to 2 Minutes.** Slide back onto cookie sheet and remove from oven to cool.

VANILLA PUDDING

POWER LEVEL: High and Medium High
MICROWAVE TIME: 6 to 10 min., total

¾ cup sugar **2 tablespoons cornstarch** **¼ teaspoon salt** **2 cups milk**	In 1-qt. casserole blend together sugar, cornstarch and salt. Gradually stir in milk, mixing well. **Microwave at High 5 to 7 Minutes,** stir every 3 minutes, until mixture is smooth, thickened and clear.
2 egg yolks, slightly beaten, or 1 egg, well beaten	Stir a small amount of hot pudding quickly into egg yolks. Return egg mixture to hot pudding, mixing well. **Microwave at Medium High 1 to 3 Minutes,** stirring after 1 minute, until smooth and thickened.
2 tablespoons butter **1 teaspoon vanilla extract**	Add butter and vanilla. Stir until butter is melted. Pour into serving dishes.

Makes 4 servings

CHOCOLATE PUDDING

Prepare Vanilla Pudding except, increase sugar to 1 cup. Add 2 squares (1-oz. each) unsweetened chocolate along with milk.

BUTTERSCOTCH PUDDING

Prepare Vanilla Pudding except, use brown sugar and increase butter to 3 tablespoons.

CREAM CHEESE PUDDING

Prepare Vanilla Pudding and cool until lukewarm. With high speed of mixer, whip 1 pkg. (8-oz.) softened cream cheese until light and fluffy. Gradually beat in pudding until smooth. Serve as pudding or pie filling.

CREAMY RICE PUDDING

Prepare Vanilla Pudding except, increase milk to 2½ cups. Into warm pudding, stir 2 cups cooked rice.

PUDDING SAUCE

Nice to serve over plain cake or gingerbread. Vanilla pudding sauce is good with fruit cake or steamed holiday pudding.

Prepare Vanilla, Chocolate or Butterscotch pudding as above, except increase milk to 2¾ cups.

BAVARIAN CREAM

This is basic custard sauce to which gelatin is added so it can be molded. It is lightened with meringue and whipped cream.

POWER LEVEL: High and Medium High
MICROWAVE TIME: 10 to 14 min., total

⅓ cup sugar **3 tablespoons cornstarch** **2 tablespoons unflavored gelatin** **¼ teaspoon salt** **2¾ cups milk**	In 2-qt. casserole blend together sugar, cornstarch, gelatin and salt, until well mixed. Gradually add milk, stirring until well blended. **Microwave at High 8 to 10 Minutes,** stirring every 3 minutes, until smooth and slightly thickened.
2 egg yolks, well beaten **1 teaspoon vanilla extract**	Stir a small amount of hot pudding quickly into egg yolks. Return egg mixture to hot pudding, mixing well. **Microwave at Medium High 2 to 4 Minutes,** stirring after 1 minute. Cool in refrigerator until mixture mounds slightly, about 1½ hours. Stir in vanilla.
2 egg whites **¼ cup sugar** **1 cup whipping cream, whipped**	When gelatin mixture has cooled, beat egg whites until foamy.

Gradually add sugar, beating to a soft meringue. Fold cooled gelatin mixture into meringue; fold in whipped cream. Pile mixture into 4½ to 5-cup mold. Chill until set. Unmold and serve with fruit garnish, such as sliced strawberries or peaches.

Makes 6 to 8 servings

NESSELRODE BAVARIAN

Definitely a holiday dessert.

1 recipe Bavarian Cream (above) **1 jar (10-oz.) nesselrode fruit mixture**	Into 2-qt. fluted mold, distribute about ¼ of Bavarian cream, ⅓ of nesselrode, ¼ of cream, ⅓ of nesselrode, ¼ of cream, last of nesselrode and last ¼ of cream on top.

(Layering technique best distributes fruit and cream.) Chill until set. Unmold onto plate which has a fairly high rim (about 1-in.). Some of nesselrode syrup will separate from bavarian upon unmolding and high rim is needed to contain syrup. Spoon syrup over nesselrode bavarian as it is served.

Makes about 8 servings

ENGLISH TRIFLE

POWER LEVEL: High and Medium High
MICROWAVE TIME: 12 to 13 min., total

½ cup sugar
½ teaspoon salt
2 tablespoons cornstarch
2½ cups milk

In 1½-qt. casserole mix together sugar, salt and cornstarch. Gradually stir in milk. **Microwave at High 7 Minutes,** stirring every 3 minutes, until slightly thickened.

4 egg yolks, beaten
2 teaspoons vanilla extract

Stir in a little over half thickened mixture into beaten egg yolks. Return mixture to casserole blending well. **Microwave at Medium High 5 to 6 Minutes** more, stirring after 2 minutes. Cool; then stir in vanilla.

1 (8-in.) microwaved yellow or white layer cake
½ cup raspberry preserves
¼ to ½ cup sherry

Split cake and fill with preserves. Cut preserve-filled cake into 12 pieces and place half in 2 to 3-qt. serving dish. Sprinkle with half of sherry and cover with half of custard. Repeat.

1 cup whipping cream
3 tablespoons confectioners sugar
¼ cup toasted, sliced almonds

Whip cream with confectioners sugar until peaks form. Spread over custard. Sprinkle with almonds. Chill 4 hours or more before serving.

Makes 9 to 12 servings

COOKING COMMERCIAL DRY PUDDING MIX

Since there is less evaporation in microwaving, microwaved pudding is often creamier in texture, lighter in color and greater in volume than it is conventionally.

POWER LEVEL: High
MICROWAVE TIME: 6 to 8 min., total

1 pkg. (3¾-oz.) pudding or pie filling mix, not instant
½ cup milk

Empty pudding mix into 1-qt. glass measure. Add ½ cup milk and stir until all mix is moistened and blended.

1½ cups milk

Add 1½ cups more milk and blend well.

Microwave at High 6 to 8 Minutes, stirring thoroughly every 3 minutes.

Pour into 4 or 5 serving dishes. Cover top of pudding with wax paper or plastic wrap to prevent "skin" from forming on top, if desired. Serve cool.

Makes 4 to 5 servings

PUDDING TRIFLE

POWER LEVEL: High and Medium High
MICROWAVE TIME: 10 to 14 min., total

1 pkg. (3¾-oz.) vanilla pudding mix, not instant
2½ cups milk

In 1½-qt. casserole place pudding. Gradually add milk, stirring to blend well. **Microwave at High 6 to 8 Minutes,** stirring every 3 minutes, until thickened.

2 egg yolks, beaten

Gradually stir half of pudding into beaten yolks. Return egg mixture to casserole, stirring well. **Microwave at Medium High 4 to 6 Minutes** more, stirring every 2 minutes, until thickened. Cool.

1 (8-in.) microwaved yellow or white cake layer
½ cup cherry preserves
¼ to ½ cup sherry, rum or pineapple juice

Split cake layer and fill with preserves. Cut into pieces and arrange half in 2-qt. casserole. Sprinkle with half of sherry and cover with half of cooled pudding. Repeat.

1 cup whipping cream
3 tablespoons confectioners sugar

Whip cream with confectioners sugar until soft peaks form. Spread over pudding. Chill 4 hours or more before serving.

Makes 8 to 12 servings

BLACK FOREST TRIFLE

This trifle combines the principle flavors of the famous Black Forest Torte; chocolate, cherries and cream.

Make Pudding Trifle above, except substitute chocolate pudding mix for vanilla and chocolate cake layer for yellow or white. Instead of cherry preserves, fill the split cake layer with 1 can (22-oz.) cherry pie filling.

Arrange filled cake in 12×8×2-in. dish and sprinkle with ½ cup rum or brandy. Pour cooled chocolate pudding over all. Top with sweetened whipped cream as in above recipe and garnish with maraschino cherries, if desired.

Pies

Because microwaved pie shells set and cook rapidly, plain pastry does not brown. Flavored pastry and toppings brushed on before microwaving have appealing color.

Plain microwaved pastry looks different from conventionally baked. From top to bottom: Conventional, Microwaved, Molasses, Maple Syrup, Chocolate Pastry, Dark Corn Syrup, Vanilla, Egg Yolk Toppings.

Check For Doneness on the bottom of the crust, which is critical. It should look opaque and dry. Top will be dry and blistered. A clear glass utensil is best because you can see the bottom.

BASIC PASTRY SHELL

POWER LEVEL: High
MICROWAVE TIME: 6 to 7 min., total

1 cup unsifted all-purpose flour **1 teaspoon salt** **6 tablespoons shortening*** **2 tablespoons ice water**	In small bowl place flour and salt. With pastry blender cut in shortening, until mixture resembles the size of small peas. Sprinkle water over flour-shortening mixture. Stir with fork to form ball.

Roll out on floured pastry cloth with rolling pin to ⅛-in. thickness. Let stand a few minutes before shaping. Use to line 9-in. pie plate shaping pastry to the edge of pie plate. Prick pastry with fork. **Microwave at High 6 to 7 Minutes,** rotating dish ½ turn after 3 minutes. Pastry is done when it looks dry and blistered and is not doughy.

Makes 1 (9-in.) pastry shell

*If desired, 3 tablespoons cold butter and 3 tablespoons shortening may be used for more flavor and color.

CHOCOLATE PASTRY SHELL

To flour add only ½ teaspoon salt along with 2 tablespoons cocoa and ⅓ cup sugar.

Crumb Crusts are perfect pie partners. Their crunchy texture complements light and airy or smooth and creamy fillings. They are also faster to make than pastry crusts. Reserve 2 tablespoons crumbs to garnish top of pie, if desired. For easy removal, set pie plate on towel dampened with hot water for a few minutes. Vary the character of pies by using different crumbs. To make 1¼ cups of fine crumbs, use 15 to 18 squares of graham crackers, 18 to 22 medium gingersnaps, 18 to 20 chocolate (not cream filled) wafers, 30 to 36 vanilla wafers. When using pecan sandies 1½ to 1¾ cups crumbs are needed, about 18 to 20 cookies.

NUT CRUNCH PASTRY SHELL

POWER LEVEL: High
MICROWAVE TIME: 6 to 8 min., total

1 cup flour **½ cup light brown sugar (packed)** **½ cup (¼-lb.) butter** **1 cup chopped pecans or walnuts**	In small mixing bowl place flour and brown sugar. With pastry blender, cut in butter until mixture is crumbly. Mix in nuts.

Place crumbly mixture loosely in 9-in. pie plate. **Microwave at High 4 to 5 Minutes,** stirring every 1 or 2 minutes. Stir again after cooking and, if desired, reserve about 2 tablespoons crumbly mixture to garnish top of pie. Press remainder of hot crumbs into pie plate. **Microwave at High 2 to 3 Minutes,** until set, rotating dish ¼ turn every minute. Cool before filling.

Makes 1 (9-in.) pie shell

TOASTED COCONUT PIE SHELL

This shell is a good one to use for ice cream pies. Use recipe to make 8-in. pie shell, then fill with 1-qt. vanilla or favorite flavor ice cream. Freeze. Drizzle sundae sauce over top and garnish with additional coconut, nuts or fruit as desired.

POWER LEVEL: High
MICROWAVE TIME: 6½ to 7½ min., total

3 tablespoons butter **1 cup (3 to 4-oz.) flaked coconut**	In 8 or 9-in. pie plate place butter. **Microwave at High ½ Minutes,** until melted. Add coconut.

Microwave at High 6 to 7 Minutes, stirring every 2 minutes, then every minute after 4 minutes, until coconut is evenly browned. Spread coconut in pie plate. Cool before filling.

Makes 1 (8 or 9-in.) pie shell

CRUMB PIE SHELL

A pretty scalloped pie shell, such as the one used in the Grasshopper Pie, page 237, can easily be made by lining the bottom of a pie plate with ½ of this recipe, then standing small whole cookies around the sides of plate.

POWER LEVEL: High
MICROWAVE TIME: 2½ to 3 min., total

¼ cup butter **1¼ cups fine cookie crumbs (vanilla wafer, graham cracker, chocolate wafer, gingersnaps, etc.)** **2 tablespoons sugar**	In 9-in. pie plate place butter. **Microwave at High ½ Minute,** until melted. Blend in crumbs and sugar. If desired, reserve 2 tablespoons crumb mixture for garnish. Press firmly and evenly into 9-in. pie plate. **Microwave at High 2 to 2½ Minutes,** rotating dish ½ turn after 1 minute.

Makes 1 (9-in.) crumb shell

FROZEN CHOCOLATE ALMOND PIE

This pie cuts well straight from the freezer. No thawing is necessary. Use a wet knife for sharpest cut.

POWER LEVEL: High
MICROWAVE TIME: 3 to 4 min., total

1 crumb pie shell made with vanilla wafers or Chocolate Pastry Shell, page 233	Microwave pie shell. Cool.
4 milk chocolate candy bars with almonds (1.15-oz. each) **½ of 10-oz. pkg. large marshmallows (about 20)** **½ cup milk**	In 2-qt. casserole place candy, marshmallows and milk. **Microwave at High 3 to 4 Minutes,** stirring after 2 minutes, until mixture can be stirred smooth. Chill in refrigerator about 30 to 40 minutes, or in pan of ice water until thickened, stirring occasionally.
1 cup whipping cream whipped	Fold whipped cream into cooled chocolate mixture. Pile into pie shell and freeze until firm.

To serve, garnish pie wedges with whipped cream, chocolate curls and/or additional almonds, if desired.

Makes 1 (9-in.) pie

ROCKY ROAD CHOCOLATE ALMOND PIE

Microwave chocolate and milk, then stir in 2 cups miniature marshmallows. Stir well, but do not melt marshmallows.

Rocky Road Chocolate Almond Pie

PECAN PIE

POWER LEVEL: High and Medium
MICROWAVE TIME: 19 to 24 min., total

1 Basic Pastry Shell, uncooked, page 233 **1 egg yolk** **2 tablespoons dark corn syrup**	Roll out pastry and fit into 9-in. pie plate. Brush inside of shell with mixture of egg yolk and corn syrup. **Microwave at High 6 to 7 Minutes,** rotating dish ½ turn after 3 minutes.
¼ cup butter	In large glass mixing bowl place butter. **Microwave at High ½ to 1 Minute,** until melted.
3 whole eggs, plus extra egg white **1 cup dark corn syrup** **⅓ cup brown sugar (packed)** **1 tablespoon flour** **1 teaspoon vanilla** **1½ cups pecan halves**	Add eggs to melted butter. Beat with fork to mix eggs well. Blend in syrup, sugar, flour and vanilla. Then, mix in pecan halves. Pour into crust. **Microwave at Medium 12 to 15 Minutes,** rotating ½ turn after 5 minutes. When done, top surface is dry and puffed, and filling is set.

Makes 1 (9-in.) pie

HOW TO MICROWAVE MARSHMALLOW PIE FILLING

Combine milk or other liquid with marshmallows. Microwave at High 2 to 3 minutes.

Air heats and expands inside marshmallows, causing them to puff up before they melt.

Stir mixture until smooth. Chill until cool and thickened before adding flavoring and whipped cream.

FLUFFY MARSHMALLOW PIES

POWER LEVEL: High
MICROWAVE TIME: 2 to 3 min., total

Crumb Pie Shell, **page 235**	Microwave Crumb Pie Shell using the flavor of cookie that best complements filling. Cool.
1 pkg. (10-oz.) large marshmallows **½ cup milk**	In 3-qt. casserole place marshmallows and milk. Cover. **Microwave at High 2 to 3 Minutes,** until mixture can be stirred smooth. Chill in refrigerator (about 30 to 40 minutes) or in pan of ice water, until thickened, stirring occasionally.
1 cup whipping cream, whipped **Special pie ingredient (see right)**	Fold in whipped cream and special pie ingredient. Pour into crust and decorate with reserved crumbs or additional whipped cream, if desired. Refrigerate several hours or overnight.

Makes 1 (9-in.) pie

FRUIT PIE VARIATIONS:

PEACH OR BERRY PIE

Fold in 1¾ to 2 cups peeled and sliced fresh peaches, sliced fresh strawberries or fresh whole raspberries.

LIQUEUR PIE VARIATIONS:

These pies are soft and creamy when served from refrigerator; for firm pieces which hold sharp cut, serve frozen. Frozen pie releases easily from bottom of pie plate if set a few minutes on towel dampened with hot water.

GRASSHOPPER PIE

Into cooled marshmallow mixture, stir ¼ cup green creme de menthe and 2 tablespoons white creme de cocoa. Garnish with mounds of additional whipped cream and chocolate curls.

BRANDY ALEXANDER PIE

Into cooled marshmallow mixture, stir ¼ cup dark creme de cocoa and 2 tablespoons brandy.

KAHLUA PIE

Add 1 teaspoon instant coffee powder to marshmallows and milk. Into cooled marshmallow mixture, stir ½ cup kahlua.

Grasshopper Pie

LEMON MERINGUE PIE

Meringue will set in a microwave oven but top will not be brown. The lemon filling, often done in a double boiler on range top, is easier to microwave.

POWER LEVEL: High, Medium High and Medium
MICROWAVE TIME: 12 to 17 min., total

1 microwaved pastry shell, page 233 **1 cup sugar** **⅓ cup cornstarch** **⅛ teaspoon salt** **2 cups cold water** **1 to 2 drops yellow food color**	In 2-qt. casserole mix together sugar, cornstarch and salt. Blend in water and food color; stir smooth. **Microwave at High 6 to 8 Minutes,** stirring after 3 minutes, until slightly thickened.
3 egg yolks	In medium bowl beat yolks well. Add sauce; mix well. **Microwave at Medium High 3 to 5 Minutes,** stir after 2 minutes, until thick.
3 tablespoons butter **¼ cup fresh lemon juice** **2 teaspoons grated lemon rind**	Stir butter, juice and rind into mixture. Pour into pastry. Finish with meringue or, if desired, cool and decorate pie with whipped cream.

Makes 1 (9-in.) pie

Meringue: Beat 3 egg whites with ½ teaspoon cream of tartar until stiff peaks form. Gradually beat in 6 tablespoons sugar to make glossy meringue. Spread over pie. **Microwave at Medium 3 to 4 Minutes,** until meringue is set (top won't brown).

APPLE GRAHAM PIE

POWER LEVEL: High TEMP:* 200°
APPROX. MICROWAVE TIME: 10 to 12 min.

½ cup (¼-lb.) butter **¼ cup sugar** **2 cups graham cracker crumbs**	In large glass mixing bowl place butter. **Microwave at High 1 Minute,** until melted. Add sugar and crumbs. Mix well. Press half of mixture firmly and evenly into 9-in. pie plate.
5 cups thinly sliced apples (4 to 6 medium) **½ cup sugar** **1 teaspoon cinnamon**	In large mixing bowl place apple slices; they should be ⅛ to ¼-in. thick. Add sugar and cinnamon, mixing well. Mound and press down into crumb crust.

Cover apples with remaining crumbs to make top crust. Press crumbs down firmly, especially at edges, to prevent boilover.

Insert temperature probe so tip is in center of pie. Cover with wax paper. Attach cable end at receptacle. **Microwave at High. Set Temp, Set 200°.** When oven signals, remove pie and let stand 10 minutes covered with wax paper. Remove wax paper so crumb topping is allowed to dry and crisp. Serve warm or cold.

Makes 1 (9-in.) pie

* On models not equipped with probe use minimum microwave time and check for doneness.

BRANDIED CRANBERRY PIE

POWER LEVEL: High TEMP:* 200°
APPROX. MICROWAVE TIME: 13 to 16 min.

2 cups prepared graham cracker crumbs **¼ cup sugar** **½ cup (¼-lb.) butter, melted**	In small bowl mix together crumbs, sugar and butter. Pat half of mixture firmly into 9-in. pie plate.
1 can (16-oz.) whole cranberry sauce **1¼ cup prepared mincemeat** **1 cup coarsely chopped pecans** **2 tablespoons sugar** **2 tablespoons butter, melted** **¼ cup brandy** **2 tablespoons cornstarch**	In mixing bowl stir together cranberry sauce, mincemeat, pecans, sugar, butter, brandy and cornstarch. Spread mixture over crust. Pat remaining crumbs firmly in wreath around outside edge of pie forming a firm unbroken crust about 2-in. wide. (Center of pie remains open for attractive finished appearance.)

Insert temperature probe so tip is in center of pie. Cover with wax paper. Attach cable end at receptacle. **Microwave at High. Set Temp, Set 200°.**

When oven signals, remove pie and let stand 10 minutes covered with wax paper. Then remove wax paper so crumb topping is allowed to dry and crisp. Serve warm or cold.

TO FLAME PIE: Measure ¼ cup brandy into glass measuring cup. **Microwave at High ¼ Minute.** Remove 1 metal tablespoonful and pour the rest over the pie. Using lighter or long match, warm and ignite brandy in tablespoon. Pour over pie to ignite brandy on top of pie.

* On models not equipped with probe use minimum microwave time and check for doneness.

DEFROSTING FROZEN PRE-BAKED PIES

Remove whole pie from foil pan to an 8 or 9-in. glass pie plate. Or cut in wedges and place on serving plates.

POWER LEVEL: **Defrost**

TYPE	TIME MINUTES	COMMENTS
Fruit or Nut Pie whole (8-in.)	8 to 10	Rotate ¼ turn every 3 minutes. Let stand a few minutes before serving.
Fruit or Nut Pie wedge (1 or 2 slices)	2 to 4	
Cream or Custard Pie whole (14-oz.)	2½ to 3	Rotate ¼ turn every minute.
Cream or Custard Pie whole (26-oz.)	5 to 7	Rotate ¼ turn every 2 minutes. Let stand a few minutes before serving.
Cream or Custard Pie wedge (1 to 3 slices)	½ to 1	

PUMPKIN PIE

POWER LEVEL: High and Medium
MICROWAVE TIME: 37 to 42 min., total

½ cup (¼-lb.) butter	In 10-in. pie plate place butter. **Microwave at High 1 Minute,** until melted.
2 cups vanilla wafer crumbs **2 tablespoons sugar**	Add crumbs and sugar; mix well. Firmly press on bottom and up sides of dish. **Microwave at High 2 Minutes,** rotating dish ½ turn after 1 minute.
1 can (16-oz.) mashed pumpkin **1 cup brown sugar (packed)** **1 tablespoon pumpkin pie spice** **1 tablespoon flour** **½ teaspoon salt** **1 can (13-oz.) evaporated milk** **2 eggs, beaten**	In 2-qt. casserole blend together pumpkin, brown sugar, pumpkin pie spice, flour, salt, evaporated milk and eggs. **Microwave at Medium 12 to 14 Minutes,** stirring every 5 minutes, until hot and thickened.

Pour hot pumpkin custard filling into prepared pie shell. **Microwave at Medium 22 to 25 Minutes,** rotating dish ½ turn after 12 minutes.The pie is done when the edges are set and the center is still slightly soft (very much like a conventionally baked pie). Let stand at room temperature about 15 to 20 minutes to set and cool before serving.

Makes 1 (10-in.) pie

2 PUMPKIN PIES: Prepare crust in 2 (8-in.) pie plates. Divide hot filling between pie shells. Microwave 1 pie at a time. **Microwave at Medium 12 to 14 Minutes,** rotating dish ½ turn after 6 minutes.

HEATING FRUIT AND NUT PIES FROM THE REFRIGERATOR

Defrosted fruit and nut pies may be heated with the temperature probe set at 120°. For a single slice, set High Power. For a whole pie (in glass pie plate), set Medium Power.

Time per slice is about ½ to 1 minute. For whole pie, allow about 2 minutes. Let stand a few minutes before serving.

TIP: Soften too-hard ice cream by placing in microwave oven briefly at Medium or Low. Allow about ¼ minute. It's easier to scoop into servings and over pie.

Chocolate Chip Bars

Cookies

Brownies and bar cookies exemplify the best of microwaving. Their taste, texture and appearance compare favorably with conventional baking and they can be ready to serve in 6 to 10 minutes. We don't recommend drop cookies for microwaving because the oven will not accommodate large batches. Instead, we've adapted some popular bar cookies for microwaving.

Small cookie has brown spots inside because cooking begins below the surface. Large cookie microwaves more evenly. Cookies are done when they are just set.

CHOCOLATE CHIP BARS

POWER LEVEL: High
MICROWAVE TIME: 5 to 7 min., total

½ cup (¼-lb.) butter, softened **¾ cup brown sugar (packed)** **1 egg** **1 tablespoon milk** **1 teaspoon vanilla extract**	In small mixer bowl cream together butter and sugar, until fluffy. Add eggs, milk, vanilla and salt. Mix well.
1¼ cups unsifted all-purpose flour **½ teaspoon baking powder** **⅛ teaspoon salt** **1 cup (6-oz.) semi-sweet chocolate pieces, divided** **½ cup chopped nuts (optional)**	Stir together flour, baking powder and salt. Add to creamed mixture. Blend well. Stir in ½ cup chocolate pieces and nuts. Spread in greased 8-in. square dish. Sprinkle with remaining ½ cup chocolate pieces. **Microwave at High 5 to 7 Minutes,** rotating dish ¼ turn every 2 minutes, until done. Cool and cut into bars.

Makes about 24 bars

BASIC BROWNIES

POWER LEVEL: High
MICROWAVE TIME: 6 to 7 min., total

2 eggs **1 cup sugar** **½ teaspoon salt** **1 teaspoon vanilla extract**	In small bowl at medium speed on mixer, beat together eggs, sugar, salt and vanilla, about 1 minute until light.
½ cup (¼-lb.) butter, melted	Add melted butter. Continue beating until thoroughly blended.
¾ cup unsifted all-purpose flour **½ cup cocoa**	Mix in flour and cocoa at low speed.
1 cup chopped nuts	Stir in nuts. Spread evenly in greased 8-in. square dish.

Microwave at High 6 to 7 Minutes, rotating dish ¼ turn every 2 minutes. When done, top looks dry and will spring back when lightly touched. Cut when cold.

Makes about 20 brownies

VARIATIONS: 1 pkg. (6-oz.) semi-sweet chocolate pieces, or 1 cup flaked or shredded coconut may be substituted for nuts.

Basic Brownies

THREE-LAYER BROWNIES

POWER LEVEL: High
MICROWAVE TIME: 6½ to 7¼ min., total

2 squares unsweetened chocolate **⅓ cup butter**	In small glass mixing bowl place chocolate and butter. **Microwave at High 2½ to 3 Minutes,** until melted.
1 cup sugar **2 eggs** **1 teaspoon vanilla extract**	Add sugar, eggs and vanilla. Beat 2 minutes.
⅔ cup unsifted all-purpose flour **½ teaspoon salt** **½ cup chopped nuts (optional)**	Stir in flour and salt just until well blended. Pour into greased 8-in. square dish. Sprinkle nuts over batter.

Microwave at High 4 to 4½ Minutes, rotating dish ½ turn after 2 minutes. Remove from oven and cool while making icing and glaze.

BROWNED BUTTER ICING

In 1-qt. glass measure or medium mixing bowl place ¼ cup butter. Cover with wax paper. **Microwave at High 5 to 6 Minutes,** until butter is golden brown. Remove from oven and blend in 2 cups sifted confectioners sugar, 2 tablespoons milk and ½ teaspoon vanilla extract. Spread over top of brownies in dish.

CHOCOLATE GLAZE

In 1 cup glass measure place 1 square (1-oz.) semi-sweet or unsweetened chocolate and 1 tablespoon butter. **Microwave at High 2 to 2½ Minutes,** or until melted. Cool slightly and drizzle over icing on brownies. Refrigerate until cool and icing and glaze are set up.

Makes about 20 brownies or
8 to 9 dessert size portions

BROWNIES FROM A MIX

POWER LEVEL: High
MICROWAVE TIME: 6 to 8 min.

1 pkg. (about 1-lb.) brownie mix **Water** **Eggs** **Chopped Nuts (optional)**	Prepare cookie dough as package directs. Spread evenly in lightly greased 8-in. round or square dish. **Microwave at High 6 to 8 minutes,** rotating dish every 2 minutes. When done, top feels firm when lightly pressed. To prevent dryness, do not overcook. Let stand directly on heat-proof counter or wooden board to cool.

Makes about 20 brownies

Family Size Brownies: Prepare cookie dough as package directs and divide between 2 8-in. round dishes. Microwave one dish at a time as directed above, except check for doneness after 5 minutes.

PECAN LOGS

POWER LEVEL: High
MICROWAVE TIME: 9 to 11 min., total

½ cup (¼-lb.) butter . . . . . In large mixing bowl place butter. **Microwave at High 1 Minute,** or until melted.

1 lb. light brown sugar
2 eggs, well beaten
3 teaspoons vanilla extract
2 cups chopped pecans
1½ cups pancake or biscuit mix
. . Into butter, mix brown sugar, eggs and vanilla. Stir well. Blend in pecans and pancake mix, mixing thoroughly. Pour batter into greased 12×8×2-in. dish. **Microwave at High 8 to 10 Minutes,** rotating dish ½ turn every 3 minutes. Center will not be quite set, but will firm upon cooling. When cool, cut into long thin bars.

Confectioners sugar . . Sprinkle top with confectioners sugar, or, cut into bars and roll in confectioners sugar.

Makes about 40 to 50 bars

CHOCOLATE TOFFEE BARS

POWER LEVEL: High
MICROWAVE TIME: 4 to 4½ min., total

11 graham cracker squares . . . . In 12×8×2-in. dish arrange graham cracker squares to cover bottom.

½ cup (¼-lb.) butter
½ cup brown sugar (packed)
. . . . . . In 1-qt. casserole place butter and brown sugar. **Microwave at High 2 Minutes.** Stir well.

½ cup confectioners sugar
1 tablespoon cornstarch
¼ teaspoon salt
1 cup coconut
½ cup chopped nuts
. . . . . Blend in confectioners sugar, cornstarch, salt, coconut and nuts. Spread evenly over graham crackers.

1 cup (6-oz.) semi-sweet chocolate pieces . . . . Sprinkle chocolate pieces over top. **Microwave at High 2 to 2½ Minutes.** Let stand a few minutes, then spread chocolate over bars. Cool before cutting.

Makes 24 bars

SWEET-TART LEMON SQUARES

POWER LEVEL: High
MICROWAVE TIME: 8 to 10 min., total

1 can (15-oz.) sweetened condensed milk
½ cup lemon juice
1 teaspoon grated lemon rind (optional)
. . . . In small mixing bowl stir together milk, lemon juice and rind, until thick and smooth. Set aside.

1½ cups graham cracker crumbs
⅓ cup brown sugar (packed)
⅓ cup butter, melted
. . . . Mix together crumbs, sugar and butter. Place about ⅔ of mixture in 8-in. square dish and press firmly into bottom of dish. Add milk mixture and spread evenly. Sprinkle remaining crumb mixture over top and pat down gently.

Microwave at High 8 to 10 Minutes, rotating dish ¼ turn after 4 minutes. Cut in small squares as cookies or in larger pieces as dessert.

Makes 16 to 24 cookies
or 9 desserts

BUTTERSCOTCH BARS

POWER LEVEL: Medium
MICROWAVE TIME: 16 to 21 minutes

½ cup butter, softened
¼ cup brown sugar (packed)
1¼ cups unsifted all-purpose flour
. . . . In a small mixing bowl, cream together butter and brown sugar. Add flour, mixing well to make soft dough. Press evenly in bottom of 12x8x2 in. dish. **Microwave at Medium 6 to 8 minutes,** rotating dish ½ turn every 2 minutes. Let stand about 5 minutes to set slightly.

2 eggs
1 cup brown sugar (packed)
1 teaspoon vanilla extract
2 tablespoons flour
1 teaspoon baking powder
½ teaspoon salt
1 cup (3 to 4-oz.) flaked coconut
1 cup unblanched sliced almonds
. . . . In large mixing bowl beat eggs, brown sugar, vanilla extract, flour, baking powder, and salt at medium speed until well blended. Stir in coconut and ½ cup almonds. Spread mixture over crust. Sprinkle remaining almonds over top. **Microwave at Medium 10 to 13 minutes,** rotating dish ½ turn after 5 minutes until set. Let cool before cutting.

Makes 24 bars.

Cakes

MICROLESSON

The growing popularity of microwaved cakes is indicated by the many new utensils being developed for cooking them. Microwave instructions are available from major cake mix manufacturers. Expect microwaved cakes to look different; they will not brown and the tops will be somewhat uneven, since they do not develop a dry crust to contain expansion. For this reason they are moist, airy, fluffy and have greater volume. Since most cakes are frosted or served with a topping you won't notice the difference in appearance but you appreciate the time saved when microwaving. Do not microwave angel food or chiffon cakes; they need the dry heat of the conventional oven.

HOW TO MICROWAVE CAKES

Cake Is Done when a wooden pick inserted in the center comes out clean. There may be moist spots on the cake surface which will evaporate as the cake cools.

Line Dish with a single layer of paper towel, cut to fit the bottom, when you wish to turn cake out. For cake served from dish, grease but do not flour.

Cakes Rise Higher. This cake was baked using only 2 cups of batter. Plastic microwave cake pans are available with deeper sides.

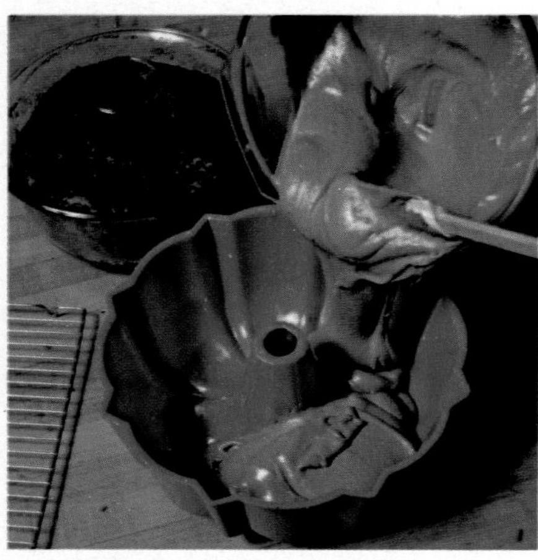

Pour batter into microwave fluted ring mold, or make your own tube pan by placing a 4 to 5-in. high glass in a large glass mixing bowl. Pour batter around it.

Prepare Dish for fruit-topped cake by buttering sides well. Coat with finely ground nuts. Line bottom with circle of wax paper; pour in ½ can pie filling. Invert finished cake.

Extra Rich Cakes and mixes enriched with special ingredients cook last in the center and bottom. Cool directly on counter top and retained heat will complete cooking.

Chocolate Cake from a Mix

MICROWAVING CAKES FROM COMMERCIAL MIXES

While some microwave experts recommend a reduction of the water called for on the package directions, we have found that the full amount of water results in a moist, eating quality cake and we recommend that cake batter be made following package directions exactly.

Amount of batter for 2-layer cake is too much for 2 round 8-in. cake layers because batter rises higher when microwaved than it does conventionally. Fill cake dishes only half full and use any leftover batter for cupcakes. You will get about ½ dozen extra cupcakes when using some mixes.

New microwave cake utensils made of plastic are designed to accommodate the greater expansion of cake batter. The round layer cake utensils hold half of batter from a 2-layer cake mix and the fluted and straight-sided molds hold all of batter from a 2-layer package. They are very convenient if you microwave cakes often.

Top appearance of microwaved cakes is uneven. Best shape may be obtained when 2-step method described below is used. However, for fastest microwaving, use High Power for all of cooking, reducing time by about 1 minute.

Immediately following this chart are recipes for some of the most popular cake mix variations. They may be microwaved according to the chart below.

DISH SIZE	AMOUNT OF BATTER	MICROWAVE AT **Medium High**	ROTATE DISH ½ TURN FINISH MICROWAVING AT **High**
12×8×2-in. (glass)	about 2½ cups	3 Minutes	3 to 3½ Minutes
8-in. square (glass)	about 2½ cups	3 Minutes	3 to 3½ Minutes
8-in. round (glass)	about 2 cups	3 Minutes	1½ to 2 Minutes
9-in. round (microwave plastic or ceramic)	about 3 cups (½ pkg.)	3 Minutes	2½ to 3 Minutes
Tube Cake (from glass mixer bowl, see left)	about 2½ cups	3 Minutes	2 to 2½ Minutes
16-cup Fluted or Straight-sided ring mold (microwave plastic or ceramic)	all of batter for 2-layer cake	For this cake **Microwave at High 11 to 14 Minutes,** rotating dish ¼ turn every 5 minutes. Let stand 5 to 10 minutes before inverting to cool.	

Microwaved Cake (second from left) looks different from conventional cake (above), until it is frosted or topped (at right).

Whipped Topping with Drizzled Chocolate

Peach Upside Down Cake, page 248

CAKE MIX VARIATIONS

Batters which start with packaged cake mix, microwave like regular cake mixes. See chart, page 243. Let stand directly on heat-proof surface to cool. The heat retained helps cook the bottom of rich cakes. Also see cupcakes, page 246. Each recipe makes 5 to 5½ cups batter.

"MIX EASY" FRUIT FLAVORED CAKE

1 pkg. (2-layer) yellow cake mix
1 pkg. (3-oz.) fruit flavored gelatin
4 eggs
¾ cup water
½ cup cooking oil

. . .In large mixer bowl, place cake mix, gelatin, eggs, water and oil. Blend on low speed of mixer until just moistened, then beat 4 minutes at medium speed. If desired, after microwaving, poke warm cake with fork and pour Lemon Glaze over top.

Lemon Glaze: Stir together ⅓ cup lemon juice and ½ cup sugar in 1-pt. measuring cup. **Microwave at High 3 to 5 Minutes,** until boiling.

"MIX EASY" SOUR CREAM CAKE

1 pkg. (2-layer) yellow cake mix
4 eggs
1 cup (8-oz.) sour cream
¾ cup cooking oil
½ cup sugar

. . .In large mixer bowl place cake mix, eggs, sour cream, oil and sugar. Blend on low speed of mixer, just until moistened, then beat 4 minutes at medium speed. If desired, top batter with Easy Streusel before microwaving.

Easy Streusel: Stir together ½ cup finely chopped nuts, ¼ cup sugar and 1 teaspoon cinnamon.

"MIX EASY" RICH NUT CAKE

1 pkg. (2-layer) cake mix, any flavor
1 pkg. (8-oz.) cream cheese, softened
4 eggs
⅔ cup soft shortening
¼ cup water
2 teaspoons vanilla extract

. . . . .In large mixer bowl place cake mix, cream cheese, eggs, shortening, water and vanilla. Blend on low speed of mixer until just moistened, then beat 4 minutes at medium speed.

½ cup finely chopped nuts

. . . .Fold nuts into batter. After microwaving, top cooled cake with Quick Glaze and garnish with nuts if desired.

Quick Glaze: Stir together 1 cup sifted confectioners sugar, 1 to 2 tablespoons milk or hot water, ¼ teaspoon vanilla extract and ⅛ teaspoon salt.

"MIX EASY" PUDDING POUND CAKE

1 pkg. (2-layer) yellow cake mix
1 pkg. (3¾-oz.) instant lemon or vanilla pudding mix
4 eggs
1 cup water
¼ cup cooking oil

. . .In large mixer bowl place cake mix, pudding mix, eggs, water and oil. Blend on low speed of mixer until just moistened, then beat 4 minutes at medium speed. If desired, top cooled cake with Chocolate Glaze.

Chocolate Glaze: In 1½-qt. casserole place 2 squares (2-oz.) unsweetened chocolate and 1 tablespoon butter. **Microwave at Low 3 to 4 Minutes,** until melted. Stir. Add 2½ cups sifted confectioners sugar, ¼ cup boiling water and ⅛ teaspoon salt. Stir smooth.

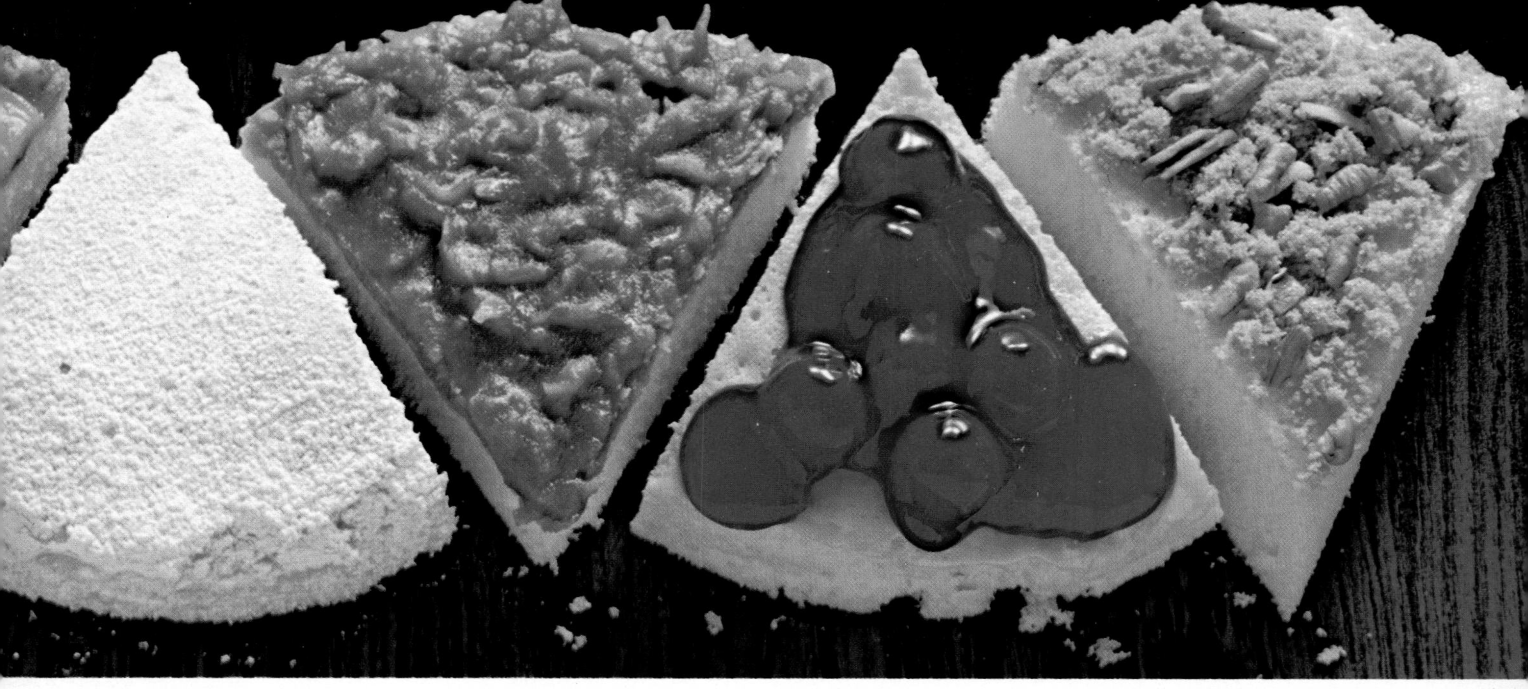

Powdered Sugar | Coconut Microwave Topping, page 251 | Cherry Pie Filling | Brown Sugar and Pecans

FRUIT-TOPPED LAYER CAKE

Some good flavor combinations to try with this technique are: yellow cake mix with peach pie filling, spice cake mix with apple pie filling and chocolate cake mix with cherry pie filling.

POWER LEVEL: High
MICROWAVE TIME: 8 to 9 min., per cake

1 pkg. (2-layer) cake mix . . Prepare cake mix according to package directions.

1 can (20 to 22-oz.) pie filling . . . Cut wax paper to fit bottoms of 2 8-in. round dishes. Pour half of pie filling into each dish. Then, pour 2 cups of prepared cake batter into each dish. If square dishes are desired, batter can be divided evenly between them.

Microwave one cake at a time. **Microwave at High 8 to 9 Minutes,** rotating dish ½ turn after 4 minutes, until toothpick stuck in center comes out clean. Let cake stand 10 minutes directly on heat-proof counter or wooden board.

If tops of cakes are not even, slice small amount from tops so they may be stacked. Invert 1 layer on serving plate. Invert and stack second layer on top. If desired, frost sides of cake with whipped cream or whipped dessert topping.

Makes 1 (8-in.) layer cake

HOW TO MICROWAVE SPECIAL CAKE MIXES

1. Prepare batter according to package directions.
2. Pour batter into greased 8-in. round dish.
3. Microwave at High and rotate dish as described in chart below.
4. Cake is done when toothpick stuck in center comes out clean.
5. Let cake stand directly on heat-proof counter or wooden board to cool.

POWER LEVEL: **High**

CAKE	TIME MINUTES	COMMENTS
Boston Cream Pie	5 to 7 ¼ turn every 2 minutes	Prepare custard filling and frosting as package directs.
Pineapple Upside Down Cake	9 to 12 ½ turn after 4 minutes	To prevent spillover, remove ¼ cup batter to make 2 cupcakes.
Snackin' Cake	8 to 10 ½ turn after 4 minutes	If ring shape is desired, place drinking glass (2-in. diameter), open side up in center of dish. Reduce time by 3 minutes.

EASY CHOCOLATE CAKE

POWER LEVEL: High
MICROWAVE TIME: 7 to 9 min., total

½ pkg. (2-layer size) fudge cake mix (about 2 cups dry mix)
1 egg
½ teaspoon vanilla extract
⅓ cup cooking oil
¾ cup water
In bottom of ungreased 8-in. square dish place dry cake mix. Add egg, vanilla, oil and water. Stir with fork until smooth and creamy.

½ cup semi-sweet chocolate pieces ... Sprinkle chocolate pieces over top.

Microwave at High 7 to 9 Minutes (no turns necessary). Serve warm or cool with ice cream or thawed frozen whipped topping.

Makes 1 (8-in. square) cake

HOW TO MICROWAVE CUPCAKES

Select a recipe from this section, or use your favorite homemade recipe (except do not use angel food or chiffon batters). For best shape, spoon into paper lined microwave cupcaker or "paper forms" described for muffins, page 208. Fill paper liners only ½ full.

You may also microwave cupcakes in double or triple thickness of paper liners only (without cupcaker or "paper forms"), but shape may be uneven. Cupcakes microwave very quickly; check for doneness at minimum time.

CUPCAKE COOKING CHART

POWER LEVEL: **High**

CUPCAKES	TIME MINUTES	COMMENTS
1	¼ to ½	If cooking more than 2, arrange in a circle on shelf.
2	¾ to 1	
3	1 to 1¼	When cooking several cupcakes, you may notice some will be done before others. If so, remove cupcakes as they are done and continue cooking the rest a few seconds more.
4	1¼ to 1½	
5	2 to 2¼	
6	2½ to 2¾	

ICE CREAM 'N' CAKE CONES

1. Spoon 2 to 3 tablespoons of chocolate or fudge cake batter from mix into flat bottomed ice cream cones. Press a cherry, nut half, caramel or a few chocolate chips into batter.
2. Microwave according to Cupcake Chart, above.

½ batter recipe makes 25 to 30 cones

BASIC BUTTER CAKE

POWER LEVEL: High
MICROWAVE TIME: 8 to 10 min., per cake

2¾ cups unsifted all-purpose flour
2 cups sugar
3 teaspoons baking powder
½ teaspoon salt
In large mixing bowl stir together flour, sugar, baking powder and salt.

1 cup (½-lb.) butter, softened
1 cup milk
1½ teaspoons vanilla extract
1 egg
Add butter, milk, vanilla and 1 egg. Beat 2 minutes at lowest speed of mixer, scraping bowl constantly for first ½ minute.

3 eggs ... Stop mixer and add eggs. Continue beating at lowest speed, scraping bowl often, 1 more minute. Batter will look curdled.

Pour batter into 2 paper towel lined 8-in. round dishes; spread evenly. Microwave 1 cake at a time. **Microwave at High 8 to 10 Minutes,** rotating dish ½ turn after 4 minutes. Let stand directly on heat-proof counter or wooden board to cool 15 minutes. Cake may then be turned out on wire rack to complete cooling, if desired.

Makes 2 (8-in. round) cakes

Nut Cake: Stir 1 cup finely chopped nuts into finished batter.

Marble Cake: After mixing batter, take out about ⅓ (2¼ cups) plain batter and drop in small mounds over bottom of dishes. To remaining batter in bowl, mix in ¼ teaspoon red food coloring; take out ½ (2¼ cups) of pink batter and drop in mounds in dishes. To remaining pink batter in bowl add 2 tablespoons cocoa and ½ teaspoon cinnamon; mix well and drop chocolate batter in mounds in dishes. With small spatula, swirl 3 colors of batter as much as desired. Microwave as above.

CHOCOLATE CHIP FILLED CUPCAKES

Batter from 2-layer chocolate cake mix
Chocolate Chip Filling (below)
Prepare cupcake liners, if desired (left). To make each cupcake, measure about 2 tablespoons batter into liner. Cover with 2 to 3 teaspoons filling.

Microwave cupcakes as shown on chart (left). As cupcakes cook, filling forms in center.

Makes 30 cupcakes

Chocolate Chip Filling: Stir together 1 pkg. (8-oz.) softened cream cheese, ⅓ cup sugar, 1 egg, ⅛ teaspoon salt, until well mixed. Blend in 1 pkg. (6-oz.) chocolate chips.

OLD-FASHIONED BUTTERMILK CAKE

POWER LEVEL: High
MICROWAVE TIME: 11 to 13 min., total

2½ cups unsifted all-purpose flour
¾ cup sugar
1 cup brown sugar (packed)
1 teaspoon nutmeg
1 teaspoon salt
¾ cup cooking oil
In large mixing bowl blend together with pastry blender, flour, sugar, brown sugar, nutmeg, salt and cooking oil to make a crumbly mixture. Reserve 1 cup of this mixture for cake topping.

2 eggs, beaten
1 teaspoon baking powder
1 cup buttermilk
1 teaspoon baking soda
To rest of crumbly mixture, add eggs, baking powder and buttermilk mixed with soda. Stir together until smooth batter is formed. Pour into greased 12×8×2-in. dish.

½ cup chopped walnuts
3 teaspoons cinnamon
Over cake batter in dish, sprinkle the reserved 1 cup crumbs, then mixture of walnuts and cinnamon. **Microwave at High 11 to 13 Minutes,** rotating dish ½ turn after 5 minutes.

¼ cup soft butter
1 teaspoon vanilla extract
1 cup confectioners sugar
3 tablespoons coffee
While cake is cooking, stir together butter, vanilla, confectioners sugar and coffee.

When cake is done, let stand directly on heat-proof counter or wooden board to cool. After cake has cooled 10 minutes, pour butter-sugar mixture over top; it will soak into cake. Serve cake warm "as is", or cool cake to room temperature; finish with Drizzle Glaze, if desired.

Makes 1 (12×8×2-in.) cake

Drizzle Glaze: Stir together ½ cup confectioners sugar and 2 tablespoons milk until smooth. From tip of spoon, drizzle over cake in fine lines. Let cake stand a few minutes until frosting sets before serving.

BANANA BUTTERMILK CAKE

Prepare Old Fashioned Buttermilk Cake, except omit nutmeg in cake batter and also reduce buttermilk to ½ cup. Add 1 cup (about 2 medium) mashed bananas along with buttermilk.

If desired, reduce cinnamon to 1 teaspoon and mix with reserved crumb mixture and nuts. Omit coffee in butter-sugar mixture.

SPICY APPLESAUCE CAKE

Good with Cream Cheese Frosting, page 251, or other favorite frosting, if desired.

POWER LEVEL: High
MICROWAVE TIME: 10 to 12 min., total

1⅓ cups unsifted all-purpose flour
1 cup sugar
1 teaspoon baking soda
½ teaspoon salt
½ teaspoon cinnamon
½ teaspoon nutmeg
¼ teaspoon allspice
1½ tablespoons cocoa
⅓ cup cooking oil
1 egg
1 cup canned applesauce
In large mixer bowl place flour, sugar, soda, salt, spices, cocoa, oil, egg and applesauce. Beat 2 minutes at lowest speed of mixer, scraping bowl constantly for first ½ minute.

½ cup chopped pitted dates
½ cup raisins
½ cup chopped nuts
Stir in fruits and nuts well.

Pour into 12×8×2-in. dish which has been greased on bottom only. **Microwave at High 10 to 12 Minutes,** rotating dish ½ turn after 5 minutes, until toothpick stuck in several places in cake comes out clean. Let cake stand directly on heat-proof counter or wooden board to cool.

Makes 1 (12×8×2-in.) cake

CHOCOLATE BEAUTY CAKE

Coconut-Nut Microwave Topping, page 251, is especially good with this cake.

POWER LEVEL: High
MICROWAVE TIME: 8 to 10 min., total

1½ cups unsifted all-purpose flour
1 cup brown sugar (packed)
¼ cup cocoa
1 teaspoon baking soda
½ teaspoon salt
½ cup water
In mixing bowl stir together flour, sugar, cocoa, soda and salt. Add water and stir to a stiff shiny batter, about 100 strokes.

½ cup water
⅓ cup cooking oil
1 tablespoon vinegar
1½ teaspoons vanilla extract
Add additional ½ cup water, oil, vinegar and vanilla. Stir until smooth and well blended.

Pour batter into greased 8-in. round dish. **Microwave at High 8 to 10 Minutes,** rotating dish ½ turn after 4 minutes. Let stand directly on heat-proof counter or wooden board to cool. Finish with favorite frosting, or as desired.

Makes 1 (8-in. round) cake

Pineapple Upside Down Cake

PINEAPPLE UPSIDE DOWN CAKE

For variety substitute peaches for pineapple and almond extract for vanilla.

POWER LEVEL: High
MICROWAVE TIME: 9¾ to 13 min., total

¼ cup butter **⅓ cup brown sugar (packed)** **1 can (8¼-oz.) pineapple slices** **4 maraschino or candied cherries, cut in half**	In 8-in. round dish place butter. **Microwave at High ¾ to 1 Minute,** to melt. Sprinkle sugar over butter. Drain pineapple (save liquid) on paper towels and arrange in dish. Decorate with cherries.
1¼ cups unsifted all-purpose flour **¾ cup sugar** **2 teaspoons baking powder** **½ teaspoon salt** **⅓ cup soft shortening** **1 egg** **Liquid from pineapple plus milk to total ½ cup** **1 teaspoon vanilla extract**	In small mixer bowl place flour, sugar, baking powder, salt, shortening, egg, liquid and vanilla. Beat 3 minutes on lowest mixer speed, scraping bowl constantly first ½ minute. Carefully spread batter over fruit in dish.

Microwave at High 9 to 12 Minutes, rotating dish ½ turn after 5 minutes. Some batter may run onto edges of dish, but will not spill. When done, toothpick stuck in cake comes out clean. Invert cake onto plate, let dish stand over cake a few minutes. Serve hot or warm.

Makes 1 (8-in.) round cake

POPULAR CARROT CAKE

POWER LEVEL: High
MICROWAVE TIME: 13 to 15 min., total

1½ cups sugar **1 cup cooking oil** **1 teaspoon vanilla extract** **3 eggs**	In large mixing bowl blend sugar, oil and vanilla. Add eggs and beat well.
1½ cups unsifted all-purpose flour **¾ teaspoon salt** **1¼ teaspoons baking soda** **2½ teaspoons cinnamon**	In small bowl, stir together flour, salt, soda and cinnamon. Add to sugar-egg mixture and mix in.
2¼ cups raw grated carrots **½ cup chopped walnuts**	Fold in carrots and walnuts. Pour batter into greased 12×8×2-in. dish.

Microwave at High 13 to 15 Minutes, rotating dish ½ turn every 4 minutes. Let stand directly on heat-proof counter or wooden board to cool. Frost with Cream Cheese Frosting, page 251, if desired.

Makes 1 (12×8×2-in.) cake

HONEY DRIZZLE CAKE

This recipe won $5,000 in a recent microwave recipe contest.

POWER LEVEL: High
MICROWAVE TIME: 16 to 18 min., total

5 eggs **¼ cup sugar** **⅛ teaspoon salt**	Separate eggs. In large mixer bowl beat egg whites until foamy. Gradually beat in ¼ cup sugar and salt until fluffy.
½ cup sugar **1 teaspoon vanilla extract**	In small bowl beat egg yolks, ½ cup sugar and vanilla until thick and pale.
1½ cups chopped pecans **1½ cups fine vanilla wafer crumbs** **1½ teaspoons baking powder** **½ teaspoon cinnamon**	Fold yolk mixture into egg whites thoroughly. Blend pecans, wafer crumbs, baking powder and cinnamon; sprinkle over top. Fold all ingredients together well.

Pour into greased 8-in. square dish. **Microwave at High 8 to 10 Minutes,** rotating dish ½ turn after 4 minutes. Remove cake and cook Honey Syrup (below). Carefully pour syrup over cake. Serve in small pieces, warm or cold, with unsweetened whipped cream.

Honey Syrup: In 2-qt. casserole stir together 1½ cups water, 1½ cups sugar and ⅔ cup honey. **Microwave at High 8 Minutes,** stirring after 4 minutes.

Makes 1 (8-in.) square cake

PECAN SPONGE ROLL

Fill Pecan Sponge Roll with vanilla ice cream instead of cream filling for a good make-ahead frozen dessert. Serve in slices with chocolate sauce.

POWER LEVEL: High
MICROWAVE TIME: 6 to 8 min., total

Prepare paper on which to microwave Pecan Sponge Roll. Cut a sheet of wax paper (which is 12-in. wide) into a 28-in. long piece. Fold in half, making a double thickness of paper 14×12-in. in size. Cut a piece of brown paper (from grocery bag, if desired) same size and place under wax paper for added support. Generously butter top of wax paper.

4 eggs, separated **½ cup sifted confectioners sugar** **2 teaspoons vanilla extract** **1½ cups ground pecans or pecan meal*** **¾ teaspoon baking powder**	In small mixer bowl, beat egg whites, until stiff. In large mixer bowl, beat egg yolks and sugar until thick and pale in color. Add vanilla. Mix pecans with baking powder and fold into egg yolk mixture. Fold in stiffly beaten egg whites.

Spread batter evenly on buttered wax paper to within 1-in. of edges. Handling carefully, place cake in microwave oven. **Microwave at High 6 to 8 Minutes,** until toothpick stuck in cake comes out clean. Let cake stand in microwave oven 1 minute, then carefully transfer to cooling rack. Cover with dish towel wrung out with cold water. Let cool.

When cool, remove towel and spread Vanilla Filling over cake. Roll up as for jelly roll starting at short side and peeling off wax paper as cake is rolled. Sprinkle with powdered sugar just before serving, or if desired, top with vanilla glaze.

Makes 12 (1-in.) slices

*Ground pecans are found packaged at grocery stores, especially at holiday time. Or, if desired, whir pecans in blender until finely ground.

Vanilla Filling: In small mixer bowl, place 2 cups well-chilled whipping cream and 1 pkg. (3¾-oz.) instant vanilla pudding mix. Beat at high speed of mixer until thick and fluffy.

Vanilla Glaze: In small bowl stir together 1 cup confectioners sugar, 1 tablespoon corn syrup and 1 tablespoon water. **Microwave at Low ½ to 1 Minute,** just until lukewarm. Stir well and pour over Pecan Roll to glaze.

NOTE: To easily transfer batter and paper to oven, place a cookie sheet under the paper. Slide batter-topped paper from cookie sheet into oven. Same cookie sheet can be used to transfer baked cake from oven.

ORANGE-GLAZED FRUIT CAKE

POWER LEVEL: High
MICROWAVE TIME: 14 to 16 min., total

1 cup (3 to 4-oz.) coconut **1 cup unsifted all-purpose flour** **1½ cups confectioners sugar** **2 teaspoons baking powder**	In mixing bowl stir together coconut, flour, sugar and baking powder.
¾ cup butter, melted **3 eggs, beaten** **½ cup milk**	Add butter, eggs and milk. Mix well.
2 cups chopped candied fruit **1½ cups chopped pecans**	Stir in fruit and nuts. Pour batter into greased 12×8×2-in. dish.

Microwave at High 14 to 16 Minutes, rotating dish ½ turn after 8 minutes. Spoon Orange Glaze over hot cake.

Orange Glaze: In 1-qt. casserole stir together ½ cup sugar and 1 cup orange juice. Cover. **Microwave at High 3 to 5 Minutes,** until boiling.

Makes 1 (12×8×2-in.) cake

STEAMED PUDDING

POWER LEVEL: High and Medium High
MICROWAVE TIME: 17 to 19½ min., total

1 cup water **1 cup seedless raisins or cranberries**	Measure water into glass measure. **Microwave at High 2 to 2½ Minutes,** until at rolling boil. Pour over fruit and let stand.
2 tablespoons butter **½ cup sugar** **½ cup molasses** **1 egg**	Beat together butter, sugar, molasses and egg.
1½ cups unsifted all-purpose flour **1 teaspoon baking soda** **1 teaspoon salt**	Stir together flour, baking soda and salt. Add flour mixture and fruit with water to creamed mixture.

Lightly grease 2-qt. casserole, then place 2-in. diameter drinking glass (open side up) in center. Pour batter around glass. Cover dish well with plastic wrap. **Microwave at Medium High 15 to 17 Minutes,** rotating dish ½ turn every 5 minutes, until pudding appears set, but glossy. Remove from oven with pot holders.

Let stand 10 to 20 minutes; twist glass to remove. Unmold onto cooling rack. When cold, wrap well and allow pudding to age about a week before slicing. Serve with Hard Sauce or Citrus Sauce, page 253.

Makes about 10 to 12 servings

EARLY AMERICAN GINGERBREAD

Serve warm, topped with Citrus Sauce, page 253, or whipped cream, if desired.

POWER LEVEL: High
MICROWAVE TIME: 5 to 6 min., total

1½ cups unsifted all-purpose flour
½ cup sugar
¾ teaspoon baking soda
½ teaspoon ginger
½ teaspoon cinnamon
½ teaspoon salt

In mixing bowl stir together flour, sugar, baking soda, ginger, cinnamon and salt.

½ cup soft shortening
1 egg
½ cup light molasses
½ cup hottest tap water

Add shortening, egg, molasses and water. Beat 2 minutes on medium speed of mixer until well blended.

Pour batter into greased 8-in. round dish. **Microwave at High 5 to 6 Minutes,** rotating dish ½ turn after 3 minutes. When cake is done let stand directly on heat-proof counter or wooden board to cool.

Makes 8 servings

CONVENIENCE CAKE DEFROSTING CHART

Cakes packaged in foil should be removed from the foil and placed on a plate, or on an all cardboard lid. Frosted layer cakes can be defrosted on the styrofoam base.

Watch icing and frosting closely as they melt easily. Defrosted cakes should be cool and easy to cut. Let cakes stand 2 to 5 minutes before serving.

POWER LEVEL: **Defrost**

ITEM	TIME MINUTES	COMMENTS
2 to 3-layer, frosted (17-oz.)	2	
1 piece, frosted	½	
1-layer, frosted, filled or topped (12½ to 16 oz.)	2 to 3	Rotate ½ turn after ½ minute.
Pound Cake (11¼-oz.)	2	
1 piece pound cake	½	
Cheesecake, plain or fruit topped (17 to 19-oz.)	5 to 6	Rotate ¼ turn every 2 minutes.
Crunch Cakes and Cupcakes (1 or 2)	½ to 1	
Crunch Cakes and Cupcakes (3 or 4)	1 to 2	
Crunch Cakes and Cupcakes (5 to 8)	2 to 3	Arrange in circle on plate. Rotate ½ turn after ½ minute.

BASIC CHEESECAKE

Cheesecake, which is a custard rather than a batter, is especially appropriate for microwaving.

POWER LEVEL: High and Medium
MICROWAVE TIME: 24¾ to 28½ min., total

3 tablespoons butter
1 cup fine crumbs (graham cracker or chocolate cookie)
2 tablespoons sugar

In 8-in. round dish place butter. **Microwave at High ¼ to ½ Minute,** to melt. Stir in crumbs and sugar. Press mixture on bottom and sides of dish. **Microwave at High 1½ to 2 Minutes,** rotating dish ½ turn after 1 minute, until set.

4 eggs
1 cup sugar
2 pkg. (8-oz. each) cream cheese
2 teaspoons vanilla extract
¼ teaspoon salt

In blender container place eggs, sugar, cream cheese, vanilla and salt. Blend on high speed 1 minute until smooth. (If mixed with electric mixer, use large mixer bowl and mix at high speed 3 minutes.) Pour over back of spoon into crust.*

Microwave at Medium 23 to 26 Minutes, rotating dish ¼ turn every 7 minutes, until center is almost set. Refrigerate at least 3 hours before serving. Garnish with Whipped Cream Cheese Topping (below) and chocolate curls, if desired.

Makes 1 (8-in.) cheesecake
8 to 12 servings

*Pouring over spoon prevents crust from breaking.

Whipped Cream Cheese Topping: In small mixer bowl place 1 pkg. (3-oz.) softened cream cheese, ½ cup whipping cream and 2 tablespoons sugar. Beat until fluffy. Serve in dollops or spread over top.

VERY CHOCOLATE CHEESECAKE

Prepare recipe above with Chocolate Cookie Crust. Add 2 squares (2-oz.) unsweetened chocolate, melted, to filling. For light chocolate, use 1 square of chocolate.

CREME DE MENTHE CHEESECAKE

Prepare recipe above with Chocolate Cookie Crust. Omit vanilla, add ¼ cup green creme de menthe to filling.

IRISH COFFEE CHEESECAKE

Prepare recipe above with Graham Cracker Crust. Omit vanilla, add 1 teaspoon instant coffee powder and ¼ cup Irish mist liqueur to filling.

REFRESHING ORANGE CHEESECAKE

Prepare recipe above with Chocolate Cookie Crust. Omit vanilla and add ¼ cup orange juice concentrate, undiluted, and 1 tablespoon grated fresh orange peel.

EASY FUDGE FROSTING

POWER LEVEL: High
MICROWAVE TIME: 3 to 4 min., total

1 cup sugar **¼ cup butter** **¼ cup evaporated milk**	In 1½-qt. casserole combine sugar, butter and evaporated milk. **Microwave at High 3 to 4 Minutes,** uncovered, stirring after 2 minutes, until bubbly.
1 cup (6-oz.) semi-sweet chocolate pieces **1 cup marshmallow creme** **1 teaspoon vanilla extract**	Add chocolate pieces, marshmallow creme and vanilla to hot mixture. Stir until well blended. Excellent on brownies or plain cake layers.

Makes about 2 cups frosting

BASIC CONFECTIONERS SUGAR FROSTING

POWER LEVEL: High
MICROWAVE TIME: 1 to 2 min., total

1 pkg. (1-lb.) confectioners sugar **¼ cup milk** **¼ teaspoon salt** **1 teaspoon vanilla extract** **¼ cup butter**	In 1½-qt. casserole place sugar, milk, salt and vanilla and stir just to blend slightly (mixture is too stiff to mix thoroughly). Add butter on top.

Microwave at High 1 to 2 Minutes, until mixture can be beaten smooth.

NOTE: Add additional 1 to 2 teaspoons milk if mixture is too stiff.

Makes enough frosting for 2 (8-in.) round or square layers

BUTTERCREAM FROSTING

Using above recipe decrease milk to 2 tablespoons and increase butter to ½ cup. Microwave as above. If mixture gets too hot, it will be runny and may run off cake. Let frosting stand in bowl a few minutes, stirring occasionally, before icing cake. As it cools, it thickens.

COCONUT-NUT FROSTING FROM A MIX

POWER LEVEL: High
MICROWAVE TIME: 1 to 1½ min., total

1 pkg. (9.9-oz.) coconut nut frosting mix **Milk** **Butter**	In 1-qt. casserole place frosting mix, milk and butter (use amounts on package). **Microwave at High 1 to 1½ Minutes,** until mixture can be stirred smooth.

Easy Fudge Frosting

COCONUT MICROWAVE TOPPING

POWER LEVEL: High
MICROWAVE TIME: 2 min., total

1 cup brown sugar (packed) **1 tablespoon cornstarch** **2 tablespoons milk** **2 tablespoons butter**	In 1-qt. casserole blend together brown sugar, cornstarch and milk. Add butter. **Microwave at High 2 Minutes,** stirring after 1 minute.
½ cup flaked coconut	Stir mixture well, then stir in coconut. Pour over cooled cake.

Makes enough frosting for 2 (8-in.) round or square layers

Coconut-Nut Microwave Topping: Add ¼ to ½ cup chopped nuts (walnuts, pecans or peanuts) along with coconut.

CREAM CHEESE FROSTING

POWER LEVEL: High
MICROWAVE TIME: 1 min., total

1 lb. confectioners sugar **1 pkg. (8-oz.) cream cheese** **6 tablespoons butter** **2 teaspoons vanilla extract**	In 2-qt. casserole place sugar. Put cream cheese, butter and vanilla over top. **Microwave at High 1 Minute,** just until ingredients can be beaten together. For a fluffy frosting, beat with electric mixer.

This recipe makes a very generous amount of frosting for top of 12×8×2-in. cake. If you desire thin layer of frosting, reserve leftover in refrigerator or freezer for another cake.

Scrumptious Butterscotch Sauce

Dessert Sauces

Delicious, smooth and creamy dessert sauces microwave with exceptional ease and speed. With conventional cooking, they require care in melting chocolate or dissolving sugar mixtures, and constant stirring to prevent scorching and lumps. With microwave cooking, stirring is minimal and sauces are ready in 2 to 7 minutes.

QUICKIE CHOCOLATE SAUCE

POWER LEVEL: High
MICROWAVE TIME: 1½ to 2½ min., total

½ cup light corn syrup **1 pkg. (6-oz.) semi-sweet chocolate pieces** **1 tablespoon butter**	Into 1-pt. glass measure, measure syrup. Stir in chocolate and butter. **Microwave at High 1½ to 2½ Minutes.** Stir until completely smooth.
¼ cup dairy half & half or milk **¼ teaspoon vanilla or rum extract**	Blend in half & half and vanilla. Serve warm or cold.

Makes about 1½ cups

SCRUMPTIOUS BUTTERSCOTCH SAUCE

Its name describes how it tastes.

POWER LEVEL: High
MICROWAVE TIME: 3½ to 4½ min., total

1 tablespoon cornstarch **1¼ cups light brown sugar (packed)** **½ cup dairy half & half** **2 tablespoons light corn syrup** **⅛ teaspoon salt** **¼ cup butter**	In 1½-qt. casserole stir together cornstarch and brown sugar. Stir in half & half, corn syrup and salt. Add butter. Cover. **Microwave at High 3½ to 4½ Minutes,** stirring after 2 minutes, until thickened and sugar is dissolved
1 teaspoon vanilla extract	Add vanilla and stir until smooth and well blended. Serve warm or cold.

Makes 1½ cups

WONDERFUL MAPLE NUT SAUCE

Prepare recipe above, substituting 1 teaspoon maple flavoring for vanilla. Add ⅓ cup chopped nuts if desired.

CRUNCHY CHOCOLATE SAUCE

POWER LEVEL: High
MICROWAVE TIME: 2½ to 4 min., total

¼ cup milk **1 square (1-oz.) unsweetened chocolate**	In 1-pt. glass measure, measure milk. Drop in chocolate. **Microwave at High 1½ to 2 Minutes.** Blend chocolate and milk.
¾ cup light brown sugar (packed)	Add sugar; stir to blend. **Microwave at High 1 to 2 Minutes,** until mixture boils.
¼ cup crunchy peanut butter **¼ teaspoon vanilla extract**	Add peanut butter and vanilla and stir until well blended. Serve warm or cool.

Makes 1 cup

FUDGE SAUCE

The kind which mounds from a spoon.

POWER LEVEL: High
MICROWAVE TIME: 5 to 6 min., total

1 cup sugar **¼ teaspoon salt** **1 can (5.3-oz.) evaporated milk**	In 3-qt. casserole stir together sugar, salt and milk, until blended. **Microwave at High 5 to 6 Minutes,** until boiling hard.
2 squares (2-oz.) unsweetened chocolate **2 tablespoons butter** **1 teaspoon vanilla**	Into boiling mixture stir in chocolate until completely melted. Stir in butter and vanilla.

Makes about 1½ cups

FESTIVE RICH BUTTER SAUCE

POWER LEVEL: High
MICROWAVE TIME: 2½ to 3½ min., total

1 cup sugar **½ cup dairy half & half** **½ cup (¼-lb.) butter**	In 1-qt. casserole stir together sugar and half & half. Add butter. Cover. **Microwave at High 2½ to 3½ Minutes,** until sugar dissolves. Stir vigorously to combine. This rich sauce may separate slightly on standing. If so, stir again.

Makes 1½ cups

NOTE: If desired, ½ teaspoon rum extract or 1 tablespoon brandy, rum, sherry or fruit flavored brandy may be stirred into sauce after cooking.

CINNAMON SUGAR SAUCE

POWER LEVEL: High
MICROWAVE TIME: 3 to 4 min., total

½ cup sugar **1½ tablespoons cornstarch** **1 teaspoon cinnamon** **1 cup hot tap water**	In 1-qt. casserole stir together sugar, cornstarch, cinnamon and water, until completely smooth. Cover. **Microwave at High 3 to 4 Minutes,** stirring sauce after 1½ minutes.
2 tablespoons butter	Stir in butter until well blended. Serve warm.

Makes 1⅓ cups

CITRUS SAUCE

Prepare recipe above, omitting cinnamon. Stir 1 tablespoon lemon or orange juice and 1 to 2 teaspoons finely grated lemon or orange rind into sugar mixture.

HARD SAUCE

POWER LEVEL: High
MICROWAVE TIME: 1½ to 2 min., total

1 pkg. (1-lb.) confectioners sugar **¼ teaspoon salt** **¼ cup rum or brandy*** **½ cup (¼-lb.) butter**	In small glass mixer bowl or 1½-qt. casserole place sugar, salt and rum. Place butter on top. **Microwave at High 1½ to 2 Minutes.**

Beat on highest speed of mixer until smooth. Sauce will be soft and creamy after beating. If a true hard sauce is desired, refrigerate until hardened. Serve over plum pudding or other baked fruit puddings, or with fruit cake, gingerbread, applesauce cake, etc. Or use as "frosting" for fruit cake.

*Or use ¼ cup milk with 1 to 2 teaspoons vanilla, rum or brandy flavoring (or use orange or lemon extract).

Makes 2 cups

TOASTED ALMOND SAUCE

POWER LEVEL: High
MICROWAVE TIME: 7 to 9 min., total

½ cup (¼-lb.) butter	In 1½-qt. casserole place butter. **Microwave at High 2 Minutes.**
3 pkgs. (2⅞-oz. each) sliced almonds	Add nuts and stir until well coated. **Microwave at High 5 to 7 Minutes,** stirring well after 3 minutes, until bubbly and golden brown.
1 jar (1-lb.) honey **Nutmeg**	Stir in honey until evenly mixed. Sprinkle generously with nutmeg. Serve hot.

Makes about 12 servings

TRUE BLUEBERRY SAUCE

POWER LEVEL: High
MICROWAVE TIME: 5 to 7 min., total

1 tablespoon lemon juice
2 tablespoons cornstarch
¼ cup sugar
⅛ teaspoon salt
1 can (16-oz.) blueberries

In 1-qt. casserole stir together lemon juice and cornstarch. Add sugar and salt. Stir in undrained blueberries. **Microwave at High 5 to 7 Minutes,** stirring every 2 minutes, until sauce is thickened and clear. Serve over ice cream, pancakes or unfrosted cake such as pound cake.

Makes about 1½ cups

TO USE FROZEN BLUEBERRIES: Place 1 (10-oz.) pouch package of blueberries in microwave oven. **Microwave at Defrost 5 to 7 Minutes,** just until berries can be separated. Substitute for canned blueberries. Add ½ to ¾ cup water for liquid, increasing cooking time, if necessary.

Mint on Mint Sundaes

CINNAMON GLAZED PINEAPPLE SAUCE

POWER LEVEL: High
MICROWAVE TIME: 6 to 7 min., total

1 can (13½-oz.) pineapple tidbits
2 tablespoons sugar
1 tablespoon cornstarch
¼ teaspoon cinnamon
2 tablespoons butter

In 1-qt. casserole place pineapple. In small cup mix together sugar, cornstarch and cinnamon. Add to pineapple, stirring well. Cut butter in 2 pieces and place over top. Cover.

Microwave at High 6 to 7 Minutes, stirring well after 3 minutes. Serve hot.

Makes 1⅔ cups sauce

MINT-ON-MINT SUNDAES

Chocolate mint sauce is also delicious on plain chocolate or chocolate ripple ice cream.

POWER LEVEL: Medium TEMP:* 140°
APPROX. MICROWAVE TIME: 2 to 3 min.

1 pkg. (6½-oz.) chocolate covered mint patties**
¼ cup whipping cream

In 1-pt. glass measure place unwrapped mint patties. Add cream.

Insert temperature probe so tip rests on center bottom of cup. Cover with plastic wrap arranging loosely around probe to vent. Attach cable end at receptacle. **Microwave at Medium. Set Temp, Set 140°.**

When oven signals, stir sauce smooth. Serve warm chocolate mint sauce over mint ice cream.

* On models not equipped with probe use minimum microwave time and check for doneness.

**6½-oz. package contains about 24 patties, about 1¼-in. diameter each.

Makes about 1 cup sauce

HOW TO WARM COMMERCIAL SUNDAE SAUCES

Commercial sundae sauces and syrups seem special when warm. Pour sauce or syrup into microwave oven-proof pitcher or measure. Avoid heating in original glass containers which might not be heat tempered.

To soften a 12-oz. jar of cold sauce topping from the refrigerator, **Microwave at High ½ Minute.** For hot fudge or butterscotch, heat about 1 minute more.

Try canned pie fillings as sundae toppings. Cherry or blueberry pie fillings are great favorites.

Jellies, Jams & Relishes

Like all fruits and vegetables cooked by microwaves, jellies, jams and relishes retain their sparkling fresh flavor. Because microwave energy heats from all sides, not just the bottom, sugar mixtures do not scorch and need very little stirring. As with range top cooking, they boil up high, so be sure to use a large casserole. Since fruit juices do not evaporate in microwaving, we recommend using fruit pectin to thicken jellies, jams and preserves. You will also obtain a greater yield for the same amount of fruit.

GENERAL RECOMMENDATIONS FOR JELLY AND JAM MAKING

1. Use High Power on all recipes.
2. Whenever pectin is added – add gradually, stirring very well.
3. Use pot holders as sugar mixtures get very hot.
4. Avoid steam burns by lifting lid away from you when removing.
5. Pour jelly into hot sterilized jars or glasses; wipe off rim well, then seal with hot sterilized lids or paraffin. Sterilizing should be done in pot of boiling water on surface unit. Paraffin manufacturers recommend melting paraffin in a double boiler.
6. If you live in a warm or humid southern climate, the United States Department of Agriculture recommends that you water-bath process the filled and sealed jars of chunky preserves and jams for about 5 minutes.

APPLE JELLY

POWER LEVEL: High
MICROWAVE TIME: 17 to 21 min., total

2 cups bottled unsweetened apple juice
3½ cups sugar .... In 3-qt. casserole stir together apple juice and sugar. Cover. **Microwave at High 12 to 14 Minutes,** stirring after 6 minutes, until boiling.

½ bottle (6-oz.) liquid fruit pectin .... Stir in pectin, mixing thoroughly. Cover. **Microwave at High 4 to 6 Minutes** more, until mixture returns to boil. Then, time for 1 minute of boiling. Stir and skim off foam if necessary. Ladle into prepared glasses. Seal.

Makes about 3 cups

Fresh Peach Jam

GRAPE JELLY FROM FROZEN JUICE

It is very important to mix pectin well with juice before microwaving.

POWER LEVEL: High
MICROWAVE TIME: 15 to 18 min., total

1 can (6-oz.) frozen grape juice concentrate, defrosted
1 pkg. (1¾-oz.) powdered fruit pectin
2 cups hot tap water ..... In 3-qt. casserole, blend together grape juice and pectin. Stir in water. Cover. **Microwave at High 8 to 9 Minutes,** stirring well after 4 minutes, until bubbles form around edge of dish.

3¾ cups sugar .... Add sugar, mixing well. Cover. **Microwave at High 6 to 8 Minutes,** stirring well after 4 minutes, until mixture boils. Then, time for 1 minute of boiling. Stir and skim off foam with metal spoon. Ladle into prepared glasses. Seal.

Makes about 4 cups

SPARKLING CHAMPAGNE JELLY

Other wines such as red, rose, burgundy, port and white may be used in this recipe.

POWER LEVEL: High
MICROWAVE TIME: 9 to 11 min., total

1¾ cups champagne wine
3 cups sugar ..... In 3-qt. casserole, stir together champagne and sugar. Cover. **Microwave at High 8 to 10 Minutes,** stirring after 4 minutes, until mixture begins to boil. Then, time for 1 minute more of boiling. Stir.

½ bottle liquid fruit pectin ..... Gradually stir pectin into hot mixture, mixing well. Ladle into prepared glasses.* Seal.

Makes about 4 cups

NOTE: Other wines such as red, rose, burgundy, port and white may be used in this recipe.

*For gift giving, place a washed bunch of fresh grapes in each glass before adding jelly. Especially pretty when sealed in custard cups with parrafin and unmolded on plate for serving. Use immediately; grapes show age after about 1 month.

FRESH STRAWBERRY JAM

POWER LEVEL: High
MICROWAVE TIME: 17 to 21 min., total

4½ cups crushed fresh strawberries (wash and stem before crushing)
1 box (1¾-oz.) powdered fruit pectin ... In 3-qt. casserole place berries and pectin. Stir well. Cover. **Microwave at High 8 to 10 Minutes,** until mixture is at a full rolling boil.

7 cups sugar .... Add sugar to boiling mixture and stir well.

Microwave at High 8 to 10 Minutes, uncovered, stirring after 5 minutes, until mixture reaches a full rolling boil. Then, time for 1 minute of boiling. Skim off foam with metal spoon, stirring jam about 5 minutes before ladling into prepared glasses. Seal.

Makes about 8 cups

STRAWBERRY JAM FROM FROZEN BERRIES

This spread can be made year round.

POWER LEVEL: High
MICROWAVE TIME: 21 to 27 min., total

3 pkgs. (10-oz. each) strawberries in plastic pouch ..... Place unopened packages in microwave oven. **Microwave at High 4 to 6 Minutes,** checking at minimum time and rearranging fruit if continued defrosting is necessary.

2 tablespoons water
½ box (2½ tablespoons) powdered fruit pectin ..... Remove fruit from pouches and place in 3-qt. casserole. Crush the fruit. Add water and pectin, stirring well. Cover. **Microwave at High 8 to 10 Minutes,** or until mixture is at a full rolling boil. Stir.

3 cups sugar .... Add sugar to boiling mixture and stir well.

Microwave at High 8 to 10 Minutes, uncovered, stirring after 5 minutes, until mixture reaches a full rolling boil. Then, time for 1 minute of boiling. Skim off foam and stir jam about 5 minutes before ladling into prepared glasses. Seal.

Makes about 4½ cups

APPLESAUCE BUTTER

Start with about 1-qt. of applesauce to make this recipe. It is very good made with microwaved applesauce, page 224.

POWER LEVEL: High
MICROWAVE TIME: 18 to 22 min., total

1 qt. (4 cups) applesauce (or 2 cans, 16-oz. each)
1 pkg. (1¾-oz.) powdered fruit pectin
1 tablespoon pumpkin pie spice
1 teaspoon cinnamon .... In 3-qt. casserole stir together applesauce, pectin, pumpkin pie spice and cinnamon. Cover. **Microwave at High 8 to 10 Minutes,** stirring after 5 minutes, until mixture boils.

4½ cups sugar .... Add sugar to hot mixture, stirring well. Cover. **Microwave at High 9 to 11 Minutes,** stirring every 5 minutes, until mixture reaches a full boil. Then, time for 1 minute of boiling. Stir well. Ladle into prepared glasses. Seal.

Makes about 6 cups

FRESH PEACH JAM

POWER LEVEL: High
MICROWAVE TIME: 16 to 20 min., total

4 cups peeled, pitted and finely chopped peaches
2 tablespoons lemon juice
1 box (1¾-oz.) powdered fruit pectin . . . In 3-qt. casserole place peaches, lemon juice and pectin. Stir well. Cover. **Microwave at High 8 to 10 Minutes,** or until mixture is at a full rolling boil. Stir.

5½ cups sugar . . . Add sugar to boiling mixture, stirring well. **Microwave at High 7 to 9 Minutes,** uncovered, stirring after 4 minutes, until mixture reaches a full rolling boil. Then, time for 1 more minute of boiling. Skim off foam and stir jam about 5 minutes before ladling into prepared glasses. Seal.

Makes about 7 cups

PEACH CONSERVE

POWER LEVEL: High
MICROWAVE TIME: 17 to 19 min., total

3½ cups peeled, pitted finely chopped peaches
½ cup dark seedless raisins
¼ teaspoon grated lemon peel
2 tablespoons lemon juice
¼ teaspoon cinnamon
1 box (1¾-oz.) powdered fruit pectin . . . In 3-qt. casserole place peaches, raisins, lemon peel, lemon juice, cinnamon and pectin. Mix together well. Cover. **Microwave at High 10 Minutes,** stirring after 5 minutes.

5 cups sugar . . . Add sugar to hot mixture mixing thoroughly. Cover. **Microwave at High 6 to 8 Minutes** more, stirring after 4 minutes, until mixture reaches a full boil. Stir, then time for 1 more minute of boiling.

½ cup brandy
1 cup sliced, unblanched almonds . . . Immediately stir in brandy and nuts. With metal spoon skim off foam if necessary. Ladle into prepared glasses. Seal.

Makes about 8 cups

SWEET CITRUS MARMALADE

Be sure to remove all of white interior portion of orange rind so sweetest, most natural orange flavor can be obtained.

POWER LEVEL: High
MICROWAVE TIME: 31 to 33 min., total

3 medium oranges
2 medium lemons . . . Prepare rind portion from oranges and lemons first; peel rind from fruit in quarters. Laying rind white-side up, scrape about half of white layer from rind and discard scraped material. With sharp knife or scissors, slice remaining rind crosswise very thin.

1½ cups water
⅛ teaspoon baking soda . . . In 2-qt. casserole place rind with water and baking soda. Cover. **Microwave at High 12 Minutes,** stirring after 6 minutes. While rind is cooking, section fruit, removing and discarding white membrane and seeds. Chop. Add this pulp and juice to the undrained cooked rind. Cover. **Microwave at High 6 Minutes.**

5 cups sugar . . . In 3-qt. casserole measure 3 cups fruit mixture. Add sugar, blending well. Cover. **Microwave at High 12 to 14 Minutes,** stirring after 6 minutes, until mixture comes to a full boil. Then time for 1 more minute of boiling.

½ bottle (6-oz.) liquid fruit pectin . . . Stir in pectin, mixing thoroughly. With metal spoon, skim off foam and stir 5 minutes to cool slightly. Ladle into prepared jars. Seal. If sealed with metal lids and band, turn upside down to prevent floating fruit.

Makes about 5½ cups

PORT WINE CONSERVE

POWER LEVEL: High
MICROWAVE TIME: 8 to 10 min., total

1½ cups port wine
1 cup chopped raisins
3 cups sugar
In 3-qt. casserole stir together wine, raisins and sugar.

3 large cinnamon sticks
1 tablespoon grated orange peel
¼ teaspoon whole cloves
½ teaspoon cardamom ground
Prepare spice bag by placing cinnamon sticks, orange peel, cloves and cardamom on a square of cheesecloth. Fold cloth around contents and tie securely with string. Add bag to wine, stir and let stand 5 minutes. **Microwave 8 to 10 Minutes,** stirring well after 5 minutes, just until bubbles appear around edge; do not boil.

½ bottle liquid fruit pectin
Remove spice bag. Immediately stir pectin into hot mixture. Ladle into prepared glasses. Seal.

Makes about 3½ cups

CUCUMBER SANDWICH PICKLES

POWER LEVEL: High
MICROWAVE TIME: 27 to 29 min., total

2 qts. ¼-in. slices small to medium cucumbers
½ cup salt
2 qts. water
In large mixing bowl place prepared cucumber slices. Sprinkle with salt. Add water and let stand 2 to 3 hours. Drain and rinse.

1 cup vinegar
1 cup water
In 2-qt. casserole place cucumber, vinegar and water. Cover. **Microwave at High 10 Minutes,** stirring after 5 minutes, until tender. Drain.

2 cups vinegar
1 cup hot tap water
1 cup sugar
1 cup light brown sugar (packed)
½ teaspoon mustard seed
½ teaspoon celery seed
½ teaspoon turmeric
In 3-qt. casserole mix together vinegar, water, sugar, brown sugar, mustard seed, celery seed and turmeric. Cover. **Microwave at High 6 Minutes.** Stir well.

Add cucumbers. **Microwave at High 11 to 13 Minutes,** stirring after 6 minutes, until mixture reaches full boil. Immediately pack into sterilized jars, leaving ⅛-in. headspace. Seal. Let stand at least 24 hours before serving.

Makes about 3 pints

SHORTCUT WATERMELON PICKLES

You will need about ¾ of a medium, round-shaped watermelon to produce 3 quarts prepared pieces for recipe below. This new recipe cuts hours of soaking time.

POWER LEVEL: High
MICROWAVE TIME: 85 min., total

3 qts. chunks white portion of watermelon (see below)
2 cups water
In 3-qt. casserole place watermelon. Add water. Cover. **Microwave at High 30 Minutes,** stirring every 10 minutes. Let stand, covered, while cooking syrup.

1 tablespoon mixed pickling spice
2 cinnamon sticks, broken
1 lemon, sliced thin
3 cups sugar
1½ cups white vinegar
1 cup water
Prepare spice bag by placing pickling spice, cinnamon sticks and lemon on a square of cheesecloth. Fold cloth around contents and tie securely with string. Place bag with sugar, vinegar and water in 2-qt. casserole. Stir and cover. **Microwave at High 20 Minutes,** stirring very well and uncovering after 10 minutes.

Just before syrup has finished cooking, drain off water from watermelon. Pour syrup, including spice bag, over watermelon in 3-qt. casserole. Cover. **Microwave at High 35 Minutes,** stirring every 10 minutes. Chunks should be tender and somewhat transparent; they will become more transparent after standing. Immediately ladle hot watermelon pickles into hot sterilized jars and seal with sterilized vacuum lids.

Makes about 5 cups

TO PREPARE WHITE PORTION OF WATERMELON: Work with ¼ of watermelon at a time. Scoop almost all of red portion from watermelon, but leave ⅛-in. of red for color. Cut rind into 1-in. strips. Cut green peel from strips, leaving white portion. Cube into about ½-in. pieces.

WHY HOME CANNING IS NOT RECOMMENDED FOR MICROWAVING

Canning should still be done on the range top and is not recommended for either the conventional or the microwave oven.

Special range top canning utensils rapidly bring the water and jars to a boil, and maintain consistent heat to each jar during the canning process. When pressure canners are used, temperatures above boiling are developed to preserve low acid or non-acid foods.

While it is an excellent appliance to use for cooking jelly and preserve mixtures, the microwave oven is not efficient in processing the canning jars.

COLORFUL CORN RELISH

POWER LEVEL: High
MICROWAVE TIME: 20 to 22 min., total

1 cup sugar
2 tablespoons cornstarch
1 tablespoon instant minced onion
1 tablespoon mustard seed
1 teaspoon celery seed
¼ teaspoon turmeric
1 cup vinegar
¾ cup hot tap water

In 3-qt. casserole stir together sugar, cornstarch, minced onion, mustard seed, celery seed and turmeric. Gradually add vinegar and water, blending well. Cover. **Microwave at High 5 Minutes.** Stir well.

3 cans (12-oz. each) whole kernel corn with chopped peppers, drained (about 5 cups)*

Add corn to sauce. Cover. **Microwave at High 15 to 17 Minutes,** stirring well after 7 minutes, until mixture boils. Stir well. Ladle into prepared glasses. Seal.

Makes about 5½ cups

*Sold as Mexicorn or Corn 'n' Peppers.

YEAR ROUND FRESH TOMATO RELISH

Delicious on hamburgers.

POWER LEVEL: High
MICROWAVE TIME: 3 min., total

1 tablespoon prepared mustard
1 tablespoon brown sugar (packed)
2 teaspoons white vinegar
½ teaspoon seasoned salt

In 1½-qt. casserole stir together mustard, brown sugar, vinegar and salt. **Microwave at High 1 Minute.**

2 cups finely chopped tomato
½ cup finely chopped celery
½ cup finely chopped green pepper
¼ cup finely chopped green onion

Add tomato, celery, green pepper and onion. **Microwave at High 2 Minutes,** uncovered. Stir well and refrigerate at least 1 hour before serving, to blend flavors. Store leftovers in refrigerator.

Makes about 3 cups

SPICY COLESLAW RELISH

Serve hot over hot dogs, Polish sausage or bratwurst.

POWER LEVEL: High
MICROWAVE TIME: 7½ to 9½ min., total

2 tablespoons butter
2 cups finely shredded cabbage
1 chopped green pepper
1 small onion, chopped
2 medium tomatoes, chopped
2 tablespoons vinegar
2 teaspoons prepared mustard
1 teaspoon Worcestershire sauce
½ teaspoon salt
¼ teaspoon hot pepper sauce (tabasco)
⅛ teaspoon pepper

In 2-qt. casserole place butter. **Microwave at High ½ Minute,** until melted. To butter add cabbage, green pepper, onion, tomatoes, vinegar, mustard, Worcestershire sauce, salt, pepper sauce and pepper. Mix together well. Cover. **Microwave at High 7 to 9 Minutes,** stirring after 4 minutes. Refrigerate leftovers.

Makes about 4 cups

SEALING AND STORING RELISHES AND PICKLES FOR FUTURE USE

Proper procedures should be taken in sealing jars of relishes and pickles to assure their wholesomeness after storage. If relishes and pickles are to be stored on the shelf at room temperature, they must be vacuum sealed in glass jars with 2-piece metal lids available for that purpose.

Sterilize the jars and lids in a kettle of boiling water and keep in hot water until just before filling. Ladling the boiling hot relish or pickle mixture into hot jars and sealing with hot lids is the best way to assure a good vacuum seal. Be sure rim of jar is clean before adding lid; wipe with damp cloth just before sealing. To completely assure proper seal, the U.S. Department of Agriculture recommends processing all relishes and pickles in water bath canner 10 to 15 minutes.

If you do not use the type of jars which may be vacuum sealed, store relishes and pickles in the refrigerator after they have cooled. Glass jars saved from purchased foodstuffs may be used as refrigerator storage jars, but do not use them for on-the-shelf storage at room temperature. Or, for gift giving, ladle relishes or pickles into attractive re-usable serving containers or glasses such as brandy snifters, unusual serving bowls, champagne glasses, etc. Cover with plastic wrap and store in refrigerator until giving.

Beverages

Heating beverages is one of the most popular uses of the microwave oven. Whether brewed or instant, it takes only 1¼ to 1½ minutes to heat a cup of coffee or tea. These water-based beverages can be heated at High.

When heating more than 4 cups, arrange them in a circle for even heating. Use a 3 to 4-qt. casserole for large quantities.

Do Not attempt to defrost or heat beverages in narrow necked bottles. Pressure builds up in the lower part of the bottle, causing it to shatter.

CALIFORNIA COCOA

POWER LEVEL: High
MICROWAVE TIME: 6 to 7 min., total

¼ cup cocoa
¼ cup sugar
3 cups milk
2 teaspoons grated fresh orange rind
¼ teaspoon almond extract

In 1-qt. glass measure combine cocoa and sugar. Add about ½ cup milk to make a smooth paste, then stir in remaining milk, orange rind and almond extract, blending thoroughly.

Cinnamon sticks

Microwave at High 6 to 7 Minutes. Pour into mugs and add cinnamon sticks for flavor and for stirring.

Makes 4 servings

Use the temperature probe, set at Medium and 140°, when heating cocoa and other milk-based beverages which boil over easily. Add marshmallow ¼ minute before cocoa is done. To heat by time, allow about 1½ to 2 minutes per cup. Time is longer than for reheating coffee because starting temperature of refrigerated milk is probably lower. Use cocoa mix or heat chocolate-flavored milk for fast cocoa.

WASSIL

The traditional English holiday drink.

POWER LEVEL: High
MICROWAVE TIME: 15 to 18 min., total

1 quart apple cider
1 teaspoon allspice
½ teaspoon ground cloves
¼ teaspoon nutmeg
2 cinnamon sticks
½ cup orange juice
2 tablespoons lemon juice
½ cup sugar
2 tart medium apples, thinly sliced

In 3-qt. casserole place cider, allspice, cloves, nutmeg, cinnamon sticks, orange juice, lemon juice, sugar and apples. **Microwave at High 15 to 18 Minutes,** until hot. Strain and serve.

Makes 8 to 9 (½ cup) servings

TWIN BERRY SHRUB

Shrubs are old-fashioned sparkling punches made with berry juice and carbonated beverage.

POWER LEVEL: High
MICROWAVE TIME: 13 to 16 min., total

2 pkg. (10-oz. each) frozen strawberries in pouch
2 pkg. (10-oz. each) frozen raspberries in pouch .....Place all 4 packages of berries on oven shelf. **Microwave at High 12 to 14 Minutes,** turning packages over and rearranging after 6 minutes. When berries have completely thawed, sieve to remove all seeds.

1 can (6-oz.) frozen lemonade concentrate ....In small glass bowl place lemonade. **Microwave at High 1 to 2 Minutes.** Add to the sieved berry syrup. Chill.

2 qt. club soda, well chilled ......Just before serving, blend berry juice mixture with club soda in festive glasses or in punch bowl. Decorate with lemon slices if desired.

Makes 3 quarts

IRISH COFFEE

POWER LEVEL: High
MICROWAVE TIME: 1½ to 2 min., total

3 tablespoons (1½-oz.) Irish whiskey
1 to 2 teaspoons sugar
1 tablespoon freeze dried or instant coffee
Water ...In 8-oz. stemmed glass, mug or coffee cup, place whiskey. Add sugar and coffee. Add water until container is about ¾ full. Mix well. **Microwave at High 1½ to 2 Minutes.** Mixture should be very hot but not boiling. Stir to dissolve all sugar.

Whipping cream ....Whip cream until almost stiff. It should be stiff enough to pour from the bowl over a spoon, onto the surface of the coffee without blending.

Fill glass to brim with cream. Do not stir. Coffee should be sipped through the layer of cream.

Makes 1 serving

Irish Mist Coffee: Use Irish Mist Liqueur instead of Irish whiskey. This variation makes a very smooth, sippable drink.

HOT BUTTERED RUM

POWER LEVEL: High
MICROWAVE TIME: 1½ to 2 min., total

1 to 2 teaspoons granulated or brown sugar (packed)
¼ cup (2-oz.) light or dark rum
Water ....In tall mug or cup place sugar and rum. Add water to ⅔ full. **Microwave at High 1½ to 2 Minutes,** until mixture is very hot but not boiling.

Butter
Nutmeg
Cinnamon stick ....Add about ¼-in. thick slice butter. Sprinkle with nutmeg and serve with cinnamon stick for stirring.

Makes 1 serving

Old Boston Buttered Rum: Substitute apple cider for water and use lower amount of sugar.

KENTUCKY MINT JULEP

This is a tradition every year during the Kentucky Derby.

To make each drink: Pour 1 tablespoon Mint Syrup (below) into tall glass filled with very finely crushed ice. Slowly add 2-oz. Kentucky bourbon whiskey. Garnish with sprig of mint and add straw.

Mint Syrup: In 1-pt. measure mix together 1 cup sugar and ½ cup water. **Microwave at High 4 to 4½ Minutes,** until hot and sugar is dissolved. Stir well. Add 1 bunch (18 stalks) mint. Stir well. Strain into small glass jar. Cover tightly and refrigerate.

SOURS

Vary the liquor to change the character of the drink.

POWER LEVEL: High
MICROWAVE TIME: 1½ min., total

1 can (6-oz.) frozen lemonade concentrate
Water
Liquor (see below) ....Remove concentrate from can to glass, microwave ovenproof pottery or stoneware pitcher. **Microwave at High 1½ Minutes,** until melted enough to stir. Add water and liquor and, if desired, ice cubes.

Makes about 4 drinks

Liquor: Use rum for daiquiris; bourbon for whiskey sours; or Scotch, orange slices and cherries for Scotch old-fashioneds.

Index

C

D

E

F

G

H

I

J

K

L

M

N

O

P

Q

R

S

T

V

W

Y

Z

Defrosting Guide POWER LEVEL: **Defrost**

MEAT	AMOUNT	FIRST HALF TIME/MINUTES	SECOND HALF TIME/MINUTES	COMMENTS
Bacon	1 package	2 to 3 per lb.	2 to 3 per lb.	Place unopened package in microwave oven. Turn over after first ½ of time. Microwave just until strips can be separated.
Franks	1 pound ½ pound	3 to 5 1½ to 2½	none none	Place unopened package in microwave oven. Microwave just until franks can be separated.
Ground, Beef & Pork	1 pound	3	3	Scrape off softened meat after second ½ of time. Set aside. Break up remaining block, microwave 2 to 3 minutes more.
	2 pounds	6	6	Scrape off softened meat after second ½ of time. Set aside. Break up remaining block, microwave 5 to 6 minutes more.
	5 pounds	12	12	Scrape off softened meat after second ½ of time. Set aside. Break up remaining block, microwave 11 to 12 minutes more. Second scraping may be needed.
Roast, Beef, Lamb, Pork & Veal	1 roast	5 to 6	5 to 6 per lb.	Place wrapped roast in microwave oven. After first ½ of time, shield warm areas with foil. Turn over and place in roasting dish. Defrost for second ½ of time. Let stand 15 to 30 minutes.
Spareribs, Pork	1 package	2 to 4 per lb.	2 to 4 per lb.	Place wrapped package in microwave oven. Turn over after first ½ of time. After second ½ of time, separate pieces with table knife. Let stand to complete defrosting.
Steaks, Chops & Cutlets; Beef, Lamb, Pork & Veal	1 package	2 to 4 per lb.	2 to 4 per lb.	Place wrapped package in microwave oven. Turn over after first ½ of time. After second ½ of time, separate pieces with table knife, let stand to complete defrosting.
Sausage, Bulk	1-lb. tray	3	3	Scrape off softened meat after second ½ of time. Set aside. Break up remaining block, microwave 2 to 3 minutes more.
	1-lb. roll	2	2 to 3	Turn over after first ½ of time.
Sausage, Link	1 pound	2	1 to 2	Turn over after first ½ of time.
Sausage, Link,	8-oz.	2	1 to 2	Turn over after first ½ of time.
Sausage, Patties	12-oz. pkg.	1	1 to 2	Turn over after first ½ of time.

POULTRY	AMOUNT	FIRST HALF TIME/MINUTES	SECOND HALF TIME/MINUTES	COMMENTS
Chicken, Broiler-fryer, cut up	2½ to 3½-lb.	7 to 8	7 to 8	Place wrapped chicken in microwave oven. After ½ of time, unwrap and turn over. After second ½ of time, separate pieces and place in cooking dish. Microwave 2 to 4 minutes more, if necessary.
Whole	2½ to 3½-lb.	9 to 11	9 to 11	Place wrapped chicken in microwave oven. After ½ of time shield warm areas with foil.
Cornish Hens	1	3½ to 4½ per lb.	3½ to 4½ per lb.	Place wrapped package in microwave oven. Turn package over after first ½ of time. After second ½ of time, unwrap and shield ends of legs with foil. Microwave 3½ to 4½ minutes more.
Duckling	1	2 to 3 per lb.	2 to 3 per lb.	Place wrapped duckling in microwave oven. After first ½ of time, unwrap and turn over into cooking dish. Shield warm areas with foil.
Turkey	1	2½ to 3 per lb.	3½ to 3 per lb.	Place wrapped turkey breast side down in microwave oven. Rotate ½ turn after first timing. After second timing, unwrap and shield warm areas with foil. Turn turkey breast side up and repeat timings.